The
JUST A MINUTE
O M N I B U S

The JUST A MINUTE

O M N I B U S

Glimpses of our Great Canadian Heritage

Marsha Boulton

McArthur & Company

First published in Canada by McArthur & Co., 2000.

Canadian Cataloguing in Publication Data

   Boulton, Marsha
     Just a minute omnibus

   ISBN 1-55278-151-8

   1. Canada – History – Miscellanea. I. Title.

   FC176.B672 2000   971'.002   C00-931319-2
   F1026.6.B686 2000

Composition and Design by *Michael P. Callaghan*
Cover by *Rocco Baviera/4 Eyes Art + Design*
Typeset at *Moons of Jupiter, Inc.* (Toronto)
Printed in Canada by *Transcontinental Printing Inc.*

McArthur & Company
322 King Street West, Suite 402
Toronto, ON, M5V 1J2

10 9 8 7 6 5 4 3 2 1

The publisher would like to acknowledge the financial support of the Government of Canada through the Book Publishing Industry Development Program (BPIDP) for our publishing activities. The publisher further wishes to acknowledge the financial support of the Ontario Arts Council for our publishing program.

TABLE OF CONTENTS

≈ ≈ ≈

Foreword xxiii

IMMIGRATION & INSPIRATION 1

A.D.1000: HUSH LITTLE SNORRI, DON'T YOU CRY 3
When Vikings sang lullabies in Newfoundland

1497: HATS OFF TO THE BEAVER 6
Castor canadensis — *our national rodent*

1535: WHOEVER HEARD OF A COUNTRY NAMED "BOB"? . 10
Where did the name "Canada" come from?

1542: SURVIVAL OF THE FITTEST 13
Marooned lovers face the Island of Demons

1606: EASIER SAID THAN DONE 16
Marc Lescarbot searches for a haven in the wilderness

1663: THE FATTEST AND THE REST 19
Women are the clue to population

1738: CLOTHES DO NOT MAKE THE MAN 23
The immigration and deportation of Esther Brandeau

1847: THE FLIGHT FROM FAMINE 26
How Irish orphans became French Canadians

1851: THE LITTLE RAILROAD THAT COULD 29
Following the drinking gourd to freedom

1851: *EÒIN A' CHUAN* 32
Norman McLeod leads Gaelic "Sea Birds" to New Zealand

1864: OH HOW WE DANCED ON THE NIGHT WE WERE
CONSTITUTIONALIZED 37
Waltzing toward a united Canada

1870: FLAMES OVER THE SAGUENAY 40
Settlers confront total desolation

1882: THE COLOUR OF THE OLD WEST 43
John Ware rides into Alberta

1890: GREEN SIDE UP! 48
Soddies: when the green green grass was home

≈   ≈   ≈

HEROES, HEROINES & THE ODD SCOUNDREL 53

1692: HOLDING THE FORT 55
The glorious inclination of Madeleine de Verchères

1813: WITHOUT A COW 58
Laura Secord's sweet heroism

1813: AN UNAMERICAN HERO 61
Billy Green and the Battle of Stoney Creek

1854: BEYOND THE CALL OF DUTY 66
Abigail Becker — heroine of Long Point

1867: CAPTAIN COURAGEOUS 69
William Jackman follows the family creed to heroism

1877: BY MANY NAMES SHALL YOU KNOW HIM 72
Crowfoot: the relinquishing of a birthright

1886: SINK OR SWIM 77
Jumping Joe Fortes of English Bay

1897: THE SAINT OF DAWSON CITY 81
Father William Judge ministers to the miners

1908: PAYING THE RENT 84
Wilfred Grenfell's mighty Mission

1915: NEIGHBOURS IN ARMS 87
Lest we forget the valour and the horror

1917: WHEN SHIPS COLLIDE 90
Heroism and the Halifax Explosion

1942: "EVERY MAN, CARRY A MAN" 93
Padre John Foote at Dieppe

1942: A MALTESE FALCON 96
Lone wolf airman George Beurling

1946: TICKLING THE DRAGON'S TAIL 102
Louis Slotin's supercritical sacrifice

1958: COURAGE DOWN BELOW 105
*Maurice Ruddick sings through the Springhill Mining
Disaster*

～　　～　　～

ORIGINS, ORIGINALS & UPSTARTS 109

1534: GENTLE BIRDS NO LONGER 111
The extinction of Canada's dodo

1811: THE ORIGINAL BIG MAC 114
All those apples from just one tree

1815: NEWFOUNDLAND NANA 117
The dog that saved Napoleon

1829: AND THEN THERE WERE NONE 120
The tragedy of the Beothuk

1849: TO WALK WITH GIANTS 124
Three towering Canadians — McAskill, Swan and Beaupré

1856: THE HANGING JUDGE 129
Matthew Begbie — have gavel will travel

1860: THE STORY OF DR. "O" 132
Oronhyatekha and the Independent Order of Foresters

1874: NO NUDDER LIKE HIM 138
Jerry Potts of the North-West Mounted Police

1878: WHERE'S JOE'S BEEF? 141
Charles McKiernan — the generous innkeeper

1908: FATHER GOOSE 144
Winging it with Jack Miner

1910: LEAVE IT TO THE BEAVER 148
Max Aitken makes hay whether or not the sun shines

1926: THE GREAT STORK DERBY 153
Charles Millar's will sparks a breeding frenzy

1930: GONE INDIAN 158
Grey Owl's life among the Beaver People

1934: A BELLY LAUGH OR YOUR MONEY BACK 162
The irrepressible Ma Murray

1938: THE SITDOWNERS 167
Steve Brodie leads a transients' strike

1955: EKOKTOEGEE 173
Judge Sissons listens to the Inuit

≈   ≈   ≈

HERSTORY 179

1852: NO PRISON IN THE WOODS 181
Mary Ann Shadd's self-reliant road to independence

1857: NO SEX PLEASE, WE'RE DOCTORS 186
The posthumous unmasking of Dr. Barry

1858: A SPY FOR THE YANKEES 190
Sarah Emma Edmonds crosses more than enemy lines

1871: "DESIST OR I WILL TELL YOUR WIFE" 194
Women medical students had to make a fuss

1882: THE RIGHT TO BE BEAUTIFUL 197
Elizabeth Arden changes the face of women

1897: FOR HOME AND COUNTRY 202
Adelaide Hoodless — Woman of Vision

1898: WOMAN OF WHEAT 205
E. Cora Hind forecasts the bushels from the breadbasket

1898: OUR LADY OF THE SOURDOUGH 208
Martha Black's "beloved Yukon" adventure

1915: "FOR THERE SHALL BE A PERFORMANCE" 211
Sister Aimee Semple McPherson finds her voice

1916: CANADA'S HYENA IN PETTICOATS 215
Nellie McClung — the activist behind the vote

1922: WOMAN OF THE HOUSE 218
Agnes Macphail, first female Member of Parliament

1926: SHE WENT WHERE SHE WANTED TO GO, DID
WHAT SHE WANTED TO DO... 221
Myra Bennett, our Florence Nightingale of the Rock

1929: "YOU'RE NOT EVEN A PERSON" 224
Judge Emily Murphy and the "Five Persons Case"

1947: LADYLIKE AND LETHAL 227
Consumer activist Dorothy Walton kept her eye on the birdie

1980: LILY OF THE MOHAWKS, GENEVIÈVE OF NEW
FRANCE 231
Kateri Tekakwitha's vulnerable venerability

≈   ≈   ≈

SPORTS 237

1838: FIELDS OF DREAMS 239
Canadians catch baseball fever

1867: ROW, ROW, ROW YOUR BOAT 242
The world-class triumphs of New Brunswick's "Paris Crew"

1880: A GENTLEMAN AND A SCULLER 246
Ned Hanlan rows to stardom

1891: FOLLOW THE BOUNCING BALL 250
James Naismith and the "invention" of basketball

1892: THE TURN-OF-THE-CENTURY TERMINATOR 253
Louis Cyr and eighteen fat men

1904: SINGING ON THE GREENS 256
George S. Lyon — Canada's golfing Olympian

1907: THE RUNNING MAN 259
Tom "Wildfire" Longboat gives his everything

1909: JUST FOR THE FUN OF IT 263
Entrepreneur Tommy Ryan introduces five-pin bowling

1912: TURN HIM LOOSE! 266
Tom Three Persons tames Cyclone

1915: SIMPLY THE BEST 268
The Edmonton Grads slam-dunk world

1920: SIR BARTON AND THE COMMANDER 271
Canada's Triple Crown winner

1922: THE BIG TRAIN THAT COULD 276
All-round all-star Lionel Conacher

1928: GILDING THE SASKATOON LILY 279
Ethel Catherwood flies through the air

1928: OUR PERCY GOES FOR GOLD 282
Olympian sprinter Percy Williams

1928: THE COMPLETE ATHLETE 285
Bobbie Rosenfeld — natural athlete and generous champion

1954: "DON'T LET THE CRIPPLED KIDS DOWN" 288
Marilyn Bell becomes First Lady of the Lake

1959: WHO WAS THAT MASKED MAN? 294
Jacques Plante changes the face of hockey

≈   ≈   ≈

ADVENTURE & DISCOVERY 299

1578: FOOLS RUSH IN 301
Martin Frobisher leads the first gold rush

1610: THE PIRATE ADMIRAL 305
Peter Easton turns Newfoundland fishermen into outlaws

1634: MANDARIN OF THE MISSISSIPPI 308
Jean Nicollet searches for a passage to China

1690: THE SULTAN OF SWASH 311
Governor Frontenac defends the fortress of Quebec

1794: A ROYAL CANADIAN LOVE STORY 314
Madame St.Laurent and her Prince in Halifax

1865: SERVING IN A HOUSE DIVIDED 319
Anderson Ruffin Abbott, Civil War surgeon

1880: ELEMENTARY, MY DEAR 322
Canada's Sherlock Holmes — John Wilson Murray

1884: ALBERTOSAURUS, I PRESUME 325
Joseph Burr Tyrrell faces a dinosaur

1895: WHITE LAMA 328
Susie Carson Rijnhart's Tibetan mission

1898: LION OF THE YUKON 334
Sam Steele — the roaring redcoat

1901: THE SPIRIT OF *TILIKUM* 337
Norman Luxton — from Samoa to saving buffalo

1914: WHO IS WHAT AND WHAT IS WHO 340
How a Canadian bear became Winnie the Pooh

1921: THESE BOOTS WERE MADE FOR WALKIN' 343
Trans-Canada hikers walk the rails

~ ~ ~

INNOVATION, INVENTION & SCIENCE 351

1535: THE *ANNEDA* SOLUTION 353
Solving the scurrilous scourge of scurvy

1684: THAT AND A GLEEK WILL GET YOU A CUP OF
COFFEE 357
A deck of cards reflects Canada's early economy

1685: THE SCENT OF A MAMMAL 360
Surgeon and natural scientist Michel Sarrazin

1824: THE MILLENNIAL TREE 363
Botanical Columbus David Douglas

1842: A HATFUL OF GRAIN 367
David Fife reaps what he sows

1846: LET THERE BE LIGHT 370
Abraham Gesner redefines the night with kerosene

1879: A MAN FOR ALL TIME ZONES 373
Sir Sandford Fleming sets a standard for the world

1890: THE HEART OF THE MATTER 376
Maude Abbott and the onward march of science

1892: H₂O + MYSTERIOUS GREY POWDER =
SUNSHINE + $$$$ 383
The alchemy of Thomas "Carbide" Willson

1907: MASTICATION AS THE MOTHER OF INVENTION . 391
Charles Saunders and the wheat that won the West

1913: ONE WITH THE SOIL 394
Charles Noble's blade takes root on the prairies

1916: RUST NEVER SLEEPS 398
Margaret Newton versus the scourge of wheat

1923: AN ALLELUIA IN THE SKY 402
The crackling candle dragon of the Northern dawn

1927: THE RAIDERS OF DRAGON BONE HILL 405
Davidson Black unearths Peking Man

1930: THE WONDER MUSH REVOLUTION 408
Pablum — the glop that makes you grow

1932: FEETS DON'T FAIL ME NOW 411
Mahlon Locke's hand to foot magic

1934: UNDISCOVERED COUNTRY 418
Wilder Penfield charts the brain

≈   ≈   ≈

ART & ARTISTS 423

1834: MARCHING THUNDER 425
Wind-tamer Joseph Casavant's passion for organs

1835: THE WISE CHILD 428
Thomas Chandler Haliburton translates "human natur"

1846: WANDERINGS OF AN ARTIST 433
Paul Kane pursues the vanishing frontier

1879: PORTRAIT OF THE ARTIST AS A YOUNG WOMAN . 436
Photography gem Hannah Maynard

1880: CANADA'S NATIONAL CONTRAPUNTAL
CANTATA 442
Calixa Lavallée composer of "O Canada"

1883: THE DIVA OF THE SACRED FIRE 445
Soprano Emma Albani conquers the world

1884: BUCKSKIN AND BROCADE 448
Mohawk princess poet Pauline Johnson

1893: *BEAUTIFUL JOE* 452
Marshall Saunders' bestselling story of a dog

1896: THE GREAT CANADIAN KISSER 455
May Irwin puckers up for the movies

1906: THE ORIGINAL ROLLING STONE 458
Yukon bard Robert Service

1914: THE PIE MAN 461
Mack Sennett — the king of comedy

1915: BORN OF FIRE AND BLOOD 464
John McCrae's poem of sacrifice and challenge

1928: THE LAUGHING ONE 467
Emily Carr paints from the forest's eye

1929: SHE DID IT HER WAY 470
La Bolduc – First Lady of Chanson

1930: THE COWBOY FROM QUEBEC 473
Will James's wild west fraud

1934: THE MAN OF STEEL 478
Joe Shuster draws Superman

1948: SPONTANEOUS COMBUSTION 481
Refus global, les automatistes and Paul-Émile Borduas

1900s to Present: MORE STARS THAN HEAVEN 488
Hollywood's Canadian connection

~ ~ ~

TRANSPORTATION 495

1862: HUMPS ALONG THE FRASER 497
Camels stink in the Cariboo gold rush

1866: "GET A HORSE!" 501
Canada enters the age of the automobile

1880: BLOOD ON THE TRACKS 504
Blasting a railway across the nation

1883: THE WRECK OF THE *MARCO POLO* 507
How tragedy inspired the creator of Anne of Green Gables

1899: THE BATTLE OF THE BLOOMERS 510
*Harley Davidson and Torchy Peden had two wheels in
common*

1921: "JUST ONCE MORE" 516
The unforgettable Bluenose

1925: GETTING THROUGH THE DRIFT 520
Ploughing through a chilly situation

1929: THE HAPPY NEW YEAR MISSION 523
A gamble with death to save lives

1929: THE PICASSO OF BUSH PILOTS 526
"Punch" Dickins wings it with style

1935: HAVE SKI-DOO, WILL TRAVEL 530
The multinational that started in a garage

1959: IS IT A BIRD? IS IT A PLANE? NO, IT'S AN
ARROW! 533
The grounding and destruction of an aviation marvel

≈   ≈   ≈

COMMUNICATION 539

1866: THE TELEGRAPH AT HEART'S CONTENT 541
Transatlantic cable and commercial intrigue

1876: THAT LONG DISTANCE FEELING 544
Phoning and flying with Mr. and Mrs. Bell

1898: PRESS PASS 110 548
War correspondent Kit Coleman

1900: RADIO MAN 553
Reginald Fessenden — the father of radio

1901: DOT, DOT, DOT...! 556
Guglielmo Marconi's "big thing" on Signal Hill

1915: THE MAVERICK MUSE OF THE WEST 559
Uncorking the conscience of Bob "Eye-Opener"
Edwards

1918: HUMAN ENGINEERING IN AN UNSEEN
WORLD 562
Eddie Baker leads the blind from disability to ability

1936: AS IT HAPPENED 565
Radio broadcasting comes of age at Moose River

1939: A MAN IN A HURRY 568
John Grierson and the National Film Board of Canada

1965: THE CROSS-DISCIPLINE DRESSER 574
Marshall McLuhan — philosopher-king of the global
village

FOREWORD

The history of Canada has been written on river rapids, mountain crags and flatland prairies. Destiny was shaped in fertile valleys, culled from the bounty of two oceans and washed with winter's snow. Native peoples blended with their environment. New immigrants confronted it. It is a story rife with adventure, adversity, triumph and turmoil.

The glimpses of our great Canadian heritage captured in this volume reveal characters and events that provide an insight into our national personality. They range from Viking sagas to consumer activism, from philosophers to frauds, and from heroes in war to Olympian triumphs and the imaginative innovation of settlers who spread across the nation.

Some of these stories even foretell. For instance, Martin Frobisher's privately and royally funded sixteenth-century quest for gold in the New World could have been a blueprint for the pre-millennium Bre-X gold stock scandal. In both cases, the gold samples were tainted and investors (including Queen Elizabeth I) were hornswoggled. As one of my personal heroes, suffragette, author, politician and "hyena in petticoats" Nellie McClung observed, "People must know the past to understand the present and to face the future."

Surprises abounded in the exploration of the jumble of geography that is Canada. When Jacques Cartier first set eye on the rocky promontory of Labrador his disappointment was palpable. "I believe that this was the land God gave to Cain," he wrote. A few months later, he pronounced Prince Edward Island to be "the best tempered region one can possibly see."

Hundreds of years down the road, artist Emily Carr noted that, "The skies out West are big. You can't squeeze them down" and she immortalized the beauty of British Columbia by painting "from the mythic eye of the forest." And twentieth-century prairie farmer Charles Noble was typical of those who worked the soil of the nation. When asked once why he chose to buy a certain plot of land, he replied simply, "The land had strength and the land lay beautifully." From tundra to coulee, from solitary spruce on the Canadian Shield to the mad-blue rush of the Fraser River, the geography of our nation is a wondrous backdrop for history.

Then there is the dressing on that geography. The first wave of immigrants to this country experienced flora and fauna they had never seen before. Everything from the Douglas fir to the skunk was new to them. The exploration of the nation is owed to an orange-toothed, tough-tailed rodent whose fur made a fashionable felt hat. The beaver, our industrious national emblem, was hunted nearly to extinction, an ignoble fate that earlier befell the flightless Great Auk of Funk Island.

A British-born fraud, Archibald Belaney in his life-long guise "Grey Owl," was instrumental in saving the beaver through his bestselling books and lecture tours. Today, ordinary citizens become local heroes when they take a stand on environmental issues — whether it is protecting the rivers where salmon spawn or recycling tin cans — the lessons of the past have provided a grassroots impetus to change.

These stories do not dwell on dates, rather they place the figure in the landscape of time, which can be far more revealing than recounting the digits of decades. To me the best gateway to history is personality. Researching these stories allowed me to study a wide range — a gamut from rogues to romantics, poets to high jumpers, opera singers to hockey players. Be it a hero who braves the icy waves off Newfoundland to save lives, a priest who heads up the Klondike trail or a blinded soldier leading the blind, these glimpses into Canada's past are tributes to our collective greatness and ingenuity.

Some of the stories you will recognize in part from the exposure they have garnered on television and in cinemas as Heritage Minutes. I was privileged to work on the development and scripting of some of those sixty-second advertisements for ourselves with Patrick Watson — a friend and colleague — who is Creative Director of The CRB Foundation's Heritage Minutes program.

Today, the Heritage Minutes and many of the stories in this book are used in classrooms across the nation to illuminate the past. The story behind the moving images is what you will find in these pages. Joe Shuster's creation of Superman turns out to be a tragic saga of one man's loss in the face of "truth, justice and the American way." Likewise, Guglielmo Marconi's much touted "first" wireless signal across the Atlantic, pales in comparison to the achievements of the Canadian-born Reginald Fessenden, the true "father of radio."

I am indebted to curators, archivists, local history boards and librarians across the nation who have indulged my obsession for uncovering stories that need telling. Organizations as diverse as the Federation of Women's Institutes, the Five-Pin Bowling Association and the Canadian Rodeo Historical Association supplied me with information and inspiration. Academically, Dr. John Thompson of the University of Alberta and Duke University served as enthusiastic historical watchdog on many of these stories.

The Internet has proved to be a useful tool in guiding me to many sources, ranging from the Canadian Museum of Civilization and Man to the *Bridge River-Lillooet News* on-line "scrapbook" chronicling the life and times of editor/founder Margaret "Ma" Murray. Along with many other encyclopaedic volumes, the redoubtable *Dictionary of Canadian Biography* has provided the solace of fact and the turntable for much storytelling.

Writing may be a singular act, but the humouring and maintenance of the author is often an extended act of goodwill. My publisher and friend, Kim McArthur, has served as a mentor and astute sounding board through many years and many stories. Her team at the brave new Canadian publishing house, McArthur & Company, includes the eagle-eyes of editors Pamela Erlichman and Nina Callaghan, the artistry of cover designer Rocco Baviera and the stylish sensibility of designer Michael Callaghan, all of whom have contributed their generous talents to this collection. My companion, Stephen Williams, has endured his own trials and tribulations wrestling with the writing of history, which has made his support all the more valuable to me.

History is all about "story," combining elements of language, geography and culture with human endeavour. From fact, it inspires fiction, drama and poetry. Like an epic adventure — a story running in a continual loop — it is always there to be dipped into; accessible, relevant and exciting.

Marsha Boulton
Mount Forest, Ontario
September, 2000

IMMIGRATION
&
INSPIRATION

HUSH LITTLE SNORRI, DON'T YOU CRY

HATS OFF TO THE BEAVER

WHOEVER HEARD OF A COUNTRY
NAMED "BOB"?

SURVIVAL OF THE FITTEST

EASIER SAID THAN DONE

THE FATTEST AND THE REST

CLOTHES DO NOT MAKE THE MAN

THE FLIGHT FROM FAMINE

THE LITTLE RAILROAD THAT COULD

EÒIN A' CHUAN

OH HOW WE DANCED ON
THE NIGHT WE WERE CONSTITUTIONALIZED

FLAMES OVER THE SAGUENAY

THE COLOUR OF THE OLD WEST

GREEN SIDE UP!

HUSH LITTLE SNORRI, DON'T YOU CRY

Newfoundland, A.D. *1000* — How many people know that a Norse baby with the sleepy-sounding name of Snorri was born around 1000 A.D. in Newfoundland? Snorri is believed to be the first European child born in North America.

The name Viking actually hails from the Norse word for raiding, and the pillage and plunder of these fierce Scandinavian pirates was felt from the stone chapels of Ireland to the Byzantine cathedrals of Constantinople between 800 and 1000 A.D.

At a time when most European sailors scarcely dared to go beyond their own shores, the Norsemen had settled Iceland and the infamous outlaw Erik the Red had discovered Greenland.

It was Erik's son, Leif, who explored the seas even further west and brought his long, wave-skimming ships called *knorrs to* the "Land of the Flat Stones," which may be Baffin Island, and *to* the "Land of the Forests," possibly Labrador, and finally to the mysterious place called "Vinland."

According to the sagas, Leif and his men stayed for the winter in Vinland, where there was little frost and the salmon were larger and more plentiful than they had seen before. Commercial grapes as we know them would not have been in evidence, but the Norse words *vin* and *vinber* may be translated to include the multitude of wild berry species that still grow in the sheltered coastal bays. Other scholars suggest that *Vin* referred to good pasture land, a valuable commodity to Norse settlers, who travelled with livestock in need of feed.

Leif's Greenlander brother Thorvald, and the respected Icelandic trader Thorfinn Karlsefni, who was descended from the legendary Ragnor Shaggypants, made the first attempts to inhabit Vinland. They set out with four ships, 160 settlers, livestock and personal effects to colonize Vinland the Good.

They may have spent their first winter near Epave Bay, much further north than the more temperate climate described by Leif. In the spring, several parties set out to explore the coastline.

A saga tells the story of a chance encounter in which Thorvald was struck by the arrow of a *Skraeling,* the Norse name for the native inhabitants. His dying words now seem prophetic: "It seems we have found a good land, but are not likely to get much profit from it."

Confrontations between the Norse settlers and the Skraelings appear to have evolved from great confusion, compounded by the Viking disposal to option warfare over communication.

On one occasion the Skraelings arrived at the settlement with intent to trade. A bull charged out of the bush and when the terrified natives sought shelter in the Norse huts, they were presumed to be attackers. Battles ensued between Vikings armed with swords and axes and Skraelings who fought with their scaling harpoons.

Discord and murder within the colonist groups led the Vikings to return to Greenland, seldom to visit again. The sagas indicate that Snorri accompanied his parents. After his father died, his mother, Gudrid, undertook a southern pilgrimage, possibly to Rome. She returned to her homeland to find that Snorri had built a church for her and she lived as a nun for the rest of her life.

For centuries, no proof of Viking settlement in Newfoundland existed beyond the sagas that pre-dated Christopher Columbus's discoveries by 500 years. Finally, after years of study, a Norwegian group led by Dr. Helge Ingstad discovered the remains of a Viking settlement at L'Anse Aux Meadows, near Newfoundland's northern tip in 1961.

Today, there is a national park at the site where a Norse baby may have slept by a fireplace while his mother spun wool and sang Viking lullabies.

HATS OFF TO THE BEAVER

New World, 1497 — If British hatmakers had been watching closely when Giovanni Caboto (John Cabot) made his landmark voyages to the New World in 1497 and 1498, the course of history might have changed. As it was, Cabot's discovery of cod in quantity off the shores of Newfoundland and New Brunswick was initially more interesting than the beaver furs he brought back to England. It took French explorers, and French fashion mavens, to recognize in the beaver a prize that would shape the future of a nation. Once word got out, it was open season on the beaver.

Native tribes used the beaver in their names and emblems long before Europeans decided to make them into hats. The Onondagas had a Beaver clan, while the Amihona, an Algonkian tribe, were known as "People of the Beaver." On the Pacific Coast, the Tsimshian and Haida claimed the beaver as their totem.

In subsequent symbolic use, *Castor canadensis* has been featured on the first Canadian stamp, the Three Penny Beaver. Its image shares the nickel coin with that of the monarch. Patriotic posters of the Second World War show the buck-toothed creature gnawing down a tree in which a terrified Adolf Hitler perches. The ubiquitous beaver is a feature in more than one thousand place names in Canada. Yet at one time the beaver neared extinction, saved in part by the silkworm, whose handiwork replaced beaver felt as the fabric of choice for nineteenth-century hats.

Hatters went quite literally mad over the fur of the beaver. Most prized of all was a pre-conditioned beaver pelt known as *castor gras d'hiver*. These were prime winter beaver pelts, skinned by native women who scraped the inner sides, rubbed them with animal marrow and cut them into manageable rectangles that were sewn together with moose sinews. Native peoples wore beaver robes with the fur against their flesh. Over a period of months, the long "guard" hairs in the fur, already loosened by the initial scraping, would fall away leaving only the downy underfur.

Felt was made by removing this duvet coat from the pelt and rolling or pounding it flat. Then it was bonded with shellac for shaping into a variety of trendy headgear from the Stetson-like *copatain* hat of the 1500s to the 1700s *tricorne*. The virtue of beaver over other furs lay in the microscopic barbs in the hairs that hooked together so a minimum of bond was required to create a fine "bever hatte."

News that their old clothes could be bartered for a bounty of foreign goods from kettles to knives came as some surprise to the natives. "You glory . . . in our miserable suits of beaver which can no longer be of use to us," one Micmac is reported to have remarked. What he did not know was that the traders were making a profit of up to 2,000 percent.

The beaver was a national staple in other incarnations. Colonists in New France compared the flavour of its meat to mutton. Boiled, peeled and roasted, the tail was considered a delicacy. The voyageurs were granted special permission from the Catholic Church to eat beaver tail on Friday, a logic which was apparently suggested by the beaver's ability to swim like a fish. Beaver pelts were also used as currency when hard coin of the realm was in scarce supply.

By 1635, beavers themselves were in short supply in the hunting grounds of the Huron. Finding new sources opened up the West. In 1794, the North-West Company built Fort Augustus near what is now Edmonton. One of the founders noted that beaver in the area "are said to be so numerous that the women and children kill them with sticks and hatchets."

Humpbacked and orange-toothed, the humble *castor* was well on its way to becoming a national symbol. In 1785, the Beaver Club of Montreal struck a medal featuring a tree-chomping beaver and the slogan "industry and persever-ance." A drinking and carousing society for the lords of the fur trade, the Beaver Club members may have required a dram of their own motto "fortitude in distress," following the evening of September 17, 1809, when thirty-two guests reportedly downed sixty-two bottles of wine, twelve quarts of beer and an untold quantity of brandy and gin.

By suppressing both its heart rate and breathing, a beaver can travel ten city blocks in fifteen minutes — pro-vided those city blocks are under water. Kits, born after a three-and-one-half month gestation period, are cared for by both parents for two years. The beaver is monogamous, a natural builder and to all intents and purposes, water-proof. Beaver dams create wetland havens for a community of birds and mammals. However, they can be fatal. Washout from a beaver dam in Northern Ontario derailed a train in 1922, killing two railway workers.

Overtrapping during the Depression led to critically low beaver stocks. Throughout the 1930s, the beaver-loving, Indian imposter known as Grey Owl made his anti-trapping epiphany into something of an industry, translating the antics of his companion beavers — McGinty, McGinnis, Jelly Roll and Rawhide — into book sales and federally funded movies. When he died in 1938, and was unmasked as English-born Archibald Belaney, the national parks department ended his conservation programs. Today, the beavers' greatest threat comes from human encroachment on their habitat.

One thing that is unlikely to change is the title of *The Beaver* magazine. Initiated by the Hudson's Bay Company in 1920 as a staff magazine, it evolved into a full-fledged magazine now published by Canada's National Historical Society and devoted to "Exploring Canada's History." When a forum over the notion of changing the title was initiated in 1996, furry opinion flew three to one against change. One reader described the title as "sacrosanct"; others threatened to cancel their subscriptions.

Canada's largest rodent — the strong, tireless and industrious beaver — was officially designated as our national emblem on March 24, 1975.

WHOEVER HEARD OF
A COUNTRY NAMED "BOB"?

The New World, 1535 — We have a flag, an anthem, and a government, but whence this moniker "Canada"? The nation's appellation can be traced back to the Iroquois word *kanata* (meaning village). The symbolism is healthy enough, and the word has a nice ring to it, but the fact is that the naming of Canada resulted more from misunderstanding than intention.

The European who is credited with providing a name for our nation over 400 years ago is master French mariner and explorer Jacques Cartier. On April 20, 1534, Cartier left the French port of Saint Malo with two ships and sixty-one men. His Royal mission on behalf of King Francis I was: "to discover certain isles and countries where it is said there must be great quantities of gold and other riches."

Instead, after thirty-three days sailing, Cartier sighted Labrador. His disappointment was palpable when he discovered little more than rock and trees. "I saw not one cartload of earth in all that northern coast," he wrote. "I believe that this was the land God gave to Cain."

Cartier's ships hauled south where they explored and charted what is now known as the Gulf of the St. Lawrence.

That June, he landed on Prince Edward Island, which he found to be "the best-tempered region one can possibly see." Still in pursuit of gold, he sailed north off the coast of New Brunswick until reaching a large, warm-water inlet that opened into a bay that Cartier called *Chaleur* (French for "heat").

It was here that Cartier reported the first formal exchange of furs between Europeans and Indians, when two groups of Micmac people approached one of his longboats in forty canoes laden with furs that they were anxious to trade. The sight of so many natives frightened the French, who motioned them away and responded to the Micmac's persistence with cannon fire. Although the Micmac were wary, they finally convinced the French that their mission was one of peaceful commerce. The nomadic Micmac had been trading with visiting Europeans for almost half a century. They were eager to barter furs for small iron tools and wares.

Upon his arrival in the Bay of Gaspé, Cartier was greeted by people from the Iroquoian village of Stadacona, who had come from the interior on a fishing expedition. Their chief, Donnacona, provided gifts and feasting.

On July 24, 1534, Cartier erected a thirty-foot, wooden cross on the shore. At the top, the words "Vive Le Roy de France" were carved in ancient lettering. The sight was unsettling to the Iroquois. Cartier explained, in sign language, that the cross was merely a marker.

Honest and direct communication was difficult, so Cartier took two of Donnacona's sons back to France for training as interpreters. Although he had not found the promised gold or riches, the King agreed to a second expedition.

The following spring, three ships left Saint Malo and Donnacona's sons ably guided Cartier past Anticosti Island

and up a broad river. On August 10, 1535, Cartier named the mighty river the St. Lawrence in honour of the saint whose feast day it was.

Proceeding up the river, Cartier finally reached a great fist of rock where he found the settlement of Stadacona, which became the site of Quebec City.

At this point, there is historic conjecture that Cartier was advised by his interpreters that the settlement at Stadacona was *kanata*, the Iroquois word for "village" or "community." Cartier, it would seem, thought it was the name of the whole country. The phrase "Kingdom of Canada" appeared in Cartier's journal on August 8, 1535. Subsequently, the name "Canada" appeared on the 1547 "Harleian" world map, which displayed the discoveries made during Cartier's second voyage.

Of course, there are other explanations for "Canada." Some have contended that Spanish explorers had sought gold around the Bay des Chaleurs. Finding none, they left after explaining to the natives: *aca nada*, which means "nothing here."

Alternately, the *Kingston Gazette* of 1811 suggested an even more fanciful proposition. The newspaper reported that the name Canada may have been derived from settlers in New France who were allowed only one can of spruce beer each day and "every moment articulated 'can a day.'"

SURVIVAL OF THE FITTEST

Island of Demons, New World, 1542 — There was a penalty for falling in love in the New World. Law books were not among Jean-François de La Rocque de Roberval's belongings when he sailed to the newly discovered territory which had been claimed in the name of France by Jacques Cartier in 1534. However, as the commander of an expedition to establish a colony, Roberval determined that the punishment for amorous indiscretion was banishment.

After an eight-week voyage, three ships with a cargo of 200 settlers, provisions, livestock and weapons sailed into the harbour of what is now St. John's, Newfoundland, on June 8, 1542.

Roberval had invited his niece, Marguerite, to join him on the daring adventure. Unknown to him, a young stowaway had also joined the expedition and his sights were clearly set more on Marguerite than the New World.

While the ships were stocked with water and supplies, Marguerite and her young man spent three weeks roaming antediluvian Newfoundland hills, gathering berries, fishing for salmon, and making love. Throughout the romantic idyll, Marguerite's servant, Damienne, acted as a guard for the lovers.

Word of the affair infuriated Roberval, who considered Marguerite's indiscretion to be a deliberate disgrace of the family name.

En route to the St. Lawrence where Cartier had established a fort, Roberval marooned Marguerite, her lover and the servant on an uninhabited island known as Ile des Demons (the Island of Demons). It may well have been Fogo Island off the northeast coast of Newfoundland. In one account, Roberval is said to have banished the nameless young man and Marguerite begged to share his fate. In another, the young man chose to be with his disgraced beloved. Damienne, it seems, had no choice.

That summer, the outcasts built a cabin. Game, fruit and bird eggs were plentiful, but they were haunted by the night calls of the unfamiliar species of birds which had given the place its demonic name.

For eight months, they did not see a ship and Marguerite's young man became depressed and physically ill. He died shortly before their child was born. Undaunted, Marguerite applied her hunting skills, using a matchlock gun her uncle had provided to harvest wild food. She told her biographer that she became so skilled that on one day she killed three bears, including one that was "white as an egg," no doubt a polar bear that had drifted south on an ice pan.

After seventeen months on the island, the servant died and Marguerite's child soon followed. A year later, lonely but in good health, she was rescued by Breton fishermen who were astonished to find the bedraggled French noblewoman.

Ironically, Jean-François de Roberval's colony at Cap-Rouge, upstream from Quebec City, was a dismal failure. Many colonists suffered from hunger, filth, cold and scurvy before the expedition disbanded.

After her return to France, Marguerite de Roberval's triumphant survival in the New World was documented by Andre Thevet, the Geographer Royal to King François I and it became popular reading.

One of those readers was Thevet's successor, Samuel de Champlain, who later helped establish a successful colony at Port Royal that was based on the theory that it was possible for settlers to live off the land. What started with a tragic love story set a pattern for survival in the New World.

EASIER SAID THAN DONE

Port-Royal, Nova Scotia, 1606 — When Parisian lawyer Marc Lescarbot sailed into the Annapolis Basin after more than a month spent crossing the Atlantic he was filled with awe at the wooded, hilly beauty of the unexplored and unexploited wilderness. "So many folk are ill-off in this world," he wrote, "they could make their profit of this land if only they had a leader to bring them."

Lescarbot was an improbable adventurer, and in this period of the early settlement of New France neither his legal skills nor his knowledge of Greek, Latin and Hebrew were likely to ensure his survival. Instead, Lescarbot utilized his talent as a writer and poet to chronicle the unfolding of events. His *Histoire de la Nouvelle-France* has been praised as "one of the first great books in the history of Canada." It is a running narrative debunking certain myths that spread from the early writings of explorer Jacques Cartier, including tales of two-footed beasts, pygmies, people who never eat food and men without recta.

A poet at heart, Lescarbot wrote about everything from conspiracy to morality. He frequently visited with the Micmac native leaders and noted their customs and chants. Contrary to the opinions of others, he found the native societies to be largely more civilized and virtuous than those of the Europeans, although he did lament their ignorance of fine wines.

The colony at Port-Royal was barely a few years old when Lescarbot arrived but boredom had already set in. Founder Samuel de Champlain recognized that a diversion was required. During that glorious winter of 1606-1607 Champlain's "Order of Good Cheer" provided an evening of entertainment once a week, and the feasting that accompanied the festivities ensured that at least one nutritious meal was had by all. Fifteen colonists took turns being Grand Master of these social events, and each took pride in trying to outdo the others in matters of ceremonious presentation of huge dinners featuring wild game and seafood.

"Whatever our gourmands at home may think, we found as good cheer at Port Royal as they at their Rue Aux Ours in Paris, and that, too, at a cheaper rate!" declared Lescarbot, who was a member of the Order. He describes the scene as one of gaiety and pomp. "The chief steward, having prepared all sorts of things in the oven, walked with a napkin over his shoulder, the baton of office in his hand, the chain of Order around his neck, with everyone in the Order right behind him, each carrying his plate."

The Order ended in the spring of 1607 when the colony was disbanded and returned to France. But the experience of this freedom-filled wilderness had whetted Lescarbot's appetite and imagination. He returned to Port-Royal and continued to document, ruminate and compose rhymes of questionable merit. Life in the colony seemed to feed his creative instincts and, in one burst of enthusiasm, he orchestrated the first theatrical presentation in North America. His play, *Thèâtre de Neptune*, featured trumpets, cannon fire and a chorus of Tritons in bark canoes.

Lescarbot spent the final decades of his life in Switzerland and France, where he became a diplomat and returned to the practice of law. He maintained contact with the colony, but never returned.

Having romanced the wilderness, Lescarbot understood the challenges that the "freedom" of life in New France presented. "Many who are ignorant of navigation think that the establishment of a plantation in an unexplored country is an easy matter but it is much easier said than done," he noted. "In vain does one run and weary himself in search of havens wherein fate is kind."

THE FATTEST AND THE REST

New France, 1663 — It was not always easy to convince settlers to come to this New World. Despite early attempts, by 1627 the population of New France was a lowly sixty-five souls. Early in the seventeeth century, settlement had been encouraged by providing land grants — feudal holdings — to groups with names like Company of One Hundred Associates and Company of Habitants. However, by 1663 when Louis XIV's reign as the "sun king" began, it was apparent that these attempts had fallen short, if not failed dismally.

As the saying goes, "it takes two to tango," and one of the problems of increasing the population had to do with the inadequate number of dancing partners. Estimates ranged as high as one woman of marriageable age for every six bachelors. The solution was simple — add women.

From 1653 to 1663 approximately eight hundred French women between the ages of twelve and forty-five received free passage to New France. Some were poor Parisian beggars and orphans, others were recruited from smaller centres such as Rouen. They were known as *les filles du roi* (the King's girls), and each arrived with a certificate from a priest attesting to her availability and moral character. Jean Talon, the first Intendant of the colony, indicated in a letter to the King's Minister Jean-Baptiste Colbert that he preferred that "those destined for this country be in no ways naturally deformed, and they have nothing exteriorly repulsive." Each young woman was accompanied by a dowry, sometimes including livestock, which also travelled on the bride ships.

Illustrations of the arrival of the *filles du roi* on the docks at Quebec often feature beautiful, apple-cheeked, wasp-waisted young women posed demurely in court dress pondering an assembly of elegant and politely eager suitors. Yet, after a crossing which often took at least two months, it is unlikely that anyone emerging from the ships smelled or looked anything close to rosy. The shipment of rouge was forbidden. In addition, manners in the colony were already at least one step removed from those in France, where urinating on the stairways of the Louvre was acceptable behaviour.

No doubt the scene on the docks was lacking in romantic idealism. In some accounts, "brides" were more or less cut out of the herd, with the fattest young women selected first on the principle that they might have the best chance of enduring a winter. Marriages were arranged quickly and within a few weeks an estimated 90 percent of each shipload of women had become wives.

There were rules to be followed after the marriage; however, they were scant and considerably incorrect by contemporary standards. For instance, a wife could only obtain a separation from her husband if he beat her with a stick that was thicker than his wrist. Farming was a subsistence occupation at best, but despite the hardships of the settlers' lives, wedlock had certain advantages. Intendant Talon denied bachelors the right to fish, hunt and trap. Unmarried women sixteen years of age and older and unmarried men of twenty and older were required to report every six months to explain their "situations."

Population became the goal of the state. In 1660, the King issued an Order in Council stating that any couple producing ten children would be eligible to receive a subsidy of 300 *livres* per child or 400 *livres* each if twelve or more births were recorded. This first "baby bonus" represented a healthy pension for parents and it produced results. A decade later, Intendant Talon reported that all of the "girls" sent the previous year were married "and almost all pregnant or mothers; a proof of the fecundity of this country." Between 1666 and 1672, the population more than doubled. The King granted a bonus to males twenty or younger and females sixteen or younger who married. Those who were not married by these ages saw their fathers *pay* a levy. Large families received the sanction of both the Church and the state. Talon returned to France, where he died in 1694 — a bachelor.

Other "bride ships" followed the pattern set by Louis XIV. During the gold rush in British Columbia the influx of thousands of miners caused a gaping disparity in the male-female ratio. In 1862, at least two shiploads of hopeful brides arrived in Victoria, B.C. They were organized at the request of the miners by the Columbia Emigrant Society, which included among its benefactors the Lord Mayor of London and the Bishop of Oxford.

The steamer *S.S. Tynemouth* carried the largest load — sixty-two women who were described as a "select bundle of crinolines" by the *British Colonist*, "varying from fourteen to an uncertain figure; a few are young widows who have seen better days." Commerce stopped on the September day when the women were greeted by the entire male population at the dock. Some were terrified by the sight of the men and some asked to leave immediately, but their reception was civil and dignified. Only one bride was claimed directly at the dock. The rest of the women walked to the Parliament buildings where they did their shipboard laundry together in pre-arranged tubs while all and sundry watched.

In time, almost all of the Victoria brides married, although it is said several chose to travel to the Cariboo gold fields to try their hand at mining or other more bawdy enterprise.

CLOTHES DO NOT MAKE
THE MAN

Quebec City, 1738 — Long before the age of the sex change, an adventurous immigrant arrived in Quebec City as a male only to be deported as a female.

Esther Brandeau had entered Canada as "Jacques La Farge." Ms. Brandeau was the first Jew to set foot in New France and she was eventually deported because she refused to convert to Catholicism.

The daughter of Jewish refugees from the Portuguese Inquisition who settled in Bayonne, France, at the age of fifteen Esther was shipwrecked while on her way to visit relatives in Holland. Following her rescue she decided not to return home, preferring adventure and the high seas.

She quickly discovered that her sex placed her at a disadvantage, so she disguised herself as a boy and signed on as a ship's cook in Bordeaux. Her ruse proved effective. Using the name Pierre Mausiette, she spent the next four years working variously as a tailor, a baker, a messenger boy in a convent and a footman to a military officer.

At nineteen, Brandeau adopted the name Jacques La Farge and set sail for New France. Officials in Quebec City were immediately suspicious of the young Frenchman who bore a polished manner but wore ill-fitting clothes. No one could put their finger on anything specific, but the La Farge fellow was definitely "different."

Under questioning by the Maritime Commissioner, La Farge finally admitted that his name was assumed — as well as his gender. To further complicate the issue, Esther Brandeau added the revelation that she was also Jewish. For this admission, she found herself placed under arrest and confined at a hospital.

According to the policy of the French, non-Catholic settlement was prohibited in the tradition of one language, one religion, one loyalty and one monarch. Any non-Catholic immigrants were to be deported or converted.

Church authorities pleaded with Brandeau to convert. For months, they used every power of persuasion, cajoling and threat, but Brandeau was unyielding. A Jew she was, and a Jew she wished to remain.

After a year of fruitless effort, exasperated authorities gave up on the notion of ever converting Esther Brandeau. "She has been as much receptive as hostile to the instructions that zealous ecclesiastics have attempted to give her," reported the perplexed Intendant Gilles Hocquart. He was confounded by Brandeau's refusal to relinquish her religion and would characterize her behaviour as "fickle."

In France, King Louis XVI was kept apprised of the bizarre situation in the colony. Finally, in 1739, on his express orders, Brandeau was shipped home at the expense of the French government. Historian Irving Abella, who documented Brandeau's New World adventures in his book, *A Coat of Many Colours: Two Centuries of Jewish Life in Canada*, reports that upon her return to France, Brandeau seems to have disappeared into obscurity.

Following the capitulation of the French in 1760, the British made the settlement of Jews in Quebec legal. Seventeen years later the first permanent synagogue opened in Montreal. Sherith Israel was built on land donated by the family of Lazarus David, whose son, David, was the first Quebec-born Jew.

In 1871, the first Canadian census in the new Dominion of Canada included statistics on religion. Out of five religions listed, there were 1,333 Canadians of the Jewish faith. This figure more than doubled within the next decade as Canada accepted thousands of refugees from the anti-Jewish pogroms in Russia.

THE FLIGHT FROM FAMINE

Grosse Isle, Quebec, 1847 — In the mid-1800s, thousands of Irish orphans were adopted by French-Canadian families. The potato famine in Ireland during the 1840s triggered the migration of over 100,000 Irish citizens to Canada in 1847 alone. Literally thousands of those poor souls died of typhus or cholera before they had a chance to settle. As a result, countless children found themselves alone, strangers in a strange land.

Most of the 1847 emigrants had been tenants on large Irish estates. In an over-populated country where the potato was the staple of the national diet, crops failed for two years in a row. Whole counties with poetic names such as Limerick, Tipperary, Clare and Cork were devastated by famine and its companion diseases.

In April 1847, more than 28,000 families were crammed into wooden transport ships bound for Quebec City, the main port of the St. Lawrence. Many of the passengers were stricken with "famine fever" (typhus) before they boarded, and once they were crammed into narrow bunks below the deck the disease spread quickly.

Food and water aboard the ships were often in scarce supply. According to one observer the straw beds were "teeming with abominations" and the bodies of the dead were often left with the living, who were too weak to carry them to the deck. Of the 240 emigrants on board one ship alone, nine died at sea and another forty on arrival at the quarantine station of Grosse Isle, forty-six kilometres downstream from Quebec City.

Dr. George Douglas, the medical officer in charge, realized that the facilities were not adequate to serve the massive Irish emigration. He begged the government to increase his staff and facilities, but was able to add only fifty beds, bringing accommodation to 200 beds.

The oppressive heat of the summer worsened an already disastrous situation, and still the overcrowded ships kept arriving — 12,000 more immigrants disembarked on June 1st, another 14,000 a week later. The number of sick at the Grosse Isle hospital totalled over 1,000. New sheds were hastily erected, but both sanitation and shelter remained woefully inadequate. The sick were sometimes left on wooden slats on the ground.

By October, when the harbour closed, four doctors had died along with eighteen medical assistants. Two Anglican ministers and four priests were also felled by disease.

The immigrant toll was awful. A plaque erected by Dr. Douglas at a mass burial site notes: "In this secluded spot lie the mortal remains of 5,425 persons who, flying from pestilence and famine in 1847, found in North America but a grave."

During that summer, it has been estimated that 35,000 Irish died during their passage to Canada or shortly after their arrival. Ultimately, the immediate victims of this tragedy were the orphaned children. According to some estimates, the children outnumbered adults fifty-four to one.

Father Charles Felix Cazeau, Vicar General of the Diocese of Quebec, who was affectionately known as "the priest of the Irish," worked tirelessly to have the destitute children taken in by parish priests and placed in foster homes. An impassioned appeal was made to the rural French-speaking population, who answered the call from neighbouring villages.

Out of sympathy for the victims and their homeland, orphanages were careful to preserve the Irish identity of the children, keeping a record of their natural parents, their parish and county of origin, and the vessel that brought them over. The records also include many of the names and addresses of the foster families, most of them French Canadian.

In Quebec City alone there are records of 619 such adoptions. For example, five-year-old Pat Noonan who entered Canada from the ship *Odessa* in 1847, son of Patrick and Mary (née Coleman) of County Westmeath, was adopted by Louis Leblanc of St. Gregoire. In fact, all six of the Noonan orphans went to families in St. Gregoire and the records show that young Pat's five sisters married French Canadians.

In 1909, 9,000 people, many of them descendants of the survivors, gathered at Grosse Isle to dedicate a monument and ponder the meaning of the past.

Several French-speaking people bore witness to the events sixty-two years before by simply stating: "I was taken as a nameless child from this land [Ireland] and given to a family who did not let me forget that I was Irish."

THE LITTLE RAILROAD
THAT COULD

St. Catharines, Ontario, 1851 — There once was a train that had no engine, no tracks but it carried 40,000 passengers. The Underground Railroad, which operated between 1840 and 1860, was the fanciful code name for a network of people with abolitionist sympathies who helped slaves escape to freedom in Canada. They were the "engine." The "tracks" followed invisible winding routes that stretched from the deep South to the Canadian border. The principal conductor of the "railroad" was a former slave named Harriet Tubman, who became known as "Black Moses."

In 1851, Tubman began using St. Catharines, Ontario, a small town near Niagara Falls and the American border, as her base. She made more than fifteen trips to the South over the following seven years rescuing more than 300 slaves, including her own elderly parents. By 1856, it was estimated that 13 percent of St. Catharines' 6,000 citizens were of Afro-American descent and nearly all of the adults were former slaves.

Tubman's daring accomplishments were not appreciated by American slave owners and the Southern states placed a $40,000 bounty on her head.

In 1850 the U.S. Congress passed a Fugitive Slave Law, which made any northerner caught harbouring or helping a slave liable to a fine of $1,000 and possible imprisonment. Sympathizers offered shelter in barns and houses called "stations." The men and women, white and black, Canadian and American, who operated this secret network of escape were its "agents" or "conductors." Slaves were concealed by day and conducted to the next station by night.

Struggling through wilderness brush on foot, the "passengers" avoided travelled roads and lit no cooking fires which might attract professional slave catchers who were notorious for their cruelty. Few had a compass to guide them. They followed the "drinking gourd" in the sky, the Big Dipper which pointed the way north to Canada, where slavery had been officially abolished in 1833. Dr. Martin Luther King described Canada as "the North Star."

One of the slaves to find a new home in Canada was Josiah Henson, who gained fame as the model for the title character in Harriet Beecher Stowe's best-selling 1851 novel, *Uncle Tom's Cabin*.

Unlike the fictional slave protagonist who was beaten to death by his master, Henson escaped from the Kentucky plantation where he had been subjected to inhuman treatment. In 1830, he gathered a small parcel of food and all the money he had (twenty-five cents) and fled north with his wife and four children.

With other fugitives, Henson established a settlement called Dawn (now Dresden, Ontario). He became a minister and served as Commanding Officer of a black company in the Essex Volunteers during the 1837 rebellion. In 1849, abolitionists in Boston published a seventy-six-page autobiographical pamphlet titled *The Life of Josiah Henson, formerly a slave, Now an Inhabitant of Canada,* which is believed to have inspired Harriet Beecher Stowe.

Canadian acceptance of black refugees was something of an affront to the United States. It served notice of the emerging nation's independence as the groundwork was being laid for Confederation.

Enthusiastic support was offered by civil-rights champions and abolitionists such as *Globe* editor George Brown through the Anti-Slavery Society; however, discrimination was widespread. A recent history of St. Catharines notes the general attitude that "as they had once been slaves, they were somehow still inferior." Local attitude aside, when twenty-three former slaves were interviewed by reporter/historian Benjamin Drew the overwhelming description of their new homeland was as a place of "refuge and rest."

Throughout the 1850s, Mary Ann Shadd, a black teacher who was active in the anti-slavery movement, edited the *Provincial Freeman* in which she crusaded for racial equality and desegregation. Her father, Abraham, became the first black to hold public office in British North America when he was elected to a town council in 1859.

As Shadd wrote in a pamphlet entitled *Notes of Canada West* as a guide to black settlers: "No settled country in America offers stronger inducements to coloured people. The general tone of society is healthy, and there is increasing anti-slavery sentiment."

The legacy of the Underground Railroad is one of tolerance, compassion and bravery. Its spirit is epitomized in the spiritual song "Follow the Drinking Gourd":

So long old Master,
Don't come after me,
I'm heading north to Canada
Where everyone is free.

EÒIN A' CHUAN

St. Ann's, Nova Scotia, 1851 — Visitors to the picturesque town of Waipu, north of Auckland in New Zealand, may be surprised to find that many of the residents call themselves "Nossies," after Nova Scotia. They are the descendants of a mass migration of Cape Bretonners who came to the North Island in the middle of the nineteeth century, led by the Reverend Norman McLeod.

For thirty-two years, McLeod ruled a colony of Scots at St. Ann's on Cape Breton Island. He came to settle there by accident. At thirty-seven, disillusioned with the Church of Scotland, he left his homeland and sailed for Pictou, Nova Scotia. By the time he landed, the charismatic but churchless preacher already had a following of shipmates who wanted to settle with him.

The lumber boomtown of Pictou was filled with rum-runners and rowdy goings-on. McLeod pronounced it "a land for shameless and daring wickedness." Instead of staying, he planned to take his followers to Ohio via the Mississippi River, and he built a ship which the Pictou natives jokingly called "the Ark."

On a trial run in the autumn of 1819, McLeod and a small crew berthed the Ark in the harbour at St. Ann's. They found the environment hospitable, the water teeming with fish — they decided it would make a perfect place to settle. Cabins were constructed, along with seven small boats. The following spring, settlers from Pictou began relocating on the island. They were joined by other Scots and soon the colony took on the aspect of a Highland clan society, complete with Norman McLeod as its ruler and latter-day biblical patriarch. He was called "Norman," his people were "Normanites" and the creed of his preaching was "Normanism."

McLeod assumed absolute power, positioning himself as magistrate, teacher and arbitrator of all things. He had no friends, only worshippers, and his cruelty became the stuff of legend. Once he punished a boy for a petty theft by ordering that the tip of his ear be cut off. Later, it was discovered that the boy was not guilty, but his parents refused to take action in court because to do so would have been to "go against God."

In McLeod's colony, the sanctity of the Sabbath was guarded with zeal. Roosters were covered with boxes on Saturday evenings so that they would not crow at dawn on Sunday. During the spring, buckets that filled with maple sap were spilled on Sunday so that no profit could be taken. Cooking was not allowed. Not so much as an apple could be picked. When McLeod's wife Mary wore a ribboned bonnet to church instead of the requisite black, she was humiliated before the congregation. One of the only signs that McLeod had any heart is reflected in the epitaph at the grave of a son who died in childhood. It reads: "Short spring; endless autumn."

McLeod was quick to ban or discipline his followers for any slight, including signs of leadership ability, but he turned a blind eye to the misadventures of his brandy-smuggling sons. Still, hundreds of followers remained faithful, finding odd solace and unity in the rule of a tyrant. They built a church at St. Ann's that reportedly held as many as twelve hundred worshippers. Their sons and daughters attended school where classes were conducted in Gaelic. That linguistic and cultural tradition remains as one positive legacy of the McLeod days. The Gaelic College of Celtic Arts and Crafts now stands on the site of the McLeod settlement.

In 1848, disaster struck the self-contained community when a late spring frost destroyed the crops. By then, McLeod had alienated any neighbourly sources of assistance. A petition to the government brought rations that staved off starvation, but the future looked bleak. Then, Norman got a letter that would change everything.

Years earlier, a black-sheep son named Donald had run away with the family ship, ending up in Australia where he became the editor of a newspaper in Adelaide. When the famine was at its worst, he sent a letter to his father describing the charms of "Down Under" and urging him to move the settlement to a continent half a world away.

Norman McLeod was seventy years old at the time. His wife was over sixty and in poor health. Nevertheless, McLeod's control over his "flock" was such that people who had barely heard of Australia prepared for a massive pilgrimage. By mid-summer the keel was laid for the first of six ships that would make the audacious voyage. Normanites were told Australia was the "destined land."

On October 28, 1851, the *Margaret* set sail with 140 passengers aboard, including 40 children. McLeod sold the family home and property for $3,000 to purchase the sails and riggings for the ship, which was named after his vivacious youngest daughter. Five months later, they landed in Adelaide, only to find that the prodigal son, Donald, had moved on to Melbourne. They caught up with him a few months later, but found Melbourne wholly unattractive.

An Australian gold rush was on, and the booming swagger that abounded in the south Australian town made Pictou look tame. The Gaels of St. Ann's took shelter in a tent-city near Melbourne called Canvastown where an epidemic of typhoid claimed some of their number, including three of McLeod's sons. When their money ran out, they were forced to sell the *Margaret*. Some of the settlers were caught up in the clutches of gold fever and left. It was not until a second ship from Cape Breton arrived that Norman McLeod came up with the idea of moving to New Zealand.

Scots had established a colony in Dunedin on the South Island of New Zealand in 1847. Word of that success had reached as far as St. Ann's. In 1853, McLeod wrote to the Governor of New Zealand, Sir George Grey, to request a block of land. He received an encouraging response. Although they were offered better land at Hawkes Bay, in 1853 the settlers chose a site on the eastern shore north of Auckland because the geography reminded them of Cape Breton. Eight hundred acres of land were purchased at the mouth of the Waipu River for £400 sterling. By 1860, more than 850 Normanites had made the exodus.

Again McLeod established himself as the colony's overlord, but this time the settlers had outside influences. The Maori people taught them how to weave roofs and walls for their log cabins out of palm fronds. Semitropical forest was cleared and converted into fields where corn, pumpkins and melons flourished along with the Nova Scotians' staples: wheat and potatoes. When a reunion of the original settlers was held in 1903, the aged survivors bore names such as McKenzie, McKay, Campbell and McLean. They called themselves *Eòin A' Chuan*, Gaelic for "The Sea Birds."

Sam MacPhee, director of the Gaelic College of Celtic Arts and Crafts at St. Ann's, is frank when he suggests that in contemporary terms, McLeod's colony was virtually a cult. Just before he died in 1866, Norman McLeod uttered his last Normanism to his followers, "Children, children, look to yourselves, the world is mad."

OH HOW WE DANCED
ON THE NIGHT WE WERE
CONSTITUTIONALIZED

Quebec City, 1864 — In photographs, the Fathers of Confederation are a solemn lot, but beneath that paternal stoicism a good many apparently had "happy feet." In fact, dancing was a critical component in the passing of the seventy-two resolutions that formed the basis of the British North America Act.

For eighteen days in October, 1864, the delegates from English and French Canada, New Brunswick, Nova Scotia, Prince Edward Island and Newfoundland met around a crimson-clothed table in the reading room of the Quebec Legislative Council. Through the dreary and rainy days, they debated and fought over issues such as representation by population and the composition of the Senate. The same issues had been discussed by many of the same delegates the previous month in Charlottetown, following long debates within their own constituencies and legislatures.

One unusual attribute of the Quebec Conference was the invitation extended to the female family members of the male delegates. The sponsors went to great lengths to organize glittering nighttime balls for their enjoyment.

So it was that five wives and nine daughters of nineteen hesitant Maritime delegates earned the nickname "Mothers of Confederation," since the tireless politicians took every opportunity to waltz away any doubts about the wisdom of a united Canada. The rewards of their ebullient evening charm were reaped at the meeting table during the following days.

"All right! Confederation through at six o'clock this evening — constitution adopted — a creditable document — a complete reform of the abuses and injustices we've complained of," cheered Liberal delegate and *Globe* publisher George Brown in a hasty note from Quebec to his wife, Anne.

Still, it had been six years since Alexander Galt had originally introduced the idea of British North American union, and it would be one more Conference and more than two years before Queen Victoria would grant Royal Assent to the British North America Act.

In fact, forming Canada's original constitutional Confederation was no easy two-step, and it bore its moments of disenchantment, discord and trod upon toes.

The unity of United Upper and Lower Canada was threatened as early as 1861 when Conservative George-Étienne Cartier insisted that "the two provinces coexist with equal powers."

Nova Scotian Joseph Howe, a once-and-future politician, published his nay-saying views in the press as "Botheration Letters." Three months after approval of the Quebec Resolutions he was predicting that Quebec would "escape from the confederacy" within five years.

Howe also tried to discredit Prime Minister Sir John A. Macdonald by sending the British colonial secretary an article George Brown had written for the *Globe* entitled

"Drunkenness in High Places," which described an inebriated Macdonald clinging to his desk in Parliament to keep from falling.

Indeed Macdonald himself came close to missing Confederation entirely when he accidentally set fire to his bed during the final meetings in London.

Then there was the question of what to call the new nation. Macdonald favoured "Kingdom" of Canada, however there was British opposition to the notion of a colony having a title that would imply equality. The issue was resolved by New Brunswick Premier Leonard Tilley. He suggested "Dominion" of Canada after noting the seventy-second Psalm: "He shall have dominion also from sea to sea."

At the second reading of the BNA Act the fandangos of its creators were confirmed. "We are laying the cornerstone of a great state," Colonial Secretary Lord Carnarvon announced in the House of Lords, "perhaps one which at a future day may even overshadow this country."

Ultimately, the dance of a federally united Canada began on July 1, 1867, when the British North America Act came into force. The Constitutional waltz continues. When it was patriated from Britain in 1982, Canadians were disco dancing.

The beat goes on.

FLAMES OVER
THE SAGUENAY

Saguenay Region, Quebec, 1870 — On the morning of May 19, 1870, as Quebec farmers cultivated their land, a dark cloud rose on the horizon. Spring had come early to the area, but there had been scant rainfall and the farmers hoped that the edge of darkness was a sign of rain. To the north, near Lac St. Jean, a sulphurous yellow rain had soaked the ground that day. But instead of welcome moisture, the cloud was the sign of a raging fire that a westerly wind had spread to the bone-dry forest.

Like many of the forest fires that occur annually in Canada today, the inferno that would sweep through the Saguenay was caused by human carelessness. A family named Savard near the village of St. Felicien started a small brush fire that blew out of control. In a matter of hours, flames had destroyed everything over a distance of 150 kilometres from the Mistassini river, near Lac St. Jean, all the way to Baie des HaHa.

There was no time for the people to contemplate ways of fighting the fire. Animals were set loose and entire families fled to the banks of rivers and lakes, where they tried to swim to safety. Others scrambled into make-shift dugouts or hid themselves in shallow basements and root cellars, while the fire raged above them with a suffocating heat.

Many families had small children and heroic efforts were made to save them. One father, Job Bilodeau, improvised a raft out of logs and branches that the fire had felled into nearby Lac Rond. He soaked the raft in water to prevent embers from setting it afire. After drenching himself and his two-year-old son, the pair set adrift while the shoreline lit up with flames.

At least five people died in the blaze, and many more suffered serious burns. One out of every three families lost everything they owned. By nightfall, the blaze had burned itself out and 5,000 people found themselves homeless and virtually cut off from the world in smouldering solitude.

A government representative reported to an inquiry that he found the area "a total and complete ruin." In the burned-out roadways he encountered weeping, half-clad families whose greatest fear was dying of starvation.

A disaster relief committee was quickly formed and $125,000 was collected and distributed to the victims, along with food, seed, clothing and other supplies sent in from parishes all over the province. The governments of Quebec and Ontario also provided assistance, and soon families were able to move from the crude huts they had carved from seared tree trunks into new homes.

The "Great Fire" left many scars, but despite the terrible toll, the resilient settlers of the Saguenay persevered. Fields were seeded again, barns were rebuilt, bridges and mills were reconstructed.

Ultimately, out of tragedy there came new hope. The destruction of the forest accelerated the clearing of the land for agriculture and contributed to the development of the entire region.

An ecological disaster transformed hundreds of hectares of northern Quebec into a scorched desolation that became productive farm land through the sheer determination of the early settlers. Some clouds do have silver linings.

THE COLOUR
OF THE OLD WEST

Highwood River, Alberta, 1882 — John Ware was born into slavery on a plantation in South Carolina in 1845, the second youngest of eleven children. Reports say that he had never worn shoes until he was twenty years old and he never learned to read or write. But John Ware knew how to sit a horse and rope a steer. Most importantly, he knew how to make his acquaintance with whites work to his peaceable advantage.

By the time the Civil War ended and American blacks were freed from slavery, Ware was living in Texas and refining his skills as a cowboy. Black cowboys were not unknown in the American West, but the Canadian West was another matter entirely.

In 1882, Ware joined a cattle drive from Idaho, where Alberta's "King of Canadian Cattle Trails," Tom Lynch, was waiting to escort 3,000 head of foundation stock to the North-West Cattle Company (later known as the Bar U) in the foothills southwest of Calgary on the Highwood River.

"Trailing" was everything and more than the Old West fantasies produced by Hollywood. Six skilled cowboys could handle 1,000 cattle, and every cowboy travelled with at least half of a dozen horses. There was always a chuck-wagon, a cook to complain about and a trail boss to hear the complaints. It was hard work to move a large herd even nineteen kilometres (twelve miles) a day. Cowboys stayed in the saddle morning to dusk supervising the "dogies."

Tom Lynch was looking for experienced cowhands to drive the herd. John Ware's name kept coming up, but Lynch is said to have hesitated at the notion of hiring a "Negro," until at least one cowboy said he wouldn't take the job unless Ware was along. Ware was assigned to a clunker of a horse and a junker of a saddle. He started the drive at the "drag end" of the herd, where there was the most dust and dirt on a dry day and the muckiest mud on a wet one.

When the herd reached its destination, John Ware was riding at the front of the herd on a horse the other cowboys had considered a handsome outlaw. And he was sitting in a comfortable saddle. Assuming that a former plantation slave would have little horse savvy, Lynch had made an entertainment out of a request Ware had made for a sturdier animal and more supple seating. Instead of falling off the wild and bucking horse as anticipated, Ware had ridden his outlaw mount to a standstill. When he accepted his pay, Ware was asked to stay on at the ranch.

Ware stayed at the Bar U for several years before hiring on at the Quorn ranch on Sheep Creek. The purpose of the Quorn was rather unusual. It was funded by The Quorn Hunt Club of Leicestershire, England, and its primary purpose was to raise hunter horses for the British market. Several hundred hunter-type mares and twenty thoroughbred and Cleveland Bay stallions were imported as foundation stock. Raising cattle was just a sideline.

While Ware did not participate in the Quorn events such as rugger, cricket and riding to hounds, he did earn the respect of the English for his uncanny horsemanship.

In 1885, a huge general round-up was held in the spring. One hundred cowboys combed the foothills, rounding up 60,000 cattle. The Quorn sent John Ware as its representative.

"If there is a man on the round-up who keeps up the spirits of the boys more than another and provides amusement to break the monotony, this man is John Ware," declared the June 23, 1885, *Macleod Gazette*. "The horse is not running on the prairie which John cannot ride."

Over the years, Ware acquired the nucleus of a cattle herd of his own, sometimes taking an animal in lieu of wages. In 1890, he started his own small ranching operation on the north shore of Sheep Creek. His brand was 9999, which was said to be his lucky number. Biographer Grant MacEwan called the Four Nines or "walking-stick" brand "hideous." Later, Ware reduced it to three nines, which charred slightly less cowhide.

In 1892, John met Mildred Lewis, whose father was a Calgary carpenter. Lightning struck, quite literally, while they were courting. A bolt killed the two horses that were pulling the buggy in which John had taken Mildred for a country ride. Tall, strong John pulled the rig back to town. Shortly afterwards, the pair were married.

Black American cowboy Bill Pickett is credited with inventing the sport of steer wrestling, but newlywed John Ware earned the distinction of being the first to demonstrate it in Canada at a Calgary fair. He learned the skill defending himself against a longhorn cow that charged a group of cowboys in a corral. Ware grabbed the enraged bovine by the horns. While she dragged him around, he managed to wrap an arm around her muzzle and pulled her to the ground by the nose until she fell under his control. At the Calgary steer roping and tying competition, it took Ware fifty-one seconds to immobilize a steer. He won $100 and a new saddle.

John and Mildred began raising a family. They appear to have integrated comfortably into the community. On one occasion Ware was apparently taunted by racist remarks in a Calgary tavern. He knocked the offender out and then graciously took him to a hospital and paid the doctor's bill.

When a Medicine Hat hotel tried to refuse him a room, Ware's friends stood up for him and "set the hotel man straight." Although he was known throughout his life as "Nigger John," even the *Canadian Encyclopedia* goes to some lengths to point out that this "was not intended pejoratively."

The mythology of John Ware's abilities with animals grew to the proportion of legend. It has been said that he could walk across the backs of a corral filled with bulls, run faster than a three-year-old steer, and leap into a saddle without touching a stirrup. The only thing he could not countenance was snakes.

The Sheep Creek area began filling up with settlers after the completion of the railway from Calgary to Fort Macleod. Ware had 300 head of cattle and he needed more grazing room, so he sold his ranch for $1,000 and moved northeast to Brooks on the Red Deer River.

In the spring of 1905, Mildred Ware died of typhoid and pneumonia despite John's efforts to obtain medicine for her during a freak blizzard. Their five young children grew up with relatives. At least two of the boys served in World War I, but afterwards the only work they could find was as railway porters.

Tragedy struck John Ware a few months after Mildred's death. He was killed when his horse tripped and fell on him after stepping into a badger hole. The Calgary Public Library's website tribute to Ware as a hero of the Old West contains this curious bit of trivia: "A young lawyer named R.B. Bennett was assigned to handle Ware's estate. Cowboys laughed at Bennett's folly of selling all of Ware's horses and then having to rent horses to round up Ware's cattle. Bennett is the only Canadian Prime Minister to have lived and worked in Calgary."

At the funeral, a Baptist minister called John Ware "one of God's most cheerful children" and noted that, "He convinced me that black is a beautiful colour . . . His example and message on brotherhood should be entrenched in our hearts."

Five years after Ware's death, 1,000 blacks from Oklahoma attempted to move to the Edmonton area but they were thwarted by public hostility against what one politician called "Dark Spots."

The Edmonton *Capital* carried a Board of Trade petition that stated: "We submit that the advent of such negroes as are here now was most unfortunate for the country, and that further arrivals in large numbers would be disastrous."

An order-in-council from the federal government barred black immigration for one year. It was ultimately withdrawn, only to be replaced by more subtle means of discouraging black immigration, including utilizing immigration agents who travelled the United States spreading the word in black communities that the climate was cold and agricultural prospects limited.

GREEN SIDE UP!

The Canadian Prairies, 1890 — How did the pioneers build houses without any wood? They cut the lawn and stacked it, green side up. Called "soddies," they were literal grass-root structures, and they all shared one thing in common — they leaked.

Lumber was a very costly commodity to obtain on the prairies during the 1890s, when the Canadian government mounted a lavish advertising campaign in Europe to attract settlers by offering 160-acre sections of land "free" to anyone hardy enough to cultivate the land for three years.

Sod houses were modest structures which usually consisted of one room that measured about twelve by eight feet. The settlers cut the sod in "bricks" which were three feet long, two feet wide and six inches thick.

The tools that were used to accomplish this task were homemade, and the measurements were never precise. The sod was cut from a slough bottom where the grass roots were thick and tough. The slabs were stacked to a height of about eight feet, and the walls gradually settled into place.

Doors and windows presented a great building challenge. The single door entry was almost always lopsided, and those settlers who were clever enough to devise windows were the envy of their neighbours.

Occasionally light prairie willow brush was used to form the roof of sod houses, and even this was covered with sod. Inside the dark soddie houses, cloth was used to partition areas for privacy and white cotton covered the walls.

Walls were lined with planks, which were whitewashed monthly. With lumber financially out of reach, the planks often came from the wagons the settlers used to bring their basic goods over the deeply rutted trails that formed the only "road system" through Canada's vast western prairies.

Floors were generally pounded earth, which was swept daily after the dust had been laid with damp tea leaves. House-proud women spread hooked rugs on the floors. Managing a soddie household was a full-time occupation. Washing clothes was particularly difficult because the hard wellwater curdled the soap. Ashes or sand were used to scour steel cutlery.

A cast-iron stove was one of the few essentials that was store-bought and trade-name brands such as the Homesteader, the Rancher, and the Grand Jewel were the pride of each household. When firewood was scarce, which was most of the time, the stove was fuelled with buffalo chips or straw twists. Every day the homemaker tended the most valuable of possessions by rubbing it with Dome or Rising Sun black lead polish to render a rich shine.

At planting and harvest time the soddie women joined their men in the field, hauling sheaves in their voluminous denim dresses and marching behind the oxen-powered ploughs. For food, they relied largely on the land and the livestock they brought with them.

Salt-pork was a continuous, and monotonous staple. Regular supplies included oatmeal, corn syrup and dried beans. A 100-pound bag of flour sold for about three dollars and sugar was five cents a pound. The dilemma was always finding a way to transport such items.

Of necessity, the homesteaders looked to the land to provide variety. The men hunted rabbits and game birds, fished the streams and sought out berry bushes.

The women became expert at gathering prairie species such as wild sage and onions. Tansy and yarrow plants were gathered for yeast, goldenrod provided dye, wormwood was used for poultices and long, purple, licorice-coloured spikes of anise were turned into cough medicine.

There is no question that the life of the soddic settlers of western Canada was one of constant toil, peppered with turmoil such as drought and grasshopper invasions. Without the determination and innovation of those thousands of settlers who lived in little grass houses and made each soddie a home, the vast prairie wheat lands would never have become the breadbasket of the world.

HEROES,
HEROINES
& THE
ODD SCOUNDREL

HOLDING THE FORT

WITHOUT A COW

AN UNAMERICAN HERO

BEYOND THE CALL OF DUTY

CAPTAIN COURAGEOUS

BY MANY NAMES SHALL YOU KNOW HIM

CLOTHES DO NOT MAKE THE MAN

SINK OR SWIM

THE SAINT OF DAWSON CITY

PAYING THE RENT

NEIGHBOURS IN ARMS

WHEN SHIPS COLLIDE

"EVERY MAN, CARRY A MAN"

A MALTESE FALCON

TICKLING THE DRAGON'S TAIL

COURAGE DOWN BELOW

HOLDING THE FORT

Fort Verchères, New France, 1692 — One of the most unusual recruiting posters of the Second World War featured a striking, stern-faced fourteen-year-old girl wearing a seventeeth-century dress and holding an ancient musket. According to the war department, the brunette vision standing on the shores of the St. Lawrence River "symbolizes the feminine heroism of Canada." Her name was Marie-Madeleine Jarret de Verchères.

There are many versions of the story of young Madeleine's heroic defence of her father's fort below Montreal on October 22, 1692. Madeleine herself added several embellishments and variations during her lifetime. There is no question that she was a young woman with a hearty survival instinct.

Madeleine was the fourth of twelve children. Her father, François Jarret, had served with the Régiment de Carignan, a 1,000-soldier force sent by France in 1665 to defend the settlers from attack by the Iroquois. After the Iroquois had been subdued by the French, the Régiment was disbanded. Two years later, in 1669, François married twelve-year-old Marie Perrot and they settled on a grant of land below Montreal called Verchères.

The family home became a fort while Madeleine was a toddler. The English and French were at war, and the British encouraged their Iroquois allies and trading partners to rekindle their attacks on French settlers. Isolated on the river, at least a day away from any military assistance, Fort Verchères was soon known as Château Dangereux. Attack was inevitable.

Madeleine was twelve when the Iroquois first stormed the stockade. Her thirty-three-year-old mother took command of a small force and drove them back with musket fire. Throughout 1690, French settlers waged their own brutal attacks on the English colonies and suffered the repercussions.

The summer of 1692 passed peacefully at Fort Verchères, which was well stocked with gunpowder and muskets. Madeleine's father left for military duty that fall and her mother felt the temper of the time was safe enough to leave her teenaged daughter "holding the fort," while she ventured to Montreal briefly for winter supplies.

From this point, the stories range freely. Some say Madeleine was gathering pumpkins when the attack began, others suggest she was on a wharf securing a water buoy when the bullets began to fly. According to the first rendition of her own story, Madeleine was running for the fort when a warrior grabbed her neckerchief, which she ripped off in the struggle to escape. Inside the fort, she rallied her meagre troops with the cry, "To arms! To arms!" In one version of her story, she discovered two cowering soldiers preparing to blow up the fort rather than risk capture, but she scolded them into taking their posts. In another, she dons a soldier's hat and takes to the ramparts herself — with an old man and two of her younger brothers firing muskets and creating the appearance of a much larger force.

Whatever diversions Madeleine created, they seemed to work on the Iroquois. When French and native allies arrived, they found only the dead in the field and the ragtag defenders of Fort Verchères under the leadership of a feisty slip of a girl.

The drama of her story sparked the interest of the French court, and when Madeleine's father died in 1700 his pension was transferred to her as a reward. By the standards of the day, she was a wealthy spinster when she married officer and seigneur Pierre-Thomas Tarieu de la Pérade in 1706. At fifty-four, Madeleine added to her legend by saving his life when he became involved in a brawl with two men.

Thirty years after the incident at Fort Verchères few eyewitnesses remained alive, so Madeleine retold her story in an apparent bid for a favour from France. Among other things, she added forty-five Iroquois to her evasive run to the fort and extended her single-handed defence to a full week rather than two days.

"Allow me to tell you that, like many men, I have feelings which incline me to glory," admitted the heroine of Verchères.

WITHOUT A COW

Beaver Dams, Upper Canada, 1813 — Laura Secord, whose name has become synonymous with boxed chocolates, was a genuine heroine of the War of 1812. However, her place in history was not recognized for many years, and even then her act of courage was often tethered to an imaginary cow.

Laura Ingersoll was born in Massachusetts in 1775. Her father, Thomas, who had been a patriot in the American Revolution, decided to take advantage of land grants offered in Upper Canada and moved his family to Oxford Township in 1793.

Laura married James Secord in 1797. He was a son of Loyalists and worked as a merchant. By 1812, the Secords maintained a modest home near Queenston Heights where they lived with their five children.

When the United States declared war against Great Britain, American troops marched on Canada and James Secord joined the Lincoln County Militia. Shortly afterward, he was wounded at the Battle of Queenston Heights.

While he was recovering under Laura's care, American officers occupied their home and Laura was required

to cook for them. It was during one particularly boisterous and well-lubricated dining session that Laura apparently overheard the enemy outlining an attack on the
British position at Beaver Dams, which was under the
command of Lieutenant James FitzGibbon.

Before dawn the following day, Secord left her home
to warn the troops. The thirty-two-kilometre trek took at
least eighteen hours. Throughout the interminably hot day,
Secord avoided travelled routes and check-points. She
forded streams, crossed snake-infested swamps and ended
her journey by climbing the steep Niagara Escarpment.

At nightfall, she was discovered, exhausted, by a
group of Mohawks, who formed the principal British fighting force. According to Secord's account, the encounter
took place by moonlight and she was terrified. "They all
rose and yelled 'Woman' which made me tremble," she
recalled. She was taken to FitzGibbon, who reinforced his
position.

With the Mohawks as their allies, the British were
victorious. Five hundred troops surrendered and the consequence was a serious reversal for the Yankees. "Not a
shot was fired on our side by any but the Indians," Fitz-
Gibbon wrote. "They beat the American detachment into
a state of terror."

Laura Secord's trek did not become common knowledge for over forty years. FitzGibbon appeared to take total
credit and, despite petitions on her behalf, Laura saw no
reward.

In 1841, James Secord died, leaving his sixty-five-
year-old wife virtually penniless and without a pension.
Her bravery was finally officially recognized when the
Prince of Wales, later King Edward VII, visited Niagara
Falls in 1860. Secord's was the only woman's name on a

list of 500 veterans of the War of 1812 which was presented to the Prince. In 1861, the Prince sent Secord 100 English pounds ($250). It was the only financial reward she received for her deed.

Fame came slowly, and often inaccurately. An early historian embellished the tale by adding a cow, which Secord was said to have used as a decoy. Following her death at ninety-three in 1868, several monuments were erected in her honour. In 1913, Senator Frank O'Connor chose her name for his new brand of chocolates. For many years the candies were marketed in white boxes adorned with a grandmotherly portrait of Secord and signed with a stylized signature.

Although her heroism may have had scant reward in her lifetime, as the wry joke would have it, had it not been for Laura Secord we might be eating Fanny Farmer sweets on Valentine's Day.

AN UNAMERICAN HERO

Stoney Creek, Upper Canada, 1813 — Canadian author/humorist Eric Nicol has noted that: "Very little is known about the War of 1812 because the Americans lost it." Maybe that is why so few Americans know that during that war, British troops burned the White House in Washington, D.C. as retaliation for American action in Niagara, York (Toronto) and in Upper Canada.

What some Americans have in retrospect characterized as a mere "border skirmish," was in fact a full-blown, often poorly executed, American attempt at the conquest of a peaceful people. In its failure, settlers north of the 49th parallel developed an appreciation of the nature of their budding nationhood and a determination not to be American.

The turning point in the conflict occurred in the predawn hours of June 6, 1813. One of the heroes of the battle, which pitted 700 British troops against 2,000 invaders, was a civilian teenager named Billy Green.

William Green is said to have been the first white child born in Saltfleet Township near Stoney Creek. Born in a log cabin on February 4, 1794, he was the eleventh child of Loyalists Adam and Martha Green who had abandoned their 6,000-acre New Jersey holdings to accept a grant of

300 acres of bush on the Niagara Escarpment. Mrs. Green died shortly after the birth and young Billy was raised by his older sisters.

By all accounts, including legend, Billy grew up attuned to his environment, ranging freely through forests of pine, oak and elm as an adventurous loner and a natural woodsman. The local people called him "Billy the Scout," and he made use of his knowledge as a member of the Fifth Lincoln militia unit.

Billy was walking on a wooded ridge trail with his older brother, Levi, in the early morning of June 5, 1813. From their vantage point, they saw blue-coated regiments of American soldiers, including light infantry and cavalry marching toward the village of Stoney Creek at noon. The Americans were two days' march away from their headquarters at Fort George on the Niagara River, which they had taken from the British just days earlier.

Whooping like Indians, Billy and Levi set off to warn the settlers, including Levi's wife and their sister, Keziah Corman. When they reached the Cormans' farm, they learned that Keziah's husband, Isaac, had been taken prisoner by the enemy who had been asking questions about the location of Indian camps.

Fearing the worst, Billy went in search of his brother-in-law, but miraculously Isaac turned up unharmed. Kentucky-born Corman had apparently secured his release by telling his captors that he was a relative of American General William Henry Harrison. The officer in charge was so impressed that when he released Corman he gave him a password that would allow him to move freely through enemy lines.

The countersign phrase is said to have been "Will-Hen-Har," based on the first three syllables of the American

General's name. Billy knew that this would be vital information to the British, who were encamped at Burlington Heights about ten kilometres away. He was determined to deliver the message.

Sentries were already patrolling the main road that Billy had to cross with the password that should have presented no problem, but at that precise and critical moment Billy Green had a stunning lapse of memory.

"I forgot it," he admitted years later. Not knowing what to do, Billy improvised a disguise. "I pulled my coat over my head and trotted across the road on my feet and hands like a bear."

Back at Levi's house on the hillside, he mounted his brother's horse, Tip, and rode as far as he could toward the British encampment. He finished the mountainous climb on foot, arriving an hour before midnight.

The British were aware of the American troop movement, but Billy was able to provide detailed information and he knew the countryside like the back of his hand. A night attack was quickly scheduled.

With Billy serving as guide, the advance party made its way toward the American camp without so much as moonlight to guide them. There was sheet lightning over the lake and a brief shower made the going muddy and difficult. Two British regiments, under General John Vincent and Colonel John Harvey, were instructed to remove the flints from their muskets to avoid the accidental discharge of weapons. The initial attack was to be a "cold steel exercise" — a silent surprise to the sleeping Americans.

Accounts vary; however, it seems that by the time the advance group reached the first sentry, Billy Green had recovered the memory of the password and used it to get close enough to the man for a bayonet to silence him.

Another guard was dispatched in a similar fashion. Only when a third sentry managed to fire off a shot while he drowned in his own blood did the Americans wake up. By that time, a church containing thirty guards had been captured while they slept in the pews.

Bayonets fixed, the British proceeded to enter the American camp. Whooping like Indians they found themselves in the midst of the dying campfires of the regimental mess, confronting a few early bird cooks and tripping over sundry cookware. One local history suggests that the Americans must have thought they had been "attacked by the entire British army and surrounded by all the Indians in Canada." The element of surprise was lost.

The Americans had been sleeping on a hill, with their loaded weapons at their sides. Before the British could fix their flints, the Americans were firing on them. For a time, disorder prevailed. Directives to the British troops were drowned in the noise. Some started to fall back.

From a nearby knoll, four American artillery guns began firing. With about twenty men, field commander Major Charles Plenderleath charged the position and captured the guns, turning them on their former owners. Confusion reigned.

"When it commenced to get daylight, we could see the enemy running in all directions," recalled Billy Green.

Both of the American generals were captured, one of them while he was attempting to rally troops he mistakenly identified as American. General Vincent fell from his horse and got lost in the bushes. He was discovered, horseless and hatless, that morning.

The battle lasted barely forty minutes. When it was over a native observer noted that corpses were strewn over the landscape like freshly caught salmon. Nearly one-third of the attacking British force were killed, wounded or missing.

American losses represented less than one-tenth of their force. However costly the victory was, it was enough to turn the Americans back, demoralized, leaderless, unaware of the diminished state of their adversaries.

On the battlefield, Billy Green and several Stoney Creek youths collected the bodies on an ox-drawn stone-boat and buried them.

Sixty-two years later, a grateful nation honoured Billy Green with a twenty-dollar gratuity. The following year, he died at the age of eighty-three.

As with his female counterpart, Laura Secord, Billy Green's bravery was barely acknowledged during his lifetime.

Ironically, following the war that defined the Canadian sense of uniquely un-American nationhood, Billy was often identified as "the Paul Revere of Canada."

BEYOND THE CALL OF DUTY

Long Point, Ontario, 1854 — The treacherous sandbars of Lake Erie have claimed many mariners to a watery grave. In 1827, three ships were wrecked at the same place off Long Point on the north side of the smallest of the five Great Lakes. Twenty-seven years later on a stormy November night, the fate of another shipwrecked crew lay in the hands of a twenty-four-year-old woman.

Abigail Becker was tending her two young children at her Long Point peninsula log cabin home that storm-tossed night. Her husband, a trapper, had gone to the mainland in the household's only boat when the heavily laden schooner *Conductor* ran aground in the blinding sleet and snow.

The ship had keeled over by morning. When Becker spotted the remains, she saw eight surviving sailors clinging to the rigging. They huddled together on a small platform near the top of the foremast in frozen clothes.

Becker's first impulse was to build a large fire to signal to the men that help was at hand. She called for the children to bring a kettle and blankets. They gathered driftwood for a blaze, but Becker could see that the situation was growing desperate as the gale ripped and pushed the exhausted men.

The ship was lodged in the shallows hundreds of metres from the shore, and a yawl boat the men might have used as a lifeboat had torn clear. Although she did not know how to swim, Becker gathered her skirt and waded out into the breakers beckoning the men to come ashore.

The sight of her rallied the crew, and Captain Robert Hackett peeled off his jacket and boots to test the waters. "If I make shore successfully, the rest of you follow," he is said to have told his crew. Using a rope, he flung himself out past the yard-arm and swam toward Becker who pulled him to the beach and sat him by the fire with a mug of tea.

One by one, Abigail Becker collected each exhausted crewman and lugged them to shore. Her crippled son was also trying to help when he was swept under, and the young woman found herself saving two lives in one trip.

Later, Lee Hays, the *Conductor*'s sixteen-year-old cabin boy, described his own experience after taking the plunge. "I could feel the strong current pushing me from shore, so I began to swim with all my might. As the waves swept over me, I went under again and again. Finally I felt myself slip beneath the waves forever. Just at that moment, a powerful hand grabbed my arm. I coughed and spluttered as the woman heaved me over her shoulder. Icy waves crashed against us, but she never let go."

By the end of the day, seven of the sailors were ensconced at Becker's home. The cook, a non-swimmer, chose to remain on board. He was rescued by raft when the storm subsided the next day.

The rescue earned Becker the title "the heroine of Long Point." She was celebrated in magazine articles and poems. Queen Victoria sent her a personal letter and a gift of fifty pounds, and the Prince of Wales presented another gift when he was duck hunting on Long Point in 1860.

The sudden notoriety surprised Becker. "I only did my duty, just as anyone else would have done," she is reported to have said. She took a $500 purse presented to her by seamen and the family bought a farm near Port Rowan. Later, she used a gold medal presented to her by the Benevolent Life Saving Association of New York to barter at the local grist mill.

When the limelight dimmed, life's duty for Becker continued to be one of day-to-day heroism. All told, she adopted two children, bore eight of her own and acquired another nine through marriage.

She may have saved seven lives, but she also raised nineteen.

CAPTAIN COURAGEOUS

Spotted Islands, Labrador, 1867 — It is part of the lore of Newfoundland that at least one mariner has expired at the mere recollection of riding out a hurricane. It was a weather disturbance of just such memorable proportion that led the schooner *Sea Clipper* into a collision with another small schooner off the shores of Indian Tickle on the craggy coastline of Labrador. The other vessel was cut down, but all hands managed to clamber aboard the *Sea Clipper*, which proceeded down the coast toward Spotted Islands.

At the height of this storm — one of the worst recorded on the coast — a burly thirty-year-old named William Jackman, who was visiting nearby, decided to take a walk outside with his friend. Captain Jackman grew up in a family that was accustomed to the perils of the sea, but his hometown of Renews was considered to be part of the "south," and the sight of the storm may have piqued his curiosity. "I felt something tell me to take that course," he said later, leading to speculation that he was mystically guided.

At the headland, Jackman spotted the *Sea Clipper*. The overloaded schooner had been driven onto a reef, where the waves tore at her in the running sea and the gale precluded any notion of launching a rescue boat. To Jackman, who grew up swimming in the Atlantic, the solution was obvious. After instructing his companion to go back to the settlement and gather ropes and men, he stripped off his coat and boots and dove into the pounding surf.

Against all odds, he managed to swim the 200 metres to the *Sea Clipper*. Hoisting a man on his back, he made the return trip. Eleven souls had been rescued in this precarious manner before help arrived. The ropes must have been a welcome sight to the tiring Jackman, who tied the lifeline to his waist and went back for more. Twenty-six men had been returned from the sea and the *Sea Clipper* deck was empty when Jackman asked the assembled survivors if there were any others left to be dry-docked.

There was one, he was told. The only woman aboard had been too ill to bring up to the deck. She was thought to be dying, perhaps even dead, and certainly too weak to survive a saltwater rescue. Despite attempts to dissuade him, Jackman's gallant response is said to have been, "Living or dead, I will not leave her there." Back he went into the icy waters for the twenty-seventh journey.

He found the woman in the aft cabin of the wreck, too sick to move even though rising water threatened to engulf her. Strapping her to his own body, he managed to bring her safely to shore where she was wrapped in his coat, but the excursion proved too much for her. She died shortly after offering her thanks.

"Captain Will" soon became known as "Captain Courageous," and the Justice of the Peace for Labrador, Matthew Warren, was quick to sing the praises of his noble conduct. Bishop Thomas Mullock of St. John's took up the cause and a year later the Duke of Buckingham sent Jackman a medal for bravery from the Royal Humane Society.

Although his countrymen wanted to celebrate his courage, Jackman was more introspective. He insisted that he was merely following the creed of his family, which demanded that one persevere until a task is completed. He gave the medal to his wife, Bridget, and never spoke of it again. His father, Captain Tom, illustrated the strength of the family creed when he told his son, "If you had not brought that woman ashore, I'd never have forgiven you."

Jackman spent the rest of his life commanding ships and men and confronting the dangers of the Labrador coast. The rigours of the rescue seemed to have tapped his great strength, however. When he died in 1877, just a few months shy of his fortieth birthday, all of the businesses in St. John's closed and flags flew at half-mast in honour of the hero of the wreck of the *Sea Clipper*.

BY MANY NAMES
SHALL YOU KNOW HIM

Blackfoot Crossing, Bow River, Alberta, September 1877
— In the culture of the Plains Indians in the late 1800s names
were sacred to each family and were earned by acts of brav-
ery and courage. When thirty-three-year-old *Isapo-muxika*, or
Crow Indian's Big Foot, succeeded Three Suns as Chief of the
Blackfoot in 1869 he had been variously known as Shot Close,
Bear Ghost and Packs-a-Knife, each name a testament to acts
that earned him the respect and reverence of his people.

By the age of twenty, Crowfoot (as he was called) had
proven himself in nineteen separate battles and sustained a
half-a-dozen wounds. But his appointment as chief was more
a consequence of attrition than acclamation. A plague of
smallpox, brought to the plains by white settlers, wiped out
thousands upon thousands of native people, including most
of Crowfoot's competition for the top job. Nothing — not his
prowess with a knife nor his willingness to do battle nor his
formidable constitution — could prepare Crowfoot for the
devastation that was brought upon his people as a consequence of the white man's inexorable westward push.

Crowfoot's visage — the chiselled profile, the dark,
weather-worn skin and piercing eyes — has made him the

prototype for the perfect "Hollywood Indian." But posterity, at least, from many native perspectives, regard Crowfoot, with troubled ambivalence if not contempt. History books most often describe him as a great visionary and peace-maker.

Most of the great chiefs saw the futility of their cir-cumstances — the European diseases to which their people had no resistance, the debilitating effects of the white man's whisky, the disappearance of the buffalo, the lethal power of the firearm. These phenomena ended native life as it had been known. But Crowfoot was unique in his seemingly infinite capacity to acquiesce and compromise. Because he was such a charismatic leader, the Blackfoot listened and obeyed Crowfoot almost until the day the Chief drew his last breath.

Instead of following Sitting Bull's imprecations to help him wipe out the North-West Mounted Police, and to cap-ture more white women and more horses than the Blackfoot could ever imagine, Crowfoot balked. He took to heart Methodist Minister Reverend John McDougall's admon-ishments about whisky trading and stealing horses and allowed the Mounties to bring the white man's law and order, not only to the whisky peddlers, but also to the Black-foot Confederacy. Crowfoot naively told McDougall, who may well have had the best of intentions, that the Minis-ter's words made him glad. "In the coming of the Big Knives with their firewater and quick shooting guns, we are weak. We want peace. When you tell us about this strong force which will govern with good laws and treat the Indians the same as white men, you make us rejoice."

And rejoice they did, for about a week. By 1871, all of Canada's Plains Indians except the Blackfoot Confederacy had signed away their lands in six treaties. On September

22, 1877, for as far as the eye could see, four thousand Blackfoot, Piegan, Stoney, Blood and Sarcee erected a thousand teepees. The Mounties were there in force. Queen Victoria was represented in the person of Lieutenant-Governor David Laird of the Northwest Territories. He was known as "The Man Who Talks Straight."

Drums throbbed. There were games of daring and chance. The government distributed copious quantities of flour, sugar and tea. Over the five days it took to get all the relevant signatures — Crowfoot's was the last — Laird told the native leaders that the buffalo would soon be extinct. He promised them rights and privileges "for as long as the sun shines and the rivers run." There would be this, that and the other thing — money, cattle, ammunition, implements, seed — for each and every native person. Chiefs would get a medal, a flag and new clothes every three years.

When Crowfoot signed Treaty Number Seven, he granted 129,500 square kilometres (50,000 square miles) of arguably the richest land in Canada stretching between Cypress Hills, Alberta, and the British Columbia border, in exchange for small change, a litany of Christian prayers and a series of empty promises. Crowfoot himself was already a wealthy and powerful man. At his peak he owned four hundred horses, had several aides on the payroll and serviced ten wives. Then he led his people to the oblivion of the reserve, where life was absolutely nothing like "The Man Who Talks Straight" had promised.

Now the white eyes could continue to wipe out the few remaining buffalo with impunity. They could sell more whisky, more successfully, into a clearly defined, stationary and demoralized target market. Crowfoot's people began starving or drinking themselves to death. Government agents turned increasingly hostile. Young native leaders, including Crowfoot's adopted son Poundmaker, rallied and readied to do or die. As Blackfoot warriors, they demanded freedom and honour or death. Even Crowfoot began to doubt his own judgment and became increasingly unhappy and depressed.

In 1883, it became apparent that the tracks upon which the "iron horse" would run were going to be laid right through the Blackfoot reserve lands west of Medicine Hat. When the great Chief and Peacemaker himself became ill, the medicine men blamed the bilious, foul smoke streaming from the locomotives' stacks — clouds of which floated like fiendish apparitions over the limitless prairie horizons.

Neither the railway route nor the installation of the rails was part of the Treaty, nor had it been discussed. Convinced that Crowfoot's illness was derived from locomotive smoke and indignant over the lack of consultation about the railway — the warrior spirit — so much a part of the Blackfoot nature — rose as billowing smoke and threatened the incipient complacency. The Blackfoot started to tear up the rails under the cover of night as fast as the legions of steeves could spike them.

Sir William Van Horne of the Canadian Pacific Railway turned to a priest for help. He knew Crowfoot respected Father Albert Lacombe. Even while the young warriors armed themselves to resist the encroachment of railway gangs on their reserve lands, Father Lacombe conferred in deferential whispers with the ailing Crowfoot over copious amounts of tea and tobacco. Crowfoot was persuaded to call off the warriors.

Crowfoot's influential intervention allowed the CPR to push through Blackfoot land. Van Horne rewarded him with a lifetime railway pass, which the Chief remained inordinately proud of until the day he died. In 1885, five years before his death, he thwarted Poundmaker's plans, averting a bloodbath by successfully persuading the Blackfoot not to join with the Métis and Cree in the second Riel Rebellion.

"The white people are as thick as flies in summer time," the aging Blackfoot Chief told his people after returning from a government-sponsored trip to the East Coast. Crowfoot's final advice to rebellious young braves was for them to think about cattle, not buffalo.

The day Crowfoot died, a mourning nation shot the great Chief's favourite horse and buried its carcass with him, adding the rifle with which Crowfoot had once been so proficient. His people believed he would need both of them on the Greater Plains to which his spirit would travel and once again be free. A bronze cross at his gravesite identified Crowfoot as "Father of His People." Buried with him was a way of life thousands of years old. Nothing would ever be the same again.

SINK OR SWIM

Vancouver, 1886 — At Alexandra Park in the West End of Vancouver there is a marble fountain depicting three children splashing in the water beneath the face of a man. The inscription it bears reads: "Little Children loved Him."

Created by Italian-Canadian sculptor Charles Marega, the fountain is dedicated to legendary lifeguard, Seraphim "Joe" Fortes, who spent most of his life patrolling the beach of English Bay and teaching youngsters how to swim. In the process, he is credited with saving at least twenty-nine lives and spreading goodwill wherever he went.

Seraphim Fortes is believed to have grown up in the Caribbean on the island of Barbados. When he was a teenager he took to the seas and sailed to Liverpool, England, where he worked as a bath attendant and swimming instructor for half a dozen years. Swimming was one thing that he excelled at and he received a medal from the daughter of the Lord Mayor of London for winning a race across the Mersey River.

In 1884, he boarded the vessel *Robert Kerr* and began a journey which was supposed to end at Victoria on Vancouver Island. Instead, the rag-tag ship lost its main mast and was towed into Vancouver's Burrard Inlet. By this time,

Fortes was seldom known as "Seraphim," that celestial first name having been reduced to "Joe" by his shipmates during the voyage. As "Joe," the strapping, stout black man took a variety of jobs in the rough and tumble landscape of "Gastown," which had been populated and carved by colourful characters with names like Hog Ned, Dumps Baker, Hans the Boatman and the voluble Gassy Jack Deighton.

Although he was in his mid-thirties when he arrived in the area that is now known as Granville, Joe is noted to have been its first shoeshine "boy." He also worked as a bouncer at the Sunnyside Hotel, before moving on to the Bodega Saloon where he served as a teetotalling bartender who discouraged heavy product abuse.

On June 13, 1886, Fortes and all of Vancouver witnessed the conflagration of their community. It was a Sunday, but CPR crews who had been clearing massive tracts of timber for a new railway terminus were busy burning stumps and debris. By this time, the entire coast had been subjected to what has been termed *silvi-slaughter*. Douglas fir trees that measured as much as four metres (thirteen feet) at the base were felled by axemen, creating a domino-effect that crushed younger trees and left storey-high jumbles of trunks and limbs cluttering the landscape.

The pall of smoke was a constant as the CPR burned the slash. It had been a dry spring, and combined with a freakish wind from the west, this allowed the fire between Hamilton and Granville Streets to grow so far out of control that comparisons were made to the volcano at Pompeii.

In less than an hour, a thousand wooden buildings were incinerated. Newspaper accounts said that wooden sidewalks burned faster than pedestrians could run. Roofs blew off buildings and flaming wood pelted down on citizens who tried to find safety in the water.

In the midst of it all, "Big Joe" was spotted helping the largely volunteer force of firefighters. Ironically, the ship that brought him to B.C., the abandoned *Robert Kerr*, had been blown from its anchorage off Deadman's Island to a reachable position near the beach. Several hundred people swam, rowed or paddled on logs to its safety. The heat was ferocious. Within minutes of the start of the fire the bell at St. James Church was ringing a warning. By the fire's end, the church was gone. Today, its melted bell is displayed at the Vancouver Museum.

In the only way he knew, protecting his fellow citizens from harm became Joe Fortes' mission as Vancouver struggled to recover from the devastation. His massive smile and stature made him a popular figure on English Bay, where he swam every morning throughout the year, consuming a cup of saltwater daily and calling it his "medicine." Three generations of Vancouverites credit him with teaching them how to swim.

"Jump! I tell you jump! If you don't jump off that raft, I'll throw you in," were the words that stuck in novelist Ethel Wilson's memory of Joe. And she jumped as did countless children at Joe's command.

"He taught nearly all the boys and girls to swim," wrote Wilson. "Joe was a heroic figure."

At the turn of the century, Fortes was made Vancouver's first official lifeguard and in 1904 he was made a Special Constable of the Auxiliary Police Force.

He lived in a tidy cottage by the beach, where he maintained the gender dividing-line between male and female bathers, and where he castigated litterbugs. The lives he is officially credited with saving are said to be far fewer than those who'd wish they could have been acknowledged. Storm waves could not keep him from a capsized boater.

When the city decided to demolish a row of squatter's cottages from the beach in the name of development, Joe's humble abode was moved to a place closer to the bandstand in the park where it was hung with a prestigious gift of the city in 1910 — an "illuminated address."

Sixty-year-old Joe Fortes died of pneumonia in February, 1922. At his packed funeral, the organ played "Old Black Joe" with all respect and the hearse towed his familiar rowboat which was filled with flowers.

Along with the fountain in his memory, there is a library named after Joe Fortes. And, of course, should you get hungry in Vancouver, you may want to try a bowl of the Westcoast Geoduck Clam Chowder "Manhattan Style," available at the restaurant that bears his Seraphim-less namesake.

THE SAINT OF DAWSON CITY

Dawson City, Yukon Territory, 1897 — Those who knew Father William Judge sometimes claimed he had a "luminescent"quality, but those who met him for the first time often thought he looked more like a cadaver. For his part, the Jesuit priest placed small value on appearances. "I remember his telling, with a chuckle, that one season while wandering in the wilds he had eaten so many rabbits that he felt his ears each morning when he awoke to see they weren't growing longer," recalled miner Karl Kaiser.

Judge was born in Baltimore in 1850 and worked as a clerk in a planing mill before deciding on a religious life. In 1890, he joined the Rocky Mountain Mission in Alaska.

He was ministering at a remote mining town called Forty Mile when George Carmack, Sookum Jim and Taglish Charlie registered the first claims on a salmon stream the native people called "Throndiuck," (meaning Hammer Water), and which later became "Klondike." Four months after their discovery, Father Judge sent a letter to his brother that carried one of the earliest messages of the find to the "outside." He noted that the discovery near Dawson City was "one of the richest and most extensive gold fields ever known." Predicting a general stampede of gold-seekers that spring, he promptly acquired a three-acre site for a church and a hospital.

"The stampeders from Forty Mile to the Klondike in the winter of '96-'97 remember overtaking a solitary and feeble old man with a single sled rope over his shoulder and a single dog helping the load along," recalled the *Klondike Nugget.* In this humble guise, Father Judge made several trips between Dawson and Forty Mile.

That summer, he replaced his tent hospital with a two-storey log-structure, followed by a church building complete with an organ. In November, he reported that 168 miners had been treated for everything from frostbite to scurvy, but despite the wealth of gold, the main topic of conversation in Dawson was "grub," and everyone was trying to secure enough food to last the winter. "If men would do half as much for heaven as they would for gold, how many saints there would be, and how much more real happiness in the world," wrote Judge. By the following spring, Dawson had grown to become the largest city west of Winnipeg and the atmosphere was hardly godly.

In June 1898, the church burned to the ground after Judge left a candle lit when he was called to the hospital during evening prayers. Dawson citizens turned out en masse to form a bucket brigade to save the neighbouring hospital. "It is a judgment on me," Judge shrugged. "I built the church too small. I had too little faith."

Judge immediately set about the task of constructing a new church. It was entirely financed by the "Klondike King" Alex McDonald, who later used the donation as leverage to achieve an audience with the Pope.

When a typhoid epidemic struck in the summer of 1898, Judge went into debt to construct a new three-storey addition to the hospital. Soon even the halls and aisles were filled with cots. Six sisters and thirty-four employees were kept busy day and night. In addition, an average of 500 attended Sunday Mass and miners continued to pour into Dawson. "I fear there will be much suffering here this winter," Judge wrote. "There are thousands still in tents, and winter is on us."

That December arrangements were made for a "minstrel" entertainment to raise funds for the hospital. It was a sober affair, since Christmas fell on a Sunday, and even in wild and woolly Dawson saloons and dancehalls were closed on Sundays. When Judge thanked the audience for helping the hospital, a five-minute ovation followed, leaving "the grand old man of Dawson" heartily embarrassed.

Judge had always appeared to be older than his years. He was only forty-eight when he succumbed to pneumonia on January 16, 1899. On the day of his funeral flags flew at half-mast and stores closed. The church was draped in mourning, and hours before the ceremony the church filled to capacity. A miner who knew him later wrote: "He died, undoubtedly the richest man in all gold-mad Dawson for there was not a soul within the valley of the Yukon not made richer for the heritage he left us."

PAYING THE RENT

St. Anthony, Newfoundland, 1908 — When it came to the service of Newfoundland and Labrador, Dr. Wilfred Grenfell was simply irrepressible. He confounded bureaucrats, angered merchants, enraged religious leaders — but he got the job done and the people loved him.

The job was never a singular issue for Grenfell. After graduating from medical school in London, he joined the National Mission for Deep Sea Fishermen serving aboard ships from the Bay of Biscay to Iceland. In 1892, he volunteered to investigate living conditions in coastal Newfoundland and Labrador. What he discovered was a large job to be done.

Poverty and disease were rampant. Merchants exploited the half-starved population and housing was seldom more than a dirt-floored hut. From the deck of his floating mission, Grenfell treated 900 patients during his three-month cruise. Most had never seen a "real" doctor, relying instead on folk cures that were no match for diseases ranging from tuberculosis to beri-beri.

Returning to England, the young doctor was determined to raise funds for proper medical facilities. Although the Mission found his zeal incorrigible, his administrative skills inadequate and his exact location unchartable, the Grenfell charm was inescapable.

He toured England addressing the desperate need he had seen. Two doctors, two nurses and enough money for two hospitals accompanied him on his return to Labrador. Then he set off to raise more money. He was particularly skilled at plucking the pockets of Americans from the Eastern seaboard, dispersing funds as he saw fit from his headquarters in St. Anthony, Newfoundland.

Grenfell's resolve was inspired by the evangelical ideology of "muscular Christianity," which favoured expressing religious beliefs through action. "The service we render to others is really the rent we pay for our room on this earth," he once noted.

Grenfell was constantly struggling to pay that rent. Money that poured in from his tours poured out almost immediately as he added facilities to hospitals, established cooperative stores, industrial workshops and experimental farms. To assist him, he accepted volunteer students during the summer. His WWP program (Workers Without Pay) saw the likes of the young Nelson Rockefeller and Henry Cabot Lodge performing all manner of menial tasks.

Because he was good at it, fund-raising became Grenfell's preoccupation. In fact, it has been suggested that Grenfell's bedside manner may have been the best aspect of his physician's skills, but his commitment to attend a young patient suffering from blood poisoning nearly cost him his life on Easter Sunday, 1908.

In a move which hindsight reflects as foolhardy, he was taking his dog team over a short-cut across Hare Bay headed for Brent Island when the ice beneath him began turning to slush less than half a kilometre from land. What followed was a series of dives and leaps from one ice pan to the next, as an off-shore wind blew Grenfell and company slowly out to sea.

To avoid freezing, he sacrificed three of his sled dogs. Using their skins as blankets and windbreaks, he huddled with the remaining dogs throughout the night. Rescue seemed remote, but he constructed a flag using a piece of his shirt tied to the frozen legs of his dead dogs.

By a sheer stroke of luck, Grenfell's pitiful presence was spotted by a seal hunter as night descended. Early the next day, rescuers in a small boat risked their own lives through the hazardous ice pans to reach Grenfell, whose "pan" had dwindled to packed snow.

Typically, Grenfell turned the tale into a instrument to raise funds. *Adrift on an Ice-Pan* became a best-seller.

Although several of his ventures were abysmal failures, including the importation of 300 Lapland reindeer, the community of St. Anthony's prospered in everything from his introduction of cottage industries to a much needed orphanage. It became the home of a mission in his own name, but still there was controversy.

Grenfell raised the ire of the Protestant and Catholic clergy when he opened Newfoundland's first inter-denominational school in 1909. As a Justice of the Peace he rendered his wrath freely to bootleggers. Politicians feared for the image (and the credit rating) of the colony when Grenfell publicly decried the squalor of the native people and the permanent residents known as livyers.

Sir Wilfred Grenfell, knighted in 1927, stood his ground against all comers for forty-five years in the service of the people. He resigned as superintendent of the International Grenfell Mission in 1937 and spent his retirement in Vermont. When he made his final visit to St. Anthony in 1939, the whole town wept when he left.

NEIGHBOURS IN ARMS

Western Front, 1915 — Lest we forget the valour and horror. After World War One, the city of Winnipeg changed the name of Pine Street. Why? To honour the individual heroism of three soldiers who, coincidentally, all lived on that quiet residential street. Pine Street is now called Valour Road in their honour.

The "neighbours" — Frederick William Hall, Robert Shankland and Leo Clarke — faced the horror of World War One with such bravery and valour that each of them received the nation's highest award for courage, the Victoria Cross.

At the outbreak of the war on August 4, 1914, Canada's "army" consisted of a mere 3,110 men in uniform and 74,213 part-time militia. The navy boasted two ancient cruisers. Experienced officers and drill instructors were in short supply. Still, there was a national will to "get on with the job," and soon recruits numbered in the hundreds of thousands.

Early in 1915, the first Canadian troops moved across the English Channel and into battle. Their first engagement was at Ypres, Belgium, and Winnipeg's Sergeant-Major Hall was there. The Allies, including twelve Canadian battalions, were outnumbered two to one. On the morning of April 24, 1915, Hall and his company were pinned down in the trenches by heavy artillery fire.

The men could hear the groans of an injured soldier on the battlefield.

Rescues were usually attempted under the cover of dark, but this time Hall and two volunteers determined to try it in broad daylight. The volunteers were immediately wounded. After helping them back, Hall determined to accomplish the mission alone. He crossed the battlefield through a hail of bullets. Then, while trying to bring his wounded comrade to safety, Hall caught a bullet in the head and died instantly.

Better than one in five Canadians who participated at Ypres were listed as killed, missing or wounded. It was a horrific initiation to battle, and one that was to set a pattern of endurance, courage and bloodshed.

Late in the summer of 1916, Canadian troops moved to the rolling hills of the Somme, where a battle had been in progress for several months. The Germans called it "the Bath of Blood." It was here that the Canadians confirmed their steadfastness under the worst conditions of warfare. Corporal Leo Clarke was there.

In the mud-filled trenches, Clarke found himself alone and under attack by twenty enemy soldiers. Instead of surrendering, he attacked, emptying his revolver twice and then firing a German rifle he picked up from the ground.

In the struggle that followed, a German officer bayonetted him in the knee. Wounded and bleeding, he kept up the attack. When the enemy fled, Clarke pursued them, killing four and taking a prisoner. Though he was ordered to the hospital, Clarke returned to battle the next day. He died in action a month later.

There were other battles in that tortured landscape — Vimy Ridge, Mount Sorrel, Courcelette, Amiens and Beaumont Hamel. Then there was Passchendaele, where Lieutenant Robert Shankland earned his Victoria Cross.

From August through November of 1917, the Allies fought in a sea of Belgian mud. The terrain was below sea level and drainage systems had been destroyed by bombardment. Heavy rains had reduced the ground to an impenetrable bog. Guns sank to their axles and horses to their bellies. Soldiers died relentlessly.

Shankland led his men to a forward position which they held during a fierce counterattack. Knowing that an accurate description of his company's position was critical to the Allied battle plan, he crossed the battlefield alone to deliver the information. He then rejoined his men and carried on until the end of the bloody battle in which 16,000 Canadians made the ultimate sacrifice. Of the three Victoria Cross recipients from Valour Road, only Shankland survived the war.

More than 60,000 young Canadians were dead before the war ended in victory on November 11, 1918. On that day, a stillness descended over the Western Front, and a soldier from New Glasgow, Nova Scotia, recalled hearing a bird singing. He wondered how it had survived.

WHEN SHIPS COLLIDE

Halifax, Nova Scotia, December 6, 1917 — The largest man-made explosion prior to the detonation of the atomic bomb occurred in Halifax Harbour during the First World War. It was not an act of war, it was an accident. The Halifax Explosion is the largest disaster in Canadian history. When two ships collided, the explosion was *felt* for over 320 kilometers.

There was a thin coat of snow on the harbour slopes that crisp winter day in late 1917. While the citizens of the booming wartime port travelled to work and school children readied for a day of studies, the French freighter *Mont Blanc* made its way toward the inner harbour. At the same time, a Norwegian steamer, *Imo,* was coming out of the narrows.

As a result of crossed passing signals, which may have been caused by the language barrier between the English and French crews, a midstream collision occurred at 8:00 a.m.

Although the ships drew apart without much damage, the *Mont Blanc* was carrying a devil's brew. In its hold there were 2,335 tons of picric acid, 203 tons of TNT and 10 tons of gun cotton. Highly inflammable benzene, stored in tins on the deck, began to burn with a flaring blue flame. The captain and crew of the *Mont Blanc* promptly took to their lifeboats, while their burning ship drifted toward one of the Halifax piers.

On the dock, most people were not aware that the burning ship was a floating bomb. Factory workers, stevedores, mothers and children rushed to the best vantage points to watch. The town fire department dispatched its new chemical engine and two boat parties fought the fire.

Train dispatcher Vincent Coleman was discussing the fire when a sailor burst into his office and announced that the ship was bound to explode. Coleman tried to warn the onlookers, when suddenly he remembered that a passenger train carrying 700 people was scheduled to arrive shortly. He returned to his post to telegraph a life-saving message.

At 9:05 a.m., the explosion came. A pillar of white smoke rose eight kilometres into the sky, unfolding into a gigantic toadstool. The *Mont Blanc* was blown apart and the *Imo* ran aground. A tidal wave swept the shore.

The force of the blast was strong enough to hurl a clock out of a tower at Truro, 100 kilometres away. In Halifax and Dartmouth, wooden buildings and homes collapsed, killing or burying the inhabitants who had barely finished stoking their morning fires. Doors blew off their hinges, and glass blasted from windows in jagged arrows. Schools and churches were demolished. Fires raged.

At the railway station, the glass-and-iron frame roof dropped in on the platform and tracks. Dockyards were shattered, foundries were ruined and a smashed brewery poured a river of beer into the harbour.

A blizzard howled that night, while 6,000 people left homeless by the blast crouched and huddled in any available shelter to survive the storm that followed.

The scene was as brutal and devastating as any wartime carnage. The Halifax Relief Commission estimated that 1,963 people were killed, 9,000 were injured and 199 people were blinded. Make-shift morgues were set up to try to identify the dead and mass funerals were conducted, while the stunned citizenry rallied to rebuild.

Tragedies can bring out the best and worst in people. Some tried to take advantage of the explosion by looting, while others, such as Vincent Coleman, sacrificed their own lives to save others. Doctors and nurses rushed to the scene and substantial help was soon on its way from outlying towns and neighbouring provinces. Halifax's historic rival, the state of Massachusetts, sent a complete relief expedition. Overall contributions totalling thirty million dollars poured in for relief and construction efforts.

Homeless Haligonians lived in temporary tents and patched-together housing Lumber was at a premium and glass was scarce during wartime, so construction was makeshift and citizens covered their windows with tar paper throughout that bleak winter.

Today the North Halifax Memorial Library stands as a monument to the victims of the tragedy. The half-ton shank of the *Mont Blanc*'s anchor still lies where it landed, three kilometres from the explosion, and at least 125 unidentified victims are buried in a common grave at Fairview Cemetery.

"EVERY MAN,
CARRY A MAN"

Dieppe, France, August 19, 1942 — Honorary Captain John Foote, chaplain of the Royal Hamilton Light Infantry, was so determined to accompany his unit into battle that he stowed away with only the tacit consent of his superiors. Then, although he could have left the horror that marked the ill-fated assault on Dieppe, he decided to stay as a prisoner of war!

Foote was a thirty-five-year-old Presbyterian minister in Cobourg, Ontario, when Canada officially entered the Second World War on September 10, 1939. He was among the earliest to apply and he pursued his duties as a chaplain with his regiment stationed in England. Before the war ended, Canada's forces grew to more than a million men and women from a professional nucleus of fewer than 10,000.

When it became apparent that Canadian troops were to finally be sent into battle on the secret mission dubbed "Operation Jubilee," Foote's commanding officer suggested that the popular padre stay back since he might be needed more than ever after the raid.

"I'll make my own arrangements, and if you see me on the beach you can order me off," replied Foote.

Along with close to 5,000 Canadian troops, Foote joined in the early morning landing at the chalk cliffs off the small port and gambling town of Dieppe. It was the first time most of the men confronted combat, and it was the first time the Allies had determined to test their ability to launch a large-scale amphibious raid on Hitler's continental fortress.

The battle lasted for nine savage hours during which the troops faced incessant, deadly fire. They were raked by machine guns and picked off by snipers. Foote attached himself to a Regimental Aid Post on the beach and set about helping the wounded, constantly exposing himself to the hail of bullets. As the tide went out, the Post moved to a stranded landing craft, and Foote hauled wounded men to its cover, only to remove them when enemy shelling set its ammunition afire.

When evacuation efforts began, the burly padre carried wounded men from the exposed beach to waiting landing craft. "Every man, carry a man," Foote shouted to all who could hear him. He may have saved as many as thirty lives and his courage set an inspirational example.

Foote had several opportunities to embark, but as the last boat departed, he waded back to the bloodied beach. "The men ashore would need me far more in captivity than any of those going home," was his belief.

More than 900 Canadians were killed at Dieppe and nearly 2,000 were taken prisoner. Padre Foote and medical officer Captain D. Clare both chose to be voluntarily imprisoned with the captured men. They led the grim column of captives on the march to prisoner-of-war camps, where they stayed until the end of the war.

Amid the squalid camp conditions, Foote organized social activities, including an orchestra in which he played a mean trumpet. He conducted regular church services, and also used the church to conceal men who were escaping. Despite threats to his life, the padre harassed the Germans for better treatment for the men.

John Foote was awarded the Victoria Cross for his heroism at Dieppe, as was another brave Canadian, Vancouver's Colonel Charles "Cec" Merritt of the South Saskatchewan Regiment. Of the thousands who served their valour and courage was singled out but they were not unique. There were many acts of heroism at Dieppe, and many more would follow, each one deserving of the everlasting gratitude of all Canadians.

A MALTESE FALCON

Verdun, Quebec, to Malta, 1942 — Heroes are heroes by any name. However, "Screwball" wasn't quite the public relations moniker the government had in mind when it sent Canadian flying ace, George Beurling, on a public speaking tour to raise money for the war effort. So, "Screwball" became "Buzz," but that made little impression on the grounded pilot. He was a flyer, an airborne killer and a ruthless lone wolf, not a fund-raiser, and certainly not a groundling.

"If I were ever asked to do that again, I'd tell them to go to hell or else ask for a commission on the bonds I sold," Beurling told a reporter. The war bond effort was better off without him. George Beurling's mission was fighting in the terrifying skies of World War II.

Born in 1921 in Verdun, Quebec, George was fascinated with airplanes from childhood. He built model airplanes with his father, becoming so proficient that he was able to sell his handiwork and use the money for flying lessons. He analyzed World War I aerial battles and tactics the way other children studied National Hockey League trades and statistics. According to his father, George "ate, drank and slept airplanes and air fighting."

By the time he had celebrated his fourteenth birthday, George was taking weekly flying lessons. At seventeen, he left his religious family behind and got a job in Ontario as a bush pilot hauling freight and accumulating enough flying hours to earn his pilot's licence. Then he rode the rails to Vancouver where he tried to enlist in the Chinese air force, which was fighting the Japanese invasion of Manchuria.

Along the way, he sought out WW I ace Ernst Udet, whose Allied kills placed him second only to the infamous "Red Baron" Manfred Von Richtofen. Udet was performing in barnstorming events, but George Beurling persuaded him (with cash) to teach him the dogfighting tactics of aerial warfare.

George never did get to China. Instead, he turned to the Royal Canadian Air Force. Despite the fact that Beurling had won a flying aerobics competition in Edmonton and beaten two RCAF pilots, he was rejected. Recruiters suggested that he would be better off completing his last year of high school.

The Finnish air force would have taken Beurling, but he was just eighteen and his parents would not give their permission. So George took a different tact. He headed for Glasgow as a deckhand on a munitions ship.

On landing, Beurling presented himself to Britain's Royal Air Force, but he was missing vital papers, including his birth certificate. He sailed back to Canada on the *Valparaiso*, dodging German U-boats and surviving a torpedo attack. After crossing the ocean three times, Beurling was finally accepted in the RAF.

During training, he impressed his instructors so much that he was asked to accept a commission and stay on as a teacher. Beurling declined. He wanted action.

In formation, he was a "Tail-End-Charlie," flying his Spit-fire aircraft behind and slightly above four other fighters. It was the most hazardous position.

To put it lightly, from the outset Sergeant Beurling had difficulty accepting authority figures. If he saw an opportunity in the air he would take it, even if that meant disobeying orders, and especially if it meant taking a chance to attack the enemy or alert his fellow-flyers to any danger. Further, when he felt orders lacked intellectual or practical merit, he expressed his opinion. One of his biographers has suggested that he volunteered for service at the height of the siege of Malta because he was "disgusted with the crass stupidity of his commanding officers."

Beurling arrived in Malta in the middle of an air raid. The Germans and Italians were maintaining a constant assault on the critically located island. Laddie Lucas was Beurling's new commanding officer in the all-Canadian RAF Spitfire Squadron and he recognized Beurling's rebellious ego, but he also saw in that some deeper sense of inferiority and a need for mutual trust.

"I judged that what Beurling needed was not to be smacked down but to be encouraged," Lucas said later. "He never let me down."

In his first month, Beurling shot down five, possibly six, enemy aircraft. He used the dogfighting tricks Udet had taught him — making tight circles, firing from what seemed to be impossible angles. His expertise lay in the "deflection shot." With deadly precision he could calculate distance, speed and angles in the air, determining in an instant when and where the line of fire between his guns and the enemy would "harmonize."

"He used to report sighting of aircraft many seconds before others saw them," said one of his fellow pilots. "And he knew whether he hit them in the front, centre or rear of their airplane and he usually used minimum ammunition."

Like World War I ace Billy Bishop, Beurling was a master of surprise and sneak attacks. He would watch an enemy squadron, assess the talents of the pilots he was confronting and then try to take out the best first.

"There is no room for softheartedness," he told *Maclean's* magazine writer Webb Waldron. "The enemy is trying to get you, it is up to you to get him first — hard and plenty."

Occasionally, Beurling would line his plane up in a head-on confrontation, shooting to kill the oncoming pilot, and then peeling away to attack any chasers. Other pilots dubbed him "Screwball," but Laddie Lucas said there was not anything wild about the way Beurling conducted himself in the air, he was just accurate in what he did.

Citations began accumulating. Despite his protests, Beurling was ordered to accept an officer's commission. Ultimately he would receive the Distinguished Service Order, the Distinguished Flying Medal with a bar for bravery and the Distinguished Flying Cross.

The war in the air over Malta that summer was brutal. Pilots were shot as they hung in their parachutes. As the temperature rose, so did tempers. The Germans and Italians attempted to cut supplies to the island and food was scarce. Pilots lived in caves or sat in their aircraft waiting for reports of a raid, conserving gasoline until a last-minute scramble was called.

Like many other exhausted pilots, Beurling lost a lot of weight and was bed-ridden for a week with malnutrition and a disease they called "the Dog."

In October, 1942, half of Beurling's squad was shot down. Raids were constant. He was flying a shift every day.

On his last flight over Malta, Beurling led an eight Spitfire squadron against eight enemy bombers and fifty fighters.

He shot down one bomber, but as it fell the rear gunner returned fire hitting Beurling's fingers and forearm. Beurling then turned his sights on a German fighter in front of him. While wounding it, he came under fire, suffering damage to the Spitfire's tail and wings.

"Screwball" went into a power dive heading straight for the sea before pulling up under the German formation and shooting down another fighter. This attracted the attention of the enemy. Beurling's controls where shot out and shrapnel ripped into one of his feet. The scene he described was the nightmare of every pilot.

"My plane was on fire, flames coming out toward me. I tried to climb out of the cockpit, but centrifugal force pressed me into my seat. I fought to get out and at the last minute I did manage to jump. Another split second and it would have been too late."

Beurling's parachute opened less than 1,000 feet above the water. When he was plucked out of the blood-stained Mediterranean, his only concern was for the Bible he always flew with, one his mother had given him.

In four months, he had shot down seventeen enemy planes over Malta. After a period of hospitalization, Beurling was shipped back to Britain and then sent to Canada on the war bond–selling mission — as "Buzz" not "Screwball."

Afterwards, the RAF wanted him as a gunnery instructor in England, but Beurling wanted to be back in the air. He transferred to the Royal Canadian Air Force in northern France. The final confirmed tally of Beurling's victories is thirty-one, although others may have fallen, wounded and out of sight.

Beurling's troubles with authority continued on in France. After facing discipline for flying too low over his own airfield, Beurling resigned with an honourable discharge.

The United States Air Force rejected him. Ottawa would not permit him to join the Chinese against Mao Tse-tung. Commercial airlines turned him down, as well. Without an airplane or an enemy, Beurling's life fell apart. At one point, he was reduced to begging in the streets of Montreal.

Postwar tension in the Middle East presented an opportunity. Beurling was twenty-seven when he hired on as a fighter with the newly formed Israeli Air Force in 1948.

What happened next remains a mystery. Beurling arrived in Rome en route to Tel Aviv. Some say that he died alone, crashing almost inexplicably on a familiarization flight. Others say he was piloting a plane carrying former Luftwaffe pilots who were also bound for Israel. In that account, an engine died after takeoff and Beurling heroically steered the plane away from a populated area before the plane stalled and crashed killing all aboard. More sinister conjecture suggests the British Foreign Service and Secret Service planted a bomb in the plane to thwart the Israelis.

When he was inducted into Canada's Aviation Hall of Fame in 1973, the citation honouring George Frederick Beurling read: "The brilliance of air fighting tactics, performed in a self-imposed area of loneliness with a structured military command, recall earlier wartime standards of heroic personal determination and have been of outstanding benefit to Canadian aviation."

He was the falcon of Malta.

TICKLING
THE DRAGON'S TAIL

Los Alamos, New Mexico, 1946 — In the time it took for a screwdriver to slip from his right hand, Louis Slotin was dealt a death sentence. The Winnipeg-born physicist was demonstrating the manipulation of two halves of a beryllium-coated sphere which formed the guts of an atomic bomb. The screwdriver that separated them was the only thing preventing a deadly chain reaction known as supercritical. Slotin called this exercise "tickling the dragon's tail."

When the simple tool dropped at 3:20 p.m. on May 21, 1946, a hot blue flash of gamma and neutron radiation filled the top-secret laboratory in Los Alamos, New Mexico. A Geiger counter clicked hysterically. Without pausing, Slotin leaned forward over the globes and pulled them apart with his bare hands. In that selfless instant, Slotin was exposed to almost one thousand rads of radiation, a lethal amount. His heroism served to shield seven observers. Although they received far lower doses, three out of the seven died years later from complications that may have been linked to their exposure.

Slotin vomited almost as soon as he left the building. He had a burning sensation in his left hand and a sour taste in his mouth. Before rushing to the hospital, the group reassembled in the laboratory, methodically plotting a diagram to determine where each of them had been standing at the time of the accident. The moment must have seemed surreal in its horror. "Everyone was wondering who had gotten most of the radiation," recalled security guard Patrick Cleary.

Nine days later, after suffering the agonies of radiation-induced trauma, Louis Slotin was dead. Citations honoured his bravery, but at his funeral in Winnipeg where three thousand mourners gathered outside his parents' home, Rabbi S. Frank recalled him as "one of the most brilliant scholars to ever come out of this city."

Louis had entered the University of Manitoba at the age of sixteen. After receiving his Masters of Science degree with Gold Medals in chemistry and physics, he pursued his studies of biochemistry in England. With his doctorate in hand, he returned to Canada in 1937, but he was unable to secure a job at the National Research Council, raising suggestions in later years that administrative anti-Semitism may have dogged his application. Instead, Dr. Slotin was welcomed at the University of Chicago, where he was introduced to nuclear physics by pioneer atomic chemist William Harkins. Although Harkins's research was underfunded, Slotin's work with an atom-smashing cyclotron attracted the attention of the Manhattan Engineer District — the cover name for America's atomic bomb program.

Slotin soon developed a reputation for skill in assembling the firing mechanism for the A-bomb. It was the product of his handiwork — a bomb code-named "Trinity" — that demonstrated the awesome destructive powers of nuclear knowledge for the first time when it was detonated in the New Mexico desert on July 16, 1945. Three weeks later, a bomb code-named "Little Boy" was dropped on Hiroshima; another followed three days later on Nagasaki.

Working on the atomic bomb presented a myriad of ethical dilemmas that would haunt many of the scientists at the nuclear research laboratory in Los Alamos. Two months before his accident, Slotin explained in a letter to a colleague, "I have become involved in Navy tests, much to my disgust. The reason for this is that I am one of the few people left here who are experienced bomb putter-togetheres." To his father, Slotin reportedly explained his involvement with weapons of destruction by simply stating, "We had to get it before the Germans."

Colleagues admitted they were aware that Slotin's procedures were unsafe, but noted that "he would always insist upon taking the greatest risk himself." Critics cited the whole affair as a scandal and secrecy shrouded the accident for decades.

The dangerous practice of conducting hands-on assembly ended following Slotin's accident. Remote control systems were constructed to separate the operating crew from their equipment by the space of approximately four football fields. If the dragon's tail was going to be tickled, it would be at a respectful distance.

COURAGE DOWN BELOW

Springhill, Nova Scotia, 1958 — Canada's "singing miner" kept the faith and what faith it was. Maurice Ruddick sang "Happy Birthday" and hymns for eight-and-a-half days to keep the hopes of his fellow miners alive when they were trapped nearly four kilometres underground in the Springhill Mining Disaster. Ruddick was one of the few black miners employed at the Springhill mine. He and 173 other coal miners were just starting their 8:00 to 11:00 evening shift in the Cumberland Pit Shaft Number Two when a small "bump" occurred.

Although the earth may not seem to move beneath our feet, it is constantly shifting. Nowhere is this more apparent than in a mine, where high pressure builds up in gaseous pockets causing pressure-releasing shifts called bumps.

An hour after the first bump, a second followed which shook even the surface of the town and created a heart-chilling rumble. It proved to be the most severe bump in North American mining history. Underground, seventy-three were killed instantly by a massive cave-in.

Rescue teams mobilized to find survivors. Within twenty-four hours, more than half of the surviving miners made it to the surface. While anxious family members crowded at the pithead, the fabled team of draegermen who were specially trained to assist in such disasters found themselves hampered by communication breakdowns and ventilation problems.

It seemed to be a miracle when, six days later, a voice was heard through a ventilator pipe that stretched over 8,000 metres below the surface and twelve more miners were saved.

Eight other miners would wait two-and-a-half more days in a metre-high pocket before being discovered in what Maurice Ruddick described as "a dungeon." For one of them, Percy Rector, help would be too late.

As the men waited, wondered and prayed, Ruddick sang. Although the forty-six-year-old father of twelve had suffered a broken leg, the trauma of crawling over fallen bodies to marginal haven, and the stun of toxic gas, he persisted in rallying his comrades' spirits with jokes and tunes.

"I cried quietly in the darkness, but I made sure nobody else heard me. It might have broken the resolve to live," Ruddick admitted in the aftermath.

When the seven men divided their last sandwich and drank the last of their water on November 1st, they also celebrated the birthday of miner Garnet Clarke with a resounding chorus of "Happy Birthday," led by Ruddick. To survive, they chewed moist bark from the pit-wall props, sucked coal, and even drank their own urine.

When the draegermen finally reached them on November 5th, one of the astonished rescuers reported that he found Ruddick "sitting on a stonetack, singing at the top of his lungs."

"Give me a drink of water and I'll sing you a song," he said in greeting, and the long ordeal came to an end.

Ruddick modestly underplayed his inspirational role, but others felt differently. "If it wasn't for Maurice, they'd have all been dead," the mother of one of the miners told Ruddick's wife. After the disaster, the Springhill mine was closed forever.

The rescue made international headlines and Canada's "singing miner" experienced the spotlight briefly in public tributes. The Governor of Georgia, Marvin Griffin, was so taken with the story that he invited the nineteen Springhill survivors to recuperate on an all-expense-paid holiday at a swank resort. The gracious invitation changed dramatically when the Governor discovered that Ruddick was black. The American South was strictly segregated in those days, and Ruddick's invitation only stood if he agreed to be segregated.

Initially, Ruddick refused the Governor's terms. When it became apparent that his fellow miners planned to refuse to go without him, he accepted the segregated invitation, suggesting to them: "We'll all have our holiday, then we'll be together again." In Georgia, he stayed at one of the few hotels that accepted blacks, while the others stayed at a vacation resort for millionaires. He could not attend functions in their honour, but the men he shared that darkened Springhill tomb with were proud to join a "segregated" celebration for Ruddick.

By popular consensus, Ruddick was named 1958's Canadian Citizen of the Year. When he presented the award to Ruddick, Ontario Premier Leslie Frost described him as "an inspiration to all . . . a man with the divine attribute of common sense." With the grace of a hero, Ruddick accepted the honour "for every miner in the town."

ORIGINS, ORIGINALS

ORIGINALS

&

UPSTARTS

GENTLE BIRDS NO LONGER

THE ORIGINAL BIG MAC

NEWFOUNDLAND NANA

AND THEN THERE WERE NONE

TO WALK WITH GIANTS

THE HANGING JUDGE

THE STORY OF DR. "O"

NO NUDDER LIKE HIM

WHERE'S JOE'S BEEF

FATHER GOOSE

LEAVE IT TO THE BEAVER

THE GREAT STORK DERBY

GONE INDIAN

A BELLY LAUGH OR YOUR MONEY BACK

THE SITDOWNERS

EKOKTOEGEE

GENTLE BIRDS NO LONGER

Funk Island, Newfoundland, 1534 — When the playful puffins dig their Atlantic coast nesting burrows they still kick to the surface the occasional bone of their long extinct cousins, the great auk. Like the Mauritius Island dodo before it, the fate of the great auk of eastern Canada was scaled by the intrusion of man. Indeed, the final gasp of the auk came at the greedy hands of man in 1844. Three hundred years before, Funk Island off the Newfoundland coast hosted a breeding colony of legendary proportion.

The great auk was the only flightless variety of its species, which includes guillemots, murres and puffins. It was a curious-looking sort of seabird that walked upright much like a penguin. While the seventy-five-centimetre-high bird may have trundled awkwardly on shore, in the water auks could "fly," propelling themselves rapidly with their rudimentary wings and steering with their powerful webbed feet to catch the fish and crustaceans that formed their diet.

They may have ranged from Greenland to Eastern Canada and as far south as Florida. Most of their life was spent in the water, and they are believed to have come ashore only during the breeding season, when the female would lay her annual, single egg after reaching maturity at four to seven years of age. The egg would be laid on bare rock. Both parents are presumed to have taken the responsibility for its incubation, and the fledgling chick may have been ready to leave the nesting ledge within ten days of hatching.

Jacques Cartier noted the birds on his first voyage to the New World in 1534 when his crew stocked up on them at Funk Island. With an estimated 100,000 pairs, the island was home to the world's largest great auk colony.

"Some of these birds are as large as geese, being black and white with a beak like a crow," Cartier says in his diary. "These birds are marvellously fat. We call them Apponatz [spear-bills], and in less than half an hour our longboats were log-loaded with them. Each of our ships salted four or five casks, not to mention those we ate fresh."

The great auk proved to be a steady and easily harvested staple for early explorers. Their feathers were sold. They were boiled to make oil, used as bait for fishing lines and their eggs were a delicacy.

By the 1700s the number of great auks was seriously depleted as thousands of the helpless creatures were simply slaughtered by passing traders, who either clubbed them to death or simply marched them up planks onto their ships. Fishermen in Newfoundland and Labrador, as well as whalers from across the North Atlantic, joined in the killing.

In 1795, one observer wrote: "It has been customary for several crews of men to live all summer on the island for the purpose of killing birds for the sake of their feathers. If a stop is not put to that practise, the whole breed will be diminished to almost nothing." By 1800, that prophecy had come true and only a few last scattered birds remained throughout their North Atlantic range. Such rarity placed them in great demand in Europe, where museums began clamouring for specimens.

One early morning in June 1844, possibly driven by a museum reward of about thirty dollars, a party of hunters went ashore on Eldey Island just off the southwestern peninsula of Iceland and killed the last two great auks on earth. Reports indicate that the auks ran but uttered no cry and offered no fight, for they were gentle birds. Today, pickled organs from those very birds are preserved at the University of Copenhagen. All told, only seventy-eight stuffed specimens of the great auk remain. Funk Island, which still thrives as a breeding colony for seabirds, continues to bear the remnants of ancient stone pounds where the great auks were once impounded before slaughter.

Although it was man who physically killed the last of the auks, modern scientists speculate that extinction may have been their ultimate destiny due to changes in environmental and climatic conditions that could have effected their feeding and breeding grounds.

The sad thing is that we shall never know what could have been.

THE ORIGINAL BIG MAC

Dundela, Ontario, 1811 — The world-famous McIntosh apple may have genetic roots to the first apple tree ever planted in Canada, but when it was discovered it was growing wild. Ultimately, it proved to be truly one of a kind.

In 1633, an apple tree called "Fameuse" was brought to New France from Normandy. It was an instant success and apples became a prized fruit on pioneer farms, since they could be stored in root cellars, dried or pressed into cider.

In 1811, John McIntosh was clearing land to build his farmhouse in Dundas County, in eastern Ontario. In the undergrowth, he discovered some seedling apple trees, which he transplanted.

One tree in particular produced exceptionally firm, red apples with sweet, juicy flesh. While other apple trees fell prey to the cold weather and disease, this particular tree was the hardiest producer in the neighbourhood.

McIntosh's son, Allan, attempted to grow seedlings from the tree in the 1820s; however, none of the seedlings bore the same crisp fruit as the old tree. The original tree was self-sterile and pollen from other apple trees that fertilized the blossoms produced a good tree, but not quite the original.

The young McIntosh knew there had to be a solution. As a Methodist minister, he travelled the countryside always carrying a supply of the unique apples, which were affectionately known as "Granny's Treats." Farmers across the countryside were impressed, but no one could solve the mystery of reproducing the tree.

Just as his father discovered the tree by chance, Allan McIntosh discovered the solution to his tree reproduction dilemma through a curious coincidence of fate.

In 1835, an American farm labourer arrived one spring day looking for work, and over a glass of "Granny" cider he learned about the McIntosh conundrum. The man suggested that the solution lay in grafting a small branch from the original tree to another variety of apple rootstock.

The hired man spent the summer instructing McIntosh in the art of grafting, budding and pruning. Then he left, never to be heard from again. Soon farmers were able to buy grafted seedlings, and the fame of the "McIntosh Red" spread.

By 1862, apple trees had been planted across the nation. Along with the McIntosh, the Baldwin, Russet, Greening and Snow apple trees flourished, while other varieties such as the Winter Codlin and Seek-No-Further all but disappeared.

At the turn of the century, half of the orchards in Ontario were producing McIntosh apples, and McIntosh Reds were finding popularity in the United States. Disaster struck in 1895 when a fire broke out and the original tree was scorched. Allan McIntosh himself propped barn doors around it to protect it from the blaze and he spent months nursing it back to health. The tree had become something of a celebrity in its own right.

The original McIntosh apple tree outlived Allan McIntosh by eleven years. It produced fruit until 1908 and finally toppled in 1910, but its progeny continue to thrive throughout Canada and the world.

NEWFOUNDLAND NANA

Isle of Elba, 1815 — Under cover of darkness Napoleon Bonaparte was escaping from exile on the Isle of Elba when he slipped from a rock, fell into the sea and floundered. As the story goes, the sailors who were escorting him to a waiting ship could not find the military strategist. Fortunately, one of them had brought along his faithful Newfoundland dog. It is this distinctively Canadian canine who is credited with plunging into the water and towing the diminutive Emperor to safety from whence he returned to power and, ultimately, met his Waterloo.

Throughout history the Newfoundland dog has been perceived as a gentle giant and a life-preserver on four legs. It is one of only four recognized dog breeds originating in Canada, including the Canadian Eskimo Dog, the Nova Scotia Duck Tolling Retriever and the Tahltan Bear Dog. Although the Labrador Retriever bears a Canadian name, its breeding was refined in Great Britain.

Theories abound about the Newfoundland dog's origins. Some say that Norse explorers brought thick-coated, black "bear dogs" with them during the Vinland quest and these mated with indigenous dogs. Basque fishermen may have introduced ancestors linked to the Pyrenees mountain dog. Arguments have been made for bloodline links to everything from the English Water Spaniel to the now extinct American Black Wolf. By 1610, when King James I granted John Guy the first charter to colonize New-foundland, the Canadian Kennel Club warrants that the physical and mental attributes of the breed had been established.

Whatever quirk of fate created this water-resistant seventy-kilogram dog, the Newfoundland soon became an international status symbol, immortalized by some of the world's giants of literature.

Sir Walter Scott's favourite Newfoundland dog was named Mungo, and Robert Burns described an aristocratic Newf named Caesar in his 1768 poem "The Two Dogs." Lord Byron's beloved Boatswain was held in such esteem that when he died in 1808, the poet constructed a brick and marble marker over his Sherwood Forest resting place.

In fiction, Nana, the faithful nursemaid of the Darling family in James Barrie's immortal, turn-of-the-century play *Peter Pan*, was played by the author's own Newfoundland. Charles Dickens delighted in the antics of his father-and-son team, Don and Bumble, and Fyodor Dostoyevsky included a Newfoundland in his novel *The Idiot*.

Above all, the Newfoundland has served its masters as a working dog. For many years, sled teams of Newfoundlands transported mail and passengers to outport communities.

Their fine sight and pre-disposition to swimming makes them excellent retrievers, both of fowl and fish. When there was deep-water fishing off the southwest coast of the island, dogs were often kept aboard fishing boats to retrieve fish that slipped off the hook at the water's surface.

Newfoundlands have even served their own kind. When the Alpine rescue dogs at the Hospice of St. Bernard were almost wiped out by a distemper epidemic in 1856, the best of the breed from Newfoundland was used to re-establish the St. Bernard.

The best of the breed was also sought in 1901 when the Duke and Duchess of Cornwall and York (later King George VI and Queen Mary) visited Newfoundland and consented to accept a dog and cart for their children. "Isn't he a beauty," Her Royal Highness said graciously, as she petted the Royal gift's massive head. "Begobs, ma'am," the trainer replied. "You won't find the likes of him no-where." Local pride in the dogs has ensured the constancy and quality of the breed.

Bravery remains the Newfoundland's main claim to fame. In the folklore of dogdom, the Newf is credited with saving more human lives than any other breed.

One of the most remarkable of these instances oc-curred in December 1919 when the coastal steamer *Ethie* was wrecked near Bonne Bay off the Newfoundland coast. Rescue boats were out of the question as the waves raged on the rocky shores. At its owner's command, a Newfound-land dog swam through the surging sea to fetch a small rope that had been cast from the ship. The retrieved rope grounded a lifeline that saw all of the passengers rescued, including a baby who made the perilous journey in a mail-bag.

Every pet is special, and the uniquely Canadian New-foundland dog epitomizes the best traits of all compan-ion animals. Lord Byron said it best in his tribute to Boat-swain:

One who possessed beauty without vanity
Strength without insolence
Courage without ferocity
And all the virtues of man, without his vices.

AND THEN THERE
WERE NONE

St. John's, Newfoundland, 1829 — When Shawnadithit died of tuberculosis in a St. John's hospital there were no relatives at her side. They were all dead.

It was the final chapter in a holocaust of atrocities that saw an entire people slaughtered like big-game hunting trophies.

Academics may suggest that extinction for these descendants of the prehistoric Maritime Archaic period was inevitable through European disease and ecological declines in food populations, but all of that remains conjecture because they were given no opportunity to adapt to anything except murder.

They were called the "Red Indians" by the Europeans, a name that followed from their custom of painting their bodies and their belongings with red ochre. From that it was a short trip to the pejorative term "redskins." Name-calling is far from the worst thing that happened to the aboriginals of Newfoundland known as the Beothuk or simply "The People." Genocide is the term most commonly applied. Historian Harold Harwood has described them as "the people who were murdered for fun."

The Vikings may have been the first to encounter the Beothuk. Sagas reveal encounters with at least two distinct native peoples, one of which was likely Dorset Inuit, and the other a taller, oval-eyed people which fits the Beothuk. Fifteen hundred years later, Jacques Cartier and John Cabot made contact. No one knows how many Beothuk lived throughout Newfoundland at that time, but the first recorded slaughter took place in 1613.

John Guy, Governor of the first English colony in Newfoundland, established trading relations at Trinity Bay in 1612. Things apparently went well. Guy arranged to return the following season to exchange goods for caribou hides and furs. When a ship entered the Bay during the approximate rendezvous period, the assembled Beothuk began dancing on the shore and launched a greeting party in ocean-going bark canoes. But it was the wrong ship. The celebration was interpreted as a war party. Grapeshot shattered the canoes. Some of the Beothuk men were killed and the rest fled.

This is not the first time such a "mistake" occurred, and it is the sort of calamitous error that might have found a reasonable resolution. However, before trading relations could resume, the Beothuk found themselves under assault by the Micmac who had migrated from Cape Breton Island and acquired guns from their French allies. According to one account, the French offered the Micmac a bounty on the Beothuk to encourage carnage and the Beothuk countered by beheading any white man they could capture.

Prior to such intrusion and skulduggery, the Beothuk had a peaceable lifestyle. Their deadliest weapons were bows and arrows, spears and harpoons. They spent their summers by the sea, collecting seabird eggs and harvesting fish. In spring and autumn, they hunted caribou along the

Exploits River. They wintered inland, where their homes were conical pole structures covered with sewn birchbark, which accommodated twenty to thirty people.

The Beothuk shared their possessions. Clothes, fire stones and amulets were their only private property. This concept contradicted that of the European settlers and opened the door for direct conflict when the Beothuk took to "liberating" items. But fishermen who suffered the consequence of vanishing salmon nets and other supplies, did not appreciate the cultural misunderstanding and decided to impose the death penalty. Europeans had already excluded the Beothuk from some of their seal and salmon hunting grounds. If men with guns had not killed the Beothuk, tuberculosis was a constant threat, coupled with malnutrition and starvation. Still, the threatened natives did not include guns in their pilfering, reportedly because they were fearful.

Until 1769, it was legal to kill the Beothuk and gunbutts were notched to keep tally of the kills. Then well-meaning administrators tried to provide deterrents, but the situation remained absurd. No court ever meted out punishment for the killing of a single "Red Indian."

The carnage was unconscionable; men, women and children were massacred while their settlements were looted and burned. Hundreds were killed, and hundreds quite literally were all that was left of the Beothuk.

In 1823, a mother and her two daughters were captured and attempts to return them to their people failed. All but the youngest daughter died. There are reports of Beothuk sightings up to 1830, but extinction was inevitable.

Ironically, the surviving Beothuk became a servant at the home of a man who participated in the murder of the last Beothuk chieftain. Called "Nancy," Shawnadithit was about twenty-three when she was captured. In 1828, she moved into the home of William Cormack, who had founded the Beothuk Institute just in time to record whatever history and mythology the traumatized woman could impart.

One of the drawings Shawnadithit left behind shows a dancing woman. Impossible as it seems, the woman, who knew as clearly as anyone could have that she was the last of her people, found it in her heart to portray an expression of joy.

TO WALK WITH GIANTS

Cape Breton, Nova Scotia, 1849 — In 1976, American comedian Mel Brooks told CBC's *As It Happens* host Barbara Frum his opinion of Canadians. "I think they are taller than Americans," he said, "they are kinder and they are more gentle." In the case of Nova Scotia's Angus McAskill, he was quite correct.

Young Angus grew up on a Cape Breton farm near St. Ann's Harbour where the McAskill family settled in 1831. They came from Harris in the Hebridean Islands of Scotland and joined a community of expatriate Highlanders in the district called "Englishtown" because its inhabitants did not speak Gaelic.

As a child, Angus was the same size as other boys but when he entered his teens he went off the growing curve. At fourteen, he was well over six feet tall and earned the nickname "Big Boy." Stories about his size and strength spread through the community. After one incident in which he knocked an antagonist unconscious at a dance, he was seldom challenged and became known for his "mild and gentle manner."

By the time Angus reached his twenties, the timber-framed McAskill house was too short for him. The roof and ground floor ceilings were raised, although he still had to duck through the front doorway. The feather or straw mattress on his eight-foot-long bed was lashed with ropes instead of a spring, and eventually even it proved too small.

Angus's strength proved a boon to his family. If a horse went lame ploughing in the field, he could take its place in the traces. One winter night when a "ceilidh" (at home) featuring music and dancing was scheduled, he was driving a team of oxen home with a load of firewood and found them too slow. So he unyoked them to find their own way and pulled the wood himself.

When he wasn't helping to clear the bush and plant the fields, Angus was a fisherman. His boat was ballasted before the mast to accommodate his weight at the stern. Onlookers marvelled when he single-handedly set the forty-foot mast. He never had to bail his half-ton boat, since he could simply set it on the beam and spill out the bilge water. Pranksters once urged him to pull on the bow of the boat while they secretly hauled back and the dory was torn apart in the tug-of-war.

At maturity, Angus was seven feet nine inches tall and weighed 425 pounds. Well-proportioned, he had curly dark hair, deep blue eyes and his voice was described as musical but hollow-sounding.

Although he was content with his life in English-town, crop failures and a freak late spring frost in 1848 wreaked hardship on the community and the McAskills. When a Yankee skipper and entrepreneur offered to tour "the big giant" as a curiosity, Angus accepted in hopes of helping his family.

Between 1849 and 1854, Angus was exhibited across Lower Canada, the United States, Europe, the West Indies and Cuba. Apocryphal tales abound about his adventures in the American West where he is said to have scared off train robbers by standing in the aisle. Likewise, in an audience with Queen Victoria at Windsor castle, McAskill tradition holds that he was presented with numerous gifts, including a Highland costume and two gold rings. During his Cuban tour, he was nicknamed "Mount Kaskill."

Wearing a cutaway coat trimmed with velvet and a Parisian-made beaver hat with a circumference of twenty-six-and-a-half inches, Angus accepted the stares of the curious, performing exercises while they gawked. His weight-lifting demonstrations were often accompanied by wagering. In one notable instance, he was challenged to lift a 2,700-pound anchor on a wharf that some say was in New York and others place as New Orleans. He successfully executed the press lift, but his grip slipped and the fluke caught his shoulder pinning him beneath it.

When he returned to Cape Breton at twenty-nine, Angus found the area transformed. Many of the families he had grown up with had emigrated to New Zealand with Reverend Norman McLeod in one of the most bizarre mass exoduses this country has ever seen. More than 850 self-described "Sea Birds" had departed St. Ann's to find a better life half a world away.

Undeterred, Angus used the "snug fortune" he had earned to open a general store across from his parents' home near the shore. The building was constructed to suit his size, and his stool was a 140-gallon molasses puncheon. He also bought a grist mill across the bay, where his strength was used by rolling the millwheels as though they were cookies. The first commercial salmon fishery at St. Ann's is also credited to his enterprise.

Much of his business was conducted in barter and he was known as a fair and friendly merchant who never refused to help a person in need. In his store, Angus sold tea by the pound or by the fistful, and tea from his foot-long palm was the best deal by far.

When he died in his thirty-ninth year after a brief illness diagnosed as "brain fever," the gentle giant of Cape Breton was mourned on a scale proportionate to his size. His gravesite, overlooking the harbour, has become a popular attraction for tourists, and artifacts from his life are displayed at the Gaelic College of Celtic Arts and Crafts at St. Ann's. By all accounts, he was Mel Brooks's epitome of a Canadian — tall, gentle and kind.

Subsequently, two other Canadians whose size made them notable became the subject of exhibition. Anna Swan of Mill Brook, Nova Scotia, was sixteen when she attracted the attention of American showman P.T. Barnum. He touted her as "the tallest girl in the world" and advertised her height at eight foot one inch although she was seven foot six in reality. In 1871, she married Martin Van Buren Bates, a Kentucky-born giant who was three-and-a-half inches shorter. They were billed as "the tallest married couple in the world." Anna bore two children, an eighteen-pound girl who died at birth, and a boy weighing twenty-three pounds twelve ounces, who succumbed after eleven hours.

In Saskatchewan, Edouard Beaupré was known as "the Willow Bunch Giant," after the town where he was born in 1881. Described as "shy, intelligent and tranquil," Edouard was the eldest of twenty children and he grew at a normal rate for the first few years of his life. However, at age nine he was six feet tall and at the peak of his growth he was an awesome eight foot two.

Edouard toured about North America on the freak show circuit and relatives accused his agent of keeping the young man drunk and of depriving him of his earnings.

While performing in the Barnum and Bailey Circus at the St. Louis World Fair in 1904, he suffered a pulmonary hemorrhage and died. His embalmed body was displayed in Montreal and ended up at the University of Montreal where it was used for medical research.

By 1967 the *Canadian Medical Association Journal* reported that the deteriorating corpse had withered to seven foot one. The Beaupré family, who had been unable to recover Edouard's body initially, demanded "respect for his body — and his soul." In 1990 the university returned his remains to Willow Bunch, where the body was then cremated. A statue dedicated to the giant was unveiled at a family reunion eighty-six years and three days after his death.

For the record, the tallest human being recorded to date was Robert Pershing Wadlow who stood one-tenth of an inch taller than eight foot eleven inches. He was an American.

A McASKILL PROPORTION SAMPLER
- Height — 7' 9"
- Width of Shoulders — 44"
- Weight — 425 lbs.
- Width of Palm — 8"
- Length of Palm — 12"
- Boot Length — 17 1/2"

THE HANGING JUDGE

Victoria, British Columbia, 1856 — When English lawyer Matthew Baillie Begbie arrived in British Columbia to serve as the colony's first judge he appeared to be the epitome of an impressive jurist. His pointed mustache was waxed and his beard trimmed into a careful wedge. He had studied at Cambridge and was fluent in French and Italian. But the dashing aura — black cloak and wide-brimmed velvet hat — did not mean that the man who was to shape the law in British Columbia was necessarily well versed in the subject.

In fact, thirty-nine-year-old Begbie had failed to make much of a living in the courts of London. His brother had usurped the affections of his girlfriend and he was reduced to being a reporter for the *Law Times* when he was offered £800 a year to pronounce justice half a world away. Legal acumen was not the foremost qualification British colonial secretary Sir Edward Bulwer-Lytton had in mind when he ordered up his first judge. He wanted a man who could "truss a murderer and hang him from the nearest tree." Begbie was given fifteen constables to help him with the job.

Crime did not come to the court room during the Fraser River gold rush, so Begbie took his court to the criminals.

The hard-riding judge kept a string of twelve horses. He carted his long judicial wig and scarlet robes with him and often meted out justice right at the crime scene. Trials were held in settlers' cabins, saloons, barns and even in open fields. When there was a scant pool of jurors, Begbie used transient Americans — which may have been an illegal practice, but it got the job done.

Sometimes the unorthodox judge even nipped crime in the bud. Arriving unexpectedly in Wild Horse Creek where a surly crew of armed miners had been fomenting a riot, he announced, "Boys, if there is a shooting in Kootenay, there will be a hanging in Kootenay." The miners named Begbie "the hanging judge." But delivering a death sentence was not something he undertook easily. Begbie often kept a chaplain at his side for moral support, and he was known to secretly lobby British Columbia Governor James Douglas to commute some sentences to life imprisonment. He had little use, however, for those who stood against him. Once he emptied a chamber pot over the heads of conspirators he overheard plotting to shoot him.

Begbie was no more charitable to some of his more obstinate juries. When a jury convicted a gambler of manslaughter rather than the "unmitigated, diabolical" crime of murder that he perceived, the judge reluctantly pronounced a life sentence. "Had the jury performed their duty I might now have the painful satisfaction of condemning you to death," he advised the prisoner in his shrill, nasal voice. "And you, gentlemen of the jury, are a pack of horse thieves, and permit me to say it would give me great pleasure to see you hanged, each and every one of you."

On another occasion, a jury acquitted an accused charged with sandbagging a companion in a Victoria barroom brawl. Begbie dismissed him saying, "You can go, and

I devoutly hope the next man you sandbag will be one of the jury."

Single-handed, Begbie was able to establish law-abiding habits in a political climate that was under pressure from the envious eye of Manifest Destiny and its anti-British sentiments. During forty-six controversial years on the bench, his detractors never won a case against him. Defying popular opinion of the day, he defended the rights of Chinese immigrants. He threw out a law that forbade native feasts called potlatches because he thought them a good and harmless custom. When British Columbia entered Confederation in 1871, Begbie became its chief justice. Four years later he was knighted.

Following his death in 1894, Begbie's small estate was left to destitute citizens whom he had quietly supported for years, and for each of clergy friends there was $100 and a case of wine. At his request, his grave was marked with the simple epitaph, "Lord be merciful to me, a sinner."

THE STORY OF DR. "O"

Brantford, Ontario, 1860 — Oronhyatekha was one very smart Mohawk. From the time he was a young brave on the Six Nations Reserve near Brantford, Ontario, in the mid-1800s, he took advantage of every opportunity made available to Reserve Indians by the equivocal benevolence of certain church organizations and the governments of Canada.

Baptized to be Peter Martin by the Anglican Church, throughout his sixty-six years he insisted that he be called by his Indian name Oronhyatekha, which means "Burning Cloud."

In 1867, he became the first native person to graduate from a university in Canada, and the first accredited native medical doctor.

Previously, Oronhyatekha had studied at Oxford University in England at the invitation of the Prince of Wales, whom he met when the Prince visited the Brantford reserve in 1860.

When Oronhyatekha returned to Canada from England in 1863, he married Ellen Hill, the great-granddaughter of Joseph Brant, and her Indian name, Karakwineh, meant "Moving Sun."

By all accounts, "Moving Sun" and "Burning Cloud" had a wonderful marriage until a son tragically died in 1881. "Moving Sun" then stopped moving and became a virtual recluse. After she died in 1901, Dr. O also went steadily downhill until he succumbed to complications from diabetes in 1907.

But his successful marriage, or the details of his education, his medical degree and the attendant success it brought Oronhyatekha, even the untimely death of his son are not at the core of his story.

Dr. O's story is of a full-blooded Mohawk Indian who ultimately made a significant career joining white men's fraternal societies typically defined by their racist policies.

As a student at the University of Toronto, he joined the secret order of Freemasons. Later, after practising medicine for a decade, he joined the ultra-Protestant Orange-men and ultimately the Independent Order of Foresters, a fraternal society based on life insurance that claimed its roots in medieval England and the attitude of Robin Hood.

To even be considered for membership in the Independent Order of Foresters, a man had to be a member of the Orange Society.

Founded in Ireland in 1795 to keep alive the memory of the "Glorious Revolution" and the Battle of the Boyne, where the Protestant succession to the British throne was secured in 1690, the Orangemen's global mandate is "the defence of Protestant Christianity and the unity of the British Empire — one school, one flag, one language."

It is surprising enough that the good doctor would want to join such a society, let alone pull it off, but that he somehow contrived to infiltrate Court Dufferin No. 7 of the Independent Order of Foresters truly boggles the mind, the more so because the constitution of the IOF openly stated (as opposed to the unspoken, unwritten racist tenets adhered to by more "secret" societies) that membership was only available to "white Christian males."

There really is no extant wholly satisfactory explanation for Dr. Oronhyatekha acceptance in any of these organizations. At six foot three, 230 pounds, with luminous copper skin, a huge head, protruding eyes and memorable basso voice, Oronhyatekha's could never have passed himself off as a white man, even had he wanted to.

The fact is Dr. O was inordinately proud of his native heritage. He never tried to hide it — the exact opposite. He wrote and published learned articles on the Mohawk language. He collected Indian artifacts from all over North America which he displayed prominently.

One thing is certain: Oronhyatekha was a beguiling, charismatic character and inveterate self-promoter. Setting up his first practice in Frankford, Ontario, he advertised his services as those of an Oxford physician who had trained with Dr. Acland in England.

Indeed, Dr. O had first met Dr. Acland when Dr. Acland accompanied the Prince of Wales on his trip to the Six Nations Reserve in 1860. What his advertisements failed to point out was the fact that Dr. Acland's degrees were in divinity rather than in Dr. O's alleged medical specialties, which the advertisements avowed were diseases of the throat and lungs as well as nervous disorders.

Regardless, since Frankford was near a large Mohawk reserve, Dr. O astutely added "Indian cures and herbal medicines" to his blurbs. He never looked back.

By 1870, three years after graduating from medical school, Dr. Oronhyatekha was well-enough positioned in the local medical establishment to be elected first secretary of the Hastings County Medical Association.

In 1871, he was invited to practise medicine in Stratford, Ontario, with a Dr. Lucas. Politically active, his new partner enticed Dr. O into helping organize a local Conservative campaign. As a consequence, Oronhyatekha met Sir John A. Macdonald, Prime Minister of the newly minted Canada.

Like the Prince and his good offices on behalf of Oronhyatekha with Oxford University, Sir John was sufficiently impressed by Dr. O to recommend him for the job of consulting physician to the Mohawks at Tyendinaga Reserve near Ottawa, a patronage appointment with some prestige.

Perhaps momentarily overwhelmed by delusions of grandeur, Dr. O immediately overextended himself when he built a mansion to house his modest family in Napanee. Within less than a year, he was essentially bankrupt.

Moving to London, Ontario, he opened a new practice and started over from scratch at the ripe old age of thirty-three.

Once again billing himself as an Oxford-educated physician and — with about the same amount of justification — a former government official, Dr. O began joining all of the fraternal, temperance and masonic organizations he could find in the area. One of them happened to be the Orange Society. The rest is history.

Whatever the reasons, however it happened, Dr. O took to the Independent Order of Foresters and their philosophy — which more than one observer has called "fraternal bunk" — like a duck to water.

He began a career of almost frantic, sometimes unsalaried, arguably fanatical activity with the IOF. His unbridled and seemingly sincere enthusiasm for the tenets of this particular kind of fraternalism were infectious. It was only a matter of months before he was High Chief Ranger of its Ontario High Court.

The Order was bankrupt — a schism had developed between the core American organization and the Canadian satellite — and all but 369 souls had jumped ship between 1878 and 1881, but Dr. O still travelled throughout the province at his own expense proselytizing fraternalism. In 1881, he was elected the first Supreme Chief Ranger of the Independent Order of Foresters, a position he held for the duration of his life.

Over the next decade, Dr. O single-handedly reconstituted the IOF as an international entity and a source of cradle-to-grave benefits for its members. In addition to life insurance, which was its schematic foundation, the Order had pension plans, weekly sick benefits, disability insurance and funeral coverage at prices with which traditional, old-line insurance companies could not compete.

Never one to shy away, Oronhyatekha proclaimed the IOF "the poor man's order."

Partly to allay public suspicion of the Order and in part to promote its products, Dr. O began to run full-page newspaper ads across the country detailing every aspect of the IOF's financial position and benefits, including its provision of up-to-the-minute "hourly sick pay-outs." He ran this campaign the way modern companies run their worldwide websites. The data was constantly changing, and was regularly updated, always to look better and better to the average citizen.

Oronhyatekha also had the sensibilities and sensitivities of the modern pollster. He seemed to be able to sense public opinion. In spite of the fact that the values of the IOF were arguably antithetical to his native heritage, Dr. O presented the IOF as a sound business operation run by sober, white, Christian men dedicated to the British Crown because that is what the majority of first-generation Scottish, Irish and English immigrants who populated the new country responded to.

The fact that he was a "Barnum let loose in the insurance business," as Dr. O was described in a 1951 *Maclean's* magazine article, does nothing to reconcile the contradictions inherent in what he did for a living and what he was.

By the time he died on August 6, 1907, the Independent Order of Foresters had become an international organization with more than a quarter of a million North American members and liquid assets in excess of eleven million dollars, making it the largest fraternal body on the continent.

The imprint of some of the more flamboyant characteristics of the IOF's Mohawk leader became bleached out by time and imperfect memory. For many years, it was regarded as a staid, stodgy, if somewhat secretive, insurance provider. However, in the 1990s, the family-values-oriented Order was rocked by a sex scandal involving none other than Dr. Oronhyatekha's 1990s counterpart, the Supreme Chief Ranger.

It seems the tall, lanky, high-living Texan executive had a penchant for certain things antithetical to Dr. O's devotion to high Anglicanism, monogamy and teetotalling. Nevertheless, evidently the Ranger from Texas shared with his predecessor a keen sense of the roll Barnums can play in the world of insurance.

When the wily, sexually active American agreed to resign in 1996 and take a multimillion-dollar golden parachute, the IOF had over 1,000 employees, over two million members, a solid balance sheet showing a $700-million-dollar cash surplus and assets of five billion dollars.

NO NUDDER LIKE HIM

Fort Whoop-Up, Alberta, 1874 — Imagine yourself in the middle of nowhere in the Canadian West, with a tight-lipped guide who carries neither map nor compass. Disoriented, perhaps concerned about the threat of attack by hostile elements, you ask the guide what he anticipates beyond the next hill. A little man with rounded shoulders and a stunted growth of whiskers, he eyes you narrowly and says, "Nudder hill." Such an experience became a familiar routine for members of the fledgling North-West Mounted Police (NWMP) when they travelled with Jerry Potts.

Potts was born in the United States at a fur trading post where his Scottish father clerked for the Hudson's Bay Company. His mother was a Blood Indian of the Blackfoot Confederacy. After Jerry's father was murdered in a case of mistaken identity, he grew up living variously with his mother's people and in white settlements.

As a young man, he fought in tribal wars and is said to have taken as many as nineteen scalps in one battle. His dress code was informal, and combined the influences of white and native cultures. Potts mixed a fedora hat with moccasins, and a bit of everything else in between. He was a superstitious man, always wearing the skin of a cat, which he believed would protect him from evil. He also refused to have a gun pellet removed from his left ear lobe because he had earned it in battle and thought it brought him good luck. He may have been right, since he died a few months after the pellet worked its way out of this lodging place of its own accord.

In the autumn of 1874, Potts was hired by Colonel James Macleod to lead the Mounties to Fort Whoop-Up, a bastion of whisky traders. As a guide, Potts was legendary. He was also said to be able to detect the smell of booze at a considerable distance, although he preferred to have the stuff close to him. Unfortunately, when Macleod and his troops arrived, the whisky runners had already fled — with their whisky.

Macleod tried to buy Fort Whoop-Up to no avail. With winter fast approaching, Potts led the weary column of troops and horses to a spot on the Oldman River, where Macleod began immediate construction of the Force's first fort in the West.

For twenty-two years Jerry Potts guided the Mounties, earning a colourful reputation along the way. One corporal reported that he had "an unquenchable thirst which a camel might have envied. If he could not get it, he would take Jamaica ginger or essence of lemon, or Perry Davis' painkiller, or even red ink." After bouts of such drinking excess, Potts and his buddy, George Star, were said to try to trim their mustaches with their six-shooters, facing each other at twenty-five paces. Potts lived in a teepee outside Fort Macleod, where he had a combination of native wives, some say as many as four at one time, including two who were sisters.

Despite his personal quirks, Potts became a great asset to the Mounties. He spoke the languages of several tribes, and he proved instrumental in establishing trust between the Blackfoot Confederacy and the NWMP. On one occasion, after Blackfoot chiefs delivered lengthy speeches of welcome and gratitude to the Mounties, Potts translated by saying, "Dey damn glad you here." Brevity was his soul.

After twenty-two years of continuous service to the Mounties, Jerry Potts's hard-lived life ended when he succumbed to tuberculosis on July 14, 1896. Calling him "a type fast disappearing," the *Macleod Gazette* noted: "For years he stood between the police on one side and his natural friends the Indians on the other and his influence always made for peace. Jerry Potts is dead but his name lives and will live. 'Faithful and true' is the character he leaves behind him — the best monument of a valuable life."

WHERE'S JOE'S BEEF?

Montreal, 1878 — You did not have to look far to find the meat in some form or other at Joe Beef's Canteen on the south side of Montreal. In the 1870s and 1880s, it was the most flamboyant tavern in the city, and probably the only one that boasted a resident live buffalo in the cellar. Opposite an open pantry piled to the ceiling with loaves of bread, there was a black bear whose chain rattled when the inquisitive came too close for comfort. For good measure, there was a spare bear downstairs and two parrots held squawk on a perch over the bar.

An account recorded by Montreal historian Edgar Andrew Collard describes the patrons almost as though they were part of the motley but well-loved menagerie of animals. "There was not a good coat, or a hat in even modest repair in the company," he suggests. "Their garb was of the poorest, but it made no difference to their spirits — all hands were happy and contented." Beer cost five cents for a pint-and-a-half mug and it was largely consumed at the upstairs bar, since the pungent odour of the buffalo was harder to take than the screeching chatter of the birds. Next door there was the Rag Shop. All along the waterfront, saloons and cafés did as brisk a business as did the sixty or so churches on the sedate north side of Montreal.

Although colourful advertising promoted "Joe Beef of Montreal" as "the son of the People," the proprietor was actually a mustachioed Irishman named Charles McKiernan, whose wit ensured a steady clientele of "the homeless and the footloose of the world." McKiernan promoted the character Joe Beef as something of a poet-renegade in search only of "coin," with scant regard for the "Pope, Priest, Parson or King William of Boyne." His handbills suggested, "If you can walk or crawl, when you go on the spree, go and see Joe Beef of Montreal."

The city itself was a marvel of extremes. On one hand, Donald Smith, the president of the Bank of Montreal and the governor of the Hudson's Bay Company, was busy building a cut-stone baronial castle, complete with a ballroom, private art gallery and marble balconies. At the same time, workers were complaining to a Royal Commission on Labour Capital that wages for a sixty-hour work week averaged about seven dollars. The disparity did not elude Joe Beef.

In July, 1878, workers on the nearby Lachine Canal went on strike for a twenty-cents-a-day raise. Six years earlier, workers in Ontario and Quebec had launched the Nine-Hour Movement in an effort to reduce working hours from twelve to nine per day. In Lachine, ten-hour days were in force and the reward was eighty cents a day. To help them hold their course, Charles McKiernan supplied the striking workers with three thousand loaves of bread and five hundred gallons of soup for their families. Then he funded two delegations to present the workers' case in Ottawa.

When his wife died, the band from his regiment played the "Dead March" from *Saul* for the procession to the gravesite at Mount Royal Cemetery. Her tombstone is marked with one of Joe Beef's impudent rhymes. On the way down the mountain, at the bereaved husband's request, the army band played a swinging rendition of "The Girl I Left Behind." The colourful innkeeper and philanthropist himself died in 1889 and the funeral was the largest ever seen in Montreal. Mourners lined the streets for blocks, and workers were given a half-day holiday.

Nobody in town had a beef with Joe Beef.

FATHER GOOSE

Kingsville, Ontario, 1908 — Jack Miner was a frecklefaced thirteen-year-old when he became a skunk hunter, earning fifty cents a pelt. This odiferous pursuit helped support his family, including eleven siblings, who moved across Lake Erie from Ohio to seven acres of brush near Kingsville, Ontario, in 1878. Young Miner became a "market" hunter. For a bounty fee, barefoot Jack and his brother, Charlie, could kill as many as a dozen rattlesnakes in a day. A bag of twenty ruffed grouse was merely average for the precocious hunter.

"Market hunting is not sport. It is murder in the first degree," Miner later wrote in his autobiography *Wild Goose Jack.* Yet the man who was to receive the Order of the British Empire for his achievements in conservation, spent fully half his life in the killing fields before devoting himself to the preservation issues that led him to establish one of the first bird sanctuaries in North America.

Most of Miner's early life was spent studying nature. His formal education totalled only three months. When he was not working in the family's tile and brick works, he was sought after as a guide for hunting parties. Without a trace of bravado, Miner noted that he and his brother, Ted, "could kill a deer about any time we wanted one."

In 1898, on a moose-hunting trip in Northern Ontario, Ted Miner was killed by a careless shot from another hunter. In his grief, Jack was persuaded to go to church, where he volunteered to teach a rowdy boys' Sunday-school class. He enthused the boys with his woodsman's adventures and prompted them to read biblical passages relating to nature. In return, the boys taught Miner to read.

Although he continued to take pleasure in hunting, Miner grew steadily more interested in befriending his prey. "Any man who isn't big enough to change his mind has nothing to change," he liked to say. Miner changed his mind about hunting when he perceived that a gaggle of Canada geese could clearly identify him as "the enemy" despite his persuasive imitation of their "khonk, khonk" clarion call.

From that day forward, he embarked on a mission to become a friend of migrating fowl. In 1904, he dug ponds on his farm, planted trees and installed four pinioned Canada geese as decoys. Neighbours snickered for three years as the brickmaker in baggy dungarees sprinkled grain for birds that did not land. Finally, in 1908, eleven geese sought sanctuary. There were thirty-two the following year. In 1910, there were 400. Gradually, the number grew to more than 50,000.

Aside from providing a safe haven, Miner also hoped to unravel the mystery of migration routes. In 1909, he banded his first duck, inscribing his address into the aluminum. Five months later he learned of the fate of the mallard, Katie, when he was notified of her death by a hunter hundreds of miles south of the sanctuary.

Miner's banding program expanded to include tens of thousands of wild ducks and Canada geese. His findings documented migration routes that spread from summer nesting grounds north of Hudsons Bay to balmy winters spent in Florida. The data contributed to the basis of the 1917 Migratory Bird Treaty between Canada and the United States, by proving that the conservation laws of the two nations had to be interrelated.

Inspired by a Salvation Army calendar, Miner began marking his bands with biblical verse as an inducement to hunters to return the bands and increase the accuracy of his migration route charts. Thousands responded to his missionary geese.

Over the next thirty years, Miner became a popular lecturer, which financed his huge feed bills and expanding conservation program. Professors compared his philosophy to that of Aristotle. He began warning of the dangers of pollution in the Great Lakes in 1927 and became the first Canadian to receive the Outdoor Life Gold Medal two years later. In celebration of the Silver Anniversary of King George V's reign, Prime Minister Mackenzie King chose Miner as Canada's representative speaker in a radio broadcast heard worldwide.

Three years after his death in 1944, the government designated the week of his birth (April 10th) as "National Wildlife Week."

His work continues through the Jack Miner Foundation, which has expanded its sanctuary from 35 acres to close to 400, accepting more than 125,000 visitors per year.

"There is no man so clean but what he will be a better thinking man if he gets well-acquainted with the pure, self-sacrificing ways of the Canada goose," Miner once wrote.

Golf course owners and farmers plagued by over-wintering giant Canada geese may disagree. With food readily available, thousands of geese no longer migrate.

But hope is never far off — in 1993, artist/environmentalist Bill Lishman launched a program to condition geese to migrate. Piloting an innovative ultra-light flying contraption, this modern-day Father Goose "led" an orphaned flock of eighteen geese 640 kilometres from Blackstock, Ontario, to a wintering site in Virginia. Of their own accord, twelve survivors of hunters and a harsh winter returned to their birthplace near the shores of Lake Scugog. The experiment will be used as a prototype to instruct domestically raised, endangered species such as the whooping crane in the "wild" art of migration. Jack Miner would be the first to "khonk" in approval.

LEAVE IT TO THE BEAVER

London, England, 1910 — A multimillionaire before he was thirty, William Maxwell Aitken's furious, flamboyant omni-presence had a profound and lasting influence on Canadian commerce. A kind of Gorden Gecko, the amoral corporate raider portrayed in Oliver Stone's award-winning 1989 movie *Wall Street*, Aitken was a mergers and acquisitions man in the nascent Canadian market. His controversial transactions dog him, like an evil twin, even to this day.

A slight man with an impish face, "Max" seemed to come from nowhere. To the civilized world, Maple, Ontario, where he was born in 1879 to strict parents of Scottish-Presbyterian descent was nowhere. Not a particularly good student, by his own admission he was an impudent son.

Aitken's early years were a testament to the axiom that it's not so much what you know, but who. As a teenager in Newcastle, New Brunswick, where his family moved shortly after he was born, Aitken had the remarkable good fortune to meet and befriend the considerably older R.B. Bennett, who was destined to become Prime Minister of Canada.

Aitken joined Bennett's law firm as a clerk, but soon dropped out. By twenty-one Max was truly nowhere. He had tried university, studied law, sold insurance, managed a bowling alley in Calgary and sold meat in Edmonton. He gambled and drank the proceeds of his labour.

Fate stepped up, in the person of John F. Stairs, a well-connected Halifax financier and politician whose acquaintance he made on a weekend fishing trip organized by R.B. Bennett. Stairs saw something in the youthful ne'er-do-well and staked Aitken as a stock promoter. Shortly thereafter, Stairs asked Aitken to amalgamate two small banks. When the youthful enthusiast made $10,000 in the process, his future was manifest. Aitken was soon managing a new investment house called Royal Securities.

In 1906, two years after his mentor's death, and under some kind of cloud, Aitken quit Royal Securities and moved to St. James Street in Montreal, then the financial heart of Canada. There he made a series of lightning fast, spectacular moves, including buying and selling Montreal Trust for a $200,000 profit. With this profit, he took over Royal Securities, facilitating a frenetic, profitable, international binge of acquisitions and mergers.

Aitkens bought and sold companies in the West Indies. He also started Calgary Power, but his most heavily rewarded talent was that of a "corporate bundler." He was to the 1920s and St. James Street what Michael Miliken was to the 1980s and Wall Street, except he was Miliken in reverse. Instead of "raiding" giant companies and dismantling them piece by piece, at an enormous profit until only a shell remained, Aitken bundled smaller regional companies in the same business to create powerful corporations.

Aitken reasoned that only large Canadian corporations, shielded by tariff protection that he coerced his pal Prime Minister R.B. Bennett to instigate, could compete with giant American rivals. Aitken went about buying all the small companies in similar businesses he could find across Canada and amalgamating them.

By 1910, there was the widespread suspicion that Max Aitken had misappropriated more than $13 million in a 1909 merger which he engineered for Canada's three largest cement companies. Instead of the three he was asked to integrate, however, he merged thirteen cement companies into Canada Cement. Skillfully and arguably illegally, he excluded one of the original three which he knew to be debt-ridden and unprofitable. The case was eventually settled out of court, with Aitken making what to him by then was a nickel-and-dime rebate of $20,000 to the Bank of Montreal.

Even as this clamour over cement churned, Aitken was on to the next deal, buying Montreal Rolling Mills, Canada's leading steel-finishing plant. To keep the deal secret, he went to the London money market for the $4.2 million he needed to secure the plant.

He told his rivals he would not take a penny less than $5 million for the Rolling Mills facility and they tried squeezing him through the Canadian banks. To their horror, they discovered Aitken had outmanoevred them with off-shore financing. His price went up to $6 million, but now included one-third of the new, amalgamated Steel Co. of Canada. On the very day Stelco came into being, Aitken packed up whatever were his cares and woes, and moved to England. There Aitken met another New Brunswick expatriate, Conservative politician Andrew Bonar Law. Law invested $100,000 in a securities corporation Aitken established and doubled his money in two years, establishing a firm friendship.

Under Law's tutelage, Aitken became a Member of Parliament in 1910. Seven years later he was granted a peerage,

moving into the House of Lords as the first Baron of Beaverbrook, a name he selected after a stream near his Canadian
home. Three years later, Andrew Bonar Law became the
first Canadian Prime Minister of England, but he was neither the first — nor the last — Prime Minister to be a
confidante of Lord Beaverbrook. Kings and dictators sought
"The Beaver" equally.

By the time Aitken was fifty, he had taken over and
revitalized the London *Daily Express*, the *Evening Standard*
and the *Sunday Express*, bought and sold Rolls-Royce,
served in Lloyd George's and Winston Churchill's wartime
Cabinets, helped oust Asquith and broken up the coali-
tion between the Conservatives and the Lloyd George
Liberals in 1922.

Embarrassingly, Beaverbrook steadfastly advocated
a policy of appeasement with Nazi Germany and made
many an approving remark about certain aspects of Nazism.
He met with Stalin and advocated for a British alliance with
Russia, jilted writer Rebecca West, befriended H.G. Wells,
advised Rudyard Kipling about money, and generally
became a master of shadow-boxing in the backrooms of
international intrigue and power.

But there were those who saw him in a different light.
Unlike Kipling, Churchill never took any of Beaverbrook's
financial advice. Lady Churchill disliked Beaverbrook
intensely, and called him a "microbe." She often scolded
Sir Winston about this "bad influence." Churchill's successor, Labour Prime Minister Clement Attlee, said Beaverbrook
was "the only evil man I ever met."

As Lord Beaverbrook, Aitken commissioned biographies about himself. For posterity, he wrote books which
sycophants described as indispensable but were, in the
words of historian Martin Gilbert, "never quite right."

Beaverbrook often governed his empire and many interests from a distance, for instance, from Villa Capponcina, his extravagant retreat in the south of France. In his hands, the telephone became a weapon. While he was chewing out his editors and barking instructions, his long-distance lackeys could often hear young women they disparagingly dubbed "Beaver's girls" giggling in the background. Beaverbrook set out to run England and the world through his newspapers. However, not one policy or issue he and his papers supported ever became public policy.

In 1947, he became Chancellor of the University of New Brunswick. He lavished approximately $20 million in gifts on his beloved Miramichi Valley. In Fredericton, he built skating rinks and libraries, an art gallery and a theatre — even a Beaverbrook Birdbath. Malcolm Muggeridge called it the "deliberate pre-humous creation of a shrine and a cult."

In spite of his philanthropies and his Zelig-like appearance in hundreds of photographs with legendary leaders, his real legacy seems to be a debatable lesson: that mass communications have little or no influence on opinion or behaviour. His daily newspapers appear to have set the precedent for their tabloid successors: contrary to being sources of reliable information and influence, they were really nothing more than entertainment.

H.G. Wells predicted that if he got the chance Lord Beaverbrook would try to merge heaven and hell. On May 25, in 1964, Lord Thomson of Fleet, a fellow Canadian-born press baron, threw a dinner party for Beaverbook's eighty-fifth birthday. Beaverbrook gave a speech in which he said that he had always been an apprentice and now it was time for him to become an apprentice once more. "Somewhere," he said, "sometime soon." He died on June 9, 1964, on his British estate.

THE GREAT STORK DERBY

Toronto, 1926 to 1936 — No one has ever been able to explain exactly just what possessed Charlie Millar when he was drawing up his last will and testament. The prominent Toronto lawyer and sportsman was considered to be a "respectable stuffed shirt," shy, irascible and thrifty. But when he died at seventy-three, he sparked a breeding frenzy in Toronto the like of which had never been seen.

Provisions in the will set forth rules for a fecundity contest that would award the bulk of the bachelor Millar's considerable estate to the Toronto woman who produced the most children "under the Vital Statistics Act" between the date of his death on Halloween Day, 1926, and the marking of that event's tenth anniversary.

The contest became known as the "Great Stork Derby." When it ended, four women who fielded families the size of baseball teams were declared the winners. Each received $165,000.

Mothers who gave birth to only eight children were out of luck. One poor woman, Mae Clark, was also a loser even though she gave birth to ten children. Five of the Clark children were sired by Mae's legal husband, but five others were of questionable paternity. A righteous court ruled the illegitimate children out of the running, but the derby winners compensated Mrs. Clark with a gift of $12,500 to stave off further legal wrangles. All of the winners were of modest means. One family had been on welfare and they promptly returned the $1,800 that they had collected from the City.

In the preamble to his will, Charles Vance Millar stated that he intended its contents to be "uncommon and capricious."

He left nothing to his relatives, and little to his faithful employees.

"If I left them money they would be glad when I died," Millar once told a friend. "I don't want anybody to look forward to my death."

In death, however, Millar loomed much larger than in life. A farm boy from Aylmer, Ontario, he became a prize-winning student. After passing the bar, he started his career as a three-dollar-a-week lawyer living in Toronto's Queen's Hotel, where the manager gave him credit. Gradually, he built a booming business in corporate law and bought a dozen houses as rental properties. He owned a houseboat with the Chief Justice of the Ontario Supreme Court and once had two racehorses place first and second in the 1915 King's Plate.

When he died, Millar's estate was valued at only $104,000. However, over the decade of the derby it grew almost tenfold when his once paltry stock portfolio sky-rocketed due to the success of the Windsor-Detroit Tunnel Co., in which he held 100,000 shares.

The few bequests that he made to individuals were almost as controversial as the Stork Derby. He left one share of a Catholic-owned brewery to every Protestant minister in Toronto.

Of the 303 clergymen who qualified, 99 applied for their share and at least three shares were turned over for charitable uses.

Only thirteen of Toronto's 114 Orange Lodges declined the same offer.

Clergymen in the Windsor area were offered one share each in the Kennilworth Race Track, which raised moral questions until it was discovered that the shares were worth less than a penny a piece.

Three lawyers who were known to dislike each other were given Millar's vacation home in Jamaica.

A devout horse-racing enthusiast and two adversaries of the betting sport — the head of the Methodist Church in Canada and a former Attorney-General of Ontario — were each offered a fifteen-hundred-dollar share in the Ontario Jockey Club provided they enrolled in the club. The two anti-gamblers joined the club for five minutes, sold their shares for a modest profit and donated the proceeds to the Poppy Fund.

A series of relatives challenged the will to no avail, but the longest running litigation was pursued by the Ontario government, which argued that it was "against public policy" and encouraged immorality.

Eleven years after Millar's death a judge finally ended the debate, stating: "I cannot find that reproduction of the human race is contrary to morals." The "Millar Will" stood as a last testament to its maker's legal skills.

Line for line, the "Great Stork Derby" received more newspaper coverage than Charles Lindbergh and the stock market crash. "The things I remember most are the smell of many children in bad houses; the unnatural talk about big money by tired women on relief; the resigned resentment of husbands whose procreative powers had suddenly become world news," one reporter told *Maclean's* magazine twenty-five years later.

In his own eccentric way, Charlie Millar may have been trying to make a statement of opposition to the government of Ontario's ban on birth control information. However, the end product caused much grief to many who could ill afford it.

A friend suggested that: "Charlie's hope was that, by turning the spotlight on unbridled breeding and making us a laughing stock before the world he could shame the government into legalizing birth control."

That ultimate distinction fell to a twenty-eight-year-old clerk from Ottawa who was arraigned on charges of distributing birth control information and contraceptive devices ten days before the Stork Derby ended.

Welsh-born Dorothea Palmer was arrested in the predominantly French-speaking, Roman Catholic suburb of Eastview (now Vanier). She had been offering requested advice about contraception on behalf of the Kitchener, Ontario-based Parent's Information Bureau, where she was employed as a part-time social worker. The Bureau was established in 1930 by birth-control advocate and rubber goods manufacturer A.R. Kaufman, who was concerned about social unrest he feared would result unless working families had the option of controlling family size. Kaufman hired the best defence counsel that money could buy.

The trial lasted a remarkable six months. Forty witnesses were called, including experts from psychologists to relief workers, professors and birth control experts. The case hinged on the notion that although Section 207 of the Criminal Code stated it was a crime to sell or advertise contraceptive drugs or devices, no person could be convicted if they could show that they were acting in the public good.

Dorothea Palmer was acquitted on March 17, 1937. Thirty-two years later, the Criminal Code of Canada was amended and the dissemination of birth control information and contraceptive devices were finally legal.

GONE INDIAN

Temagami, Ontario, 1930 — He wasn't a grifter in the classic sense; he grew into his con and stayed with it for the duration. Among other things, he was a drunk, a fraud, a philanderer, a bigamist, and a wife-abuser— but he liked beavers, a fact that stood him in good stead with English Royalty and posterity.

The author known as Grey Owl had other good qualities, such as his inordinate love and understanding of the wilderness and its inhabitants. When he wrote about nature, he wrote about what he knew and infused his stories with an essential sincerity that defies the make-believe mask of the Noble Savage that he wore to his death. His was a lifetime of performance art.

Grey Owl told anyone who would listen that he was a half-breed, born in Mexico to a Scottish-American father and an Apache mother. In fact, he was plain old Archibald Stansfeld Belaney from Hastings, England, the son of a dipsomaniac and his teenage bride. He was raised by aunts, but even as a child he apparently acted out his fantasies. A history of the English grammar school he attended describes eleven-year-old Archie as "a delicate boy but full of devilment; and fascinated by woods and wild animals

. . . What with his camping out, his tracking of all and sundry, and wild hooting, he was more like a Red Indian than a respectable Grammar School boy."

Disillusioned, confused and spellbound by the romantic tales of James Fenimore Cooper, Belaney came to Canada in search of adventure when he was eighteen years old. By 1930, the war veteran, trapper and forest ranger had completely assumed the mantle of the Noble Savage and become Grey Owl, or Wa-Sha-Quon-Asin meaning He Who Flies By Night. In fact, by this time Belaney had demonstrated his "fly by night" predilection to several wives.

Belaney began writing under his birth-name, and selections from his diary as a trapper and forest ranger first appeared in *The Hastonian* in 1913. Sixteen years later, his first "professional" magazine article appeared in the British weekly, *Country Life.* He was encouraged to write more, and gradually began an elaborate process of configuring himself as a bona fide Indian. In a native ceremony, he married an Iroquois woman eighteen years his junior. Anahareo, who joined Grey Owl in the wilderness of Temagami instead of fulfilling a scholarship to Loretto Abbey (a toney private girls' school in Toronto), urged him to quit trapping and helped determine the conservationist course of action that proved to be his lasting legacy.

In 1933, his first book, *Men of the Last Frontier,* was published, and Belaney had begun writing and speaking publically as Grey Owl. The federal Parks Department took such an interest in Grey Owl's stories that they made a film about his life with the beaver. Jelly Roll, a female beaver who was almost as much of a showman as Grey Owl, starred with him in a display of trust and affection that won the attention of the world.

The story of Grey Owl and the beavers had begun years before with two orphaned kits named McGinty and McGuinness. The adopted beavers captivated Grey Owl and he became preoccupied with the idea that the beaver was facing extinction. He set his classic children's story *Sajo and Her Beaver People* in the great Temagami forest where they lived in a rustic cabin. The tale of native children and two baby beavers remains in print and has been translated into nearly twenty languages.

While he was writing his children's book, Grey Owl was also completing his autobiography *Pilgrims of the Wild,* which was published in 1935 by Australian-born Lovat Dickson, who grew up in Canada. Dickson organized a lecture tour for Grey Owl in Britain. At a time when the economics of Canada and England were depressed, Wall Street had crashed, Hitler was mobilizing for war, Mussolini was ranting and raving, and industrial pollution was choking European cities, Grey Owl was a breath of fresh air from an enchanted wilderness. He spoke about forests that had the size and sanctity of medieval cathedrals; about a land where mankind could begin again, where the air was pure and animals roamed free. The crowds loved it. Regardless of the purity of his message, Grey Owl was still a fraud, and for his efforts the consummate con began earning in the princely neighbourhood of $30,000 a year. He drank whisky almost non-stop on his return crossing. Before he had such an outstanding income, his substance abuse of choice had been vanilla extract.

His final book, *Tales of an Empty Cabin,* was published in October 1936 and one month later, tired of being neglected while he incessantly wrote out his stories, Anahareo left Grey Owl. A few weeks later, the much-married and seldom-divorced Archie wed Yvonne Perrier, whose native name was Silver Moon.

A second tour of England and the United States was scheduled for the winter of 1937 through 1938. Once again, Grey Owl was spellbinding, and he looked more "red" than ever, thanks to a sun lamp. He appeared in a command performance for King George, Queen Mary and the Royal Princesses, Elizabeth and Margaret Rose. Eschewing protocol, Grey Owl insisted that all members of his audience be seated before he made his dramatic entry. In his braids, beads and fringed leather costume, the British-born imposter greeted his King in the Ojibway language, which he translated as "I come in peace, brother." Then he showed his films and told his stories. Princess Elizabeth was apparently so enthralled that when it was over she jumped up and cried, "Oh, do go on!" Publisher Lovat Dickson attended the Royal event and notes in his biography *Wilderness Man, The Strange Story of Grey Owl* that "he was more than ever the Indian, proud, fierce, inscrutable."

Months later, on April 13, 1938, Grey Owl died at his cabin in Prince Albert, Saskatchewan, and the world soon learned that he was a hoax. There was surprise, but no shock wave of disapproval. His masquerade as the Noble Red Man was one of the great thespian performances of the century and his environmental concerns are as relevant today as they were in his lifetime. What better grift than to get away with it in the end.

A BELLY LAUGH
OR YOUR MONEY BACK

Lillooet, British Columbia, 1934 — She called herself "Ye Ed" but to most everyone else, Margaret Murray, the editor of British Columbia's *Bridge River-Lillooet News* was known as "Ma." Cut from a cloth which was both delightful and maddening to her readers, Ma Murray was an original and as irrepressible as *Calgary Eye Opener* editor Bob Edwards. In fact, the two mavericks were acquainted. In 1913, when Margaret Lally married her boss, editor George Murray, Bob Edwards sent champagne to their wedding table.

"Guarantees a chuckle every week and a belly laugh once a month or your money back," proclaimed Ma's masthead. The circulation of the community newspaper might have peaked at 2,000 but "every bloody one of 'em paid for" was proclaimed with blunt pride.

Irreverent, sometimes even shocking, Ma Murray had spiced her editorials with words like "craporini," "damshur" and "snaffoo." She freely admitted that she was not a writer, rather she "told things." At the beginning of the year, readers who insisted on proper grammar were rewarded with two inches of punctuation marks to position as they saw fit.

A child of Irish immigrant parents, Margaret was raised on a farm in Windy Ridge, Kansas. Her childhood education stopped at grade 3, but she washed dishes to pay tuition fees to attend secretarial school and graduated with honours.

While working at a saddlery company in Kansas City, Margaret started sending notes along with the invoices to Alberta cowboys, and was rewarded with return correspondence that included pictures of broad-shouldered Westerners, invitations and even marriage proposals. In 1912, her curiosity got the better of her and she headed for Calgary "to catch a cowboy." Her money ran out in Vancouver and she decided to stay.

She started out in the newspaper business selling subscriptions to *B.C. Federation*, a labour publication. This led to a bookkeeping job at a south Vancouver weekly called the *Chinook*, where she was soon writing community news.

"My boss is a nice young man, a little vague and annoying but real handsome," Margaret said in a letter home. Less than a year later, she married *Chinook* editor George Murray.

Two children and a series of newspapers followed, with poverty a constant companion. Margaret and the children homesteaded in a small tar-paper cottage on Burrard Inlet until George got a steady job as the managing editor of the *Vancouver Morning Sun*. Back in Vancouver, Margaret started *Country Life in B.C.* magazine, an enterprise that involved her in the activities of Women's Institutes and saw her reporting on everything from beekeeping to rug hooking.

Margaret claimed the Depression hit the Murray family a full year before the stock market crashed in 1929. George's salary was halved, the children were placed in boarding school and Margaret tried selling her homemade handicrafts. "Times were very hard," she recalled later. "My tongue was stickin' out a foot for a taste of a strip of bacon." But the characteristic Murray optimism never failed.

George felt strongly about the need for development in B.C. and improved transportation corridors to the north. With Margaret's help and a $200 campaign budget, he was elected to the provincial legislature in 1933 as the Liberal member for Lillooet, a small interior community that was noted as Mile One during the Caribou gold rush.

"Well hell's bells, we're here aren't we, so we may as well start a newspaper," announced Margaret.

According to her daughter, Georgina, the family settled in "a house that looked ready to slip into the Fraser River before dinnertime." The salt-box, frame house ringed with porches was the heart of the newspaper Margaret founded in 1934 to help supplement George's meagre salary as an MLA.

An upstairs bedroom served as the editorial office. A hole was cut in the floor so that copy could be lowered to the waiting press, a Klondike gold rush artifact that shook the whole building when it rolled. Margaret sold advertising and subscriptions, sometimes accepting chickens in lieu of cash. At fifty-three, she was running her own newspaper and Margaret Murray felt she had come into her own.

Other people may have thought that "Ye Ed" came a bit too close to coming into their own. The *Bridge River-Lillooet News* was cited in seven divorce actions after publishing a local hotel's guest registry. And Margaret's expansive editorial language raised legal hassles. The *News* paid legal costs when a retraction on behalf of an individual who was described as a "crooked horse trader" and a "gypsy," was not forthcoming.

Margaret found news everywhere she looked. She covered everything from gold strikes to prostitution and pulled no punches.

"I'm the editor of the dinkiest paper in British Columbia," she once told a television interviewer. "The place I live in is so isolated you gotta scrape the bottom of the barrel. My God, there isn't a week I don't have slivers in my fingers scrapin' up the news."

A Toronto writer provided the moniker "Ma" and even though Margaret disliked it at first, her weekly column "My Week, A Digest of the More Homely Things in Our Everyday Life," was soon signed "Ma Murray."

The Murray publishing empire expanded to include at least two more newspapers, which were soon under management of their children. The Second World War brought changes to British Columbia. In 1942, Lillooet became an internment centre for more than 3,000 Japanese Canadians. At the same time, George Murray's dream of a highway to Alaska was being realized as American dollars poured into the construction of a defence road following the Japanese occupation of the Aleutian Islands. The Mur-rays decided to move where the action was, settling in Fort St. John, north of Dawson City in the Peace River Valley where the first issue of the *Alaska Highway News* appeared in 1944.

Coincidentally, during that period George was defeated after serving eight years in the legislature, and prosperity in Fort St. John declined when American troops stationed along the new highway pulled out.

"What kind of heebie jeebies has hit this town anyway?" Ma wrote of the slump. "Checks in this town are bouncing like popcorn and pockets are empty."

Although Margaret had briefly flirted with developing her own political career as a Social Credit candidate, George remained staunchly Liberal. In 1949, he was elected as the federal member in the Cariboo riding. Ma, however, did not last long in Ottawa. Although her son Dan had agreed to run the newspaper, apparently the two could not see eye-to-eye on editorial or subscription policy. When she returned for a visit, he had gone and she stayed to run the paper.

In 1958, the Murrays decided to retire in Vancouver and their children took over the *Alaksa Highway News*. Three months later, seventy-one-year-old Ma Murrary informed her daughter that she felt "no sap flowing inside." The couple returned to Lillooet and bought back the old newspaper. A few years later, George died, but "Ye Ed" continued to produce her newspaper well into her eighties, including the popular column "Chat Out of the Old Bag." She never lost the "dinging away" edge that both delighted and infuriated her readers.

"Governments are like underwear. They start smelling pretty bad if you don't change them once in a while," Ma told the *Toronto Star* at the 1981 premiere of Eric Nicol's play *Ma! A Celebration of Margaret Murray*. The following year Margaret Murray was buried beside her husband in Fort St. John. She was ninety-five.

THE SITDOWNERS

Vancouver, 1938 — Ironically, Steve Brodie's early exposure to politics would have been to hardline Conservatism and the lionizing of that triumvirate of earthly authority: God, King and Empire. But the lack of any godly grace in Brodie's life and the cruel Canadian prairie soon undermined the youthful Scot's naive beliefs.

The son of a preacher, Steve Brodie was born Robert Brodie in Edinburgh in 1912. "Steve" was a nickname he acquired later from his legion of rail-riding unemployed comrades in the Dirty Thirties in Canada. Brodie's relentless, never-say-die style reminded them of another Brodie named Steve — a working man's hero in the bleak, Depression landscape who plunged off the Brooklyn Bridge to win a bet.

Orphaned during the 1919-1920 influenza epidemic, Brodie came to Canada at age thirteen. Part of one of many mass orphan migrations organized by the Salvation Army, he walked off the boat onto an Eastern Ontario farm as an itinerant worker. Hearing there was work and a better life in the West, Brodie caught the last of the harvester excursion trains.

Reality was otherwise. The Canadian prairies had fallen prey to drought and desolation. When a Saskatchewan farmer introduced him to some socialist pamphlets, the seeds of revolt fell on fertile ground. Proudly, Brodie espoused his new views to his next employer. An Alberta rancher and no socialist, the man dumped the hapless farm-hand on dead-of-winter Edmonton streets with ten dollars and the clothes on his back. That winter, like prairie per-mafrost, socialism sank deep into Brodie's soul.

Although he was a physical lightweight, Brodie had uncanny powers of persuasion with the single, unemployed drifters who travelled the rails, sharing the collective over-the-rainbow dream of steady work. Prime Minister R.B. Bennett told them they were lucky to get twenty cents a day building roads and levelling airfields. Brodie began to argue about the injustice of it all.

In the winter of 1933, Brodie rolled into the Rocky Mountains where he spent the time building fire trails and clearing beaver dams in a forestry camp near Banff, Alberta. In the early spring, he moved south to Vancouver, where the weather suited his clothes. He was not alone.

By 1938, the prosperous but provincial city of 246,000 had an unemployment rate of almost 30 percent. The city alone could not give relief to the thousands upon thousands of Steve Brodies sleeping fitfully under its viaducts and bridges. But there was no help and little sympathy from other quarters.

The transients were denounced by the Mayor and the Prime Minister of Canada as dangerous, cold-blooded, Bol-shevik agitators. They were deemed ruffians, who refused to be hungry and destitute with the quiet dignity reduced means traditionally commanded.

Brodie had joined the Communist Party and became an influential figure. Early in the summer of 1938, he and a select coterie of labour organizers plotted a mass demonstration.

The idea was to organize a march and then surreptitiously, stealthily, with two thousand men, occupy three strategic buildings: the Vancouver Art Gallery, the Post Office and the Hotel Georgia. These stately edifices symbolized the civic, public and private interests that comprised the city's lifeblood.

Nineteen years earlier, the Winnipeg Strike had been marred by extreme violence. In Brodie's view, although that strike had immobilized a city, the violence largely negated its point. Neither violence nor agitation were on the agenda for Vancouver. The sitdown was to be a peaceful demonstration.

Although RCMP infiltrators attempted to keep tabs on pending insurgencies, Brodie's scheme stayed under wraps. One minute — business as usual — the next, two thousand men squatted throughout three grand premises. When the local police chief, Billy Foster, requested Brodie take his men out, Brodie politely refused. Recognizing the seriousness of the situation and its inherent flaws, Foster immediately made arrangements with the Canadian Pacific Railway station for the use of its washrooms by the sitdowners.

Brodie's men occupied the large, marble-floored lobby of the Post Office. Once they regained their composure, postal clerks continued to transact business at their brass wickets. For the next thirty days, the public calmly threaded their way around and over Brodie and his increasingly bored band of sitdowners.

The peaceful demonstration display at the Hotel Georgia ended quickly. A group of city aldermen, concerned about the effect of bedraggled protesters on tourism, raised $500 and bought the men out. Brodie considered this a victory and an indication that the city accepted some responsibility for its population of transient unemployed. The money went to support the balance of the demonstration.

Meanwhile, the Art Gallery and the Post Office took on the semblance of a siege. Supportive women's organizations delivered hot meals. The YMCA opened its shower rooms, and a linen company provided towels. Local restaurants and churches offered free meals. A bakery donated bread and pies. A music store gave the men two radios, and a department store chipped in five hundred pairs of socks. There were even a few cots scattered among the bedrolls. And the protest had its own weekly newspaper. *The Sitdowner's Gazette* sold for donations ranging from ten cents to five dollars per copy. Its editorials were simple: the cure to the sitdowners' problems was work.

Brodie took time out to address a revival meeting, pleading the men's case from the pulpit and bringing tears to the congregation's eyes with his references to "that other Transient."

The Vancouver Sun complimented the protesters' "amazing restraint" and, after more than three weeks, Brodie's peaceful sitdown was beginning to attain its goal of shaming government into recognizing the men's demands for work and wages. However, it was naive in the extreme to expect that the authorities would ultimately respond with anything but disdain.

The buck was being furiously passed. From his cottage on Bowen Island, Vancouver Mayor George Miller disavowed responsibility for the demonstrators. From Victoria, the Premier of the province, Duff Pattullo, said the sit-in was the concern of the Prime Minister, William Lyon Mackenzie King. King said the federal government was going to stick to its policy — and do nothing. But that was only a pose. Following orders that undoubtedly originated in Ottawa, RCMP Sergeant Bob Wilson lobbed the first Lake Erie Jumper — the popular moniker for tear gas — across the marble floor of the Post Office lobby. Hundreds of men, temporarily blinded by the gas, stunned by fear, leaped through the windows into the street where the Mounties and the city police began wailing on them mercilessly.

Brodie was the last man out. He wasn't difficult to identify in his trademark orange sweater. Sergeant Wilson and a group of Mounties began beating the defenceless Brodie in shifts. Finally, an RCMP constable stopped it. Brodie was staggering to his feet when a plainclothes detective with a rubber hose battered him back into the gutter.

Nearby, a photographer recorded the event. The brutality finally ended when the detective became self-conscious. Motionless, Brodie lay in the street, his orange sweater streaked with blood. Firefighters, who had been ordered to the site with their wagons, cursed the police for refusing to call an ambulance for the injured protestor. At great personal risk, a passing motorist picked Brodie up and delivered him to a hospital.

The beatings cost Brodie an eye, but otherwise he recovered. The single, transient unemployed men were given what they had been asking for all along — emergency relief, and jobs — five thousand of them, miraculously created by the provincial government in the name of public works. Briefly, Brodie became as heroic a figure as his bridge-jumping namesake.

The RCMP and the city police — under savage criticism — quarrelled volubly over whose brutality had turned a peaceful demonstration into an ugly riot. Daily newspapers placed the blame "squarely on the institution of the government in Canada." Much later, there were some questions in the House of Commons.

During the Second World War, Sergeant Bob Wilson found work infiltrating various ethnic groups in British Columbia and then ratting them out to an increasingly paranoid government. Brodie served in the merchant marine. In peacetime, he worked on federal weather ships. Still later, he found gainful employment at the Victoria shipyards.

One day, Brodie raised a fuss in a government office over some injustice and found himself, twenty-nine years after his fifteen minutes of fame, unknown, unsung and unemployed — again.

EKOKTOEGEE

Yellowknife, Northwest Territories, 1955 — When the police arrived, they found a gun within arm's reach of the lifeless body of Allan Kaotak's father. Closer examination revealed a piece of twine tied to the trigger.

Allan Kaotak, an Inuit from Cambridge Bay on Victoria Island, explained the string. He said he had done what any dutiful, loving son would do. He had rigged the gun to help his ailing, aged father commit suicide.

The Royal Canadian Mounted Police charged Kaotak with murder. His Yellowknife trial took place half a territory away from Cambridge Bay.

The Crown argued that Kaotak had murdered his father after a dispute over an arranged marriage. The defence said it was assisted suicide and assisted suicide was *de rigueur* in Inuit culture.

This dramatic conflict of culture, custom and law was the first case presented to John Howard (Jack) Sissons, the first judge of the Territorial Court of the Northwest Territories.

Sissons was born in Orillia, Ontario, in 1892. A survivor of childhood polio, he walked with a limp for the rest of his life. He grew up living on the grounds of the local mental asylum where his father was chief superintendent. On his mother's side, Sissons was related to the Scottish explorer David Livingstone. Stories about Livingstone's adventures in Africa shaped Jack's youth.

In his memoirs, *Judge of the Far North*, Sissons wrote that it was Livingstone's "hatred of injustice, his anger at the abuse of colonial power . . . his understanding and affection for the native African and his respect for their natural human rights" that held sway over him. This sway led to landmark decisions in the North.

Sissons graduated from Queen's University in 1917 and moved to Alberta where he studied law. In 1921, he opened a practice in Grande Prairie. In 1929 he married an Irish visitor, Frances Johnson. They had two children, a son Neil and a daughter Frances.

With the help of a Métis campaign manager, the staunchly Liberal Sissons won the Peace River seat in 1940. As a Member of Parliament, Sissons sought and won inclusion for the seven hundred Métis of the Lesser Slave Lake area in treaty arbitration. Because they were considered half-breeds by blood Indians and ignored by Ottawa, this was quite a victory. Defeated in 1945, the following year Sissons was named to the district court in southern Alberta by Prime Minister Mackenzie King.

During his years as a judge in Alberta, Sissons earned a reputation that often placed him at odds with bureaucracy. Critics called him unorthodox, cantankerous and "a stubborn old coot." Sissons was sixty-three and had never been north of the sixtieth parallel when he accepted the appointment to the Territorial bench.

Uncharacteristically for appointed officials of the day, Sissons decided to research the culture of the people he would judge. In the case of Allan Kaotak, he discovered that suicide was an accepted Inuit solution for old age, infirmity and chronic illness. It was also considered a relative's duty to assist the afflicted.

Out of the gate, Sissons arranged that six non-native jurors were replaced by Inuit from Cambridge Bay. The jury took only twenty minutes to find Kaotak not guilty.

"Justice to every man's door" became Sissons's credo. "The flying judge" took his court on the road over a land mass that stretched from the Yukon to the eastern bluffs of Baffin Island. For eleven years, travelling by single-engine Otter aircraft and dogsled, he meted out justice in the landscape of the accused. Understanding that justice had to be seen to be done, the media-savvy judge often invited reporters to accompany him on his circuit. Cases were tried in kitchens, cockpits and igloos, with Sissons in full robes and the dignity of justice maintained.

In 1958, Sissons presided over a trial involving murder, child abandonment and negligent death. *Regina vs. Kikkik* was a tabloid journalist's dream and received a great deal of coverage in the United States, as well as Canada.

Kikkik, an Inuit woman, was accused of murder and abandoning her children, causing one of them to die unnecessarily. In the Chief Justice's opinion, the "bright boys in Ottawa" — a Sissonsism for the mandarins in the nation's capital — were the ones who were most responsible.

Amid questionable reports that the caribou herds were dwindling in the interior barren lands, the Department of Indian and Northern Affairs decided to move the Ihalmiut Inuit from the interior to the coast of Hudson Bay.

On their way to Eskimo Point on Hudson Bay, Kikkik, her husband Hallow, her five children and her half-brother Ootuk, became stranded in a blizzard several days' travel from an outpost at Padley. Hallow left the igloo to ice-fish but was shot and killed on the ice by Ootuk, who wrongly believed that his travelling companions were withholding food.

When Ootuk returned, Kikkik sensed something was wrong because he refused to surrender the gun that had been loaned to him. A struggle ensued and shots were fired. Unaware that Hallow was dead, Kikkik restrained Ootuk and sent her daughter Ailoyoak to get Hallow. When the daughter returned with news of Hallow's murder, Kikkik tried to stab Ootuk but her knife was too dull. She got another knife from her daughter and fatally stabbed Ootuk in the heart.

In the following days, Kikkik set out with her children to try to reach Padley despite desperately cold temperatures. They met some relatives who were also starving, but after a few days of travel Kikkik and her children were unable to keep up. One night she and her children remained behind, sleeping in the open. When they finally caught up with the relatives, Kikkik was told to stay in the igloo they had built and wait for help. After five days without food, Kikkik and her family once again set out for the outpost at Padley.

Realizing that she was not strong enough to manage all five children, Kikkik left her two youngest behind, wrapped in caribou hide in a snow house she built using a frying pan as a tool. Later that day, a search plane found Kikkik and her three remaining children. Kikkik was afraid and she told the authorities she thought the two children she had left behind were dead. The following day the RCMP found the infants — only one of them had survived.

At the beginning of the trial, Sissons explained to the jury that Kikkik was "a woman of a Stone Age society," and that if justice was to be served, everyone had to try and understand her behaviour in that context. A jury of four whites and two Inuit acquitted Kikkik on all charges.

Judge Sissons presided over many precedent-setting cases which dramatically put Inuit culture at odds with the white man's mores and law. He recognized the legitimacy of Inuit marriages, which the Department of Indian and Northern Affairs characterized as unlawful due to lack of formal registration. "White Christendom does not have a monopoly on virtue," he said. In accordance with native treaties, he defended aboriginal hunting rights. Sissons asserted the validity of Inuit customs, decrying Ottawa's "colonial bureaucracy," which he once described as "seeking to control everything but the Northern Lights."

To the Inuit, Chief Justice Sissons was known as *Ekoktoegee* — "He Who Listens." To Sissons, the Inuit were "the people par excellence." He died in 1969, two years after the Northwest Territories became self-governing.

HERSTORY

NO PRISON IN THE WOODS

NO SEX PLEASE, WE'RE DOCTORS

A SPY FOR THE YANKEES

"DESIST OR I WILL TELL YOUR WIFE"

THE RIGHT TO BE BEAUTIFUL

FOR HOME AND COUNTRY

WOMAN OF WHEAT

OUR LADY OF THE SOURDOUGH

"FOR THERE SHALL BE A PERFORMANCE"

CANADA'S HYENA IN PETTICOATS

WOMAN OF THE HOUSE

SHE WENT WHERE SHE WANTED TO GO,
DID WHAT SHE WANTED TO DO...

"YOU'RE NOT EVEN A PERSON"

LADYLIKE AND LETHAL

LILY OF THE MOHAWKS,
GENEVIÈVE OF NEW FRANCE

NO PRISON IN THE WOODS

Windsor, Canada West, 1852 — The perception of the life that settlers could expect in Canada was often dramatically different. When English "gentlewoman" Susanna Moodie's book *Roughing It in the Bush* was published in 1852, the author noted that her "melancholy narrative" was written "in the hope of deterring well-educated people" from settling "in the Backwoods." In contrast, that same year another woman — a Quaker-educated teacher — published a twelve-page pamphlet recommending emigration.

"No settled country in America offers stronger inducements to coloured people," said the pamphlet. "The general tone of society is healthy, and there is increasing anti-slavery sentiment."

What Susanna Moodie described bleakly as "the green prison of the woods," represented freedom and hope to Mary Ann Shadd, author of "Notes of Canada West."

A freeborn black American, Shadd was twenty-eight when she came to Windsor, Canada West in 1851. The eldest child of a prominent black abolitionist, Abraham Doras Shadd, Mary Ann grew up in Wilmington, Delaware. After attending a Pennsylvania boarding school, she organized her first school for black children when she was sixteen.

Constantly involved in many anti-slavery initiatives, she viewed education as a tool for black independence and self-respect.

President Millard Fillmore signed the Fugitive Slave Act in 1850. It allowed slave owners the right to reclaim their runaway "property" and subjected abolitionist workers in the "Underground railroad" to fines or imprisonment. Thousands of blacks crossed into Canada, landing everywhere from Saltspring Island on the West Coast to the heartland of southern Ontario in Raleigh Township where a former Louisiana landowner, Reverend William King, established a colony for refugees.

Mary Ann Shadd wanted to help black emigrants adapt to this new environment. Although slavery had been officially abolished in British Empire colonies in 1834, Shadd also felt her mission was "to inculcate a healthy anti-slavery sentiment in a country which, though under British rule, is particularly exposed, by intercommunication, to pro-slavery, religious and secular influence."

Provincial legislation passed in Canada West in 1850 laid the groundwork for segregated schools. Blacks began establishing their own private school, while continuing to protest the poor quality of education their children could obtain in common schools. One Hamilton-area protester suggested that children left such schools "knowing but a little more about the grammar of their language, than a horse does about handling a musket."

In the autumn of 1851, Mary Ann Shadd was hired by the black community to conduct a school in a ramshackle building that had once been a Windsor barracks. Attendance was lower than expected and some students could not afford even the most modest fee which was to be paid toward their teacher's salary.

The American Missionary Association stepped in to guarantee Shadd an annual salary of $125. After a shaky start, which was aggravated by a cholera epidemic, approximately two dozen pupils were enrolled. Shadd taught all ten classes, covering everything from botany to mathematics. Her pupils ranged in age from four to forty-five.

During the same period, Shadd became embroiled in a controversy with another black abolitionist and his wife.

Henry Bibb was the son of a white father and a slave mother. Born in Kentucky, he has been described as a "discontented slave" and was reportedly sold for figures ranging from $350 to $1,200 before escaping and fleeing to the North. Bibb and his second wife, Mary, settled in Sandwich (near Windsor).

In January, 1851, Henry began *The Voice of the Fugitive*, the first black newspaper published in Upper Canada. At the same time, Mary opened a school. To all intents, the Bibbs' goals and Shadd's seemed to be syncopated.

However, along with newspaper and his work in the Canadian Anti-Slavery Society, Henry Bibb also founded the Refugee Home Society. The RHS collected donations to purchase land for refugees. Shadd denounced this as "begging," and ultimately accused Bibb of fraud. It seems that some of the land acquired never found its way to fugitive ownership and "agents" who collected the funds kept as much as 63 percent for themselves.

Although she described it as a painful duty, Shadd denounced Bibb to the American Missionary Association. "It is no slander to say that Henry Bibb has hundreds of dollars belonging to fugitives, probably thousands would be nearer the truth," she wrote. "Henry Bibb is a dishonest man, and as such must be known to the world." She expressed disappointment at the situation "involving as it does loss of confidence, in coloured men, who assume to be leaders of their people."

Bibb struck back at Shadd in the pages of *The Voice of the Fugitive*, accusing her of concealing funds she was receiving from the American Missionary Association. Shadd was also falsely accused of refusing to accept white children at her school, even though her views on integration as a means of ensuring that blacks were not ghettoized were well known. Ultimately, the AMA withdrew Shadd's funding. In a letter to the association Shadd said: "This whole business is really sickening to me."

On March 24, 1853, the first issue of the *Provincial Freeman* was published. Well-known American abolitionist Samuel Ringold Ward was listed as the editor of the weekly newspaper "Devoted to Anti-Slavery, Temperance and General Literature," but that was simply a ruse to boost circulation. Mary Shadd was the functioning editor, and as such became the first black woman on the continent to found and edit a newspaper. After one issue, publication was suspended while Shadd spent a year raising money through a lecture tour.

The *Provincial Freeman* resumed publication in Toronto in 1854. The paper's motto was "Self-Reliance is the True Road to Independence." In the *Freeman*, Shadd discussed all aspects of the black experience in Canada, exposing bigotry and decrying compromises on slavery. She opposed any notion of second-class status urging blacks to assimilate and not isolate themselves in self-segregated communities.

Publication was somewhat sporadic and in 1855 the paper moved to Chatham, Ontario, under a new editor. That year, Shadd became the first woman to speak at the National Negro Convention, where she earned the admiration of activist Frederick Douglass.

In 1856, Mary married a black businessman, Thomas Fauntleroy Cary. They had a son in 1858, but Cary died before the birth of their daughter in 1861. The *Freeman* continued publishing until 1859, with Mary serving as one of three editors and her sister, Amelia, and brother, Isaac, assisting. Their father, Abraham, became the first black man to hold public office when he was elected to the town council of Raleigh Township.

Whether she was meeting with John Brown while he plotted his rebellion in Chatham or wrenching a child away from slave-hunters, Shadd remained at the centre of black politics and social assimilation.

When the Civil War broke out, she returned to the United States to serve as an enlistment recruitment officer. After the war, she resumed her teaching career in Washington, D.C., returning to Canada briefly to organize a suffragist rally.

At forty-six, she became the first woman law student at John Howard University, but she was not granted her degree until 1883 due to sexual discrimination. In America she crusaded for women's rights to vote alongside Susan B. Anthony and Elizabeth Cady Stanton, and testified before the Judiciary Committee of the House of Representatives. She holds the distinction of being the first black woman to vote in a national election.

The citation inducting Mary Ann Shadd Cary into the National Women's Hall of Fame at Seneca Falls, New York, in 1998 concludes: "As an educator, an abolitionist, an editor, an attorney and a feminist, she dedicated her life to improving the quality of life for everyone — black and white, male and female."

They might have added "American and Canadian."

NO SEX PLEASE,
WE'RE DOCTORS

Montreal, 1857 — The first woman to work as a doctor in Canada caused a sensation when she drove through the streets of Montreal in 1857 with her black manservant and small white dog in a red sleigh complete with uniformed footman and coachman. She wore a musk ox fur coat and favoured hats with plumes. Her skin was smooth and red hair framed a tiny face, dominated by large expressive eyes and a proboscis of considerable dimension. Petite and trim, she tended to strut — even into her sixties — although sometimes her movements seemed awkward since her sword clanked perilously close to the ground. She was the chief military doctor for all of Upper and Lower Canada in an era that did not permit the nation's women to study medicine, but her real name remains a mystery — to the men who served under her she was known as Dr. James Barry.

The "great revelation" of Dr. Barry's sexuality was made known only after a staff surgeon had recorded her as a male on her death certificate in 1865. A char woman who was preparing the body for burial determined the truth. She began spreading gossip about Dr. Barry's bosom and abdominal stretch marks, which suggested that "he" had once given birth.

To explain the oversight, the doctor in charge began insisting that Barry was a hermaphrodite, but no autopsy was ever performed to support this conjecture. As medical biographer Carlotta Hacker points out in her book *The Indomitable Lady Doctors*, the only reasonable explanation for Dr. Barry's masquerade is that being a male was the only way any woman of the period could practise medicine.

James Miranda Stuart Barry's parentage is also a mystery. She is believed to have been the niece of artist James Barry, a freewheeling intellect who taught at London's Royal Academy and followed the vision of English feminist Mary Wollstonecraft, author of *A Vindication of the Rights of Women*. The incorporation of the feminine appellation "Miranda" related to a family friend, General de Francisco de Miranda.

When Barry entered Edinburgh University in 1809, her masculine identity was firmly established since the university would not have considered accepting a female student in any area of study, let alone medicine. Her chaperone for that first year in Scotland was a Mrs. Bulkeley and Bulkeley is believed to have been Dr. Barry's true surname. Speculation aside, the cross-gendered doctor's origins may never be known since she was as secretive about her past as she was her undergarments.

Certainly, Dr. Barry's sexuality had nothing to do with her medical abilities. After graduation from Edinburgh University, she rose quickly through British army medical ranks and served as Assistant Surgeon to the Colonial Inspector and Physician to the Governor's Household during her first overseas posting in Cape Town, South Africa. While there she performed one of the first Caesarean operations in which both mother and child survived. She is also said to have saved the life of the typhus-stricken Governor, which led them to become close friends. In fact, the friendship between the two men caused gossip. When George Thomas Keppel, then Lord Abelmarle, first met the Governor's medical advisor he wrote, "There was a certain effeminacy in his manner, which he seemed to be always striving to overcome." Some comments were a bit too much for Dr. Barry to stand for and demanded "his" participation in at least one duel.

As much as Barry succeeded in the art of disguise, she failed in the dance of politics, outraging the army hierarchy with her outspoken letters and demands. Barry's goals, however, were irrefutably in support of better treatment for the everyday soldier, and she was acknowledged as an excellent surgeon. She received consistent promotions, serving in the West Indies, Corfu and Crimea, before embarking on her reform of Canadian barracks and dietary conditions. Among other things, she insisted that feathers replace the straw in pillows. Although she maintained a vegetarian regime, she commanded that the soldiers' diet be varied and include "a cheering change of a roast instead of eternal boiled beef and soup." She also insisted on private rooms for conjugal visits, a notion that apparently had eluded generations of army doctors before her.

Following the revelation of her sex, numerous attempts were made to discredit Dr. Barry's achievements. The scandal was shocking enough, but the notion that a woman had functioned admirably and professionally in the male sanctum of medicine was intolerable to Victorian sensibilities. Still, the troops Dr. Barry tended in Canada must have appreciated her contribution to a soldier's well-being.

Eighteen years after Dr. Barry's posthumous unmasking, Dr. Augusta Stowe became the first woman to graduate from a Canadian medical school. Other Canadian women, including Augusta's mother, Emily, had already paved the way for the acceptance of women doctors by taking their degrees in the United States where universities were more liberal in attitude. Dr. Stowe was under no pressure to keep her sex a secret. She married classmate John Benjamin Gullen while the ink on her diploma was still fresh.

A SPY FOR THE YANKEES

Moncton, New Brunswick, 1858 — Sarah Emma Edmonds was more than likely not the sort of young woman to wear fancy hats. At the age of seventeen, however, she and a friend established a ladies' hat shop in Moncton. Known as "Emma," Edmonds was raised on a farm in the bush near Magundy. She was always a bit of a tomboy, able to out-ride and out-shoot her peers and her siblings. It was a hard-working lifestyle, and Edmonds's father was known to be something of a vengeful tyrant. When she was barely a teenager, he tried to force her into marrying an elderly farmer. With the help of her mother she ran away, finding anonymity in Moncton as a milliner's apprentice.

By 1858, she was managing her own business, but she was constantly worried that her father would find her. He did. Before he could take her back to the bush, she moved to Saint John. There she took on the first of many disguises, cutting her hair, changing her wardrobe and adopting the persona of a young man, Franklin Thompson. From that time forward, Edmonds became a skilled practioner of gender deception.

A New Brunswick newspaper carried an advertisment from an American publisher who was looking for an agent to travel the countryside selling Bibles and other religious books. It was a job that apparently suited "Franklin" quite well. "Mr. Thompson" ended up working at the head office in Hartford, Connecticut, before moving to Flint, Michigan.

When the American Civil War broke out in 1861, twenty-year-old Edmonds was one of thousands of Canadians from coast to coast who enlisted. Canadian sentiment ran so high that some Canadians, such as the all-black Victoria Pioneer Rifle Company of Victoria on Vancouver Island, formed their own units. All Edmonds had to do was convince the medical examiner at Company F of the Second Michigan Regiment that she was a male, something she had years of practice in doing.

"Private Thompson" volunteered to work at the regimental hospital, an unpopular assignment since it meant exposure to epidemics of measles, mumps and chicken pox, which killed many Union soldiers before they even saw battle. Later she joined in combat herself, fighting at the battle of Bull Run and other major engagements.

She then joined the secret service, a move her memoirs suggest was simply to "serve her adopted country." To avoid suspicion in the ranks, she was appointed as the regimental mail carrier. This ruse explained her absence from the regiment and allowed her to courier messages to the high-ranking officers who had selected her because she was such a capable young "man." Her first mission as a spy was in 1863. Using what she described as "chemicals," she darkened her face and other visible extremities. Wearing a black wig and the clothing of a male slave, she infiltrated a Confederate fort at Yorktown, Virginia, and collected information about troop strength and artillery stocks. This disguise was used with success on several other such missions. Alternatively, she would pose as an escaped female slave, and even as an Irish peddler woman, complete with an accent she recalled from her childhood in New Brunswick.

A chance encounter with a Confederate officer, who thought he recognized her as Franklin Thompson, led Edmonds to an even more dangerous assignment in counterespionage. Posing as a young boy, she got a job with a Louisville, Kentucky, merchant who hated all things "Yankee." While in his employ, she identified three Rebel spies, two of whom were eventually captured.

Malaria ended her military career. Knowing that she could not seek treatment at an army hospital without having her true sex disclosed, she entered a civilian hospital in Cairo, Illinois, as a woman. Shortly afterward, much to her regret, Emma learned that Franklin Thompson had been officially declared a deserter, an offence punishable by death.

She wrote a book about her experiences called *Unsexed: or the Female Soldier*, which was published by the Bible-sales company she had worked for. In later editions, to suit the temper of Victorian times, the title was changed to *Nurse and Spy*. The book became a bestseller, and she donated all of her royalties to the Sanitary and Christian Commissions, an organization that preceded the Red Cross in caring for wounded veterans.

She married a New Brunswick carpenter, Linus Seelye, in 1867. They settled in the American midwest, where the newly incarnated "Sarah Seelye" gave birth to three children, all of whom died in infancy. Later the couple adopted two sons.

In the 1880s, she determined that she would have to come clean about her status with the Army in order to receive the pension that was her due. Her old comrades in the Second Michigan Regiment helped to have an Act of

Congress passed granting her an honourable discharge and the rights that went with it. In 1889, Sarah Emma Edmonds Seelye became the first — and only — woman to be granted membership in the Civil War Veterans' Association.

Representatives of the Grand Army of the Republic conducted her funeral in 1898 and she was buried in the veterans' section of a cemetery in Houston, Texas. Even in death, she adopted a disguise. At her request, her headstone was inscribed simply, "Emma E. Seelye, Army Nurse."

"DESIST OR I WILL TELL YOUR WIFE"

Toronto, 1871 — When Jennie Trout and Emily Stowe managed to obtain restricted permission to attend a session of lectures at the Toronto School of Medicine, Canadian universities would not allow women to study medicine. In fact, the two women were only allowed to attend on the absolute condition that they agreed "not to make a fuss."

However, the "restricted" sessions were virtually designed to incite a "fuss." With the professors' collusion, their fellow male students jeered the women and took to placing dissected body parts on their chairs. From a hole in the wall between the lecture hall and an anteroom, the aspiring female doctors would check their seats before entering to determine what tricks their classmates had been up to. Obnoxious sketches were drawn on the walls of the lecture room with such frequency that the classroom had to be whitewashed four times during that first semester.

Trout and Stowe endured all this and more. Both were ultimately instrumental in establishing medical colleges for women. The only evidence approaching a "fuss" occurred when one lecturer who persisted in telling sickening and smutty stories, inspired Trout to admonish him to desist or she would advise his wife of exactly what he had said. Apparently, this tactic was effective.

Jennie Trout and Emily Stowe both grew up on Ontario farms. Both excelled in school and went on to become school teachers. At one point, they lived on the same Toronto street. They became friends and shared in discussions of women's rights.

Stowe was a more aggressive personality. In addition to becoming the first Canadian woman to graduate from a medical school, she also founded Canada's first suffrage group, which operated under the title of the Toronto Women's Literary Club for many years.

Trout was ten years younger, and preferred to avoid publicity. Like Stowe, she completed her medical studies in the United States, where medical colleges for women were first established in 1850.

Stowe graduated as a doctor in 1867, and Trout followed eight years later. However, according to an 1869 Act of Parliament, graduates of American colleges could only be licensed to practise in Ontario if they attended a session of Canadian lectures and a matriculation exam.

Emily Stowe chose to ignore the licensing requirements. She practised openly and illegally for thirteen years and most likely paid the $100 penalty that was levelled for such violation more than once. Although she had qualified in her sessional studies, the feisty Stowe may well have felt that she could not tolerate the second indignity of taking the oral section of the exam before yet another group of hostile men. She was forty-nine when her licence was finally granted in 1880.

Trout, on the other hand, took the exam immediately following her graduation in 1875. As a sign of the times, when her husband picked her up following the oral exam, *he* was complimented on having such a talented and creditably intelligent wife. She became the first Canadian woman to be licensed to practise medicine. However, when she died in 1921 the *Canadian Medical Journal* did not even record the fact.

Emily Stowe and Jennie Trout confronted a system that was designed to thwart their desires to serve the physical needs of all humanity and, using different tactics, they both won.

THE RIGHT
TO BE BEAUTIFUL

Township of Vaughan, Ontario, 1882 — As a child growing up on the outskirts of Woodbridge, Ontario, Florence Nightingale Graham set a challenging career goal. "I want to be the richest woman in the world," she told anyone who would listen. Although others may have surpassed her wealth through inheritance or royal status, when she died she left an estate worth tens of millions and an imprint on the face of women. Little Flo grew up to be Elizabeth Arden, the queen of a cosmetics empire and one of the most astute retailing entrepreneurs of the twentieth century.

She was one of five children born to Susan and William Graham. In England, her Scottish father made his living racing horses, an enterprise that was frowned upon by his future wife's upper-class family. The pair eloped and came to Canada, where their first child was born in 1871. William became a vegetable peddler, although he still dabbled in horses. Florence, his second youngest daughter, was his best stable helpmate.

It was through her ability at nursing sick horses that Florence determined to follow the path of her famous English nurse namesake. But the rigours of the profession were not for her. "I found I didn't really like looking at sick people. I want to keep people well, and young and beautiful," she explained when she dropped out of school.

According to a biography by Alfred A. Lewis and Constance Woodworth, *Miss Elizabeth Arden: An Unretouched Life*, a chance encounter with a hospital biochemist who was working on a skin cream remedy for acne led her to begin experimenting with beautifying potions of her own in the Graham family kitchen. Strange odours were soon emanating from the wood stove and into the community, causing a local clergyman to fear that the poor family was reduced to cooking rotten eggs. After a hamper of fresh eggs and provisions was dropped at the doorstep, father Graham advised his daughter to get a real job.

Approaching thirty and bored with office work, Graham decided to follow in her brother's footsteps and move to New York City. She started out as a bookkeeper for the Squibb Pharmaceutical Company, but the research laboratories held more fascination for her than numbers. Then, as a beauty parlour trainee, she learned a trendy therapy called "facials," which involved strapping the customer's multiple chins tightly and massaging the skin with glycerin water. She knew there had to be something better.

In 1910, Graham found a kindred spirit in Elizabeth Hubbard, who had developed skin creams, tonics and oil that had marketing potential. Together, they planned to open an upscale "salon" on Fifth Avenue where fashionable women would be pampered and artfully packaged beauty products would be for sale. The partnership fell apart while the gold lettering on Elizabeth Hubbard's name was still drying over the salon's door, but Graham determined to continue alone. Instead of removing the sign she decided to work with it. "Elizabeth" pleased her, but she felt her own last name was too drab for the world of beauty. Reflecting on her favourite poem, Alfred Lord Tennyson's *Enoch Arden*, she settled on "Elizabeth Arden," adding "Mrs." for respectability.

As Elizabeth Arden she prospered. Wealthy socialite clients dubbed her the "little Canadian woman with the magic hands." Through skillful marketing of skin cream products and absolute control of her business, she soon became what she beheld — a wealthy woman who could hold her own in society.

In 1915, she married Thomas Jenkins Lewis, who shared her flair for advertising and marketing. When the marriage ended nineteen years later, Lewis betrayed her trust by promoting the products of archrival Helena Rubenstein. "There is only one Mademoiselle in that world, and that is I," legendary fashion designer Coco Chanel once said. "One Madame, and that is Rubenstein, and one Miss, and that is Arden."

Another marriage, to Russian-born Prince Michael Evlanoff, also ended in divorce in 1942. But whether she was the consort of pseudo-royalty, or married to a pitch man, a Miss or a Mrs., Arden or Graham, the business continued to flourish. By 1944, the U.S. Federal Trade Commission reported that Arden was marketing approximately one thousand different products, and salons featuring her famous red doors were strategically located all over America and in Europe.

The love of horses that her father had fostered also endured. In the early 1930s, Arden-Graham bought a farm in Maine and began raising thoroughbreds. Racing her horses under the name Mrs. Elizabeth Graham, she had an impressive record, which culminated in the 1947 Kentucky Derby win of her stallion, Jet Pilot. Even in her stables she maintained complete autonomy, although her stablehands jokingly called her "Mrs. Mud Pack." Jockeys were instructed to spare the whip on her "darlings."

Wealth allowed her to move in international circles. She had homes all over the world including a castle in Ireland and a ten-room apartment in New York entirely decorated in pink. At five-foot-two, perennially fit, impeccably coiffed and attired, Arden-Graham never looked her age. For many years the slogan of her company was, "Every woman has the right to be beautiful," and Arden did everything she could to claim that right. She is alleged to have gone as far as having her passport photograph retouched.

Fortune magazine once suggested that Arden-Graham "earned more money than any other businesswoman in the history of the United States." She also donated a considerable amount to charity. In 1954, she was honoured by the Canadian Women's Press Club of Toronto. That year, the *Woodbridge News* noted that "Miss Elizabeth Arden" (who was also referred to as "Mrs. Elizabeth Nightingale Graham") attended the opening ceremonies of Dalziel Pioneer Park in Ontario's Humber Valley and planted a tree in the land that had once been her playground.

When she died of a heart attack in 1965, Arden-Graham's age was a mystery. A corporate spokesperson suggested she was eighty-one, born December 31, 1884. However, early Canada Census records indicate that she was probably born in 1882.

Her fortune was estimated at between $30 million and $40 million. Disposing of the business empire proved a complex affair, but Arden-Graham had ensured that her family and faithful employees received substantial bequests. Likewise, her darlings were not forgotten. She insisted that the race horses in training be sold first and that "mares should be sold last, and those with foals should be sold together with their foals." It was hardly a businesslike gesture, but quite beautiful, indeed.

FOR HOME AND COUNTRY

———◆———

Stoney Creek, Ontario, 1897 — The turn of the century was a time for maxims, and one that became known throughout the nation was, "You purify society when you purify the home." The maxim-user was a woman with a broad brow, a lush wave of curls and a mission.

Adelaide Hunter was the youngest of twelve children who were raised near Brantford, Ontario, in a clapboard house called "The Willows." Her father, a refugee of the Irish potato famine, died when she was an infant, leaving her mother to struggle to maintain the family farm while instilling in her children a sense of well-being and self-reliance.

Adelaide was twenty-four when she married Hamilton furniture maker John Hoodless and settled into a comfortable middle-class life, which eventually included four children. All may have seemed right with the world to the handsome and poised young mother before tragedy struck in 1889. Her youngest child, John Harold, died of the mysterious ailment known as "summer complaint." In those days, graveyards were filled with tiny headstones. Statistically, one out of every five Canadian children died, and Adelaide set out to discover the root cause of such heavy casualties.

When she learned that her child's death may have been caused by something as innocuous as milk, she began a crusade that would last her lifetime. Without benefit of refrigeration, farmers delivered their milk in open cans to populated areas. Flies that swarmed in summer streets found their way into kitchens where ice boxes were inefficient and rare. Hoodless was convinced that the high infant mortality rate had more to do with ignorance of good nutrition and sanitation than it did with "God's will."

Within months, the grieving mother appeared before the fledgling Young Women's Christian Association in Hamilton with a proposal to include cooking and domestic science in their courses. Soon the local school board was sending pupils to the YWCA and teachers were being provided with instruction.

In 1893, YWCA delegate Hoodless attended the Columbian Exposition in Chicago where issues such as suffrage and women's working conditions were hot topics. She met a kindred spirit in Lady Aberdeen, the wife of Canada's new Governor General, and a tireless organizer of causes relating to women. Consequently, Hoodless set wheels into motion that helped create the YWCA as a national organization. Lady Aberdeen called on her in Hamilton after the Chicago experience and the result was the formation of the National Council of Women, which held its first annual meeting in April, 1894.

Over the following two years, Hoodless gave more than sixty speeches about the importance of domestic science. Through her platform she was able to encourage the development of courses in schools across the country. She wrote a guidebook on nutrition that became a nationwide fixture in the kitchen. It was apparent that her goals were far larger than any food fad, and she was able to enlist support and donations for the establishment of an Institute of House-hold Science at the Ontario College of Agriculture in Guelph.

In February 1897, 101 women and one man (farmer Erland Lee) attended a meeting at Stoney Creek, Ontario, where the formation of a sister organization to the national federated Farmers' Institute was discussed. Under Hood-less's guiding hand and with the banner slogan "for home and country," Women's Institutes soon formed all over the country. Members were committed to the notion that "a nation cannot rise above the level of its homes." The Institute became an international organization that expanded to include country women in more than one hundred nations.

Hoodless had a definite knack for getting things started. With Lady Aberdeen she helped form the Victorian Order of Nurses to provide care in frontier communities. She excelled at fund-raising and her poised presentations made her a popular speaker.

In the middle of a speech to a Toronto audience of the Federation of Women's Clubs in 1910, fifty-two-year-old Adelaide Hoodless, who had been bothered by a headache all day, smiled, took a sip of water and fell lifeless to the floor. At the time, she was just beginning to investigate the possibility of establishing technical and trade schools for young women, which explains why she is universally acknowledged as Canada's "Woman of Vision."

WOMAN OF WHEAT

Winnipeg, 1898 — When Aunt Alice announced she was "going west" her niece, E. Cora Hind, joined her in the spirit of adventure. Hind had grown up on farms in Flesherton and Orillia, Ontario. She was orphaned early in life and, at the age of twenty-one, she was ready to become a pioneer of sorts.

Hind longed to be a newspaper reporter. The day after her arrival in Winnipeg in 1882, she presented herself to the editor of the *Winnipeg Free Press.* He reportedly was "not interested in skirts" on his reporters, which only stiffened Hind's resolve to one day work for the newspaper.

Early on, Hind displayed a keen eye for trends. When she discovered that no one in Winnipeg knew how to use a typewriter, she promptly rented a machine and mastered the craft, becoming the first typist west of the Great Lakes. With this invaluable skill, she found employment in a law office, bringing her in contact with many land deals, as well as individual farmers. She made it her business to understand what she was typing and conversed knowledgeably with farm clients, who were impressed by the young woman's wide-ranging interest in agriculture.

In 1893 Hind set up her own stenography office. Farm organizations began asking her to report on their meetings and conventions. In those days, wheat prices fluctuated wildly according to the size and quality of the crops. Millers and financiers, along with farmers, were intensely anxious for information. Soon she was preparing reports about agricultural conditions and markets.

Finally, in 1898 she was given her first chance to report on the wheat crop by Colonel J.B. Maclean, founder of Maclean Publications in Toronto. She boarded a train west for Moose Jaw the very night she received his telegram requesting a survey of the fields. This was one of many trains Hind was to take over her long career.

In 1901, she was hired by the *Winnipeg Free Press.* Her knowledge of agriculture rapidly removed her from the "Women's Page," and she was made the paper's agriculture editor. Farmers and businessmen from across the West sent her crop condition reports, but Hind never strayed far from the source for her data. Riding the rails, she questioned everyone she met. Along the way she would stop off at stations, hire a horse and buggy, and journey along the endless prairie roads, climbing a fence now and then to poke the soil to judge its moisture and grab a head of wheat to thresh in her small hand.

Hind's ability to forecast the wheat crop grew to legendary proportions and her reports were telegraphed to markets all over the world. Bankers and grain companies took her estimates as gospel. Her accuracy effected the entire economy.

Her reports were never candy-coated. When she predicted a poor crop, she was nicknamed "Calamity Cora." Her estimate remained unchanged and the official tally showed Hind to be correct. "No one loves the West more than I do," she said, "but very early in my career, I learned that the West was big enough and strong enough to have the truth told about it on all occasions."

When the Canadian Wheat Board took over the task of marketing grain in 1933, it announced that Hind's total of twenty-nine estimates had reflected more accurate forecasting than any government or other official statements.

Hind's love of agriculture was not limited to wheat. She championed western beef and dairy cattle and served as a director of the Canadian Co-operative Wool Growers. As a livestock judge and as a speaker, she cut a dashing figure wearing her beaded buckskin jacket and odd assortment of hats.

Cora Hind received many honours throughout her career, including a Doctor of Laws degree from the University of Manitoba. She travelled the world, wrote two books about her adventures and spent forty-one years as a reporter.

In 1932, seventy-one-year-old Hind realized a lifelong dream when she accompanied the first cargo of Canadian wheat from Churchill, Manitoba, to Great Britain. As the *London Morning Post* reported: "A woman who can go around and look at wheat fields and then come home and estimate the Canadian wheat crop, forecasting it so accurately that bankers and grain companies take her estimate as gospel— such a woman is not met every day."

OUR LADY OF
THE SOURDOUGH

Dawson City, Yukon Territory, 1898 — When Chicago socialite Martha Louise Munger Purdy set out over the Chilkoot Pass in 1898 with thousands of other Klondike dreamers, she was looking for adventure and whatever came her way. In the thrall of gold fever, the refined thirty-two-year-old had arranged for her two sons to stay with her parents in Chicago. At the last minute, her wealthy businessman husband, William Purdy, decided to head for the Sandwich Islands instead. Their failing marriage ended when Martha boarded the steamer *Utopia* bound for Skagway. Martha Louise had embarked on a life-transforming journey far from the froth and frivolity of America's Gay Nineties that would eventually see her become the First Lady of the Yukon and the second woman to sit in the Canadian Parliament.

When her party cleared the North-West Mounted Police checkpoint at Lake Tagish, it was logged as the 14,405th to enter the rapids that led to wild and woolly Dawson City. Her money and her mettle had helped her to get that far, driven by a rumour of a million dollars in gold dust, a legacy she would share if she could find it and lay the claim.

When this failed to happen, however, Martha staked a few claims and settled into a log cabin across the Klondike River in a district known as "Lousetown," famous for its brothels. To complicate matters, she soon discovered that she was pregnant. Considering the scarcity of food and medical assistance, the odds were stacked against her survival, but on January 31, 1899, she gave birth to a healthy son named Lyman.

Neighbours rallied to supply food, fuel and bedding, and grit-eyed miners crowded the cabin to marvel at the simple beauty of a baby. "We became self-reliant," Martha noted years later. "We knew what it was to get along without the amenities of so-called civilized life."

The winter saw a typhoid epidemic and a fire all but consume Dawson City. By spring, those "cheechakoos" (tenderfoots) who had survived were elevated to the more respectful status of "sourdoughs," in honour of the yeast-less bread that was their dietary staple.

That summer Martha returned to her father's home after a landslide came within thirty metres of sweeping her cabin into the river. She found life in Chicago stifling. In 1901, with some profits from her claims and the support of her family, she returned to her "beloved Yukon" and started a sawmill business.

At thirty-eight, the now divorced mother of three married a Dawson lawyer who was seven years her junior. George Black had spent a couple of years mining before returning to his law practice and the pursuit of Conservative political ambitions. In 1912, he was appointed Commissioner of the Yukon and, for the next four years Martha Black served as chatelaine of Government House. At her first reception she served one thousand sandwiches and forty cakes, accompanied by massive quantities of salads and plenty of ice cream. Although her staff was astounded, the new First Lady understood the appetite of the hardy souls of the Yukon.

George Black resigned as Commissioner in 1916 and began recruiting the Yukon Infantry Company, in which he was a captain. Martha bucked bureaucracy to travel with the men when they left to serve in Europe during the First World War. While George and company fought in France, Martha crusaded for the Yukon in London, giving lectures and assisting volunteers. Her knowledge of Yukon flora earned her a fellowship in the Royal Geographical Society. Lyman, the son she bore in Dawson, was invested with the Military Cross by King George V.

When the war ended, George Black resumed his political career, representing his Yukon constituency from 1921 until 1935, when he was sidelined by illness. Friends pressured Martha to run in his place, and the seventy-year-old sourdough rose to the challenge, campaigning vigorously throughout the territory to win by 134 votes, although the majority of other Conservative candidates suffered a rousing defeat by William Lyon Mackenzie King's Liberals.

For the next five years, Martha Black and parliamentary pioneer Agnes Macphail were the only females in the House of Commons. When George regained his health, he also regained his seat, which Martha insisted she had merely been "keeping warm."

The transformation of the Chicago socialite was complete by 1949, when she received the Order of the British Empire for her contribution to Yukon life.

"FOR THERE SHALL BE A PERFORMANCE"

Mount Forest, Ontario, 1915 — When evangelist Jean Sharpe learned that Aimee Semple McPherson was coming to her Victory Mission in the rural, southwestern Ontario town of Mount Forest, she was inspired by the writings of the apostle Luke. "Blessed is she that believeth, for there shall be a performance of those things that were told her from the Lord." However, McPherson's first "performance" was somewhat of a disappointment, since it attracted a paltry audience of two men and a boy. Four sermons later, the attendance was no better and Sister Aimee was getting antsy.

"I surveyed the scene and sought to lay my plans for a siege of souls," McPherson wrote in her memoir, *This and That*. With that, the slender brunette hit upon an idea that was to prove her trademark for the next quarter-century — she pulled a stunt.

Garbed in white, McPherson hauled a chair to the middle of town. As the sun set, she stood on the chair with her eyes closed and her arms raised to the heavens. A crowd of curious onlookers gathered and when McPherson felt the time was ripe she jumped off the chair and shouted, "People follow me!" Then she ran down the street to the meeting hall, hustled her followers inside, locked the door and commenced preaching. The captive audience was soon captivated.

"If you are annoyed over attendance, why not try the chair-and-prayer method at some busy intersection? I can heartily recommend it and practically guarantee that it will work," McPherson later advised wannabe sermonizers. Her stunts, combined with her charisma, created an indomitable force in evangelism that would lead her to become the most famous and infamous preacher of the Roaring Twenties and the Dirty Thirties.

Sister Aimee grew up near Ingersoll, Ontario, the daughter of a Methodist father and a Salvation Army mother. At seventeen, she married Robert Semple, a Pentecostal preacher and blacksmith. In 1912, they travelled to China where Robert planned to become a missionary, but he died of malaria soon after their arrival, leaving his pregnant widow to fend for herself. Returning to the continent with her newborn daughter, Aimee married a grocery clerk, Harold McPherson. Following the birth of their son, Aimee began her itinerant preaching and Harold divorced her on the grounds of desertion.

There was no particular organization to accompany the professional preacher. Fire and brimstone gypsies travelled what became known as "the Sawdust Trail" after the ground cover that they spread over the dirt floors beneath their tents. With her mother, Minnie Kennedy, serving as her business manager, McPherson barnstormed across the continent, starting on the Atlantic coast and ending up in California in 1918.

From dingy halls, she soon graduated to huge auditoriums and tours that took her to Europe and Australia. By 1923, her coffers had swelled enough to allow the construction of a $1.25 million, 5,000-seat church in Los Angeles.

The Angelus Temple became the home of the Church of the Foursquare Gospel, complete with its own radio station and Bible school. "I don't like the tinkle of silver, but the rustle of paper," McPherson announced when the collection plates circulated.

Whether embroiled in lawsuits or organizing soup kitchens, Sister Aimee made the most of every publicity opportunity. Her most famous "stunt" occurred when she vanished from a California beach on May 26, 1926. Thousands showed up to comb the sand, along with boats and search planes. When she finally surfaced a month later in Mexico with a bizarre tale of kidnapping and torture, it raised more than eyebrows. A grand jury hearing convened to look into allegations that included perjury and conspiracy to perpetrate a hoax. Ultimately, no charges were laid, but the front page coverage — and the speculation that McPherson's disappearance was related to her involvement with the temple's married radio operator — filled her pews more than ever.

McPherson's personal life was as fraught with breakdowns as her public persona. A rift with her mother ended in a $100,000 settlement after Aimee reportedly broke Minnie's nose in a slugfest. In 1936, she accused her daughter and other church associates of conspiring to wrest control from her. McPherson lost the bitter court battle that ensued. Her third marriage was also doomed to failure. None of that stopped her from preaching and building more churches.

Sister Aimee was in Oakland, California, on September 26, 1944. She led a parade, preached to a packed house and planned to dedicate a church the following day. Her Sunday sermon, "Going My Way," had already been announced, but the next morning she was found dead in her hotel room at the age of fifty-three. Although initially reported as a heart attack, the cause of death was later revealed as the apparent consequence of an accidental over-dose of barbiturates.

Sister Aimee Semple McPherson's performance had ended.

CANADA'S HYENA
IN PETTICOATS

Winnipeg, Manitoba, 1916 — What event roused the Manitoba Legislative Assembly to celebrate by singing "For They Are Jolly Good Fellows"? The uncharacteristic outburst was prompted by the passing of a law that granted Manitoba women the right to vote. The political activist who spearheaded the suffrage campaign was Nellie Mooney McClung.

McClung was born in Chatsworth, Ontario, and spent most of her childhood in Manitoba where she became a teacher. "Women's roles" fascinated her at an early age, and McClung signed her first petition on behalf of women's suffrage in 1890 at the age of sixteen.

At twenty-three, she married pharmacist Wes McClung and they eventually raised a family of five. During this time, McClung was active in the Woman's Christian Temperance Union and she became a popular speaker. She also pursued a writing career, producing her first novel *Sowing Seeds for Danny* in 1908. It became a national best-seller.

After moving to Winnipeg in 1911, McClung became involved in the city's active and vocal women's rights and reform movement. She lobbied Conservative Premier Sir Rodmond Roblin for better working conditions for female factory workers. It was to be her first confrontation with Roblin, but not her last.

In 1914, McClung led a delegation of women to ask for the right to vote. "I don't want a hyena in petticoats talking politics to me. I want a nice gentle creature to bring me my slippers," advised Premier Roblin. The meeting ended as Roblin concluded: "Nice women don't want the vote."

McClung's response was to stage a mock Parliament in which the subject of the debate was whether or not men should have the vote. "Man is made for something higher and better than voting," declared McClung in an excruciatingly humorous and deadly accurate parody of the Premier. "Politics unsettles men, and unsettled men mean unsettled bills — broken furniture, broken vows — divorce."

The mock Parliament was a huge success. Although there was some public backlash to her rabble-rousing style, as well as vicious attacks by critics who accused her of neglecting her children, McClung maintained her posture through reasonable discussion and irrepressible wit and charm.

"Never retract, never explain, never apologize — get the thing done and let them howl," became McClung's motto. While her critics nicknamed her the "Holy Terror," her supporters and her family cheered her as "Our Nell."

On January 27, 1916, Manitoba's new Liberal government passed the Bill for the Enfranchisement of Women. What McClung had called "a bonny fight, a knockdown drag-out fight, uniting the women of Manitoba in a great cause," was resolved in a victory that paved the way for other provinces and the federal government to determine that women should be granted the vote.

McClung moved to Edmonton, where she continued the struggle for the right to vote in that province. She gained a seat in the Legislature in 1921 and lobbied for everything from free medical and dental treatment for school children to improved property rights for women. Defeat in 1926 did little to curtail her public activities. The following year she became one of the "famous five" who launched the "Persons Case."

"Women are going to form a chain, a greater sisterhood than the world has ever known," said McClung. As an author, lecturer and grandmother, she continued to advocate rights and reforms for women until her death in 1951.

WOMAN OF THE HOUSE

Ottawa, 1922 — Agnes Macphail, Canada's first female Member of Parliament, was chided by the press for failing to wear headgear in the House. In those days, hatlessness was next to political incorrectness. All of Macphail's nineteen years as an Honourable Member were characterized by such unfair derision.

Agnes Macphail was born in a log cabin in Proton Township in Grey County, Ontario, near the southern shores of Georgian Bay in 1890. She was always proud of her rural upbringing, and spent most of her life speaking on behalf of farmers.

After teaching school for several years, Macphail expanded on her rural interests as a member of United Farmers of Ontario. She defeated ten men to become the UFO candidate in the 1921 federal election. When losing nominees decided to stir up trouble by asking her to resign and call another convention "in which saner judgement would be possible," Macphail stood her ground. She was thirty-one when she won her first election.

Women had been allowed to vote in federal elections since 1918, but Macphail was the first to take a seat in the House of Commons. Her presence created quite a stir. While many members rose to greet her and welcome her formally in speeches of flowery praise, Macphail discovered that a welcoming bouquet of roses placed on her desk was actually the penance of a man who was paying off an election bet that she would fail.

Outside of the House she was subject to constant staring. The ordeal of eating in the parliamentary restaurant caused such strain that by her own admission she lost twelve pounds during the first session. Above all, her recollections of parliamentary initiation were of "a miserable time." In her own words: "Some members resented my intrusion, others jeered at me, while a very few were genuinely glad to see a woman in the House."

The press was of no help. Reporters decided that Macphail was stiff and severe. They preferred analyzing her blue serge suit to the policies she pursued on protective tariffs, her investigation of labour relations and her commitment to penal reform which led to the Archambault Commission.

So hurtful were the attacks that Macphail ensured that several love letters written to her be stored among her papers for eventual inclusion in the National Archives. She could not bear the thought of being remembered as the stern, frigid spinster the contemporary press made her out to be. In fact, according to Durham, Ontario, poet/author Wilma Coutts, who spent her childhood singing at parties in Macphail's riding: "Our Aggie could dance up a storm with the best of them."

She received several marriage proposals, but the institution did not seem to suit her. "One of the outstanding features of this age is the number of intelligent women who do not marry," she noted. "I have talked to hundreds of these fine, alert and very capable women in business, the professions, and the arts, and their reason was the same as mine: *the person* could not be subjected."

Macphail was a "feminist" for her time. She argued for equality and fulfillment for all, with the same vehemence that she argued in favour of world disarmament in a pro-military environment. "When I hear men talk about women being the angel of the home I always, mentally at least, shrug my shoulders in doubt," she told the House during a debate over the Divorce Bill. "I do not want to be the angel of any home; I want for myself what I want for other women, absolute equality. After that is secured then men and women can take turns at being angels."

Macphail remained in the House of Commons until her defeat in 1940. Undaunted, she entered provincial politics, where she sometimes won, and sometimes lost as a member of the Co-Operative Commonwealth Federation (C.C.F.). Politics was her life.

SHE WENT WHERE SHE WANTED TO GO, DID WHAT SHE WANTED TO DO...

Daniel's Harbour, Newfoundland, 1926 — For more than fifty years, Newfoundland nurse Myra Bennett was the only medical aid along almost 400 kilometres of rugged coastline on the northern peninsula. She set broken limbs, performed kitchen table operations by lamplight and sutured and dressed wounds of every description. Throughout the province she was known as the "Florence Nightingale of the North."

The war-trained, English nurse was twenty-nine when she volunteered for a Newfoundland posting from the British Overseas Nursing Association. She had hoped to be sent to Saskatchewan, a faraway place she read about in a two-penny weekly nursing publication.

Both Lady Grey, wife of Governor General Earl Grey, and Lady Harris, wife of Newfoundland Governor Sir Alexander Harris, convinced her that there was a great need for nurses in Newfoundland. In preparation for her new job, the young nurse took a course in midwifery and she acquired some limited tools of her trade, including a device for extracting teeth, a "universal forceps," which was to prove invaluable.

She arrived at Daniel's Harbour in the spring of 1921 and immediately began ministering to everything from difficult childbirths to tuberculosis. Her salary was seventy-five dollars a month, and she worked long hours travelling up and down the coast in all kinds of weather.

In 1922, "Nurse" married Newfoundland sailor and businessman Angus Bennett. He built a large home, which also served as a surgery education centre and hospital for half a century. Bennett was three months' pregnant with their second child when she received one of her most dramatic calls to duty in the middle of a snowy February night in 1926.

Her brother-in-law, Alex, was working at a lumber camp about eight kilometres from Daniel's Harbour and his foot had been almost completely severed by a saw at the mill. A thin strip of flesh was all that held the foot to the rest of the leg above the exposed ankle joint. Using snow as an anesthetic, Bennett cleaned the foot of splinters and bone and stitched the foot back onto the leg as best she could.

The following morning, Myra and Angus set out on a 100-kilometre journey to take the injured man to a doctor at Woody Point. The journey took three days, winding across the ocean on drifting ice and dodging ragged coastal ice. The Bennetts walked beside the sled to make it lighter for the horse as they battled drifting snow, howling winds and exhaustion.

Telegraph wires hummed with news of their journey. They spent the first night at Parson's Pond, where a group of men carried the patient and sled from the ice-encrusted cliffs to a warm home with steaming soup awaiting the weary travellers.

When they finally reached the doctor at Woody Point, he was amazed at Nurse Bennett's handiwork. There was no need to amputate. After a lengthy recovery, Alex was able to walk again.

Before she retired at sixty-eight, Bennett trained five midwives, raised her own family of three children and fostered four others. She delivered more than 5,000 babies and extracted at least 3,000 teeth in a career that did not end with the formality of retirement. Indeed, the last child she delivered was one of her own grandsons, and she was ninety-two when she performed her final extraction at Daniel's Harbour. "Mum always had strong arms and hands," recalled daughter Barbara Laing of Wawa, Ontario. "Once she got a hold of a tooth, she didn't let go."

Nurse Bennett received the Jubilee Medal from King George V, Coronation medals from both King George VI and Queen Elizabeth II, the Medal of the British Empire, the Order of Canada and an honorary doctorate in science from Memorial University. In 1967, Dr. Bennett was made a life member of the Association of Registered Nurses of Newfoundland in tribute to her "half-century of noble and notable service."

"I went where I wanted to go and I stayed there because I was needed," Myra Bennett once explained. She died in 1990 at the age of 100, leaving a legacy of dedication that honours the best tradition of Canadian nursing.

"YOU'RE NOT EVEN
A PERSON"

London, England, 1929 — To say that the fact that women were not considered "persons" in Canada irritated a Canadian magistrate named Emily Ferguson Murphy would be a gross understatement.

The first woman magistrate in the history of the British Empire, Emily Murphy had her legal status as a "person" belligerently challenged on her first day in court in 1916. If that arrogant defence lawyer Eardley Jackson could have imagined the consequences of his challenge, he might have held his tongue. Magistrate Murphy went on to spearhead a thirteen-year effort to change that stupefying state of affairs.

Emily Murphy was born in Cookstown, Ontario, in 1868. She was the daughter of well-to-do parents and enjoyed an excellent education. At nineteen, she married an Anglican minister twelve years her senior. They served in parishes throughout Ontario and spent several years in England. During that time Murphy raised a family of young daughters. She became a journalist and later an author, writing under the pen name "Janey Canuck."

In 1904, the Murphys moved to the Swan River area of Manitoba and then to Edmonton in 1907. In Alberta,

Murphy lobbied fiercely for the cause of women's rights and she was instrumental in framing the Dower Act of 1911, which provided property rights for married women.

In 1916, women observers were asked to leave a court session in which a group of prostitutes were being tried. Crown Counsel argued that the evidence would be unsuitable for a mixed audience. This prompted Murphy to argue that the city of Edmonton needed a court in which offenders could be tried by women in the presence of women. The Attorney General agreed with her, and promptly appointed Murphy as the first woman Police Magistrate in the Empire.

Murphy found her first day in court "as pleasant an experience as running a rapids." Not surprising, since Eardley Jackson turned on her as she sentenced his bootlegger client.

"You're not even a person," he shouted. "You have no right to be holding court!" Jackson persisted, quoting a statute of British Common Law which stated: "Women are persons in matters of pains and penalties, but are not persons in matters of rights and privileges." Since the position of magistrate was one of "privilege," Jackson concluded that Murphy was sitting "illegally" and no decision of her court could be binding.

In 1917, the Supreme Court of Alberta ruled that as far as it was concerned women were "persons." But the matter did not end there for Murphy, who discovered that according to the British North America Act women were not considered "persons" and as such could not be appointed to the Senate.

On a national scale, women's groups spent years urging the federal government to appoint a woman to the Senate, to no avail. "Whenever I don't know whether to fight or not, I always fight," Murphy once said.

By 1927, Murphy's fighting blood was up. She discovered that under the BNA Act any group of five citizens could petition the Supreme Court of Canada to rule on a constitutional point, and she determined to have an answer to the "person" issue. Four prominent Alberta women joined Murphy in the petition, which became known as the "Persons Case."

When the Supreme Court of Canada ruled that since women held no public office of any kind in 1867, the Fathers of Confederation could have had no intention of including women among the "persons" qualified to be summoned to the Senate, Murphy and her fellow petitioners decided to take their case to the Privy Council in London. Five judges joined a battery of bewigged lawyers from Canada and England in four days of debate over the interpretation of a seven-letter noun.

On October 18, 1929, the the Supreme Court's decision was reversed. Lord Sankey announced that in the view of the Council, the BNA Act had "planted in Canada a living tree capable of growth and expansion." The judgment ruled that "the word person includes members of the female sex," and Sankey noted that: "The exclusion of women from all public offices is a relic of more barbarous times."

Thus, Canadian women were accorded legal status as "persons" and were entitled to sit in the Senate for the first time. If history were devised to construct happy endings, Murphy's supporters would have relished her appointment as the first woman Senator. However, in 1931, Prime Minister Mackenzie King selected a well-known Liberal party worker, Cairine Wilson of Montreal.

Undaunted, Murphy urged women "to rejoice" at the ultimate consequence of their hard-won personhood. She was some kind of a woman.

LADYLIKE AND LETHAL

Ottawa, 1947 — It might seem a circuitous route from the badminton court to the politicized arena of consumer advocacy, but Dorothy McKenzie Walton was both a world-class badminton player and a leading force in the Canadian Association of Consumers. On and off the court, she had a confident stride and she never took her eye off the "birdie."

When she was a student at the University of Saskatchewan during the 1920s, Swift Current–born Dorothy was known as "the girl with the million-dollar smile." She excelled in athletics, participating in everything from hockey to the high jump. A member of fourteen intercollegiate sports teams, she was the first woman to qualify for the university's top athletic honour, the Oak Shield.

An above-average student, Dorothy was also the only female member of the university debating team, a team that won the Western championships and out-pointed the English and Australians. Years later, as a sought-after public speaker, she summed up her technique: "Have something to say, say it and shut up."

Her father, Edmund, was a successful merchant and a leading local Liberal. The only hint of rebellion Dorothy seems to have exhibited in her youth was participating in a Conservative election campaign when she was seventeen. She said she did it to get out of the family "rut."

Between 1924 and her marriage to Toronto businessman Bill Walton in 1931, Dorothy won more than fifty provincial and Western Canadian tennis titles and several badminton titles. She also earned a master's degree. Her thesis was on Canadian immigration.

After giving birth to a son, John, Dorothy began playing badminton in earnest. By 1939, she had won every major singles title in North America, along with numerous mixed doubles titles and a half-dozen tennis titles. She was thirty years old when she travelled to England to participate in the World's Amateur championship.

Even though Great Britain was the cradle of the game — the Duke of Bedford having named it after his country estate, Badminton House, in the late nineteenth century — the British would have done well to be wary of this racquet-carrying Canadian. In 1930, four top British players had been roundly trounced by Guelph, Ontario's Jack Purcell. Dorothy Walton proceeded to duplicate the feat.

"Mrs. Walton achieved Number One ranking because of a rare combination of abilities," wrote S.F. Wise and Douglas Fisher in *Canada's Sporting Heroes*. "The intelligence and deception of her play, especially at the net and in the production of beautifully paced, tantalisingly soft drop shots, enabled her to seize and hold the psychological edge that gives mastery in any sport."

At the top of her game, Walton's athletic career was cut off by the Second World War. In 1940, she was the runner-up for the Lou Marsh Trophy, an oversight that sports historians have attributed to the lack of publicity granted badminton. A decade later the Canadian Press hailed her as one of the top Canadian female athletes of the half-century.

Birds and racquets were in short supply throughout the war and Walton restricted her play to exhibition games for the troops. More importantly, she was involved with a variety of wartime initiatives, including the Wartime Prices and Trades Board (WPTB).

The idea of a consumer group sprang up after the war. A survey conducted by the National Council of Women showed that 80 percent of Canadian women favoured continuing the information flow about products that had begun with the WPTB.

In 1947, a handful of women, including Dorothy Walton, approached the government for funding to bring together fifty-six women's organizations from across Canada.

The meeting took place in Ottawa. It was a curious combination of clubwomen and housewives. There were representatives of political, business and professional associations and church groups, including the matronly leader of the Salvation Army and an opinionated Communist.

While Lady Ishbel Aberdeen's founding meeting of the National Women's Council in 1893 floundered initially over controversy concerning the opening prayer, this meeting was all business.

A constitution was drafted and dues were set at fifty cents. The all-woman Canadian Association of Consumers was launched with the motto: "In unity there is strength."

Early initiatives dealt with everyday issues. For example, clothing sizes would vary enormously. A woman who thought she wore a size twelve dress might purchase the same size from another manufacturer and find that it required substantial alteration. The sizing of children's clothing was mind-bogglingly stupid.

In 1949 the CAC began drafting a universal labelling system for clothes. They discovered that the U.S. army had drawn up a standard measurement system after systematically analyzing millions of male and female figures for the purpose of churning out wartime uniforms. Using this data, the CAC set about standardizing clothing sizes. Then they turned their sights on the textile industry, demanding "true labelling" about the content and care of garments.

Dorothy Walton became president of the CAC in 1950. Whether she was challenging deceptive bacon packaging or lobbying hosiery manufacturers to list the leg length on their product packaging, Walton was unrelenting.

In a 1952 article for *Maclean's* magazine, June Callwood described Dorothy Walton's leadership of the CAC as "a ladylike but lethal warfare against carelessness, fraud, ennui and ignorance in high places."

The CAC persuaded the government to require that soap and detergent manufacturers accurately list the weight of their product. They checked the accuracy of butcher scales and they demanded that a twenty-four-ounce loaf of bread weigh twenty-four ounces.

There was nothing too mundane to escape their concern, whether it was the price of eggs in April or the vitamin content of apple juice. In the Supreme Court of Canada, the CAC argued that a federal ban on margarine violated the British North America Act. They won.

Ralph Nadar was still a teenager in 1953 when Dorothy Walton was awarded the Coronation Medal for her service to the Canadian public. Behind that million-dollar smile Walton maintained a gutsy determination that made her both a champion athlete and a champion of the people.

LILY OF THE MOHAWKS, GENEVIÈVE OF NEW FRANCE

Caughnawaga to Rome, 1980 — "Catherine Tekakwitha, who are you? Are you (1658–1680)? Is that enough? Are you the Iroquois Virgin? Are you the Lily of the Shores of the Mohawk River? Can I love you in my own way?" Thus begins Leonard Cohen's elegiac, controversial, some say pornographic, 1966 novel *Beautiful Losers*, which, among other things, is an evocation of the first Indian saint, Kateri (Catherine) Tekakwitha.

Kateri Tekakwitha was venerated by Pope Pius XII in 1943 and subsequently beatified by Pope John Paul II on June 22, 1980. The history of the Catholic Church in Canada is, like Cohen's novel, controversial, nowhere more so than in Quebec. But it is a seminal history. The Church was hugely influential in Canada's settlement and its establishment as a nation. In no single story is that influence more confounding, more resonate, than in the story of Kateri Tekakwitha. The daughter of a Christian Algonkin squaw and a pagan Mohawk, Kateri was born in 1656 near what is now Auriesville in Albany, New York State. Her mother had been brought up by French settlers at Trois-Rivières, then captured by the Mohawks around 1653. Instead of being killed, she was taken as a wife and Kateri was conceived.

Along with religion and fire water the Europeans also brought disease to the New World. In 1660 Kateri Tekakwitha's mother succumbed, as did her husband and their last-born child, to a smallpox epidemic. Young Kateri survived, but barely. She was, from then on, an exceedingly frail creature, with badly damaged eyes and a heavily scarred, pock-marked face. Kateri was taken in by her uncle, the first chieftain of the Turtle Clan village called Gandauoque (Caughnawaga). Ironically, her uncle was a vociferous and dedicated enemy of the white man and the Christian faith.

In the fall of 1666 Prouville de Tracy came down from Quebec, burned and plundered these centres of the Mohawk population and their stores. Decimated, the Mohawk begged for peace and dutifully asked for missionaries to placate the maurading French. Three black-robed Jesuit emissaries arrived in Gandauoque in September 1667. During the three days they were there, eleven-year-old Kateri was charged with their care. Whatever happened during those three days, a change came over the young Indian child that not even her avuncular uncle could reverse.

Her piety and refusal to marry, as her relatives frequently tried to arrange for her to do, is not necessarily as miraculous as zealous Catholic chroniclers would have the student of Canadian history believe; two-thirds of the population of Gandauoque was composed of Christian Algonkins and Hurons who undoubtedly proselytized the religious life and spoke to Kateri about the Ursulines of Quebec in glowing terms. Kateri was not without a "support group," in spite of her uncle's disapproval.

Kateri formally converted to Catholicism in 1675. Her conversion brought with it the wrath of her uncle and those in her community who felt as he did. Legend has it that there was active persecution of the young girl — death threats and beatings — all of which left the fragile Kateri physically more challenged but emotionally more resolved.

The priests advised her to pray unrelentingly and if her prayers did not stay the savages, to flee her village and go and live at the mission near Lachine Rapids more than 320 kilometres (200 miles) away. There her faith would be readily accepted.

In the fall of 1677, at the age of twenty-one, with the aid of three Indian neophytes, Kateri fled. It was at the Saint-Francois-Xavier mission at Sault St. Louis near Montreal that Kateri prepared herself for the chaste life as a devout Catholic. Anastasie Tegonhatsiongo, who had been her mother's friend at Ossernenon (Auriesville, N.Y.), was recruited as Kateri's spiritual guide.

In the spring of 1678, she was received into the Confrérie de la Sainte-Famille (The Holy Family), despite the fact that she was a very young novice. She continued to live the full Indian life, accompanying her people on the great winter hunts, up until the last two years of her life. However, her commitment to chastity and strength of purpose gave the caretaker French priests an impression of exceptional spirituality.

On the feast of the Annunciation, March 25, 1679, she was permitted to take in private the vow of perpetual chastity. Thus neo-Catholic posterity gave her the moniker, Lily of the Mohawks.

As it is obsessively and imaginatively documented in Cohen's novel, Kateri adopted a penitential lifestyle — long periods of enforced silence, fasting, standing in the cold dawn for hours with little protection from the elements, self-mutilation — all of which invariably hastened her early demise a mere three years after her arrival at the mission.

Her sainthood has rightfully met with skepticism, even hostility, by some native peoples and non-Catholics, who contend that an imperialistic Church had co-opted a "Native Person" for its own purposes.

The Catholic Church's Congregation for the Causes of Saints (the Vatican department that attends to the business of selecting and recommending veneration, beatification and canonization to the Pope) puts a priority on candidates who represent occupations or peoples who have no saints to celebrate. Until the twentieth century, the Church had never put a priority on women. Only 20 percent of the saints canonized up to 1900 were female. That number has increased.

It was Kateri Tekakwitha's "pastoral priority" that determined her beatification, despite the fact that all of the miracles attributed to her intercession lacked certification.

The fledgling church in North America was unequipped in the seventeenth century to carry out the formal investigations necessary to establish a miracle's validity, normally a prerequisite for sainthood. According to the French Jesuit historian Father Charlevoix, miracles took place at Kateri's humble tomb, which became a place of pilgrimage for the parishes around Montreal. He recorded a story about a newly arrived parish priest named Father Rémy who refused to lead the annual pilgrimage to Kateri's grave because, the new priest avowed, such worship was not acknowledged by the Church. According to Father Charlevoix's story, the priest fell gravely ill that very day and only recovered when he relented and agreed to lead the procession. Pope John Paul II decided when he made Kateri a saint in 1980 that her reputation for producing miracles was sufficient.

Kateri died on April 17, 1680 at 3 o'clock in the afternoon. Her last words are said to have been "Jesos Konoronkwa" (Jesus I love you). According to the Jesuit priests who were present fifteen minutes after her death, the ugly pox marks and scars on her face suddenly disappeared and she was made beautiful.

In 1688, Bishop Saint-Vallier, the second bishop of Quebec, declared Kateri "the Geneviève of Canada." In 1744 Father Charlevoix wrote that she was "universally regarded as the Protectress of Canada."

A Joan-of-Arc figure, Kateri's legend grows, nurtured by papal authority. She is a patron saint of exiles, orphans and people ridiculed for their piety. Each year sees more pilgrimages to Auriesville, where the American Catholic Church has built The National Shrine of the North American Martyrs presided over by the Lily of the Mohawks, and to the François-Xavier mission at Caughnawaga where Kateri Tekakwitha's relics are maintained.

SPORTS

FIELDS OF DREAMS

ROW, ROW, ROW YOUR BOAT

A GENTLEMAN AND A SCULLER

FOLLOW THE BOUNCING BALL

THE TURN-OF-THE-CENTURY TERMINATOR

SINGING ON THE GREENS

THE RUNNING MAN

JUST FOR THE FUN OF IT

TURN HIM LOOSE!

SIMPLY THE BEST

SIR BARTON AND THE COMMANDER

THE BIG TRAIN THAT COULD

GILDING THE SASKATOON LILY

OUR PERCY GOES FOR GOLD

THE COMPLETE ATHLETE

"DON'T LET THE CRIPPLED KIDS DOWN"

WHO WAS THAT MASKED MAN?

FIELDS OF DREAMS

Oxford County, Ontario, 1838 — Although American Abner Doubleday is often credited with "inventing" baseball in 1839, the fact is that on June 4, 1838, two weeks before Queen Victoria's coronation, and six months after the Mackenzie King Rebellion in Toronto, Canadians played their first recorded game on a smooth pasture behind Enoch Burdick's shops at Beachville, near the southwestern Ontario town of Ingersoll.

Canadian baseball had its origins in English games like rounders and cricket, which also feature a pitcher, catcher, fielders and batters running to bases. The history of the game is imprecise. Drawings found in Egyptian tombs appear to indicate that a few innings may have been enjoyed by the likes of King Tut, and games utilizing balls and sticks in medieval times often coincided with spring fertility rites.

When the assorted Beachville village players of Oxford County met the neighbouring township team from Zorra, the rules and the implements of the game were slightly different from those we know today. Four bases, called "byes" marked the infield area and eleven players formed a team. The batter was known as a "knocker," while the bat itself was referred to as a "club."

Early bats were fashioned out of cedar, blocked with an axe and finished with a drawing knife. Wagon spokes and barrel staves were also used. The relatively small baseballs were made out of double and twisted woollen yarn covered with calfskin and stitched with waxed thread.

No gloves were worn and the real fun of the game came in "plugging," which involved hitting the runner with a thrown ball. This hazardous practice was revised in the 1860s when a "standard" set of rules was adopted by the Canadian Association of Base Ball Players, and the gentler art of "tagging" the runner for an out came into effect.

Scores were kept on a notched stick and games lasted six to nine innings, or finished when one of the teams achieved a designated number of runs. Hits and runs were numerous, since batters were allowed to wait for their choice of pitches. When the Woodstock Young Canadians played the Atlantic Club of Brooklyn, New York, in the first ever international baseball game, their resounding defeat was scored at 75-11.

From its small-town and rural roots, Canadian baseball evolved as a working-class sport. Players on the first organized team — the Hamilton Young Canadians — included five clerks, three shoemakers, a marble cutter, a tinsmith, a painter and a saloon-keeper, along with makers of everything from brooms to carriages.

Although players were praised for their "gentlemanly bearing," games between communities became heated affairs and fights in the bleachers were not uncommon. The popularity of the game was confirmed in 1869, when the town of Woodstock hosted a three-day tournament and attracted 5,000 spectators, which was at least 1,000 in excess of the southwestern Ontario town's entire population.

In 1876 the Canadian Base Ball Association was formed. It featured a five-team league, including the London Tecumsehs who went on to defeat the National League champion Chicago White Stockings in an exhibition match. The following year the Tecumsehs defeated Pittsburgh to become champions of the National League's principal rival organization, the International Association.

Baseball fever spread across Canada. Games with U.S. teams were prevalent in Victoria and New Westminster, B.C. By the mid-1880s, inter-town matches were played in New Brunswick. In Manitoba, Winnipeggers were said to be suffering from "baseball mania" and open gambling on the games raised public concern.

Canadians, such as players George "Moon" Gibson and James Edward "Tip" O'Neil and managers Arthur Irwin and Bill Watkins, went on to enjoy substantial professional careers in the United States as part of the first "foreign invasion" of the game in America.

Although the vast majority of professional league players in Canada were recruited from the United States, by 1900 baseball was the most popular and most publicized sport in the country.

The imagination of Canadians has been seized in the field of dreams ever since.

ROW, ROW,
ROW YOUR BOAT

Paris, France, 1867 — Three fishermen, and a lighthouse keeper — that was the "Paris Crew." Believe it or not, this ragtag rowing team from Saint John, New Brunswick, won the prestigious Paris Regatta in 1867. Just weeks after Confederation, they became a newborn nation's first world-champions.

"With their flesh-coloured jerseys, dark cloth trousers, leather braces and bright pink caps, they were in striking contrast to their neat competition," was how the *Manchester Guardian* euphemistically understated the spectacle these rough-hewn, freshly minted Canadians presented at this most élite of events.

But it was not only the appearance of Elijah Ross, the lighthouse keeper, and fishermen Robert Fulton, George Price and Samuel Hutton that struck an odd chord. Instead of the sleek shells that were used by the likes of the Oxford Blues rowing team and the French Geslings, the Paris Crew had two, homemade, lime-green boats that weighed a good fifty kilograms more than those of their competitors

Furthermore, the Canadians had the audacity to argue publicly amongst themselves, which did not sit well in "civilized" rowing circles. Reporters balked at their short-stroke rowing style — "by no means in accordance with received ideas." And to defy convention even further, they chose to compete without a coxswain, the diminutive individual who traditionally provides instructions from the bow of the boat. Reception, perception and eccentricities aside, the Paris Crew had the unwavering support of their countrymen. To send the foursome to Paris, the citizens of Saint John raised $4,000 and the provincial government subscribed another $2,000. These were staggering sums of money in those days, but the vigour of gambling potential may have spurred the goodwill.

Sheriff Harding of Saint John accompanied the rowers to the "sinful" city to protect the "investment" and to levy tens of thousands of dollars in wagers on behalf of his constituency.

The Crew was entered in two races, one for heavy in-rigged boats and the other for out-rigged shells. They triumphed in both!

According to one English description of the first race: "The Canadians were not supposed to have a chance . . . Yet they won by three lengths with London second and Oxford third. At the finish, they were ploughing away, clear of the others, laughing and talking in the easiest possible manner."

The victories became a national inspiration to the new country. "Perhaps nothing since Confederation has occurred which so thoroughly brings home to the broad mass of our people that our bold Maritime friends are now our fellow countrymen in name and in fact," noted *The Toronto Globe.*

In 1868, the fabulous four did it again, and beat the best America had to offer. They appeared indomitable.

During a race against a Toronto crew, the New Brunswickers were so far ahead that they paused to share a bottle of wine and still won their race.

When the Paris Crew was surprised by defeat at the 1870 Lachine Regatta in Quebec, Saint Johners demanded a rematch against the victorious team from Tyne, which was stroked by the great English single sculls champion James Renforth.

The race was scheduled for August 23, 1871, over 9.7 kilometres of the Kennebecasis River, just east of Saint John. Race day was declared a public holiday and a crowd of more than 20,000 celebrated. In those days rowing was such a huge spectator sport that throngs gathered just to observe the team practise.

The Paris Crew, stripped to the waist and rowing at forty-two strokes a minute, had taken a commanding lead when the English boat suddenly veered off course. Renforth had collapsed. Shortly afterward, the twenty-nine-year-old champion was dead.

Confusion reigned. Rumours spread, with some accounts suggesting that Renforth's last words had been: "Oh Harry, I've had something." English newshounds rushed to the conclusion of murder most foul — by poison!

At the inquest that followed, medical experts in Boston absolved the good citizens of Saint John. No poison was found. The cause of death has been cited variously as either heart failure or asphyxia, attributed to congestion in the lungs brought on by mental and physical stress.

Later, in tribute to the fallen rower, a town at the river's edge was named Renforth. But after the tragedy, the Paris Crew never raced again. No one would accept their challenge, and the Saint John Four went into rather ignominious retirement.

Nine years later, in 1880, Canada earned its second world championship, when Toronto oarsman Edward "Ned" Hanlan beat Australia's Edward Tickett in a race viewed by more than 100,000 spectators on the River Thames in England.

In 1984, Canada's rowers earned gold at the Olympics and, after the success of our rowers in the 1992 Barcelona Summer Olympics, there can be no doubt that our nation is blessed with a tradition of golden oars.

A GENTLEMAN
AND A SCULLER

River Thames, 1880 — When Canada's "Boy in Blue" rowed to victory, the effect was so seamless that one reporter said "his boat seemed to be pulled through the water on a string." Compact and charismatic, Edward "Ned" Hanlan became Canada's first international sports personality and the Champion Oarsman of the World.

He grew up surrounded by Lake Ontario, on the Toronto Island whose western arm now bears the name Hanlan's Point. As a child, Ned rowed across the harbour to school in a marginal craft made out of thick planks sharpened at each end. When he was five years old, he created a local sensation by threading a skiff through throngs of vessels awaiting the arrival of the Prince of Wales.

Fishermen taught him, and time spent on the water honed his skills. He was a teenager when he won his first race. After that, a blue jersey, blue shorts and a red bandanna became his uniform and a soup-strainer moustache his trademark.

Sport aside, rowing was also big business. Hanlan's talent attracted the attention of a consortium of wealthy speculators who formed the Hanlan Club in a syndicated effort to boost his championship efforts and enhance their side-betting odds. At twenty-one, Hanlan had a trainer, a sleek English shell and the latest in rowing innovations — a sliding seat and swivel oarlocks.

Crouched with his arms extended, he mastered the "slider," enhancing his stroke and relieving him of the uncomfortable buffalo skins and greased chamois pants that less technologically astute competitors used to gain extra leverage from their stationary seats.

Hanlan's syndicators had high hopes. In 1876, they entered him in the prestigious International Centennial Regatta in Philadelphia. Young Ned departed for the United States earlier than scheduled when he discovered that there was a warrant out for his arrest on charges of bootlegging. He was eventually cornered at the Toronto Rowing Club.

In a scene that could have been scripted for the Keystone Kops, Hanlan relieved the boathouse of a skiff and took off across Lake Ontario while the flat-feet stomped their heels in dry dock. A steamer filled with revellers from Toronto's German Club picked Hanlan up and he partied with them all the way to the American side of the lake.

In Philadelphia, Hanlan trained quietly with Billy McKen, a fellow-Canadian who doubled as the betting agent for the Hanlan Club. After Hanlan took the first two heats, New York gamblers are said to have been determined to prevent the young Canadian from competing. Their plot to poison Hanlan was foiled when McKen was mistaken as the target. McKen ended up drinking a doctored beer that landed him on a stretcher back to Toronto the next day. Hanlan won the race in record time and returned to the first of many celebrations in his honour. The warrant for his arrest was shredded by the chief of police.

In 1877, Hanlan won the Canadian championship. The U.S. championship followed in 1878. Hanlan outclassed all comers. During his first race in England he actually stopped to bail out his boat and still finished four lengths ahead of his rival.

He won the English championship handily, breaking the course record by fifty-two seconds. Hanlan's return to Canada was celebrated by a flotilla of yachts, sidewheelers and small craft filled with well-wishers who greeted his arrival on the steamer *Chicora* with screams, whistles and bands playing "Hail the Conquering Hero."

Match races were both crowd pleasers and big money events. In three matches with American Charles Courtney, Hanlan won thousands, but every encounter was marred by the hint of scandal. When they first raced at Lachine, Quebec, in 1878, Hanlan's margin was slight and Courtney's backers claimed their man would have won if he had not accidentally strayed into Hanlan's lane.

A rematch at Chautaqua Lake in New York State attracted 50,000 spectators to the hamlet of Mayville (population: 1,000). Unbeknownst to Hanlan, some of his backers had promised Courtney a victory in the second heat. When Hanlan got wind of the plan he refused to be a party to the "fix." On the morning of the first match, Courtney's racing shell and his practise boat were discovered sawn in half.

Hanlan raced alone, covering the five-mile course in a record-breaking thirty-three minutes and fifty-six-and-a-quarter seconds. But all bets were off and his prize money was a rubber checque.

Courtney denied any impropriety on his part, leaving the world press to speculate about who was responsible. When Hanlan and Courtney met for the final time in a race on the Potomac River, Courtney claimed to have a headache and dropped out of the race.

Ned Hanlan's finest hour came on the River Thames in November, 1880. Canada's five-foot-eight-and-three-quarter-inch, 150-pound "Boy in Blue" was pitted against Australia's Edward Trickett, who was seven inches taller and fifty pounds heavier. Wagering was fierce, with half a million dollars riding on the outcome of the four-and-a-half-mile race. Torontonians alone bet $42,000 on their favourite son.

Trickett had arbitrarily declared himself the world's champion oarsman, but all of his arrogance was no match for Hanlan's prowess. A supremely confidant Hanlan took the early lead and never looked back.

Crowds lining the banks and bridges of the course cheered as he clowned his way to victory, rowing in a zig-zag pattern, blowing kisses, feigning a collapse and even pausing to chat with by standers.

Despite the debilitating effects of two bouts of typhoid, Hanlan successfully defended his world title six times over the following four years. On the international stage he was an entrenched symbol of Canada's "muscular nationalism."

When Ned Hanlan retired from competition in 1897, he had won more than 300 races and suffered fewer than a dozen defeats. He went on to serve two terms as an alderman in Toronto and held a seat on the Toronto Harbour Trust.

The father of eight died of pneumonia in 1908 at the age of fifty-two. Eighteen years later, a towering statue of Ned Hanlan was unveiled at the Canadian National Exhibition grounds on Toronto's waterfront. It is dedicated to "the most renowned oarsman of any age whose victorious career has no parallel in the annals of sport."

FOLLOW THE
BOUNCING BALL

Springfield, Massachusetts, 1891 — It all started with two peach baskets, a soccer ball and a few Americans. They wanted to call it "Naismith ball." Typical of many Canadians, James Naismith was too modest to allow them to name a game after him. So they called it "basketball" instead.

This most American of sports, and now the world's most widely played game, was indeed invented by a young physical education teacher from Almonte, Ontario.

Very few sports have actually been "invented." Hockey, another uniquely Canadian game, evolved from the native peoples' fast-paced game of lacrosse. Football is a rugby derivative.

James Naismith, a doctoral graduate in theology from McGill University and Presbyterian Theological College in Montreal, practised his faith in the belief that a healthy mind was inseparable from a healthy body.

In 1891, Naismith found himself in charge of a bored and rebellious gym class made up of mature men at the YMCA training school in Springfield, Massachusetts. Where other instructors had failed, he was determined to discover an indoor sport that would fill the gap between the football and baseball seasons.

"All of the stubbornness of my Scottish ancestry was aroused, all of my pride of achievement urged me on," he once recalled.

Naismith tried modifying traditional games, but tackling and full-bore running proved hazardous on the hard gymnasium floor. One by one, Naismith thought out the elements of the new game.

He recalled a childhood game that involved knocking a rock off another rock with a stone.

He also remembered an off-season rugby exercise he had practised at McGill that involved throwing a ball into an empty box at the end of a gymnasium.

Why not elevate the goals? A soccer ball was light enough to be thrown and caught. To make the goals, he borrowed two peach baskets from the janitor.

On December 21, 1891, he posted thirteen rules on the YMCA bulletin board.

When the men came by to while away a few hours with the intense but likable doctor of divinity, they found that all the traditional gym apparatus had disappeared.

Rings and climbing ropes were slung out of the way to clear "air space" over the sloped peach baskets that were nailed to the balconies at either end of the room.

At first, they were skeptical. One may even have had the audacity to ask: "Is this some kind of Canadian joke?"

Early games must have been amusing to watch. The traditional gym uniforms of the day consisted of long grey trousers and short-sleeved jerseys, worn by players who favoured full beards or walrus mustaches.

In the beginning, there were nine competitors on each team. When a player was cornered too closely to throw, he would roll the ball and run after it. The first game of basketball ever played ended in a score of 1-0, a far cry from the NBA scores of today.

As the game caught on, refinements were made; the skill level increased and the "dribble" was introduced. However, the janitor quickly grew tired of climbing up and down a ladder to retrieve the soccer ball from the peach baskets.

"Let's cut the bottom out of the baskets," Naismith declared and the "hoop" as we know it took shape at each end of the "court."

Although his students preferred "Naismith ball" as a title, the inventor just laughed. "I told them I thought that name would kill any game." A student came up with "basketball."

A truly egalitarian sport, basketball stresses skill over strength, speed and power. The same sport that is played in $200 spring-loaded sneakers and satin shorts is also played in wheelchairs.

James Naismith, a man from a country where the climate forces its population indoors half the year, invented a pastime that has become one of the most popular sports in the history of human endeavour.

THE TURN-OF-THE-CENTURY TERMINATOR

Montreal, Quebec, 1892 — Nothing could have prepared the thugs who roamed the toughest district of Montreal for the newest police recruit. Louis Cyr was a massive man and a virtual block of muscle. At his peak, the fair-haired strongman had a 152-centimetre (60-inch) chest, 84-centimetre (33-inch) thighs and biceps that were the size of a fit woman's waist. When he confronted the underworld ruffians of Sainte-Cunégonde, he had no weapon other than brute strength. "At first the arrested ones endeavoured to put up a fight," reported the Montreal *Star*. "Cyr, taking one under each arm and carrying the other in a vice-like grip in front of him, marched off to the station with all three prisoners off the ground." But lifting three men was a fractional display of Cyr's strength. In 1895, he backlifted a platform holding eighteen fat men weighing 1,967 kilograms (4,337 pounds).

From birth, the Canadian Hercules seemed destined for big things. When he entered the world on October 10, 1863 at St-Cyprien-de-Napierville, south of Montreal, the eldest of the seventeen Cyr children weighed an astounding 8.2 kilograms (18 pounds). His father was a farmer of unremarkable stature, but his mother was statuesque. She could hoist two full grain sacks at a time. This was a feat that her fair-haired son (baptised Noe Cyprien) matched at twelve years old, when he abandoned all formal schooling to take his first job working in a woodlot.

The family moved to Lowell, Massachusetts, when Noe was fifteen. Lowell was a textile centre and the bustling town attracted so many French-Canadian workers that it became known as "Little Canada." In preparation for the trip, young Cyr learned English. His mother decided that he should have a name more in keeping with the Anglo-Saxon tongue and selected "Louis" in honour of the French kings. She also took it upon herself to apply curling irons to his long blond hair. Although his age would normally have precluded him from heavy work, Louis Cyr impressed the first foreman he met by hoisting a 170-kilogram (350-pound) roll of cloth. At the age of eighteen, he won his first strongman contest. He lifted a Percheron horse on his back and was promptly declared the strongest man in Massachusetts.

At the celebration in honour of this triumph, Louis met Melina Comtois, a wisp of a woman who took over the curling iron chores after she became his wife in 1882. Melina had also been targeted for courtship by another French-Canadian, David Michaud, Canada's reigning undefeated strongman for a decade. When Michaud challenged Cyr to a title match in Quebec City, it was said to be as much a challenge of romantic revenge as it was a desire to maintain control of his title.

The champion chose boulders as the challenge. They were marked with weights from 45 to 227 kilograms (100 to 500 pounds), with one huge rock identified only by a question mark. Rain created a muddy playing field for the two giants, but both were able to raise the second-largest rock.

The showdown came over the rock of questionable weight. When it was over, Cyr was victorious and the answer to the question of the rock's weight was 237 kilograms (522 pounds).

Louis Cyr was formally designated the "strongest man in the world" in 1896 when he confronted Swedish champion August Johnson in a competition that lasted more than three hours. "I can defeat any man in the world; but no man can defeat this elephant," Johnson is reported to have commented.

For all his strength, Cyr also had weaknesses — the greatest being gluttony. From childhood, he associated food with physical power and his heroic eating habits became part of his legend. During a twenty-three-month tour of England, the gentry were almost as impressed by his 9-kilograms (20-pounds) a day meat capacity as they were with his ability to lift 250 kilograms (551 pounds) with the middle finger of one hand. Ultimately, diet proved the erstwhile Samson's downfall. By the age of thirty-seven, he suffered from Bright's disease and subsisted on a diet of milk.

In 1906, Cyr participated in his final championship. The debilitated, forty four year old met the challenge of superbly conditioned, twenty-nine-year-old Hector Decarie. Surprisingly, the two gladiators ended in a tie, after Cyr hoisted a 1,302-kilogram (2,8700-pound) platform that Decarie could not budge. Then in a measure of grace, Cyr retired forever. One month after his forty-ninth birthday, he died.

"He used power . . . nothing but power," wrote Ben Weider, the founder of the International Federation of Bodybuilders, who spent his own Quebec childhood imitating the feats of the legendary Louis Cyr. "What a modern coach could do with a man of his muscular power heaven only knows."

SINGING ON THE GREENS

St. Louis, Missouri, 1904 — Golf was played as an Olympic event only once in the history of the Games, and top honours went to a forty-six-year-old Canadian. George Seymour Lyon, a golfer of unconventional swing and attitude, accepted his gold medal and commemorative silver cup after walking through the dining room of the Glen Echo Country Club on his hands.

Lyon did not hold a putter until he was thirty-eight, but by then he was already one of Canada's most accomplished athletes in a variety of other sports, including rugby, baseball, soccer, lawn bowling, curling. At eighteen he set a Canadian record in the pole vault. He represented Canada at cricket eleven times and once scored 238 not out for his club, another Canadian record.

Golf was a game he took up on a dare in 1896. He never looked back. His swing has been described as "a haphazard, if ruthless, swipe at the ball," and his stance owed more to cricket than golf. Lyon played the game aggressively rather than pensively, and he took great delight in walloping the ball. Beneath his unconventional form was a truly competitive temperament. After only one season of play, he made the semifinals of the Canadian amateur championship, a title which he eventually won eight times.

The Third Modern Olympiad in 1904 was held in St. Louis, but the Games themselves were almost totally overwhelmed by other events, including the Russo-Japanese War and the St. Louis World's Fair. There were no opening or closing ceremonies; many European nations did not even bother to send a team.

In the golf competition, Toronto's George Lyon placed in the top half of the thirty-six-hole qualifying round that reduced the field of mainly American golfers from seventy-five to thirty-two. It was during this time that reporters twigged to Lyon's "coal-heaver's swing," as well as his penchant for singing on the greens when the round was over and for telling jokes to his competitors.

In his semifinal round against U.S. Pacific Coast champion Francis Newton, Lyon's pin-high drive was recorded at an amazing 273.4 metres (299 yards). When the personality-packed Canadian triumphed over twenty-three-year-old American amateur champion Chandler Egan to win the event, the St. Louis *Globe Democrat* cited his "iron nerves" and "prepondering wisdom, born of longer experience."

Lyon could have had two Olympic victories to his credit. In 1908, he was scheduled to play in the London Olympics; however, an internal dispute among British golfers led them to boycott the games. Lyon was the only other entrant, but he refused to receive a gold medal by default. Golf has never since been entertained as an Olympic event.

As the veteran captain of his home course, the Lambton Golf and Country Club in Toronto, Lyon continued to play golf and encourage newcomers to the sport. In 1924, his son, Fred, took the Ontario Junior Championship.

Lyon himself went on to win the Canadian Senior Championship ten times, placing second on four other occasions.

Until the age of seventy-eight, George S. Lyon, Canada's only golfing Olympian, shot his age for eighteen holes. He died the following year in 1938. To this day, the members of the Lambton Golf and Country Club open and close their season with the song that George S. would sing with gusto at the slightest provocation, "My Wild Irish Rose."

THE RUNNING MAN

Boston, Massachusetts, 1907 — Greed and racial innuendo peppered the career of Canada's first national sports hero of the twentieth century. In other circumstances, marathon runner Tom Longboat might have become a wealthy and venerated athlete. Instead he ended up working as a garbageman. "Maybe all I'm good for now is sweeping leaves, but if I can help the kids and show them how to be good runners and how to live a clean life, I'm satisfied," Longboat told the Toronto *Globe* thirty years after running the Boston Marathon in record time.

Tom Longboat's Onondaga name was Cogwagee, meaning "Everything." He was born in a log house on the Six Nations Reserve near Brantford, Ontario, in 1887. His father died when Tom was five, and much of his childhood was spent helping his mother on their small farm. He resented the English-language education provided by the Anglican mission boarding school that drew him away from his own culture and the aid of his family. At twelve, his formal education ended and he became a transient farm labourer.

Mohawk runner, Bill Davis, took Longboat under his wing after watching him finish second at the Caledon Fair in 1905. Longboat began training every day, extending his distances gradually. The following Victoria Day, he won the Caledon 8-kilometre (5-mile) race by more than 400 metres.

The booming steeltown of Hamilton held a prestigious 30.5-kilometre (19-mile) foot race around Burlington Bay every year. In 1906, the crowd chuckled as a tall, native competitor took his place at the starting line wearing cheap canvas running shoes, threadbare cotton bathing trunks and a baggy sweatshirt. Although he ran awkwardly, with his feet kicking sideways and his hands held hip high, the onlookers' laughter turned to cheers when Longboat beat the field by a full three minutes. Two more victories that year confirmed his abilities.

On a cold April morning in 1907, Tom Longboat became a national hero when he sailed past more than one hundred competitors to win the Boston Marathon. He was showered and eating steak before the other runners finished.

Longboat's winning streak continued, but coping with fame and the wiles of the world was not his forte. The YMCA suspended him for a curfew violation, and for breaking smoking and drinking restrictions. Two Irishmen, Tom Flanagan and Jim O'Rourke, took an interest in him and Longboat began running for the Irish-Canadian Athletic Club, all the while dodging suspicions that his caretakers were placing bets on the side. The U.S. Amateur Athletic Union declared him a professional. Flanagan gave Longboat a job in a cigar shop to show Canadian authorities that the runner had independent means.

Despite a case of boils that caused him to miss the Olympic trials, Longboat was named to the 1908 Canadian team. He was among the leaders in the marathon when he collapsed in the final quarter of the race. Rumours flew that he had been overtrained, undertrained or drugged by gambling interests. A disappointed Longboat suggested that he had run his last race.

Not surprisingly, Flanagan persuaded him otherwise. Soon afterward he was winning races throughout Ontario and setting new records, prompting Canadian Athletic Union president William Stark to declare him "the greatest long distance runner of the century."

Tom Longboat turned professional on December 15, 1908, when he raced Olympic gold medalist Dorando Pietri at Madison Square Gardens. He won $3,000 when the Italian collapsed six laps from the finish. Again, Longboat was claimed as a Canadian hero. He and his Mohawk bride, Lauretta Maracle, were given a wedding reception at Toronto's Massey Hall.

One of the biggest match races in history took place on February 5, 1909, when the Canadian dubbed "Wildfire" met international champion Alfie Shrubb in the run for the professional championship of the world. Shrubb conceded after 39 kilometres (24 miles) and Longboat jogged to a standing ovation.

Meanwhile, Flanagan cashed-out, selling his contract to an American promoter for $2,000. Longboat lost his next race, and his contract was sold again, this time for $700. No longer invincible, he was tarred by the press as "lazy," and a suspended sentence for drunkenness in 1911 tarnished his image.

Interest in marathon running paled with the outbreak of the First World War in 1914. Longboat was one of 292 Six Nations warriors to go to the front. In France, he ran dispatches through the trenches. Twice wounded, he was once declared dead during a debacle in Belgium. When he returned home, he discovered that his wife had taken the news seriously enough to remarry. He started a new family and took whatever work he could find. When he died of pneumonia at the age of sixty-one, the funeral service was conducted in Onondaga, a language Tom Longboat never forgot.

JUST FOR THE FUN OF IT

Toronto, 1909 — Imagine how it must feel to forget to
patent a million-dollar invention — a game that has become
Canada's largest participant sport, enjoyed by millions and
profitable to many. "I was hustling so much . . . well, I forgot," admitted Tommy Ryan, an elfin, jovial entrepreneur,
who favoured wearing a bow-tie that squirted water.

The game Ryan created was five-pin bowling, a com-
paction of the ten-pin game. Bowling artifacts have been
unearthed in Egyptian tombs. An outdoor version of the game
played on grass with wooden pegs became such a popular
diversion from field work that King Henry III of England
passed a law forbidding it. Variations of the game have been
played by Celtic Helvitii and by ancient Polynesian cultures.
Ryan's refinements, however, were uniquely Canadian.

The Canadian 5-Pin Bowlers' Association dates the
invention of this game as November, 1909, although Ryan
could never be pinned to an exact date. He was promoting
boxing matches, dabbling in horse racing and running his
own ten-pin bowling alley when he devised the game. "I
was the biggest sucker in the world," Ryan said on reflection. He was also one of the game's greatest boosters for
more than half a century.

Thomas Francis Ryan was born in Guelph, Ontario in 1872. From an early age, he was good at games that involved throwing spheres. While he was working as an invoice clerk in Toronto, his after-hours skill as a baseball pitcher attracted an offer from the Baltimore Orioles. Instead, Ryan opened a billiards academy that catered to his many friends in the sporting fraternity. In 1905, he diversified, installing the first ten-pin bowling lanes in Canada above a jewellery store not far from the business district.

Ryan intended to attract a toney crowd. At a time when bowling alleys were considered something akin to the devil's work, he offered an emporium featuring potted tropical plants, a string orchestra and private memberships. The ten polished wood alleys designed by Chicago experts at a cost of $45,000, however, failed to earn their keep.

Although his carriage-trade patrons included the likes of retail magnate Sir John Eaton and the elite legal minds of Osgoode Hall, the rigours of the game proved too taxing. "The ten-pin ball was too heavy for the type of person I had induced to bowl," Ryan told sportswriter Al Nickleson. "Some hadn't used their muscles in years. They'd bowl one or two games, then play bridge in my office while I supplied adhesive tape for their thumbs."

Ryan's solution was obvious. Instead of a 7.2-kilogram (16-pound) behemoth of a ball, he opted for a palm-held, lightweight ball without any troublesome digit-holes. He even supplied the balls, eliminating cartage problems for his white-collar customers.

Smaller balls meant smaller pins. Ryan's father, a practical mechanic, whittled down five ten-pins with a lathe. Then Ryan figured out a new scoring system for a game that asks its players to knock down five pins configured in a 91-centimetre (36-inch) triangle by rolling a ball down a narrow 18.3-metre (60-foot) solid surface. Each bowler was allowed ten "frames" per game and a maximum of three balls per frame. A score could only be counted if the bowler knocked over the Number Four corner pin, a stipulation that Ryan found resulted in no uncertain "blasphemy."

Noise and damage control characterized the first few riotous years of five-pin bowling. The lighter pins fairly flew through the air, sending the setters (young men known as pin-boys) scurrying for cover. By 1912, numerous complaints had arisen over errant pins crashing through windows and endangering passers-by on the street below. Ryan responded with innovation, adding a rubber collar to the belly of each pin. This served as a shock absorber and lowered the decibel level. Players also saw their scores soar, since the added girth of the collar allowed the ball to connect with greater frequency. In 1921, Bill Bromfield knocked off the first perfect game, scoring 450 points. The sport thrived and "trundlers" were soon flocking to bowling centres across the country.

In later years, Tommy Ryan found other diversions to capture his imagination, including judging beauty pageants and conducting antique auctions from his sprawling three-storey mansion, once the home of farm implement mogul, Hart Massey. At the age of seventy-eight, he spearheaded the drive that ended an eighty-five-year ban on Sunday sports in Toronto. A decade later, in 1960, he was honoured at Canada's first Civic Bowling Week celebrations. When he died the following year, he did not regret the lost profits he might have taken from the game. In the words of Tommy Ryan, "I don't care, as long as people are having fun."

TURN HIM LOOSE!

Calgary, 1912 — There is an old prairie adage that suggests, "There never was a horse that can't be rode, or ever a cowboy that can't be throwed." Ultimately, that is the spirit of rodeo — a contest between human and animal, which combines sport and entertainment with commerce and romanticism for the Old West. There have been many confrontations between those with two legs and those with four, but when Tom Three Persons met a black bronco named Cyclone, the ride went down in history.

Three Persons, a Blood Indian from Cardston, Alberta, was the only Canadian to make it to the finals of the saddle bronc riding competition at the first Calgary Stampede in 1912. Under the guiding hand of vaudeville rodeo maestro Guy Weadick of Wyoming, hundreds of cowboys showed up to vie for prize money put up by Alberta's Big Four — Pat Burns, A.E. Cross, George Burns and A.J. Maclean — but the majority were experienced American cowboys and hard-riding Mexican vaqueros. To make matters worse, Three Persons drew Cyclone, a horse that had thrown 127 cowboys in seven years of bucking. There was no eight- or ten-second time limit in those days; the ride simply ended when the horse stopped bucking or the rider stopped riding. Cyclone had never stopped.

Three Persons was the last competitor in the event and thousands crowded the stands to watch. The infield betting held that the brawny twenty four year old would not last four jumps. With his gravity-defying leaps, Cyclone had already beaten one of the best cowboys in the country, Pirmez Creek's Clem Gardner. When Three Persons shouted "turn him loose" there was no turning back.

"Bucking, twisting, swapping ends and resorting to every artifice of the outlaw, Cyclone swept across the field," reported the *Calgary Herald*. "The Indian was jarred from one side of the saddle to the other, but as the crowds cheered themselves hoarse he settled every time into the saddle and waited for the next lurch or twist."

When bucking did not work, Cyclone turned to his trademark vertical rearing tactics, but Three Persons was ready for the acrobatics. He let out a bellow that brought Cyclone down to earth. Soon the pair were galloping across the field like old friends in a hurry.

Spectators cheered wildly and hundreds of native people galloped their own horses up and down the field in celebration. When he was inducted into the Canadian Rodeo Historical Association's Hall of Fame in 1983 it was acknowledged that "Tom Three Persons became a hero that day."

For years afterward, Three Persons returned to the Calgary Stampede, but never won another world title. He became a successful rancher, raising purebred Hereford cattle and thoroughbred horses. At sixty, he suffered a broken pelvic bone while trying to stop a young horse from breaking a corral, and he died three years later in 1949. It was the largest funeral ever seen in Cardston. In his obituary, the *Albertan* said that when Tom Three Persons tamed Cyclone he "rode into a niche in the hearts of westerners who will remember him as long as cattle graze in the foothills and cowboys ride after them."

SIMPLY THE BEST

Edmonton, 1915 — In the history of sport there has never been anything like Alberta's legendary Edmonton Commercial Graduates women's basketball team. The statistics speak for themselves: they won 96 percent of their games, held the title of "World Champions" for seventeen consecutive years and had a winning streak that lasted for 147 consecutive games. Scarcely a generation after James Naismith invented the game, his countrywomen formed a team that many contend was "simply the best."

"They are champions because they are the most whole-hearted, sport-loving girls that it would be possible to find," said the man who served the Grads as both teacher and coach. "They have won because the spirit of the Prairies is born and bred in them."

Basketball had evolved considerably from its peach basket beginnings, when Percy Page introduced the game to his girls' physical education class at Edmonton Commercial High School in 1914. Enthusiasm ran high when the school team won their first city title.

In 1915, Page organized a senior team which combined the talents of students and former students who wanted to continue playing. In their first season the Grads won the Alberta title, and they held onto it for twenty-four out of the next twenty-five years.

Their horizons broadened in 1922, when the first Canadian women's basketball championships were held in London, Ontario. Once again the Grads won on their first try. They retained the title for eighteen years.

The Underwood Typewriter Company put up a challenge cup in 1923, which was tantamount to the women's world championships since it involved teams from all provinces and every state. The Edmonton Grads never lost a series. When the team disbanded in 1940, the Underwood Trophy was awarded to its only winner.

The Grads had an uncanny cohesion and coach Page ran a tight ship, establishing a "farm system" that gradually moved players from high-school basketball positions on to the Gradettes, and finally the Grads.

Page insisted on the importance of physical conditioning — two practices weekly during the season, and no drinking or smoking. "You must play basketball, think basketball and dream basketball," he told his players, and they rewarded him with complete loyalty, and dazzling shooting skills.

"He's a perfect dear, but we don't have to do a thing he tells us unless we like," one of the Grads once remarked.

Wherever they played the Grads drew big crowds. Over the years they travelled more than 200,000 kilometres, attending four Olympic-related competitions in Paris, Amsterdam, Los Angeles and Berlin.

Unfortunately for Canada, basketball did not become a sanctioned event until 1976. In their exhibition matches at the 1924, 1928, 1932 and 1936 Olympic Games, the Grads never lost a match and they out-scored their opponents a remarkable 1,863 points to 297.

The team financed itself from gate proceeds, but the players never received a penny. Their only motivation was a love of basketball. When the all-time high-scorer, Noel MacDonald, was inducted into the Canadian Sports Hall of Fame in 1971, she admitted that she was "not altogether comfortable" at being singled out. "We were a team," she said. "We were closer than sisters."

As part of the war effort, the team's playing facility was appropriated by the Royal Canadian Air Force in 1940. The Edmonton Grads disbanded — every one of them a winner.

Percy Page went into politics and ended up becoming the Lieutenant Governor of Alberta in 1959.

James Naismith was a long-time fan of the Grads. He called them "the finest basketball team that ever stepped out on a floor."

The Grads took their compliments with grace. In everyday life they were filing clerks, stenographers and school teachers. When alumnus Winnie Martin was asked if she thought Naismith would have changed the game in any way after seeing the Grads play, she responded: "I think it's obvious. He'd have put the basket higher."

SIR BARTON
AND THE COMMANDER

Windsor, Ontario, 1920 — It was billed as "The Race of the Century." Two stallions would meet in Windsor, Ontario, before a crowd estimated at 30,000 to determine who was the fastest horse of all.

Representing the United States was the great Man o' War, who had won nineteen out of twenty races and had been voted the "Three-Year-Old of the Year."

Canadian hopes were on another chestnut horse, Sir Barton, the first winner of racing's Triple Crown, owned by Montreal millionaire Commander John Kenneth Levenson Ross.

Commander Ross was one of the most flamboyant characters ever seen in Canadian horse racing. Born in Lindsay, Ontario, he was the son of railway baron, James Ross, who earned his fortune as one of the "Big Four" who blasted the Canadian Pacific Railway through the Rocky Mountains. The same vigour his father applied to making money, his son applied to spending it.

An only son, Ross was educated at Bishop's College School in Lennoxville, Quebec, and earned a Bachelor of Science degree from McGill University, where he was best-known as a star lineman on the football team. While the father was grooming the heir apparent in matters of business, the son took time out to learn sleight-of-hand card tricks and delighted in producing an ace of spades from the left ear of any new acquaintance.

As the assistant general manager of the Dominion Coal Company, which his father purchased in 1901, Ross divided his time between head office in Montreal and the mines in Sydney, Nova Scotia. At his summer home in Cape Breton, he devoted himself largely to sailing his seventy-five-foot yacht and fishing for world-record tuna.

Ross's father died in 1913, leaving an estate estimated at sixteen million dollars, which his son would inherit when he turned forty in 1916. In the interim, the will provided a generous annual allowance of $75,000 and allowed Ross to use up to one million dollars for purposes of business or property acquisition. Ross seems to have interpreted this liberally, using it to acquire a 106-foot, custom-built motor yacht.

When the First World War broke out, Ross loaned the yacht to the sadly undershipped Canadian navy and donated $500,000 to the government toward the war effort. In the early days of the war, he bought two more steam yachts and gave them to the navy.

Ross served on one, *Grilse*, as a reserve lieutenant and commanded the ship on patrols between Halifax and Bermuda for two years. Then the government seconded him to serve as Chairman of the Dominion Board of Pension Commissioners. In 1917, the navy promoted Ross to the rank of commander in recognition of his generous contributions.

Ross began acquiring race horses in 1914. Two years later, he built a million-dollar breeding stable at Verchères on the St. Lawrence River. The barns were painted in his racing colours — black and orange — and he had a string of nearly fifty horses.

Once the operation was in full swing, Ross was known to ferry his friends to racetracks in his private railway car. He was also known for his bold wagers.

In 1918, a front-page headline in a Chicago sporting journal reported that a Canadian navy officer had bet $50,000 on a horse named Canso and parlayed the winning bet into a million dollars.

The New York Jockey Club reportedly asked Commander Ross to ease up.

That same summer, Ross bought a winless, American-bred, two-year-old colt named Sir Barton for $10,000. Samuel Riddle of Philadelphia paid half that amount for an awkward colt named Man o' War.

The first Canadian owner to win the Kentucky Derby was not in attendance on the day of the 1919 run for the roses. Ross was in Toronto attending his dying father-in-law when Sir Barton led the field of twelve by five lengths for the win. Another Ross Stable horse, Billy Kelly, finished second. Then four days later, Sir Barton won the Preakness Stakes at Baltimore.

For a horse who had never won a race before, whose hooves were so "shelly" (brittle) that he could lose four shoes in a race, Sir Barton was on a prestigious winning streak. That June he won the Belmont Stakes in a three-horse race. Although now recognized as the first winner of racing's "Triple Crown," the designation and trophy for Sir Barton's achievement was not created until several decades later.

Commander Ross cleared more than half a million dollars in 1918 and 1919 between the purses his horses won and the bets he successfully wagered. He established a second breeding farm in Maryland and became one of the top winning owners in America.

In 1920, the racing world clamoured for a match race between Sir Barton and the sensational Man o' War. American racetracks vied to host the spectacle, but Kenilworth Park in Windsor won the day by offering the largest payday racing had ever seen at the time — a $75,000 purse to the winner. General admission tickets were five dollars apiece.

On the afternoon of October 12, the two horses met. Man o' War was a year younger than Sir Barton and he was the crowd's betting favourite.

Sir Barton had the rail position and for a brief instant at the start of the race his head was even with the rangy stallion that was affectionately known to America as "Big Red."

Alas, the day did not belong to Sir Barton.

He finished seven lengths behind Man o' War, who broke the track record by six seconds even though his jockey had him on a tight rein.

Man o' War retired to stud after the race. Sir Barton never regained his stature as a winner. He, too, was put out to stud, but he failed to sire any notable winners.

The only Canadian-owned horse to win the Triple Crown was shuffled off to the breeding shed at a U.S. cavalry remount farm, where his fee was a measly ten dollars. Sir Barton died in 1937 and he is remembered every year at Pimlico Raceway in a stakes race named in his honour.

Like his stallion, Commander Ross faced setbacks in the years that followed the race. He spent lavishly, remodelling his forty-room mansion on Peel Street in Montreal and holding a "house-warming" party that included the Duke of Windsor, who was then the Prince of Wales. But the expenses of horse racing, the maintenance of the breeding farms, the thirty or more servants, the seven or eight Rolls-Royces and all of the yachts began taking their toll. What he later termed "unwise investments" led to Ross's bankruptcy in 1928.

It seems Ross had fallen into the thrall of an American promoter and financier who had involved him in vastly unprofitable investments in oil. "I had never seen an oil field in my life. I don't pretend to know anything about oil or oil wells," he told a meeting of his creditors.

A story in the Montreal *Star* headlined "Most Regrettable Local Insolvency," described Ross as "victimized by designing people," and recounted his many philanthropic contributions. In a dozen years, Ross managed to whittle his sixteen-million-dollar legacy to $300 in cash.

Fortuitously, a codicil in his father's will had set up a trust fund of one million dollars to provide income for Ross during his lifetime and later for his two children.

With a guaranteed income of at least $50,000 a year, the former millionaire was able to live comfortably on a sunny estate in Montego Bay, Jamaica, which was later sold to another flamboyant Canadian millionaire, Max Aitken (Lord Beaverbrook).

Commander J.K.L. Ross died, horseless, in 1951.

THE BIG TRAIN
THAT COULD

Toronto, 1922 — Although his formal schooling never went beyond the eighth grade, Lionel Conacher may have owed one of Canada's most illustrious sporting careers to the education system. There were ten children in the Conacher family. Money was tight and the working-class streets of Toronto were rough and tumble. A wise headmaster at Jesse Ketchum Public School, where Lionel was a student, realized that mandating a program of organized sports could help preserve some sense of order. Through sports, young Lionel saw a way out of poverty, and he excelled in every one he tried. When he was named Canada's Male Athlete of the Half-Century in 1950, it was for outstanding achievement in wrestling, boxing, football, lacrosse, hockey, rugby and baseball.

Conacher played football in the Toronto Rugby League when he was twelve. At sixteen he won the Ontario 125-pound wrestling championship. By 1920, the twenty-year-old Conacher had boxed himself to the light-heavyweight championship of Canada. The following year, he stood his ground in an exhibition match with world heavyweight champion Jack Dempsey.

Football was his favourite game. He could run the 100 yards in less than ten seconds. When the Toronto Argos defeated the Edmonton Eskimos 23 to 0 in the 1921 Grey Cup, Conacher contributed fifteen points.

No one sport was big enough for Conacher. On one legendary day in 1922 he hit a triple in the final inning of the Ontario baseball championship for the winning Hillcrest team. Still holding the victory wreath, he jumped into a car, changed uniforms and led the Toronto Maitlands to a provincial championship in lacrosse.

Hockey was where the money was, and Conacher turned pro in 1925 as a member of the Pittsburgh Pirates in the expanding National Hockey League. He had only been skating for seven years. "I laced on skates for the first time at the age of sixteen, and you'll never know the humiliation and utter weariness of the long hours which I spent on the rink with younger and much more skilled players before I won a post in junior circles," Conacher admitted. He compensated for his awkwardness on the ice by becoming a great tactician, stopping pucks with his knee and calculating angles with split-second timing. There was always some steam left in the player who was known as "the Big Train." In his eleven-year NHL career as a defenceman he scored 80 goals and 105 assists. His name was engraved on the Stanley Cup twice. By the end of his playing days, Conacher's battle scars chronicled a saga of victory and confrontation. He bore as many as 600 stitches patchworked over his six-foot-one frame, including 150 from the shoulders up. His nose had been rearranged eight times.

In 1937, Conacher moved to the political backbenches as the Liberal MPP for Toronto Bracondale. For twelve years, constituents brought their problems to the office he kept just a block from where he was born. Appropriately, he served as chairman of the Ontario Athletic Commission and devoted himself to championing needs he understood, such as recreational facilities in city parks.

In 1949, the federal Liberals pitted popular hero Lionel Conacher against Communist Party leader Tim Buck for the working-class Toronto Trinity riding. Conacher held that seat until he died.

It was May 24, 1954, and the Members of Parliament were playing their annual softball game with the parliamentary press corps. In the sixth inning, Conacher lifted a flyball for a triple. He was racing to third base when his heart failed. Twenty minutes later, "the Big Train" stopped forever.

GILDING THE
SASKATOON LILY

Amsterdam Olympics, 1928 — The high jump was the last
event in which Canada had an entry in the Ninth Olympiad.
As nineteen-year-old Ethel Catherwood attempted to stretch
and flex in the chilled Dutch air, the Canadian women's
team already led the forty-nation points standing. Cameras
poised to capture the moment in which the lanky and lithe
Catherwood was suspended over the bar. She was the most
photographed athlete at the 1928 Games, and she remains
the only Canadian woman to have won an individual gold
medal in Olympic track and field competition. *The New York
Times* called her "the prettiest of all the girl athletes." Canadians knew her as "the Saskatoon Lily."

Ethel Catherwood was born in Haldimand County,
Ontario, in 1909, but she was raised in Saskatchewan. Her ability in what was then known as the "running high jump"
became evident when she entered the Saskatoon city championships in the summer of 1926 and equalled the Canadian
record of 1.511 metres (4 feet, 11½ inches). That Labour Day,
the third-year high-school student went to Regina and broke
the world high jump record. "Her performance overshad-
owed the championship events for men," noted her hometown

newspaper the *Saskatoon Phoenix*. "Even the auto races failed to furnish the thrill that spectators derived when she beat her old record."

Mining millionaire Teddy Oke, a noted patron of amateur sport, quickly transported Ethel and her sister, Ginger, to Toronto. He sent them both to business school and gave them jobs in his brokerage offices, which were largely staffed by female athletes. Catherwood became a member of the Parkdale Ladies Athletic Club and Oke hired veteran coach Walter Knox to hone her technique.

Sportswriters were soon as smitten with the long-legged Western Canadian as Oke. "From the instant this tall, graceful girl from the Prairies tossed aside her long, flowing cloak of purple and made her first leap, the fans fell for her," wrote one. "A flower-like face of rare beauty above a long, slim body clad in pure white . . . she looked like a tall, strange lily — and was immediately christened by the crowd 'The Saskatoon Lily.'"

The Lily blossomed at the final Olympic trials held during a heat wave in Halifax in July of 1928. Five thousand spectators showed up to cheer what the *Halifax Chronicle* called "the greatest collection of women athletic stars in Canada." Ethel Catherwood jumped 1.6 metres (5 feet 3 inches), reclaiming the world record from South Africa's Marjorie Clark and setting a mark that stood as the Canadian record until 1954.

The 1928 Olympics were a triumph for Canada's six-member women's team. By the time Catherwood's high jump event took place on the final day, the track team had taken one gold medal, two silver medals and a bronze. All eyes in the stadium focused on the Canadian beauty, who carried a rag doll and a ukulele with her wherever she went.

There were twenty-three contestants in the high jump, including Holland's own Carolina Gisolf who had beaten Catherwood's world record by a fraction of an inch. Wrapped in her red Hudson's Bay blanket, the Canadian contender tried to stay warm between jumps on the uncharacteristically cold August day. Only the competitors were allowed on the field, so Catherwood had to fend for herself until friendly members of the Belgian team took it upon themselves to cloak her after each jump. She only placed seventeenth in the qualifying events, but in the afternoon final her grace and co-ordination proved unstoppable.

The leap that gilded Catherwood was a full half-inch less than her personal best, but that final gold medal gave the Canadian women's team an overall victory. "She was lifted to the shoulders of Canadians, athletes and spectators alike, and smilingly received the plaudits of the huge crowd," crowed the Toronto *Evening Telegraph*.

The first Olympic Games in which Canadian women participated was almost their last. Pundits from the Pope to McGill University's Dr. A.S. Lamb argued that strenuous sport was physiologically and psychologically unsuitable for women. The proof of the performance of Catherwood and her teammates resoundingly refuted such theories.

After her hero's homecoming welcome, Catherwood was courted for stardom, but she rejected Hollywood's beckon. In 1929, she and her sister moved to the United States, where Ethel married and settled in San Francisco. Her benefactor, Teddy Oke, was said to be so disheartened by the departure of his dream athlete that he abandoned plans to build a women's sports palace in Toronto.

The once-soaring high jumper never competed again.

OUR PERCY GOES FOR GOLD

Amsterdam, 1928 — Few Canadians had heard of Vancouver's Percy Williams when he crouched in the blocks preparing to sprint against the best runners in the world at the 1928 Olympics in Amsterdam. His double victory in the 100- and 200-metre track events stunned the world. In 1964, Saskatchewan's Harry Jerome would flash for silver in the 100 metre and Ontario's Ben Johnson would lose a gold in the sports humiliation of the 1988 Games, but Williams took home the ultimate prize in both of his events.

Percy Williams was an unlikely Olympian. He suffered from a damaged heart as a result of childhood rheumatic fever and he had no all-consuming ambition to be a runner. When his coach, Bob Granger, first spotted Williams at a high-school meet in 1926 he described him as "a puny 110-pound [50-kilogram] kid."

Nevertheless, Granger saw the spark of talent. When he took Williams under his wing it was with the express resolve to win Olympic gold in 1928. The coach had theories about training and conditioning to go with his vast experience. The modest protegé took instruction without questioning.

Modern coaches might well question some of Granger's techniques. He made Williams give up swimming because he felt it affected his speed, and instead of gruelling regimens Granger believed in conserving energy. For example, it has been reported that on a cold day before a race, Granger would dress Williams' body with coconut butter and force him to wear layers of track suits and sweaters to conserve body heat.

Williams ran most of his races in British Columbia, and by the spring of 1928 he was clocking some remarkable times for a schoolboy. When he went east to compete in the Canadian Olympic trials at Hamilton, Ontario, in 1928, he won the 200-metre race. His victory in the 100 metres equalled the 10.6-second Olympic record of the day.

Still, only Granger believed that Williams had a chance against the best in the world. When the Canadian Olympic Committee refused to pay his passage to Holland, Granger worked his way across the Atlantic on a cattle boat, arriving three days after the team.

Williams was drilled in technique right up to the eve of the races. In his hotel room, Granger piled a mattress against one wall and rehearsed starting procedures, sending the now 121-pound (55-kilogram) Williams bursting across the room into the bedding.

The practice paid off on July 30th. The unknown underdog shot off the blocks leaving five world-class runners behind him for the entire 100 metres. The stadium erupted. Canadian Olympic chairman P.J. Mulqueen rushed onto the field and kissed Williams, whose first words after the race were said to be: "Won't Granger be pleased."

Two days later, the focused Canadian won the 200 metres in a driving finish. General Douglas MacArthur, then the president of the U.S. Olympic Committee, declared Williams "the greatest sprinter the world has ever known."

Williams' triumphant return was celebrated across the country. In Vancouver, school was let out for the day. Before a cheering throng, Mayor Louis Taylor presented Williams with a sports car and Granger with $500 in gold. The favoured snack of the day became the Our Percy chocolate bar.

In the following two years, Williams defeated all of the great American sprinters. He set world records of 4.9 seconds in the forty-five-yard dash and 10.3 seconds for the 100 metres.

On August 23, 1930, during the 100-yard final at the British Empire Games in Hamilton, Williams pulled a muscle in his left thigh. Although he won the race, the injured leg was never right again. He failed to qualify in either of his specialties at the 1932 Olympics.

The slim and unassuming young man, who had come out of nowhere to beat the established athletes of the world, quietly dropped out of competitive sport and devoted himself to a business career in Vancouver.

With the glory behind him, Williams admitted no regrets in a 1954 interview. "I was simply bewildered by it all," he said. "I didn't like running. I was so glad to get out of it all."

THE COMPLETE
ATHLETE

Amsterdam, 1928 — She won Olympic gold in 1928 and was named Canadian Woman Athlete of the Half-Century, but little Fanny Rosenfeld never had a coach. Popularly known as "Bobbie," she has been described as "the complete athlete." In fact, her biographers suggest that the most efficient way to summarize her career is to say that she was not proficient at swimming. In hockey, baseball, basketball, tennis and track and field, Rosenfeld was a champion.

She was born in 1903 in Russia and came to Barrie, Ontario, as an infant with her parents. Early on she attracted the attention of the sporting establishment when she beat the reigning Canadian 100-yard champion, Rosa Grosse, at a small track meet in Beaverton, Ontario. Later, Rosenfeld and Grosse shared the world record for 100 yards at eleven seconds flat.

In 1922, Rosenfeld moved to Toronto and entered active competition. Constance Hennessey, one of the founding members of the Toronto Ladies Athletic Club, recalled the determination of the diminutive Rosenfeld. "She did not look powerful, but she was wiry and quick. Above all she went after everything with full force."

Although hockey was her first love, Rosenfeld's prowess was multi-dimensional. In 1924, she won the Toronto grass-court tennis championship and throughout the 1920s she played on several Ontario and eastern Canadian championship basketball teams.

In 1925, her "club" won the points title at the Ontario Track and Field Meet, with firsts in the discus, the 220 yards, the 120-yard low hurdles and seconds in the javelin and the 100-yard dash. This was particularly impressive since the "club," which was sponsored by the chocolate factory where Rosenfeld worked, had only one "member" — Bobbie Rosenfeld.

Rosenfeld established Canadian records in the long jump, standing broad jump and the discus which stood until the 1950s. Wearing her brother's t-shirt and swim trunks, and her father's socks, she thrilled 5,000 spectators at the Olympic Trials in Halifax. She was a character, and the people loved her.

The Amsterdam Olympics of 1928 marked the first time women were admitted to track and field competition — overcoming arguments that vigorous physical activity would damage female reproductive organs and was "unseemly."

The Ninth Olympiad was the highlight of Bobbie Rosenfeld's career. As the anchor runner in the four-member, 400-metre relay team, Rosenfeld brought home a gold. Photographers could barely capture a picture of the exuberant Canadian team, as the women celebrated in a whirl of exhilarated motion.

The 100-yard dash was another matter. Three Canadians faced two Germans and an American. Tension was high, and Rosenfeld's undefeated teammate, Myrtle Cook, was disqualified after two false starts, as was one of the

German competitors. The race was over in 12.5 seconds and witnesses suggested that Rosenfeld was robbed of a gold in a tight finish that placed her second to the American runner.

Ultimately, it may be her fifth place finish in the 800 metres that shows the true mettle that Bobbie Rosenfeld was made from. Although she had not trained at that distance, Rosenfeld was entered to encourage seventeen-year-old teammate, Jean Thompson. From ninth position, the more mature runner watched as the teenager began to falter, and she moved up to coax her on. Then, as team manager Alexandrine Gibb noted: "She refused to go ahead of the youngster." Thompson took fourth. Rosenfeld had quietly demonstrated the generous spirit of a champion.

Less than a year later, she was stricken with arthritis. Although bed ridden for eight months and on crutches for a year, in 1931 she was back as the leading home-run hitter in a major softball league. The following winter, she was the outstanding player in Ontario women's hockey.

In 1932, Rosenfeld coached the Canadian women's track team at the British Empire Games. Arthritis forced her to retire from active sports in 1933. She became one of the first inductees to the Canadian Sports Hall of Fame in 1949. In the same year, a Canadian Press poll named her Woman Athlete of the Half-Century.

Rosenfeld blazed many trails. For over twenty years she wrote a sports column in the *Globe and Mail*, covering everything from horse-racing to wrestling with an irreverent humour. When she died in 1969, the newspaper paid tribute to her as "that rarity, a natural athlete."

"DON'T LET
THE CRIPPLED KIDS DOWN"

Lake Ontario, 1954 — Before she started her marathon swim across Lake Ontario, Marilyn Bell said she thought she would scream if she felt an eel on her body. But when it happened — when a pencil-long lamprey eel fixed its disc-shaped excuse for a mouth to the stomach of her black silk and nylon bathing suit, in the middle of the night, in the pitch blackness of Lake Ontario — Marilyn just hauled back and punched the sucker. Three more lampreys would assail her thighs, but the young woman calmly beat them off and kept on swimming.

There were other slippery creatures in the boats that surrounded her, but Marilyn never had to hit a newspaper reporter. They were too busy battling among themselves for her story. She was headline news; an unknown schoolgirl attempting to become the first swimmer to conquer Lake Ontario.

When she kissed her parents and dove off of a retaining wall in Youngstown, New York, at 11:07 p.m. on September 8, 1954, Marilyn Bell was a sixteen-year-old grade 12 student at Toronto's Loretto College School. Just 155 centimetres (five-feet-one-inch) and 54 kilograms (119 pounds), she was a finely tuned, blue-eyed pixie with a toothsome smile.

Her father, Syd, taught her to swim when she was four. By the age of ten, she was winning awards and medals. At thirteen she was teaching swimming lessons to children who had been crippled by polio and at fourteen she became a professional instructor.

Training under Gus Ryder, one of the top coaches in the country, she won numerous amateur races. As a teen-aged professional, she was the first woman to complete the twenty-six-mile Atlantic City Marathon.

Still, veteran sports reporter Trent Frayne once noted: "Marilyn looked like somebody's baby-sitter."

The whole idea of the swim started with the Canadian National Exhibition, which hoped to attract crowds by featuring an American champion in a solo swim. They paid thirty-four-year-old, Californian Florence Chadwick $2,500 in advance, with a guarantee of $7,500 if she succeeded. The Toronto *Telegram* co-sponsored the promotion of the event. If there was a story in Chadwick's attempt, the *Tely* would have the inside edge.

However, marathon swimming was now considered past its prime. In 1927, seventeen-year-old Torontonian George Young gained some margin of fame for swimming the Catalina Channel in California. The Catalina Kid's last successful marathon had gone virtually unnoticed in 1931.

When Marilyn Bell and St. Thomas, Ontario's Winnie Roach Leusler, twenty-eight, announced their plans to challenge Chadwick for free, the *Tely* wasn't much interested in the story, even though Winnie was the only Canadian who had swum the English Channel.

Gus Ryder offered both the *Telegram* and its arch rival, the Toronto *Star*, the opportunity to sponsor his swimmer and help underwrite costs including the $700 per day boat rental. The *Star* seized the opportunity. Marilyn also had the moral support of *Star* sports reporter Alexandrine Gibb, founder of the Women's Amateur Athletic Federation of Canada.

The race would begin when Florence Chadwick entered the water. Marilyn had made it known that her only fears were eels and swimming in the dark. For two days, weather delayed the start. When it finally cleared, Chadwick announced that she would start swimming shortly before midnight.

Marilyn Bell had not slept all day. Now she was facing 50 kilometres (32 miles) of unlit, open water. She was only seven minutes behind Chadwick when she started, sprinting after Chadwick with her white bathing cap bobbing in the searchlights. Underneath it, tucked in her short blond hair, Marilyn had a four-leaf clover.

Five hours later, after stroking against the wind and confronting waves twice her height, a gaunt Marilyn treaded water while coach Ryder passed her a cup of corn syrup on a stick. She told him she was numb and cold, but he assured her things would be better once the sun came up.

In the light of day, Marilyn looked rough; she was crying and her body ached. This time Coach Ryder passed her a cup of liniment to rub on her aching legs. The other swimmers were already out of the race, Flo overcome by nausea and Minnie pulled sobbing and cramp-riddled after two attempts.

At 10:30 a.m., after she had spent almost twelve hours in the water and gone more than twenty-four hours without sleep, Ryder pulled out a blackboard and wrote "FLO IS OUT" to offer Marilyn some encouragement. By noon, he turned to a more diabolical psychological ploy.

The blackboard now read: "DON'T LET THE CRIPPLED KIDS DOWN."

Radio stations announced progress reports every half hour, while boatloads of reporters swarmed to get close enough for a photograph. People began flocking to the lakefront. Marilyn's classmates joined them, flowers in hand. By the time rush hour hit, the whole town knew the name "Marilyn Bell."

Having lost their American drawing card, CNE officials announced that the $7,500 Flo Chadwick had forfeited would now go to Marilyn if she finished.

Gus Ryder dutifully wrote the sum on his blackboard, but Marilyn could barely see it through her half-closed, bloodshot eyes.

Safety concerns grew amid a mounting flotilla of watercraft ranging from the tugboat *Ned Hanlan* to rowboats. The Toronto Harbour Commission sent lifeguards in dinghies to row alongside the wearying Marilyn. The waves had calmed but strong currents in the lake pushed her westward. Her stroke had slowed to fifty per minute.

Reporters in the Toronto *Star* boat ferried a fellow swimming instructor, Joan Cooke, out for moral support. Wearing a blouse and pedal-pushers, she swam to the coaching lifeboat and shivered out calls of encouragement to her friend.

Around five o'clock, Marilyn announced that her legs were totally numb and she had constant pain in her stomach. At Ryder's urging, Joan stripped down to her bra and panties, joining a dozing Marilyn in the lake, where she cajoled the exhausted teenager into following her pace for a few minutes.

As darkness fell, chill winds picked up. CNE officials became concerned that instead of landing at the Exhibition grounds where pink flares lit the sky, Marilyn seemed to be on a course to the west and Sunnyside Park. With just three kilometres (approximately two miles) to go, Syd Bell screamed at officials to "get out of here." He was ready to take his sobbing child out of the water, but Gus Ryder shouted to Marilyn, asking her for just fifteen minutes more.

A huge headline in the *Tely* read "ONLY YARDS TO GO." Across Canada, radio audiences were glued to their sets. A crowd estimated at 250,000 whooped and roared, while the motley armada on the lake let off whistles and sirens. The only thing missing was a fledgling media called television. The local CBC station opted to cover a social event rather than the human interest story of the year.

Unbeknownst to Marilyn, the Harbour Commissioner had decreed that Marilyn's swim would be deemed successful if she reached the offshore breakwater. After almost twenty hours in the water, her left hand touched the concrete at 8:06 p.m. Fireworks filled the sky. Two lifeguards had a difficult time removing Marilyn from the water. She kept insisting she was "all right."

Marilyn didn't know that she had legitimately succeeded in her goal until she was in the back of an ambulance.

Right down to the wire, the *Telegram* and the *Star* vied for the story. *Tely* editor J.D. MacFarlane even went so far as to have a female reporter disguised as a nurse attempt to lure Bell into the *Telegram* ambulance and take her away. The attempted kidnapping was foiled when *Star* reporters discovered that the untended *Tely* ambulance had been left at curbside with the keys in the ignition. They moved it a few blocks, pocketing the keys and the distributor cap for good measure. That didn't stop the *Tely*'s intrepid "Nurse" Dorothy Horwath from trying to sneak aboard the *Star*'s official ambulance. She was ejected. However, the next day, the *Telegram* appeared to have scooped the *Star*. It ran a first-person story next to the signature "Marilyn Bell," which had been lifted from the inside cover of one of her school books.

Marilyn became an instant celebrity, receiving $50,000 in prize money, gifts and contracts. Despite concerns about her health, she was in fine shape after a few days' rest. The following year, she crossed the English Channel. In 1956, she swam the Juan de Fuca Strait, reaching Victoria, B.C., in eleven hours and thirty-five minutes on her second attempt.

"It's okay if you fail at something," she once said, "as long as you don't give up — as long as you say — 'Okay, I will try it again!'"

Since 1954, more than thirty Canadian swimmers have crossed Lake Ontario. Their names are etched on a monument at Niagara-on-the-Lake and the list continues to grow. After the tragic loss of an American swimmer in 1974, all races are carefully monitored for the safety of the athletes. Some swimmers, such as Kim Middleton and John Scott, have made the swim more than once. Vicki Keith holds the record at five, including one all-butterfly crossing and a remarkable two-way swim in 1987.

Twenty years after Marilyn Bell's epic effort, another sixteen year old became the second Canadian woman to make the swim. Mrs. Marilyn Bell-DiLascio, the "Queen of the Lake," was on hand to congratulate Cindy Nicholas on a record time of fifteen hours and ten minutes.

"It's your lake now," she said with the aplomb of a champion.

WHO WAS THAT
MASKED MAN?

New York, November 1, 1959 — Although it looked like something out of a Stephen King nightmare, there came a time when Jacques Plante would not step near a goal crease without his homemade face mask. The immortal Montreal Canadiens' goalie's invention literally changed the face of hockey.

Plante was a player who dared to be different. Wearing protective headgear went against all of the game's "macho" traditions. He also had a habit of knitting in the dressing room before games.

As the oldest of eleven children in a Shawinigan, Quebec, family during the Depression, his youthful education included learning to cook and sew and make his own sweaters.

A sports columnist recalled seeing twenty-two-year-old Plante wearing a toque and jersey of his own creation when he was playing with the Montreal Royals. Plante continued to knit throughout his career, contending that it helped him relax and refine his supple hands.

Throughout his career Plante was considered something of an eccentric and a loner. Some suggested that he was a hypochondriac. In fact, he suffered from asthma. To avoid smoke-filled rooms, he would often divorce himself from the team, especially when they were on the road.

He was not one to mince words, particularly on the topic of the stress of goalkeeping. "How would you like it, if you were doing your job in an office and you made a little mistake?" he once asked. "Suddenly a bright light flashed on, a loud buzzer went off, and 18,000 people started screaming: 'Get the bum out of there!'"

On the ice, Plante was a study in focus. When a teammate scored on him in practice, he would stare straight ahead as though the puck had not gone in.

Plante revolutionized the net minder's position by pioneering the move behind the net to stop the puck and leaving it for a defenceman or passing it off to a teammate along the boards. His risky style outside of the "cage" unsettled coaches and drove fans to distraction. The press nicknamed him "Jake the Snake."

Goaltenders of that era often suffered from the pressure of "seeing too much rubber," a sporting euphemism for laceration, concussion and general contusion caused by the repetitious collision of speeding pucks and goaltenders' skulls. Plante finally saw too much "rubber" during a game at Madison Square Gardens on November 1, 1959, when a powerful shot by the New York Rangers' Andy Bathgate redefined his profile, inflicting a deep gash that took seven stitches to close.

After receiving a total of 200 previous stitches in the face, Plante decided he had paid his dues to the gods of the national sport and stubbornly held his own against Canadiens' coach Toe Blake, who believed a player had to "fight for his life" to play well.

That night, with his face sewn from nose to lip, Plante agreed to return to the ice only if he was allowed to wear the homemade face mask he had been wearing in practices since 1955.

This cream-coloured mask drew a mixture of criticism, admiration and wisecracks. Nevertheless, the team went on to win the game 4-1.

To keep his mask, which he was supposed to give up once he healed, Plante outdid himself by leading an eleven-game winning streak. The Canadiens won the Stanley Cup the following spring.

With a keen sense of showmanship, Plante appeared in public wearing a plastic or fibreglass mask looking like something from a Frankenstein film. And he made the masks as well.

Overall, he produced several models for himself and fellow players, constantly improving their strength, visibility and lightness. In the 1960s and 1970s, protective face masks with captivating graphics flourished in the NHL, and were even the subject of art exhibitions.

Today, the goalie face mask is mandatory gear for anyone courageous and agile enough to assume that critical place in the game.

Jacques Plante's playing career spanned two decades, during which he won the prestigious Vezina Trophy seven times. His legacy is part of hockey's history, and his "moves" are imitated by players from peewee to professional in the game that formally became Canada's national winter sport in 1994.

ADVENTURE
&
DISCOVERY

FOOLS RUSH IN

THE PIRATE ADMIRAL

MANDARIN OF THE MISSISSIPPI

THE SULTAN OF SWASH

A ROYAL CANADIAN LOVE STORY

SERVING IN A HOUSE DIVIDED

ELEMENTARY, MY DEAR

ALBERTOSAURUS, I PRESUME

WHITE LAMA

LION OF THE YUKON

THE SPIRIT OF *TILIKUM*

WHO IS WHAT AND WHAT IS WHO

THESE BOOTS WERE MADE FOR WALKIN'

FOOLS RUSH IN

Kodlunarn Island, Northwest Territories, 1578 — Klondike poet Robert Service said it best when he wrote: "Strange things are done in the midnight sun by the men who moil for gold." In three remarkable voyages to the Canadian Arctic, adventurer and master mariner Martin Frobisher proved this to be true. His quest for gold cost forty lives, and the ton of ore that his crew excavated by hand turned out to be worthless "fool's gold." Even his search for a northwest passage proved to be folly — the "strait" he thought was a transcontinental channel turned out to be the bay that now bears his name.

As a teenager, Frobisher left his native England to crew aboard various Elizabethan expeditions. Like many of the daredevil marine careerists of the day, he dabbled in piracy. Early on, it became apparent that Queen Elizabeth I had a soft spot for Frobisher and his impetuous plundering of Spanish ships, especially since a share of his booty went to Her Majesty's coffers. When Frobisher decided that he wanted to find the legendary northwest passage to Cathay, he took his plan to the Queen's court. "It is still the only thing left undone, whereby a notable mind might be made famous and remarkable," he noted.

Although the privately owned Muscovy Company held the licence for such exploration, the Privy Council prevailed to give Frobisher a crack at it. Michael Lok, a Muscovy director, became Frobisher's champion. He corralled eighteen investors and personally contributed £700 to finance shipbuilding and outfitting.

On June 7, 1576, the Queen waved a farewell. Foul weather drove them to the shores of Greenland, where four men were lost in a pinnace accompanying the two main ships, the *Gabriell* and *Michaell*. Captain Owen Griffyn of the *Michaell* decided to turn back. Arriving in London, he reported the rest lost.

But Frobisher continued, noting that "the sea must needs have an ending." Finally, he found a "great gutte, bay or passage" which he thought was the route to Asia.

Five of Frobisher's seamen disappeared after going to shore with a native. No trace of them was ever found; however, native folk lore indicates that "they died in our land . . . we did not harm them." In an apparent attempt to counter his loss, Frobisher lured an Inuit aboard, whereupon the terrified man bit off his own tongue.

The return to England that October was cause for celebration. Frobisher handed Michael Lok a chunk of glistening black rock which he said was the "first thing that he found in the new land."

Three assayers identified the rock as marcasite, a crystallized version of iron pyrite commonly known as "fool's gold." However, a fourth, an Italian named Agnello, announced that he found gold in the samples. Whether the sample had been doctored or whether gold actually existed remains a subject of debate.

"It is necessary to know how to flatter nature," explained the enigmatic Agnello.

Within months, a second expedition was fully funded. Queen Elizabeth threw £1,000 of her own into the pot and lent Frobisher a ship capable of hauling 200 tons of ore from the newly discovered country that she called "Meta Incognita — Land Unknown." Three ships set out in May of 1577 with strict instructions to search for gold, and gold alone.

By late August they had laboriously retrieved their stockpile of black rock. Frobisher took several Inuit hostage, but hopes of trading them for his missing sailors faded after a skirmish that left an Inuit arrow puncture in the admiral's backside.

Returning to England, the cargo was hoarded under quadruple lock in the Tower of London and at Bristol Castle. Controversy over its value raged, but before it was even assayed, a third expedition was mounted. Fifteen ships departed with instructions to establish a settlement and to return with 2,000 tons of ore.

Ice, fog and mistaken navigation delayed their arrival at Kodlunarn ("Island of the White Men") off the coast of Baffin Island. Fortune frowned again when the bark carrying building materials and supplies for the colony sank. Nevertheless, miners hauled aboard tons of ore in wicker osier baskets. Frobisher left a lime and stone cottage on the island, and buried remaining supplies in one of the mine trenches, with hopes of returning to retrieve more gold.

No triumphant welcome awaited Frobisher in England this time. Assayers had pronounced the whole lot of black rock to be fool's gold. Michael Lok was sent to debtor's prison, the company went bankrupt and the Queen found herself out of pocket for her contributions.

Frobisher would never moil in the Arctic again. He went on to serve as a commander in the defeat of the Spanish

Armada, a role that earned him a knighthood from his all-forgiving Queen.

The first gold rush in the New World ended when the worthless ore from the Arctic barrens was unceremoniously dumped into Bristol Harbour.

THE PIRATE ADMIRAL

Harbour Grace, Newfoundland, 1610 — Maritime outlaw Peter Easton, a short, dark man with a glib tongue and a cruel streak, offset by his good cheer and generosity, remains a folk hero in Newfoundland. The town of Happy Adventure is named for his flagship, and many of his adopted pirates took the Easton name in his honour.

While Samuel de Champlain was still struggling to found his colony at Quebec, commerce was booming in St. John's. The Basques, Portuguese, French and English gathered at the harbour to trade and refit their ships.

Easton's first visit to Newfoundland was during the reign of Queen Elizabeth I. He came with her blessing as a privateer. When James I took the throne, he eliminated the legal plundering of foreign ships by privateers, which led to a massive transition to outright piracy.

Easton made the transition quite successfully. By 1610 he commanded forty ships and he was the recognized leader of a loose federation of pirates engaged in looting ships in the English Channel.

Merchants petitioned the government for relief from Easton's depredations, and Sir Henry Mainwarring prepared a squadron of ships to pursue Easton. However,

Easton avoided any engagement by embarking for New-foundland.

He arrived with ten armed ships and built a fort at Harbour Grace, where he proceeded to recruit — or press — fishermen into his service.

Although he used Harbour Grace primarily as a base, he found time to raid Basque and French ships for their arms, commandeered cargoes of salt fish and "liberated" at least one shipload of French wine.

In Conception Bay he took two ships and thirty ships were pillaged in St. John's. The colony at Cupids was spared after rendering two pigs to the buccaneer. Easton even stored and protected the colonists' valuable fishing supplies and tons of salt during the winter. Often accompanied by trumpeters and minstrels, his loyal followers dubbed him the "Pirate Admiral" and he was perceived as a defender of common folk.

By 1612, Easton had amassed a considerable navy. He is said to have taken 500 fishermen into his employ. *The Happy Adventure* alone required a crew of 150.

Easton's greatest coup of this period was a raid conducted in Puerto Rico. Although the Spanish colony at Moro Castle had withstood an attack by Sir Francis Drake, Easton and his Newfoundland pirates made off with stockpiles of gold and returned with a Spanish ship filled with treasure

Basques had captured his fort in his absence, and the triumphant return ended in a battle on land and sea. Forty-seven men died regaining Easton's fort and they are buried at nearby Bear's Cove, in a place still known as "the Pirates' Graveyard."

Although he was an outlaw in England, Easton applied to King James for a pardon, and apparently paid well for it. In fact, he received two pardons.

En route to his retirement, Easton paused to intercept the Spanish plate fleet which was transporting the annual loot of the empire from Central America.

When he finally settled in a palace on the French Riviera, Easton was one of the richest men in the world. He became a marquis, and lived in the lap of luxury.

Easton never returned to Newfoundland, but his fishermen pirates did and the Easton name remains popular in that part of Newfoundland where pirates once reigned.

MANDARIN OF
THE MISSISSIPPI

Lake Michigan, 1634 — Twenty-year-old Jean Nicollet was fresh from his studies in Paris when he arrived in Quebec in 1618 with a handful of fellow citizens and four priests. He had been hired to live among the native people, and to encourage them to collect furs to trade with the French.

In the early seventeenth century, the beaver-pelt trade created a heated rivalry among the French, English and Dutch. While the English and Dutch tried to attract native people to their trading posts, the French lived among them, learning their languages and customs, and converting them to Christianity.

Samuel de Champlain, who had established the first upriver trading post on the St. Lawrence in 1608, sent Nicollet to Allumette Island, a strategic outpost on the Ottawa River. His assignment was to create friendly relations with the Algonkians, an allegiance the French needed to counteract the Dutch influence with the Iroquois to the south.

For Nicollet it meant entering a strange and harsh new life. He accompanied the Algonkians on canoeing, hunting and trapping expeditions; acquiring their language and adapting to their customs in the process. He carted heavy

pelts through deep snow, ate raw game and learned to portage in bare feet. Although the solitude was not easy for the
young Parisian, Nicollet's endurance, resourcefulness, and
patience earned him the respect of the Algonkians. He was
even able to help them negotiate peace with the Iroquois.

Next he was sent northwest to Lake Nipissing where
he founded a trading post. He spent nine years doing business with various tribes and journeying into the Great
Lakes region where he collected precious geographical information. In the spring, he sent pelts to Quebec.

Since Jacques Cartier's first expedition in 1534, explorers had dreamed of finding a passage to China that would
give Europeans easy access to its spices, silks and precious
metals. One hundred years later, Champlain challenged
Nicollet with a dual mission. The Winnebagoes, who lived
on the western shore of Lake Michigan, had strained relations with the Algonkians and threatened to ally themselves
with the Dutch. Along with his diplomatic duties, Nicollet
was commissioned to verify reports of "the great water"
called "Mississippi," which he presumed led to China. The
Winnebagoes were known as the "people of the sea," and
rumour had it that they "had neither hair nor beards" and
had come from the Orient. Nicollet set off to cross Lakes
Ontario, Erie and Huron by canoe in search of the route to
untold riches.

When the eager explorer reached the Winnebagoes,
the scene may have resembled something out of a slapstick
comedy. Nicollet was so convinced he had reached the gateway to China that he donned a dress of Chinese damask
embroidered with coloured birds and flowers. Dressed for
success and brandishing two pistols, he disembarked.

The Winnebagoes had never seen a European, let
alone one who was dressed to meet Chinese mandarins.

However, once they became accustomed to the charming ambassador, Nicollet convinced them to join in peaceful trade. Unfortunately, Nicollet's "great water" turned out to be Lake Michigan, but he had ventured further west than any other European. Others would follow to chart the heart of the continent.

In 1642, Nicollet accidentally drowned in the icy waters of the St. Lawrence. Ironically, the adventurer who had spent most of his life travelling the lakes, rivers and streams of the New World had never learned to swim.

THE SULTAN OF SWASH

New France, 1690 ——Even as he strode down the gang-plank, Governor Frontenac was a swashbuckling vision. His wig was perfectly curled and his scarlet hat sported an appropriate plume. He exuded courage and confidence and was determined to rule his colonial posting as a "high and mighty lord."

In fact, Louis de Buade, Comte de Palluau et de Frontenac, was a bit of a poseur and deadbeat. Although he was the godson and namesake of King Louis XIII, and had earned a rank equivalent to that of a modern brigadier general, he also managed to amass a debt that has been estimated in excess of 800,000 livres (two million dollars). His arrival in Quebec in 1672 as the new governor was a highly calculated career move that effectively blocked his creditors' attempts to seize his French properties.

Governor Frontenac was a man of many weaknesses. He was proud, vain, stubborn and impatient. All of these attributes, plus his agility in avoiding formal channels of approval for such items as the building of new fur-trading posts, led to his recall to France after a decade.

In the years following his retirement, the colony of New France was eroded by weak leadership and Frontenac had once again accumulated vast debt. In 1689, sixty-nine-year-old Frontenac was returned as Governor of Canada to the delight of the colonists.

During his absence the Iroquois had allied themselves with the British and the *Canadien* colonists had come under constant attack. Shortly before his arrival, raiding Iroquois had killed twenty-four settlers and taken ninety captives at Lachine, Quebec.

Frontenac determined that the only way to defeat the British was to defeat them in the eyes of their native allies. He mounted a series of surprise attacks on outposts of the New England colonies that spread terror throughout the English frontier settlements. The tactics of this warfare were brutal. Both the British and the French offered rewards for scalps. In Massachusetts, the cry went out for revenge and an English fleet of thirty-four warships under the command of Sir William Phips set out from Boston to capture the French colony.

Frontenac made immediate plans to defend the fortress of Quebec, which was the gateway of the St. Lawrence and guarded the rest of the colony.

The siege of Quebec began on October 16, 1690. Hoping to avert a bloody assault, Phips sent his emissary, Major Thomas Savage, to order the government to surrender. At this point, Frontenac achieved a brilliant stroke of tactical deception.

Savage was blindfolded and led through the town to Frontenac's headquarters. Along the route, citizens and soldiers raised a great commotion, giving the impression of a large and willing garrison readied and eager for battle. Governor Frontenac received the emissary in a splendid room, surrounded by officers who wore their most elegant attire. The letter of demand from Phips was translated for

Frontenac. It ended with a request for a "positive" answer to be made by the sounding of a trumpet within one hour. But Frontenac was not about to blow any horn of defeat at the British. "My only reply to your general will be from the mouth of my cannon," was his blustering response.

The report delivered to Admiral Phips had the effect of a cold shower. It is even said that the message was punctuated by a cannon shot which took down the British flag.

The British launched an attack with 1,400 troops, but Frontenac's psychological ploy proved so effective that the solid stand of his small but valiant force of less than 500 *Canadiens* saw the British beat a hasty retreat after three days of siege.

Despite his human frailties, Frontenac proved himself a gallant Governor and his exploits have become the stuff of legend. When he died in 1698, one who knew him well wrote: "He was the love and delight of New France."

A ROYAL CANADIAN
LOVE STORY

Halifax, 1794 — Although she never saw it, the heart-shaped pond that ripples like a permanent valentine on the grounds of Prince's Lodge overlooking Bedford Basin is commonly known as Julie's Pond. There is also a street called Julie's Walk in her honour. "Julie" was a woman of many names — the longest of which was Alphonsine Julie Thérèsa Bernardine de St. Laurent de Montgenêt, Baronne de Fortisson. Most often she is called Madame St. Laurent, and for almost three decades she was known to be the mistress of Edward, Duke of Kent, fourth son of King George III — and the man who fathered Queen Victoria. Edward was twenty-seven when he arrived in Halifax to assume command of the forces of Nova Scotia. His mistress was thirty-four.

They had met three years earlier in Gibraltar, where Edward was cooling his heels after a scandal involving a French actress and an illegitimate child, not to mention his considerable debts. She was French from a bourgeois family in Besançon, and she had a history of romantic entanglements. For his part, the Prince was lonely. He had written his brother, the Prince of Wales, that he was "looking for a companion, not a whore." When Madame St. Laurent arrived in his life, he wrote to another of his brothers that she met his "every qualification . . . good temper, no small degree of cleverness, and above all, a pretty face and a handsome person." In 1791, they sailed to Canada together, settling first in Qubec.

In her definitive account of the romance, *The Prince and His Lady*, author Mollie Gillen notes: "The pretty girl from Besançon would live all her days with her prince in a strange sort of twilight, flitting like an almost invisible woman in and out of personal letters but never appearing in official reports or the public press." One of the few public records that identifies Madame St. Laurent as "Julie" is a 1792 Quebec baptismal record showing that the Prince and his consort were godparents to the son of their friends Ignace-Louis and Catherine de Salaberry. In the margin of the document, near Madame's exhaustive full name, someone wrote "Julie."

While Prince Edward busied himself with his regiment, Madame St. Laurent tended to matters of the household. She served as a discreet hostess, removed from ceremonial duties and public functions. Still, word of her existence caused tongues to wag. In England, the *Morning Chronicle* of April 25, 1793, reported: "An illustrious Prince, it is said, has formed an attachment with a beautiful Marseilloise, who is highly spoken of for mental as well as personal accomplishments. She is one of the *rank and file* in the garrison of Montreal."

During the American War of Independence some forty thousand Loyalists fled to British territory, with the largest preponderance settling in the area of Nova Scotia. Through their enterprise, the colony flourished. It was also no stranger to British Royal Princes and their romantic proclivities.

Beginning in 1786, William, the Prince of Wales, spent three summers in Halifax where he was a naval captain. William was said to have a romantic relationship with Frances Wentworth, a married woman of ambitious character. Her husband, John, was appointed as Nova Scotia's governor when the Prince returned to England. The Wentworths were among the first to welcome Prince Edward and Madame St. Laurent when they arrived in 1794, and it was their country home that would become Prince's Lodge.

The main residence was an Italianate villa with large windows that looked out over the sheltered harbour of Bedford Basin. Prince Edward immediately set to work on improvements to the property, transforming the rugged bedrock landscape into gardens suitable to an English estate. An artificial lake was created by diverting a stream — but its heart-shape would be crafted much later, in celebration of visits by the Prince's grandsons Edward and Arthur. On a rise, he built a wooden rotunda known as the "Round House" which served as a music room.

The relationship between Madame St. Laurent and her Prince became quite public. The couple delighted in attending the theatre. On one occasion, the *Halifax Chronicle* published a flowery rhyming verse that rhapsodized about Madame's "bewitching eyes" and "fragrant lips." Although some straitlaced members of society made it clear that the Prince's courtesan was not welcome in their company, Madame St. Laurent accepted the rebuffs with quiet grace. In a private letter to the Undersecretary of State in London, Governor Wentworth noted, "She is an elegant, well bred, pleasing sensible woman, far beyond most . . . I never yet saw a woman of such intrepid fortitude yet possessing the finest temper and refined manners."

The Prince was never thoroughly satisfied with colonial life, or with the climate. He worked hard at fortification projects, dabbled in telegraphy experiments and continually shaped his troops, always hoping that his efforts would earn him a transfer. There were occasional respites from what he described as "the dreariness of Nova Scotia," such as his trip with Madame back to England for his investiture as the Duke of Kent. However, it was an injury suffered during a horseback riding accident that proved to be his ticket out.

Madame accompanied her Duke on subsequent travels to England, Gibraltar, Belgium and France. As they aged, the relationship changed, but the friendship, affection and trust endured.

When Princess Charlotte, the daughter of the Prince Regent died in childbirth, there was a scramble to marry the aging bachelor princes and produce heirs. On May 8, 1818, Edward set out the terms of a security fund he had established for Madame St. Laurent, hoping this would be "proof of how dear she will always be to me . . . to my last breath, as a true and faithful friend in every eventuality." A long-time friend from Nova Scotia, James Putnam, was one of the trustees. Shortly afterward, Edward married a German princess. Their daughter, Alexandrina Victoria, was born the following year.

Even as a newlywed, the Duke maintained a correspondence with his former mistress, whom he knew was stricken with grief. It is often reported that Madame St. Laurent ended up in a convent. In fact, she appears to have stayed in France, uncloistered and close to her family.

The Duke died from complications caused by a persistent cold in 1820. Immediately upon his death, the Duchess of Kent wrote a letter to the mistress she knew would also be grieving. The two women never met; however, correspondence from Madame St. Laurent to her lover's widow is said to have moved the Duchess deeply.

The woman Haligonians called Julie was three weeks shy of her seventieth birthday when she died in Paris in 1830. At her side was a friend who had visited Madame and Edward in happier times at Prince's Lodge. He was Louis-Phillipe, the new King of France.

SERVING IN
A HOUSE DIVIDED

Washington, D.C., 1865 — More than 50,000 Canadians served in the American Civil War. One of them, Anderson Ruffin Abbott, distinguished himself by becoming one of only eight black surgeons to administer to the wounds of Union soldiers. He became a friend of the family of Abraham Lincoln, and he appears to have been the first black man to attend a White House levee. Following Lincoln's assassination in 1865, his wife, Mary Todd, presented Abbott with the black-and-white Shepherd Plaid shawl that the sixteenth President had worn on the day of his first inauguration.

Abbott's father, Wilson, was born of free parents in Richmond, Virginia. As a young man, Wilson and his wife, Ellen, operated a general store in Mobile, Alabama. When the city council of Mobile passed a law requiring free blacks to wear a badge indicating that they had posted a bond signed by two white men guaranteeing their good behaviour, Wilson Abbott refused to comply. An anonymous threat followed, and the couple decided to relocate quickly. Shortly afterward, their store was burned to the ground.

They came to Toronto in 1835. Two years later Anderson Ruffin was born. The couple was active in church and anti-slavery organizations, and Ellen Toyer Abbott founded the Queen's Benevolent Society, which aided black refugees.

When his tobacco shop failed, Wilson Abbott began to buy property and rent houses. He had learned to read and write from his wife, and he possessed a natural ability in mathematics. Over the next forty years, he acquired more than seventy-five properties in Toronto and throughout southwestern Ontario. The value of his holdings is impossible to estimate, however, among the tracts that he once owned in Toronto are the sites of the City Hall and the Eaton Centre.

The Abbotts raised three children, all receiving the best possible education. Anderson Ruffin attended the prestigious Buxton School in Chatham, Ontario, the Toronto Academy and Oberlin College in Ohio before enrolling in the Toronto School of Medicine. In 1861, he became the first Canadian-born black to be licensed in the practice of medicine.

Dr. Abbott was determined to join the Union Army. When blacks were finally permitted to participate in 1863, he was appointed as a surgeon at Freedman's Hospital in Washington. Soon afterward he became Surgeon-in-Charge of the 2,000-bed military hospital at Camp Baker.

Even Abbott's surviving family are uncertain about his connection to Lincoln. He was known to have been the personal physician to Mary Todd Lincoln's dressmaker. Whatever circumstances forged the friendship, it was powerful enough for Mrs. Lincoln to feel that her husband's shawl should be passed to Abbott as a token of appreciation to all Canadians who had joined the Civil War effort.

Many blacks who had sought refuge in Canada prior to the Emancipation Proclamation moved back to the United States, but Abbott returned to his Canadian roots.

He married and settled in Chatham where he practised medicine and became the first black coroner in Canada. He was constantly investigating new medical techniques and promoted high standards among his colleagues. As president of the Wilberforce Educational Institute, Abbott lobbied for equal education for all races.

In 1894, he moved to Chicago, where he served as Medical Superintendent of the Provident Hospital which had been founded by the black community as both a hospital and a nurses' training school.

When he retired in Toronto, Abbott continued to lecture in medicine and wrote articles protesting discrimination wherever he found it.

Toward the end of his life, Abbott reflected on his participation in the Civil War. "I am a Canadian, first and last and all the time, but that did not deter me from sympathizing with a nation struggling to wipe out an inequity," he wrote. "It was not a war for conquest or territorial aggrandizement, nor for racial, social or political supremacy. It was not a war for white men or black men, red men or yellow men. It was a war for humanity, a conflict between beautiful right and ugly wrong, between civilization and barbarism, between freedom and slavery. Canadians have a right to claim a full share in the honour and glory of that achievement."

ELEMENTARY, MY DEAR

Toronto, 1880 — Detective John Wilson Murray was the Canadian version of Sherlock Holmes. For most of his thirty-one-year career during the late 1800s, he was the only provincial police detective in a jurisdiction that extended east from Montreal to Rat Portage in Manitoba. He never gave up on a case and his tenacity earned him the nickname "Old Never-Let-Go."

Murray was born in Scotland in 1840 and moved to New York as a child. At seventeen, he enlisted in the United States Navy and he had his first taste of detective work during the Civil War. In 1862, he uncovered a complicated plot to free 4,000 Confederate prisoners.

After working as a special agent for the Navy he joined the Erie police force and, ultimately, came to Canada as Head of Detectives for the Canadian Southern Railway. In 1874, Ontario Attorney General Sir Oliver Mowat persuaded him to accept the position of Provincial Detective of Ontario. Murray proved to be a tireless investigator who was far ahead of his time in scientific criminal detection. Many a conniving soul found themselves convicted literally by their soles, since he was one of the first detectives in the world to realize the importance of footprints.

He regularly requested an autopsy on murder victims and had clothing and murder weapons chemically tested for clues.

Between 1875 and 1880, counterfeiters embarked on a bold effort that sent over one million dollars in phony bills into circulation throughout North America. The plates used to make the bills were so finely crafted that even the bank officials could not identify the fakes. In the far northwest $200,000 of such money was used to pay for furs that were shipped to England, Montreal and New York.

After contacting known "con" men in New York, Murray determined the bills to be the work of John Hill and Edwin Johnson, who were masterful engravers. After discounting Hill as an active suspect, Murray spent months tracking Johnson and his family to Toronto.

He staked out the Johnson house, and began conducting covert interviews with everyone from the family's butcher to the milkman to determine patterns of behaviour.

Everything appeared normal, until one day Murray followed Johnson on a boozy, bar-hopping session from Toronto to rural Markham. After many stops, the tipsy Johnson paid for a drink with a counterfeit one-dollar bill, and continued to do so at various stops, culminating in a four-dollar purchase of a necktie. Johnson was arrested.

Plates valued at $40,000 were unearthed in a north Toronto wood lot, where they had been carefully wrapped in oilcloth and encased in a protective coating of beeswax. There were twenty-one separate copper plates used to recreate seven different bills, including a U.S. five-dollar note. Johnson's wife and seven children had all been involved in the creation and distribution of the phony money, which was printed only once a year and quickly turned over to wholesale dealers known as "shovers."

Johnson's fatal flaw was his penchant for using the counterfeit money when he was inebriated. His nemesis, Detective John Wilson Murray, noted: "Crime lost a genius when old man Johnson died."

ALBERTOSAURUS,
I PRESUME

Alberta Badlands, 1884 — Even with the success of Hollywood blockbuster movies like *Jurassic Park*, few people are aware that at least twenty-five species of dinosaurs mysteriously ended their reign over large areas of Saskatchewan, Alberta and British Columbia at the epilogue of the Mesozoic age. The Plains Indians called them the "grandfathers of the buffalo" and one of those egg-layers, which became extinct over sixty-five million years ago, bears the name of the province in which its mortal remains were discovered.

It is called Albertosaurus and it was a close cousin to the most fearsome of all dinosaurs, the carnivorous Tyrannosaurus. Scientists estimate that Albertosaurus may have grown up to nine metres long and weighed as much as two tonnes.

Its fossilized remains were discovered in 1884 by a young Canadian geologist and explorer named Joseph Burr Tyrrell. At twenty-five, he worked for the Canadian Geological Survey, whose job it was to map the vast territories of Canada in the last century.

Tyrrell and his assistant were paddling their canoe between the steep banks of the Red Deer River, south of

Drumheller in southern Alberta. In the layers of ancient rock, the geologist found seams of coal, outcroppings of one of the largest deposits in North America.

On June 9th, Tyrrell set off on his usual routine of examining the river banks when a peculiar brown substance sticking out from the valley wall caught his attention. He scaled the steep slope and, with mounting excitement, he began to clear away the dirt. Using his bare hands and his geologist's hammer, he gradually uncovered the fossilized skeleton of a dinosaur.

Dinosaur remains had been unearthed in western Canada before, but as Tyrrell explored the valley he recognized that nothing like this dinosaur graveyard had ever been found.

One memorable day, after a month of surveying and collecting fossils, Tyrrell looked the ancient past directly in the face. Sixty-nine years later, at the age of ninety-five, he recounted the instant of his most dramatic discovery. "I was climbing up a steep face about 400 feet [120 metres] high. I stuck my head around a point and there was this skull leering at me, sticking right out of the ground. It gave me a fright." Tyrrell had found the first skull of Albertosaurus.

The "find" was to become the site of the world's richest palaeontological discovery. The skeletal remains of more than 475 dinosaurs have been recovered from the barren valley walls of the Red Deer River.

Although the word *dinosaur* stems from the Greek *dino saurus* meaning "terrible lizard', recent advances in technology have led scientists to speculate that, unlike reptiles, the dinosaurs may have been warm-blooded creatures more closely linked to animals and birds than lizards and crocodiles.

Dinosaur "nests," fossilized eggs and the remains of baby dinosaurs have furthered our understanding of the "community" of dinosaurs, and scientific examinations of ancient layers of rock may one day lead to a final understanding of why the dinosaurs disappeared.

Today, the Royal Tyrrell Museum of Paleontology in Dinosaur Provincial Park in Drumheller, Alberta, pursues the work Joseph Burr Tyrrell started when he took Albertosaurus's skull out of the badlands on the back of a buckboard wagon and gave it to the world.

WHITE LAMA

Chatham, Ontario, to Tibet, 1895 — Bounded by the Yang-tze River and three sets of mountains, the Himalayas, the Karakoram and the Kunlun, Tibet has been called "the Roof of the World." The spiritual homeland of the Dalai Lama was an exotic half a world away from the rural southwestern Ontario town of Chatham where Susanna Carson was born in 1868. But she would go there — twice — as a medical missionary.

Active in the Methodist church throughout childhood, the young woman who was known all her life as "Susie" had decided by the age of fourteen that she wanted to become a doctor. In fact, Susie was barely eleven when her progressive father, who was a principal and school inspector, began making inquiries about a Canadian medical course for women doctors. At the age of twenty, Dr. Carson graduated from the second class of female students at Women's Medical College in Toronto. With her sister, Jessie, another graduate of Women's Medical, she practised in Strathroy, Ontario, until her marriage six year later to a Dutchman named Petrus Rijnhart.

Petrus had already travelled to China as a part of a non-denominational mission, but he was turfed when his credentials were scrutinized and found lacking. In Toronto, he learned English by working at a factory and soon found supporters to back his idea of a mission to Tibet (Xinjiang province in the People's Republic of China).

Responding to what she viewed as a calling "to do pioneer work," Susie joined him on the odyssey across the ocean and across China, armed with everything from dental and surgical implements to copies of the scripture in Tibetan and a bicycle.

The Rijnharts settled in Lusar, a border town in Outer Tibet that was the trading centre for the lamasery of Kumbum, home to more than 4,000 lamas who followed the teachings of Buddha. Although foreign missionaries were generally regarded with suspicion, the Rijnharts were allowed to build a house and establish a medical clinic. A young lama taught them the language and they adapted to local customs, including drinking tea mixed with rancid butter and salt which they found less than savoury.

Their evangelic efforts were deliberately subtle. Although the Rijnharts' mission was to convert Tibetans to their vision of Christianity, they recognized Buddhism as a religion worthy of respect. "In every religious service, however absurd or degraded from the Christian point of view," Susie noted, "there is some feeble acknowledgement and groping after the one great God."

By decorating the walls of the surgery with provocative biblical illustrations, such as the story of Lazarus being risen from the dead, the Rijnharts were able to engage Tibetans in discussion. Their reputation as healers and the tactful way in which they introduced their religion without imposing it or attacking alternative forms of worship earned them the interest of curious Tibetans and a powerful friendship.

The kanpo (abbott) of the lamasery, Mina Fuyeh, invited Susie and Petrus to attend his ailing treasurer at his residence, an unheard-of privilege for a foreigner. Mina Fuyeh, a lively twenty-seven year old, was the highest dignitary in northeastern Tibet and ranked as a "living Buddha." He was interested in knowing everything about the Rijnharts' religion and studied the scriptures closely, finding many Christian precepts to be compatible with Buddhism. Naively, the Rijnharts held hope that Mina Fuyeh would convert, but their "firm friend" was not about to abdicate a position that had taken him many reincarnations to achieve.

When a Muslim rebellion threw the countryside into turmoil, Mina Fuyeh offered the Rijnharts sanctuary in the lamasery. From safety, they watched as thousands of lamas wearing red and yellow robes and silk turbans marched off to join Chinese troops in putting down the revolt. While the Rijnharts treated a diphtheria outbreak in the refugee-crowded monastery, villages were destroyed in brutal fighting that saw 100,000 killed. The "white lamas," as the Rijnharts were known, ended up going to the battlefields to treat the wounded.

The army surgeon and her public health officer endeared themselves to the Tibetan people, treating thousands of patients and never asking for payment. But Susie and Petrus never lost sight of the purpose that brought them to Tibet. On Wednesdays and Sundays they ran a Bible school. It was a popular gathering place for women and children, who sang the hymns they were taught to the accompaniment of Susie's violin and Petrus's concertina. Still, there were no converts.

Life in Lusar was good, but since the Rijnharts considered their mandate to be spreading the gospel, they accepted an invitation to take their work to Tankar, a trading town in Inner Tibet.

When Petrus was called away to Peking (Beijing) for several months, Susie felt comfortable and secure enough to stay alone in Tankar. In a country where foreigners sometimes disappeared or were murdered, this unusual circumstance surprised visiting Swedish explorer, Sven Hedrin. He might have been even more "astonished" at meeting the "bareheaded young lady wearing spectacles and dressed after the Chinese manner," if he had known that she was also pregnant. Charles Carson Rijnhart was born in July of 1897.

Restless and relentless, the Rijnharts conducted a number of itinerant missions, distributing gospels throughout the countryside. But they knew that the ultimate prize would be to enter the "Sealed Land," and carry the word of their God to Lhasa, the site of the most sacred of all Buddhist monasteries.

"The Lord had opened many doors for us in China, and we were confident He would open others," Susie wrote in her narrative memoir *With the Tibetans in Tent and Temple*. With their ten-month-old son and dog, Topsy, they set off with three guides to lead them through the mountains, a dozen pack horses carrying food for a year, and 500 copies of the New Testament.

After travelling for two hellish months through bogs, hail, torrential rains and snow with the constant threat of wild animals and thieves, they were about a week's journey away from their goal. It was late August when Susie wrote that "the darkest day in our lives arose bright and full of promise." By the end of it, their ailing baby was dead, despite all of Susie's efforts. The Rijnharts buried their "darling" with a bouquet of wild asters and blue poppies in their emptied drug box and covered it with a boulder.

At this point they had already lost five of their pack horses to thieves and their guides had deserted them. A government patrol tried to stop them, but they pressed on stealthily until they were finally turned back.

Reprovisioned with guides and horses, the Rijnharts were on their way to China when they were attacked by robbers who killed all but one of their horses and scared off their guides. Travelling through deep snow they came across a tented camp across a river.

On September 26, 1898, eleven days after the couple's fourth anniversary, Petrus left Susie alone with a revolver for protection. His plan was to swim across the river and enlist help. Susie never saw him again. Revolver in hand, she waited for three days, searching the river bank with her telescope.

It took Susie two months to reach a branch of the China Inland Mission at Tachienlu (Kangdon) in Szechuan province. Convinced that her husband had been murdered, she spent six months trying to find the culprits, to no avail.

Her health was failing and, at thirty-two, her hair was completely white when she returned to Chatham in 1900. She wrote her book and embarked on a lecture tour, but two years later she returned to Tibet. In 1905, she married a Scottish missionary, James Moyes, who had been the first white man to speak to her following Petrus's disappearance.

In 1907, Susie and James returned to Chatham. The following year, Susie died two months after giving birth to a daughter. Her sister was her attending physician. The mission she had founded in Tibet was closed, having recorded seven converts.

"If ever the gospel were proclaimed in Lhasa," Susie wrote, "someone would have to be the first to undertake the journey, to meet the difficulties, to preach the first sermon and perhaps never return to tell the tale — who knew?"

LION OF THE YUKON

Dawson City, Yukon Territory, 1898 — Superintendent Sam Benfield Steele of the North-West Mounted Police was as square of jaw and as forthright of conviction as Dudley Do-Right. He was a lawman who could bring order out of chaos, which was just what Prime Minister Wilfrid Laurier's government had in mind when Steele was dispatched to preserve peace on the Canadian side of the border during the Klondike Gold Rush.

The situation was ripe for trouble. In Skagway, Alaska, on the American side of the border, gangster Jefferson Randolph "Soapy" Smith and his gang of thugs had a stranglehold on all things outlaw. "It seemed as if the scum of the earth had hastened here," noted one traveller. Steele, himself, found it to be "little better than hell on earth," a place where "robbery and murder were daily occurrences." Such behaviour would not be countenanced in Sam Steele's jurisdiction.

Steele made his first indelible imprint on the *cheech-akoos* (tenderfoots) in the spring of 1898. He had established headquarters at Lake Bennett, where a tent city of more than 10,000 "argonauts" was waiting for the spring break-up to free the river for the final leg of their journey to Dawson. By the time he arrived, about 150 boats had been wrecked in perilous rapids and at least five people had drowned. "Many of your countrymen have said that the mounted police make up the laws as they go along," announced Steele. "I am going to do so now for your own good."

With that, Steele established Mountie checkpoints and everything that attempted to float toward Dawson was inspected for seaworthiness. Women and children walked around the rapids. No more lives were lost.

The thousands who made it to Dawson City had to first pass muster with Steele's border posts on the legendary "Trail of '98." Customs duties were collected, handguns were confiscated and anyone who did not have the requisite 522 kilograms of food was turned back. Unruly intruders into Canadian territory were dealt with firmly.

One night Steele heard two shots near his cabin. The culprit was brought before Steele, who found marked cards and loaded dice in his saddlebags. "I'll have you know that you can't lock up a United States citizen and get away with it," the gunman boldly announced.

"Well seeing you're an American citizen, I'll be very lenient," replied Steele. "I'll confiscate everything you have and give you half an hour to leave town."

Amid the carnival ambience that marked the tent city that billowed at Dawson, Steele was a force of reason. What he initially found to be "a city of chaos" was quickly whipped into an orderly state, complete with a board of health and a dutiful respect for Sunday. Prostitution was confined to a red-light district, gambling was licensed, and comedians were prosecuted for disparaging remarks about the Queen. There was still plenty of room for "whooping it up." Indeed, in his 1958 book *Klondike*, author Pierre Berton notes that during the '98 season 120,000 gallons of liquor were imported into Dawson. But at the peak of the Rush, Steele reported: "Only three homicides have taken place, none of them preventable."

Something so simple as a monetary punishment for behaviour outside of the law would have been too easy in a community where fortunes were made (and lost) overnight. When Steele imposed a fifty-dollar fine on a gambler, the response was often laughter. Steele's response was to add sixty days' labour on the wood pile. "Have you got that in your vest pocket?" he would ask.

Soon Dawson boasted a stack of firewood nearly three kilometres long. Rounders who really irritated Steele earned a "blue ticket," which banished them from the town and curtailed their lucrative prey on newly rich miners.

When Sam Steele roared, people listened. In political matters, however, the "Lion of the Yukon's" direct approach may have been his Achilles heel. When he tried to clean up the corrupt practices of bureaucrats, the Tory Steele ran up against Liberal powerhouse, Sir Clifton Sifton, who had friends with vested interests in securing powerful liquor licensing commissions and meat contracts.

On September 8, 1899, Steele was relieved of his command in a terse telegram signed by Sifton as the minister in charge of Mounted Police affairs.

Protests and petitions from the citizens of Dawson were to no avail. When Steele left town, prospectors, piano-players, dancers in petticoats and out-and-out whores lined the wharf The departing redcoat was judged by the *Klondike Nugget* to be "by all odds the most respected man in the Yukon."

THE SPIRIT OF *TILIKUM*

Nootka, British Columbia, 1901 — A Canadian adventurer taught the Governor of Samoa to play poker and ended up playing a major role in saving the buffalo from extinction in western Canada, but does anyone remember his name?

Norman Luxton was a man of many careers, travels and travails. He was born in Winnipeg in 1876 and his father, William, was one of the founders of the *Winnipeg Free Press.*

Young Luxton tried his hand at the newspaper business in Calgary and Vancouver, and prospected for gold in the Kootenay area of British Columbia in the early 1900s.

Adventure beckoned when he encountered a kindred spirit in a Danish mariner, Captain F.C. Voss. The pair made plans for a South Seas expedition. Luxton purchased a nine-metre, red-cedar dugout canoe from a Nuu-Cha-Nulth craftsman. Its ungainly renovations included a small cabin, three masts, four sails and an ancient Spanish cannon.

The distinctive craft was christened *Tilikum* — meaning friend. The adventurers departed Nootka, British Columbia, on July 6th, 1901, with rudimentary navigational technology, including a sextant with a cracked mirror and a chart showing their approximate destination. On a good day, they could cover 240 kilometres.

By the time Luxton and Voss reached the South Seas, their friendship was strained and they spent most of their time sitting at opposite ends of the vessel clutching their guns, but they were determined to continue.

Finances ran thin when they reached Samoa, so Luxton set himself up as a professor of card games, specializing in poker — which became the particular affection of the Governor.

All told, Luxton and Voss stopped at forty-two South Seas ports to a variety of receptions. One king was so taken with Luxton that he offered him a choice of daughters for marriage and a coconut grove of his own. On another island, a confrontation with hostile residents who were presumed to be "cannibals" called the ancient cannon to their defence.

Luxton abandoned the expedition to recover from injuries suffered in a shipwreck off Australia, but Voss successfully guided the *Tilikum* to England, arriving in September 1904.

Luxton returned to Canada and settled in Banff, Alberta, where he began a publishing business, a trading post and a year-round hotel. He committed himself to the community, leading his biographers to nickname him "the oracle of Banff." During a card game, he helped conceive the Winter Carnival and in the summer Luxton conducted the annual Indian Days Festival in conjunction with the Stoney.

When an influenza epidemic struck near a trading post Luxton operated in northerly Morely, he supplied much-needed food and medical supplies to the isolated native population without compensation. The business failed, but Luxton was named an Honorary Chief of both the Blackfoot and the Stoney tribes.

In 1909, Luxton suggested that the Canadian government purchase a herd of Montana buffalo to replenish the prairie herds which had been hunted almost to the point of extinction. These animals provided the foundation stock for the herds at Wainwright National Park.

Norman Luxton's legacy of adventure and open-hearted vision of the true meaning of "tilikum," continues to thrive. Today, the original dugout *Tilikum* is permanently berthed in Victoria, B.C., and every year thousands of visitors enjoy the spirit of place and the spirit of this unique Canadian adventurer at the Luxton Museum, which is housed in a log building beside the Bow River at Banff.

WHO IS WHAT
AND WHAT IS WHO

White River, Ontario, 1914 — The Second Canadian Infantry Brigade was on its way east from Winnipeg to Quebec and the front lines of the First World War when army veterinarian Harry Colebourn bought the bear. It was a warm August day when the train carrying Prairie soldiers stopped for water and fuel at White River, a Northern Ontario lumber town. Colebourn spotted a trapper on the platform with a small black bear cub. As the story goes, the trapper had killed the cub's mother but the cub was so endearing he kept it. For twenty dollars, she was Harry's.

The bear became the soldiers' unofficial mascot. Colebourn named her "Winnipeg" after his hometown, but this was soon abbreviated to the endearing "Winnie." When the brigade was shipped overseas, the bear went with them. While the troops trained at Salisbury Plains outside of London, she slept under Colebourn's cot and dutifully ate her rations from his hand.

In December of 1914, Colebourn was scheduled to transfer to the "Big Fight" in France, which he knew would be no place for a pet bear. He approached the London Zoo and released Winnie to their temporary custody.

Soon hundreds of children and adults were flocking to the zoo to see her. Although the zookeepers had to keep a wary eye on all of the other bears, they would not hesitate to enter Winnie's cage and give her a pat on the head. Children were given "bear-back" rides on her, and she delighted the crowds by fluffing her pillow and pulling her blanket over her great huge shoulders when she took a nap.

After the war ended, Captain Colebourn tried to retrieve his bear, but when he saw the incredible affection the British people had for her, he officially donated her to the zoo in January, 1919. Over the years, the Winnipeg veterinarian maintained a steady correspondence with the zoo and he was assured that Winnie was in good hands.

Colebourn's bear was not the only Canadian bear to find a home in the London Zoo. Records show that five of the species *ursus americanus* were placed at the zoo for safekeeping by Canadian soldiers during a six-month period in 1914-15. However, there was something quite special about this Winnipeg bear. Not only was she the first, she was also a crowd-pleasing ham.

Among the many visitors who thrilled to the famous Canadian bear's antics were author Alan Alexander Milne and his young son Christopher Robin. In 1925, Milne was commissioned to write a Christmas story for the *London Evening News*. He wrote a story about a teddy bear named Edward who went "bump, bump, bump" down a staircase and ended up as that most treasured Bear of Very Little Brain — Winnie the Pooh.

Although golden in colour and anatomically incorrect in the illustrations drawn by E.H. Shepard, the storybook Winnie was modelled after the huge, black she-bear in the London Zoo who was famous for coming out to greet the crowds when a child so much as knocked on the Bear House door. "Pooh" was a word Milne's son is said to have used to show his disdain for a local swan that would not come when the child called.

Winnie the Pooh became a bestseller in 1926. Seventy years later, A.A. Milne's four volumes of stories about a boy and a bear who loves HUNNY, who has great adventures with his pals, Eeyore, Rabbit, Piglet, Kanga and Owl remain a "warm and sunny spot" among the classics of children's literature.

Back in Winnipeg another little boy, Harry Colebourn's son Fred, grew up hearing real-life stories about his father's bear, Winnie. When Captain Colebourn died, Fred inherited six wartime diaries containing all of the bear facts. In 1987, through sheer coincidence, Fred learned that the London Zoo had contacted Calgary's Princess Patricia Light Infantry regarding "their" Winnie. History had become blurred after the lovable bear's death from old age in 1934. When sixty-year-old Christopher Robin Milne dedicated a bronze statue of his father's famous character in 1980, the plaque that accompanied it had attributed Winnie's origins to the wrong Canadian army company!

Fred Colebourn rushed to the breach, reclaiming his father's bear for the soldiers of the Second Infantry. In 1989, the citizenry of White River rallied to celebrate the birthplace of Winnie the Canadian Pooh in a festival that has become an annual event on the third weekend of August. Saskatchewan artist Bill Epp created a sculpture of Captain Colebourn and his bear for the City of Winnipeg and in 1995 a duplicate was presented to the London Zoo.

As A.A. Milne wrote in the final lines of *The House at Pooh Corner*, "Wherever they go, and whatever happens to them on the way, in that enchanted place on the Top of the Forest, a little boy and a bear will always be playing."

And that is the story of Harry and his bear, Winnipeg.

THESE BOOTS
WERE MADE FOR WALKIN'

Halifax to Vancouver, 1921 — It might not be everyone's idea of a stroll, but in the middle of the winter of 1921 Charles Burkman decided to walk across the country. He was twenty years old and he had just lost his job at the Halifax shipyards. An acquaintance, Sid Carr, was also out of work. The footloose pair formulated an equally loose plan to tred the railway tracks west until something better came along or they waded into the Pacific.

When they announced their plans to the Halifax *Herald*, the adventurers anticipated the trip would take seven months at a leisurely pace. Along the way, they planned to sell commemorative postcards for a dime, a princely sum considering that a turkey dinner cost about twenty cents.

The *Herald* must have been having a slow news year. Seizing on the story as though it was "news," they offered to pay for reports and made Charlie and Sid front-page news.

On January 17, Pathé News filmed the duo's departure in fog and rain, but no one guessed how big the story would get.

As they walked, a pattern emerged involving free meals, lodging and gifts of everything from boots to long johns. Hundreds of postcard-buying well-wishers offered them encouragement and they plodded on despite freezing temperatures. But on January 21, they had competition.

John Behan, a forty-four-year-old postman from Dartmouth, proposed a father-son challenge. He told the *Herald* that he and his twenty-four-year-old son, Clifford, could reach Vancouver in six months. Burkman and Carr had a nine-day advantage by the time they set out, but team Behan proclaimed that they would be in the lead by Montreal. Carrying their own stash of commemorative postcards, the Behans gave hot pursuit. They were at Truro composing their own dispatches to the *Herald* when a third team of hikers threw their soles in the ring.

Windsor, Nova Scotia, foundry worker Frank Dill and his wife, Jennie, added a whole new dimension. Married less than two years, they both enjoyed the outdoors and Frank had earned a modest reputation as a runner.

Dark-haired, diminutive Jennie was the wild card. A muscular fisherman's daughter, she was a good shot and a notable speed skater. Joining the race was her idea and she created a sensation by wearing men's clothing — riding breeches and high leather boots. The *Herald* dutifully noted that there was "not a single suggestion of mannishness in her personality."

Before the Dills got started on February 1, Sid Carr dropped out. "I won't be forced into racing across Canada," he told the press, who promptly romanticized Charles Burkman as "the lone hiker."

Two thousand Haligonians saw the Dills off in a heavy snowfall. That day, Burkman crossed into Maine and the Behans were gaining ground on him near Saint John. Although doubters argued that no woman could hike beyond Truro, Jennie Dill's report from Truro said that she was hoping to walk past Moncton the following day, "if Frank can stand it."

Wagering on the outcome became frenetic. Despite offers of rides in everything from sleighs to railway cars, the contestants kept walking.

Halifax businessmen sympathetic to Burkman's solitary plight pledged $500 if he reached Vancouver in six months. Meanwhile, three wildcats attacked the Behans and John shot one of them. Although huge crowds turned out to shower the Dills with notes, newspapers and food, Jenny never let Frank slow the pace.

Burkman had gone through sixteen changes of boots when he reached Montreal on February 19. He stayed at the swank Windsor Hotel, delighting Montrealers by dancing all evening despite his blisters.

At the end of February, Burkman had travelled 1,490 kilometres (926 miles) in forty-two days. The Behans were hard on his heels, clocking 1,382 kilometres (859 miles) in thirty-four days. Despite waist-high snow in Maine, the Dills made 928 kilometres (577 miles) in twenty-two days.

In Halifax, a $1,000 bet was placed that the Behans would overtake Burkman by March 12. The Dills hardly seemed to be in contention.

Father and son Behan walked the snowy rails with a pole held between them to help keep their balance. Jennie was small and Frank was tall, so they could not effect the same device. Somewhere between North Bay and Sudbury, Burkman found a roller skate. Tied to a spanning rod, it ran on the opposite rail and Charlie balanced against it. On March 12, he was only a few hours ahead of the Behans. Someone lost $1,000.

Two days later, the Burkman–Behan paths crossed in the depths of Northern Ontario. They spent that day walking together, a pleasurable respite for Burkman, whose only dialogue with human company usually occurred when he was exhausted after a day's hike. For the rest of the month, the two teams engaged in a foot duel — sometimes gaining, sometimes losing ground by trying false shortcuts — but the Behans were the first to reach Lake Superior.

Way back in Ottawa, the Dills enjoyed a meeting with Prime Minister Arthur Meighen and Liberal leader William Lyon Mackenzie King. Jennie thrilled readers with news that she had killed a timber wolf with a single shot after it leapt out of the bushes at Frank. They were picking up the pace despite heavy storms and white-out conditions.

Sometimes the newspaper would not hear from Burkman for days, but he was always dogging the Behans. In sub-zero temperatures north of Superior, they spent several days walking together. Wolves howled at the door of a cabin where they took shelter.

Port Arthur (now Thunder Bay) was Burkman's hometown, so he stopped to spend some time. The Behans savoured their lead; crossing the halfway point at Savanne, Ontario, they were "feeling like two jack rabbits." Jennie Dill titillated the nation by suggesting that her husband was jealous of letters she received from Charlie Burkman and thought that the lonely hiker might be slowing down so that he could walk with her. Burkman had slowed down, but only because he hurt his hip slipping off a rail.

Warm weather brought its own strains. Frank Dill suffered from sunburn, while Burkman opted to walk at night to avoid the heat. Despite heat waves, mosquitos and prairie sandstorms, the hikers made good time on the flat land.

Blisters slowed Burkman down. When the Dills over-took him, Jenny said she was sorry but he would have to take care of himself. Noting that "this wonderful hike" had taught her a lesson she intended to share with other women, she wrote: "The subject is not what men can do women can do, but what men have done women CAN MORE THAN DO."

What Jennie Dill could not do was prevent Frank from carousing with friends in Calgary. The Behans were barely two days ahead and she was furious when Frank "went out with the boys." After hauling him out of the Kiwanis Club in the late afternoon, they walked 16 kilometres (10 miles) in a hailstorm before stopping.

In the Rockies, John and Clifford Behan suffered nose-bleeds. John had lost almost 10 percent of his bodyweight and Clifford caught a chill sleeping outdoors at Lake Lou-ise. When a painful spasm stopped him at Albert Canyon, Clifford took a train west to Revelstoke for a prescribed rest. Returning to Albert Canyon, he resumed the hike toward his father, who reached Revelstoke in the interim.

Charlie Burkman was effectively out of the race but he decided to stick it out, acknowledging that, "Some might criticize me for letting a woman pass me."

Jennie Dill was pushing Frank hard, even though his feet were bothering him. At one point outside of Kamloops she accused the Behans of cheating so that they would not be beaten by a woman. The charge could not be substanti-ated.

On June 11, after walking twenty-two hours straight covering a remarkable 98 kilometres (61 miles), the hag-gard Behans arrived in Vancouver. Two days later, the Dills followed and Jennie reportedly "looked more as if she had been on a picnic." Burkman joined them on July 16.

In the end, the Dills were the winners. They had travelled the 5,872 kilometres (3,650 miles) in 134 days, bettering the Behans by two days. At 150 days, Charlie Burkman outdid his original "leisurely paced" estimate by two months, but the promised $500 never materialized.

There was no pot of gold at the end of the rainbow. In Monopoly terms, the Trans-Canada hikers simply passed "Go" and started at zero. That July, an attempt at a high-stakes footrace with John, Frank and Charlie foundered when one dropped out and the others suffered heat prostration. They were finished as "news" and dropped from public view.

Ultimately, the notion of walking the country enjoyed its finest hour in 1980, when a youthful, one-legged victim of cancer named Terry Fox announced plans to make his way from Newfoundland to his home province of British Columbia.

Terry's unforgettable "Marathon of Hope" ended tragically in Thunder Bay when doctors diagnosed that the cancer had spread to his lungs. He died the following summer, leaving a legacy of courage that resounds to this day in the annual "runs" that are held in his name, raising millions to fight the disease that challenged him to greatness.

INNOVATION, INVENTION & SCIENCE

THE *ANNEDA* SOLUTION

THAT AND A GLEEK WILL GET YOU A CUP OF COFFEE

THE SCENT OF A MAMMAL

THE MILLENNIAL TREE

A HATFUL OF GRAIN

LET THERE BE LIGHT

A MAN FOR ALL TIME ZONES

THE HEART OF THE MATTER

H_2O + MYSTERIOUS GREY POWDER = SUNSHINE + $$$$

MASTICATION AS THE MOTHER OF INVENTION

ONE WITH THE SOIL

RUST NEVER SLEEPS

AN ALLELUIA IN THE SKY

THE RAIDERS OF DRAGON BONE HILL

THE WONDER MUSH REVOLUTION

FEETS DON'T FAIL ME NOW

UNDISCOVERED COUNTRY

THE *ANNEDA* SOLUTION

Stadacona (Quebec City), 1535 — One of the ugliest diseases to afflict early explorers also has one of the ugliest names ever to apply to a human condition. Scurvy was a scourge that plagued generations of seafarers. On his first trip around the Cape of Good Hope (1497-1499), Vasco da Gama lost half of his crew to the illness. In the New World, the ravages of scurvy might have stopped French explorer Jacques Cartier from venturing further than the present-day site of Quebec City had it not been for an Iroquois native named Domagaya.

Cartier and his crew of 110 spent the winter of 1535-1536 living aboard their icebound ships near an Iroquois village they called Stadacona. In his journals, Cartier wrote of "a pestilence" that ravaged the crew to such a degree that "on all our three ships there were not three men in good health." The symptoms he describes started with swelling in the legs which spread painfully into the upper body and the neck. In gruesome detail he notes "the flesh peeled off down to the roots of their teeth, while the latter almost all fell out in turn." Cartier tried psalm singing and prayer, but twenty-five crew members died that winter.

In the village, more than fifty natives also died, likely due to European diseases. The natives also suffered from scurvy, and Cartier observed the disease in Domagaya, who was the son of Iroquois chief Donnacona. He noted that one of Domagaya's knees had swollen "as big as the body of a two year old child" and his teeth had decayed to the gums. Less than two weeks later, Cartier saw Domagaya again. He was walking purposefully across the river ice in extreme cold and he appeared to be in perfect health. After some prompting, Cartier learned that Domagaya had healed himself by drinking a tea made from the ground bark, twigs and fronds of a tree the natives called *anneda* — probably eastern white cedar.

Within weeks, Cartier's crew was restored to health thanks to this simple remedy. The reason for the cure would remain a mystery for several centuries, but it was the vitamin C from the plant material that prompted such seemingly miraculous recovery. Dutifully, Cartier recorded the cure in his journals, with one critical omission — he failed to provide a description of the *anneda*.

In his early explorations, Samuel de Champlain also encountered problems with scurvy. While travelling in the area of the Kennebec River in 1605, he met a native chief whose name was pronounced *anneda*. "I was satisfied from the name that it was one of his tribe that had discovered the plant called *anneda*, which Jacques Cartier said was so powerful against the malady called scurvy," Champlain wrote, hopefully. However, the chief had no cure to offer. Since *anneda* was the Iroquois word for spruce tree, supposition has it that the native Champlain encountered was from a different tribe. The introduction of farming to the colonies was finally instrumental in solving much of the scurvy problem.

In the far North, the Inuit had their own unique solution for scurvy — the Willow ptarmigan. A relative of the grouse, ptarmigan feed on the vitamin C-rich buds and

twigs of the hardy dwarf willow bush. By eating the giz-
zards and intestines of the ptarmigan, scurvy could be
avoided. In addition, the Inuit would eat partially digested
seaweed found in the stomachs of seals and other sea mammals that they hunted. Unsavoury, perhaps, but markedly
preferable to the agonies of scurvy.

Solutions that native peoples had figured out centuries
earlier continued to elude Europeans. During the eighteenth
century, scurvy was responsible for more fatalities in the
British navy than enemy action. In 1747, Scottish surgeon
James Lind began studying the effects of diet on sailors with
scurvy and found that feeding them oranges prompted dramatic results. Six years later, he published his findings in
A Treatise of the Scurvy, recommending citrus fruit as a treatment and preventative. Although it took the British navy
forty-two years to heed the advice, when lime juice was
distributed as part of the regular ration to sailors on long
sea voyages, scurvy was eliminated. From then on, British
sailors had to live with the moniker "limey."

Unfortunately, ascorbic acid (vitamin C) is prone to
oxidize over time and it deteriorates under temperature
stress. This phenomenon haunted most nineteenth-century
polar explorers and may have contributed to the loss of Sir
John Franklin's third expedition in 1847.

Scurvy also afflicted soldiers during the First World
War. Dr. Murrough O'Brien from Dominion City, Manitoba,
confronted the disease while serving as a medical officer to
a railway unit in northwest Russia. He had the foresight to
include lime juice in his supply order, but it had been
dumped off in freezing temperatures and spoiled. In Donald Jack's authoritative Canadian medical history book,
Rogues, Rebels and Geniuses, O'Brien admits that he found
himself in "a bit of a pickle," until he remembered having

read that potato peels were also effective in treating scurvy. His patients were Russians, but O'Brien did not feel he would have much success commandeering potatoes from the local authorities. "I took the easiest way out," he said. "I called in three or four of my best filchers and sent them after tubers. I got my potatoes, fed the patients skin scrapings, and the scurvy cleared up like magic." Such a simple solution to such an ugly scourge that is now all but forgotten.

THAT AND A GLEEK
WILL GET
YOU A CUP OF COFFEE

New France, 1684 — As the Intendant of the colony, one of Jacques de Meulles' responsibilities was to supervise the operating budget and pay the troops. Apparently, he was a man who took his responsibilities seriously. So when the coin coffers were bare, he was determined to find a short-term solution, and he found it in a deck of playing cards.

Although Europeans were using paper money backed by gold bullion in the seventeenth century, colonists in New France relied largely on the barter system due to a scarcity of coins. Most of the settlers were subsistence farmers and they traded their goods and services for whatever they required. Such trading was formalized in September 1670, when a decree issued by the Sovereign Council set a standard for measuring the value of beaver pelts, moose hides and other furs. Although it may seem ecologically unfriendly today, one blanket could be purchased for eight wildcat pelts.

Members of the garrison were paid in coins which were sent from France, and in 1670 silver and copper coins were minted for specific use in New France. In the spring of 1684, the French government neglected to ship coins. This left de Meulles in an uncomfortable position, since the men under his command were kept busy with their military responsibilities and had not acquired the pelts to pay for their board and lodging.

In desperation, de Meulles determined to issue paper money based on playing cards endorsed by him, which would be redeemable the following year when coins would surely arrive. It was a bold gamble, but one that paid off.

Card playing was a popular activity in the barracks of Quebec City, where active games of "maw" involved elaborately illustrated cards with names such as Tiddy, Gleek, Tup-tup and Towser. De Meulles collected decks of durable cards and cut each one into four pieces, which he marked and stamped as "good" for specific amounts of currency under his seal and signature.

This imaginative solution to a shortage of coin worked quite well for many years and suffered vagaries typical of modern paper money, including a devaluation to half its face value in 1719. Thirty years later, the King of France authorized the issue of card money to be increased from 720,000 to one million livres.

The conclusion of the Seven Years' War in 1763 saw an end to playing-card currency in favour of British sterling. A hodgepodge of currency followed including Nova Scotia provincial money, American dollars, Spanish dollars and U.S. gold coins.

Paper money was introduced in 1792 by the Canada Banking Company, but it lacked a certain credibility. It was considered to be about as valuable as a U.S. continental dollar, which was virtually worthless at the time. Coins were again at a premium during the War of 1812, and the government of Lower Canada issued paper "army bills" to purchase supplies.

In 1837, William Lyon Mackenzie signed the first ten-dollar note issued by the provisional government of Upper Canada. Swindlers issuing bogus, but colourful, three-dollar notes were quick to follow.

Bank notes which were not backed by gold did not become legal tender throughout Canada until August 3, 1914, the day before Britain declared war on Germany. The rest is a crumpled history of bills folded in wallets at values dictated by global circumstance. In this nation, it all started with a deck of cards.

THE SCENT OF A MAMMAL

New France, 1685 — New France represented a cornucopia of new plant and animal life to its explorers. Among these never-before-seen oddities, the skunk was no uncertain surprise to settlers who had never experienced its "nature."

Michel Sarrazin, the colony's first natural scientist, abandoned an attempt to analyze the creature's anatomy because "it had a frightful smell, capable of making a whole canton [district] desert."

The twenty-six-year-old French surgeon came to New France in 1685 and became Surgeon-Major of the troops at Ville-Marie and Quebec City. He also served the civilian population and treated several well-known citizens for wounds they received during duels.

Sarrazin's hobby was scientific endeavour and he devoted himself to investigating the indigenous flora and fauna, which presented many uncharted species. Initially, he would risk Iroquois ambush while roaming the woods, fields and bogs, gathering specimens and assembling countless notes and sketches which he forwarded to scientists in France. "I could more easily traverse the whole of Europe, with less danger, than I could cover 100 leagues in Canada," he wrote.

In 1699 the Royal Academy of Sciences in Paris honoured Sarrazin by naming him as a corresponding member. Attempts were made to ship potted bushes and plants to France on the King's ship. Sailors were instructed to maintain them on the deck, and in the absence of rain they were to utilize precious reserves from the ship's meagre water supply. This proved futile, since the plants were often drenched by waves of saltwater and Intendant Bochart de Champigny received correspondence indicating that the samples arrived "dry, or more exactly dead." Seeds fared better, and samples of Canadian flora were soon growing in the King's royal garden.

Sarrazin's "hobby" did not interfere with his duties as a doctor and he was considered quite competent. Although surgical techniques were far from advanced and anesthetics quite primitive, in 1700 Sarrazin performed a breast cancer operation on a nun. It may have been the first of its kind in New France and his biographer, Arthur Vallée, cites this as an example of Sarrazin's "professional conscience, surgical ability and religious and moral valour."

Epidemics of flu and yellow fever were a constant problem. In his quest for cures and remedies, Sarrazin gained the trust of the native people and sought their suggestions. Following a smallpox epidemic in 1702 that killed 2,000 people, Sarrazin employed his botanical skills to discover a smallpox treatment through the common pitcher plant, whose scientific name became *Sarracenia purpurea*.

Industry in the colony also benefited from Sarrazin's love of nature. His investigation into the properties of the sugar maple laid the foundation for the harvest of maple syrup, which reduced the need for expensive, imported sugar. By 1704, Sarrazin had submitted more than 200 specimens to the Royal Academy, including exhaustive anatomical studies of the beaver, porcupine and muskrat.

As a member of the Superior Council, his knowledge of plant life was applied to agriculture and he was charged with the responsibility of examining the milling and cooking of wheat. Although Turkish wheat was initially considered, Sarrazin obtained hardier wheat specimens from Sweden which yielded better results.

At fifty-three, Sarrazin married a woman thirty-three years his junior. The marriage certificate shows Sarrazin's age as only forty, which may have been a touch of coquettish gallantry on his part. Although he owned many properties, medicine was not particularly lucrative due to the lack of hard currency in New France. When he died at seventy-five from typhus brought over on one of the ships, Michel Sarrazin was a pauper.

"He exercised his art with a rare and unselfish charity; serving all who sought his help with kindness and grace which he dispensed equally and with great success," reported the Sisters of L'Hôtel Dieu hospital.

The skunk may have eluded Sarrazin, but his contribution to the health of New France and the understanding of its unique natural world set a precedent of excellence for others to follow.

THE MILLENNIAL TREE

Pacific Coast, 1824 — It is the largest tree in Canada, achieving heights of twenty storeys. More than 1,000 growth rings have been counted on stumps as wide as an average single-lane roadway, making it a truly millennial tree.

The Douglas fir (*Pseudotsuga taxifolia*) is a majestic, blue-crowned tree. Its wood became the core of British Columbia's forest products industry. The botanist whose name it is taken from first discovered the tree at Mount St. Helena in Washington State on one of his many expeditions to discover new species.

Today, groves of Douglas fir mark David Douglas's 1799 birthplace in Scone, Scotland and the site of his mysterious death in 1834 in northern Hawaii. But the Douglas fir is not his only legacy, since in his short lifetime David Douglas contributed approximately 7,000 previously unknown species of plants to our understanding of the natural world. He has been called a "Botanical Columbus."

The son of a Perthshire stonemason, Douglas was attracted to nature from an early age. By the age of eleven he was serving as an apprentice gardener on large estates where access to botanical libraries stimulated his interest in exotic plants. Further study took him to the Glasgow Royal Botanic Garden and at the age of twenty-four, Douglas became a field collector for the Horticultural Society of London.

In 1823, the Society sent him on a four-month expedition that began in New York and saw the intrepid Scot travelling as far as Amherstburg in Upper Canada and Sandwich (now Windsor, Ontario). Despite the fact that he was robbed of his money and his coat while climbing a tree, Douglas managed to return to Britain with an impressive array of samples.

The following year, he was sent to explore the Pacific coast of North America. Fort Vancouver, a Hudson's Bay Company outpost on the Columbia River, served as his headquarters. One of the many samples he sent back to London in his first shipment was his namesake evergreen, whose wood Douglas suggested "may be found very useful for a variety of domestic purposes."

Indeed the multi-faceted Douglas fir had not gone unnoticed before Douglas. Native people used the flat-needled boughs as covering on the floors of their lodges and as fuel for their cooking pits. The sturdy wood was useful for making everything from fish hooks to handles.

In 1778, Captain James Cook cut spars for one of his ships from the abundant forest near present-day Duncan, B.C. Exceptionally durable, Douglas fir has been used in heavy construction such as wharves, trestles and bridge parts. When thin layers are bonded together the result is a tough plywood.

In 1827, Douglas accompanied the Hudson's Bay Company's annual express to York Factory on the shores of Hudson Bay. While he got along well with fur traders and native people, Douglas had little use for the HBC, which he

considered a soulless "mercenary corporation." When travelling by canoe he said that he felt "molested out of my life
by men singing their boat songs." Fortunately, much of his
work was a solitary endeavour.

"Being well rested by one o'clock I set out with a view
of ascending what seemed to be the highest peak on the
north," he wrote during his travels through the Athabasca
Pass.

That day the rugged Scot climbed a 9,156-foot mountain in five hours alone and without benefit of climbing
equipment. It was the earliest recorded climb in the Canadian Rockies. Douglas named his conquest Mount Brown
in honour of botanist Robert Brown, the first head of the
British Museum's botanical department.

He returned to England in 1827, having survived a
violent storm in Hudson Bay that nearly took his life. The
plants and seeds he brought with him were the largest collection ever gathered by one person.

Although he was notably shy, Douglas became an
instant celebrity.

Three years later, he returned to Fort Vancouver and
continued to botanize despite diminishing eyesight caused
by the blowing snow, sand and glaring sun experienced
during his previous adventures. Still, one of his travelling
companions noted that he would "scramble like . . . a cat
upon rocks" when a specimen attracted his attention. A few
years later, he lost sight completely in his right eye, but was
determined to return to England, travelling through British
Columbia, to Alaska and then across Siberia.

His ambitious journey was foiled in a misadventure
on the Fraser River when he lost his canoe over a cataract
near Prince George, B.C. Douglas and his guide were
caught in a whirlpool and washed up on the rocks. While

he was lucky to be alive, more than 400 specimens and his meticulous notes were lost. Five days after the incident, Douglas was bound for the Sandwich Islands, reaching Honolulu just before Christmas, 1934.

What happened next remains something of a mystery. Douglas apparently continued to collect specimens with his usual vigour in Hawaii. In July, he was exploring on the slope of Mauna Kea in northern Hawaii. His body was ultimately recovered from a pit-like cattle trap holding an enraged bull. He had been gored and trampled.

The unusual circumstances advanced a variety of theories ranging from accident to suicide. Kenneth Favrholdt, a Kamloops museum co-ordinator who has been researching the life and travels of David Douglas, believes that foul play is the most likely explanation. He visited the stone cairn that marks the site of Douglas's death on the Parker Ranch in Hawaii. At the museum there, Favrholdt was greeted with stony silence when he tried to discuss local lore, which suggests that the night before he was killed Douglas camped with an Australian convict who may have been his murderer.

Embued with a curiosity and enthusiasm for what he called the "great operations of nature," Douglas's contribution to the world of botany is evident today in gardens all over the world where species of lily, phlox and lupine bloom.

"There is scarcely a spot deserving the name of a garden in which some of the discoveries of David Douglas do not form the chief attraction," noted one twentieth-century horticulturist. "To no single individual is modern horticulture more indebted."

A HATFUL OF GRAIN

Otonabee, Upper Canada, 1842 — Scottish settler David Fife had a problem growing a good crop of wheat. There were some years when he lost his whole crop to an early frost, and others when a fungus known as "rust" decimated his production. Fife was experiencing the same problems that had plagued pioneers since European settlers first set seed to sod at Port-Royal in Acadia in 1605, but he was not about to give up.

Farmers had experimented with different varieties of wheat trying to find one suitable to the Canadian climate and growing conditions. They tried varieties that grew everywhere from India to Siberia, but new seed stock was difficult to obtain. Fife believed that northern European varieties might hold the clue. He had a friend who was working as a clerk in Glasgow and he enlisted his aid to obtain seeds direct from the ships that passed through the dockyards.

Security was tight at the Glasgow docks, but somehow the Scottish clerk managed to talk his way into a stroll aboard a ship carrying a bounty of wheat from Danzig (now Gdansk, Poland). While peering into the cargo hold, his hat apparently fell into the bin. No one could criticize the good

Scot for wanting to retrieve a perfectly good hat. And no one could have predicted that the handful of wheat kernels that became "accidentally" lodged in the lining of the headgear would change the complexion of Canadian wheat fields from rust to gold before the turn of the century.

In the spring of 1842, David Fife sowed the seeds he had received from Scotland in an experimental garden plot on his farm near what is now Peterborough, Ontario. Except for one, all of the resulting plants perished. The sole survivor produced five fine seed heads. However, reports in the *Canadian Agriculturist* dryly note that two of these "were destroyed by cattle." More lively accounts describe Mrs. Fife confronting a gorging ox in the experimental garden and salvaging just one head — enough seed to fill an egg cup.

The Polish wheat stock thrived in succeeding years and soon neighbours were pleading for seed. It became known as Red Fife, as much for David's red hair as for the seed's own rosy complexion. Less than a decade after its first planting, the plump-berried, rust-resistant strain of wheat was being endorsed by farmers throughout Upper Canada, and it soon spread to spring wheat belts in Michigan, Illinois and Wisconsin. By 1862, the *Canadian Agriculturist* was hailing the golden grain that yielded twenty to thirty bushels per acre as "the glorious Fife . . . rather hard to grind, but it makes good flour. Why sir, ten years ago, it would have been considered incredible."

In 1876, Red Fife was planted for the first time in Manitoba's Red River Valley. That year's harvest was to mark the first shipment of wheat out of Western Canada, coinciding with a crop failure in Ontario caused by a dry growing season and a wet harvest. On October 13, the *Winnipeg Free Press* advised that "Steele Brothers, Seedsmen,

Toronto, arrived last night . . . for the purpose of obtaining 5,000 bushels of Manitoba wheat for seed in Ontario."

The firm of Higgins and Young, "Dealers in Boots and Shoes, Crockery and Glassware," were assigned the task of filling the order that promised to pay farmers eighty cents per bushel. In previous decades, wheat had been traded much as beaver pelts — for goods rather than cash, and the prospect of hard currency caused considerable excitement. When the available grain was finally assembled for shipment at McMillan's Mill on the banks of the Red River, there were only 417 two-bushel, white cotton bags on the dock, less than a fifth of the order. Just one step ahead of freeze-up, the precious cargo moved circuitously by riverboat, rail and lakeboat before reaching Toronto.

By the following year, Red Fife had established a firm following among the Red River settlers and twenty thousand bushels were shipped to eastern buyers on October 17, 1877. One of the contractors was Barclay and Brand of Glasgow, Scotland, which received the first overseas shipment of wheat from the Canadian West. The birth of a viable wheat industry in Canada can be celebrated from that point. Coincidentally, that year also marks the death of David Fife, the red-headed Scot who started an industry with a hatful of grain.

LET THERE BE LIGHT

Charlottetown, Prince Edward Island, 1846 — Long before the light bulb, kerosene would change the nocturnal habits of nations. It was the discovery of a failed horse trader and self-taught geologist named Abraham Gesner. More than kerosene, his methods and processes of distilling oil from hydrocarbons led to the establishment of the entire petrochemical industry. In 1933, Imperial Oil erected a monument honouring him as the "American inventor" of kerosene, but Abraham Gesner was a true Canadian genius.

He was a farmer's son, born in 1797 and raised near Cornwallis, Nova Scotia. In his youth, he collected rocks and dabbled in chemistry. When several of his "experiments" resulted in explosions in the homestead, a makeshift laboratory was established in a shed. Young Gesner impressed some local farmers with homemade matches, while others were convinced his destiny was to blow himself to smithereens.

Jobs were scarce, so Gesner turned to horse trading. He planned to ship horses to the West Indies for profit, a concept that was as risky as it was inhumane. His first venture barely broke even, nevertheless he returned with mineral samples, including a curious black "pitch" from Trinidad which proved to be asphaltum. In his early experiments with the sticky substance, Gesner discovered that it burned with a hot, steady flame. If the problems of smoke and smell could be eliminated, it might even make an illuminant.

But commerce called. Gesner was anxious to earn enough money to marry a doctor's daughter, Harriet Webster. His subsequent horse-trading ventures floundered, quite literally, and instead of being penniless, he found himself in debt.

Although he managed to marry Harriet, Gesner's father-in-law sent him to medical school in England to avoid disgrace at the hands of his creditors.

Returning to Nova Scotia in 1827, he chose Parrsboro as the location for his practice, more for its interesting terrain than for its medical prospects. During this time, he travelled the countryside on horseback in the company of Micmac Indians, playing the flute while they helped him gather geological specimens.

His treatises on the geology and mineralogy of Nova Scotia established his reputation and from 1838 to 1842 he served New Brunswick as its first geologist. His enthusiastic reports led several speculators to rush into ventures that went bankrupt and the government refused to pay Gesner for his final year.

This time Gesner confronted debt with the novel idea of opening a paid-admission museum. In Saint John, he assembled 2,173 artifacts from his private collection, including numerous fossils and oddities such as the air bladder of a sturgeon. When the museum failed, his creditors accepted the collection in place of payment and it formed part of the foundation of the New Brunswick Museum.

Gesner returned to medical practice in Cornwallis, devoting his spare time to refining hydrocarbons in the same laboratory shed he had enjoyed as a child. At an 1846 lecture in Charlottetown, Prince Edward Island, he introduced a substance he called "keroselain" after a Greek word meaning "wax oil." It was a clear, white oil that he distilled from the treated vapours of heated coal.

Candles, whale oil and other illuminants of the day produced dingy light and greasy, odorous smoke. "Burning fluid" composed of turpentine and alcohol produced a bright light, often accompanied by explosions. Gesner's oil could be handled easily and burned with a brilliant yellow light that produced almost no smoke. He refined his process further when he identified a previously unknown mineral, albertite, a bitumen found in Albert County, New Brunswick. Gesner bought a large tract of land containing the mineral, only to have that venture land him in court when another man claimed the coal rights. A jury was bamboozled into believing that albertite and coal were one and the same. Gesner's loss turned into a multimillion-dollar profit for his adversary.

Embittered and impoverished, Gesner left Canada. He had secured patents in the United States and wealthy developers in Long Island, New York, set up a factory under his guidance in 1854. "Kerosene" became the most successful lamp oil ever produced, but Gesner was never a partner in the profits. His patent was challenged and, once again, Gesner lost.

He died in 1864, just as he was about to become the first chemistry professor at Dalhousie University.

A MAN FOR
ALL TIME ZONES

Toronto, 1879 — When it is 6:00 p.m. in Prince George, British Columbia, it is 10:30 p.m. in Grand Falls, Newfoundland. Why? The answer is Standard Time, the globally recognized system of telling time which was invented by a Scottish-born Canadian, Sir Sandford Fleming.

Fleming was eighteen when he arrived in Canada prepared to take up a career as a draughtsman and surveyor. After completing the survey of several small Ontario towns, he set about mapping the city of Toronto, producing the first usable chart of Toronto's harbour by taking soundings both from a boat and through holes drilled in the winter ice.

Fleming's interest in developing a universal system of time developed during his work as the Chief Engineer of the Inter-Continental Railroad and the Canadian Pacific Railroad.

In Canada and other countries 12:00 noon was designated as the time when the sun was directly overhead. As a result, if it was noon in Kingston, it was twelve minutes after noon in Montreal and thirteen minutes before noon in Toronto. Local people were perfectly content with local time. After all, they did not have programmable VCRs to concern themselves with. They worked according to the cycle of the season and the placement of the sun.

The variations became more significant when railroads allowed longer distances of travel over shorter time periods. The results were confusing. For example, a journey by train from Halifax to Windsor involved having to re-set your watch ten times!

Fleming had a talent for spotting a simple solution to an inconvenient problem. After missing several trains himself and recognizing the headache transcontinental travel would pose, he began examining the history of time. He discovered that most ancient civilizations had computed day and night in twelve-hour cycles. He combined this into a twenty-four-hour clock and proceeded to divide the globe into twenty-four equal zones.

When he first presented the concept of Standard Time to the Canadian Institute for the Advancement of Scientific Knowledge at Toronto in 1879, Fleming was variously denounced as an Utopian and a promoter of notions which were "contrary to the will of God." Persistence and persuasion finally won governments and the scientific community to the practicality of his idea.

Canada adopted Standard Time in 1883, along with all North American railway companies. The following year twenty-five nations adopted the proposition at a conference in Washington, D.C. Greenwich, England was designated as the Prime Meridian (line of longitude) as the base for calculation, since it had served as the standard for two-thirds of the world's shipping industry for many years.

By the late nineteenth century, inhabitants of all but the remotest corners of the world had adopted Standard

Time. Coordinated Universal Time, based on atomic clocks established in Paris in 1972, has been the foundation of Standard Time since 1985.

Sandford Fleming was a man of many accomplishments. He designed Canada's first postage stamp, the Threepenny Beaver in 1851. He also lithographed the first accurate large-scale surveyor's maps of Canada and promoted a submarine telegraph cable from Vancouver to Australia. In 1897, Fleming was knighted, but he always contended that his greatest honour was to serve as Chancellor of Queen's University for thirty-five years. Somewhere between his writing of scientific papers and his abiding interest in a good game of chess, Sir Sandford Fleming also wrote an interdenominational prayer book, hymnal and psalter.

"Nothing can be recalled what is past, no not even a second ago," the "Father of Standard Time" once wrote in his diary. "Every action is as it were recorded on the minute of time for ever and ever! I do not regret the time I have spent."

THE HEART OF THE MATTER

Montreal, 1890 — She was to all intents a fortunate orphan, raised by loving grandparents who provided a governess for her early education. A conventional child in many respects, she read *Little Women*, kept a diary full of her dreams and delighted in a Christmas stocking that included "a silver thimble, a black-handled tooth brush, half a dozen handkerchiefs." But by the time she was fifteen, Maude Abbott clearly had more on her mind than shopping for the contents of the first catalogue published by Timothy Eaton.

"Think of learning German, Latin and other languages in general," she wrote to herself in 1884. "Think of the loveliness of thinking that it entirely depended on myself whether I got on."

Applying herself to the process of "getting on" was not a problem for Maude Abbott. She had a boundless enthusiasm for learning, which would see her studying in Germany, Austria and Scotland before she settled into her life's work as a medical curator and a world authority on congenital heart ailments.

The Abbott surname belonged to Maude's grandparents. Their daughter, Elizabeth, married the Reverend Jeremiah Babin but the marriage failed before Maude was even born. She was seven months old when her mother died of tuberculosis, leaving Maude and her sister, Alice, to be legally adopted by her grandparents.

Reverend William Abbott came to Canada in 1818 with his brother, Joseph, who was also an Anglican clergyman. They occupied charges in St. Andrews East and what is now known as Abbotsford, Quebec. Young Maude thrived in what she recalled as "the genial social atmosphere of old world culture and refinement" of her childhood. The Abbott family achieved prominence in the area, most notably through Maude's second cousin, John, the first Canadian-born Prime Minister in 1891.

But having relatives in high places was not going to help Maude realize her dream of attending McGill University. For years, McGill opposed "mixed classes" on moral grounds and claimed that separate sex classes were not economically feasible.

A hero appeared in 1884 in the figure of Donald Smith (later Lord Strathcona) who endowed the university with a total of $120,000 specifically for the higher education of women. Two years later, Maude Abbott received a scholarship to enter the arts program, the only program McGill offered to female students.

When Grace Ritchie delivered the first valedictory address to McGill's "Donalda" students, she distinguished herself by challenging the university to expand its enlightened attitude by starting a medical course for women. She herself pursued medical studies at Kingston's Women's Medical College, which had opened its doors in 1883.

Around the time of Grace Ritchie's speech, Maude Abbott was beginning to consider what her options would be after graduation. The story goes that Maude sought her grandmother's counsel.

"May I be a doctor?" she asked.

"Dear child, you may be anything you like," Mrs. Abbott told her. What the progressive grandmother did not tell her eager charge was that McGill University would have to be pixillated by a lot of fairy dust and a World War before a woman would graduate from their medical school.

Maude started petitioning the faculty of medicine to open classes to women before she graduated in the arts. The idea was summarily rejected, even when Maude and her supporters raised $12,000 toward the expense.

One professor threatened to resign. Another despaired that while women might have some useful place in certain areas of medicine, they "would not have the nerve" in "difficult work" such as surgery. He added: "And can you think of a patient in a critical case, waiting for half an hour while the medical lady fixes her bonnet or adjusts her bustle."

Although she considered anything less than a McGill education to be "inferior," Maude elected to attend Bishop's Medical College in Montreal. It was as close to McGill as she could get, since many McGill professors provided hospital instruction at Montreal General Hospital.

Access to hospital instruction was a critical issue to women attending medical college in those days. Grace Ritchie had paved the way for Maude at Bishop's. A knowledgeable, likable student, Ritchie impressed Bishop's staff when she spent a summer as a clinician at Montreal General Hospital, gaining a "ticket" permitting access to the wards. Bishop's lured Ritchie away from Kingston to spend her final year with them. She was a feather in their cap to wave at their McGill rivals.

What Montreal General had done for the amiable Ritchie began to have repercussions. Other women medical students from Kingston began applying for summer "tickets" to the teaching wards. Before graduating from Bishop's, Ritchie told Maude Abbott to send her twenty-dollar fee and her application right away.

Sure enough, the hospital started backtracking on entry for women, allegedly fearing an onslaught of ticket requests from women. Maude was caught in a "Catch-22" situation. On one hand, she had started classes at Bishop's without a hitch, but on the other she could not graduate without hospital experience. The hospital had taken her money but now they would not give her the ticket to teaching ward access that she had paid for.

She was contemplating a transfer to medical school in Philadelphia when her story hit the newspapers. At a delicate moment in Montreal General's annual fund-raising process, several of the largest subscribers refused to pay until Miss Abbott received her ticket. Her ticket arrived in the mail.

In 1894, Maude Abbott graduated with honours and accolades. It had been a lonely four years, in which she found herself decried by her fellow students as an aggressive "swot." Although shy by nature, apparently Maude would not hesitate to elbow her way to the front of any demonstration. In keeping with her passion for being at the forefront, Maude embarked on postgraduate studies in Vienna, accompanied by her sister, Alice, who was pursuing music studies. She spent two years taking courses, including internal medicine and pathology, which were her special interests. When the Abbott sisters returned to Montreal in 1897, Alice was recovering from a bout of diphtheria. A few years later, she suffered a nervous breakdown. Maude would care for her chronically invalid sister all her life.

To support the two of them, Dr. Abbott opened a practice for women and children. This drab follow-up to her European sojourn was brightened when two professors associated with McGill took an interest in clinical studies she had conducted in Vienna and assigned her to research projects. Although it was mandated that women could not present academic papers, Maude's statistical study on heart murmurs gained her recognition and unprecedented membership at the society where it was read. Another paper was delivered by a male colleague on her behalf to the Pathological Society in London, England, the first time research by a woman was recognized.

McGill finally began to see Dr. Abbott's scholarship and energy as a potential asset. In 1898, she was appointed as assistant curator of the university's medical museum. Since its beginnings in 1823, "specimens" had been accumulating in jars and bottles. Maude's task was to catalogue, classify and organize seventy-five years of pickled neglect.

On a tour of American museums, she met the Canadian physician who inspired her career as he did generations of medical practitioners. By then, William Osler was chief of medicine at Johns Hopkins Hospital in Baltimore. Dr. Osler shared Dr. Abbott's passion for pathology, and he was responsible for a good many of the specimens at McGill which she would be maintaining. He told her that the museum was a great opportunity and one that would provide a valuable teaching tool. "He gently dropped a seed that dominated all my future work," said Maude.

In 1905, Osler was compiling the book *System of Medicine* and he asked Maude to contribute on the topic of congenital heart disease. The monograph she submitted included a statistical analysis of more than 400 cases. Osler declared it "far and away the best thing ever written on the subject" and Abbott became known internationally as an authority. A dozen years before the first female doctors would graduate from McGill in 1922, the university granted Maude an honorary degree M.D., C.M. (*honoris causa*), and she began lecturing in pathology.

The museum also flourished. Students enjoyed stopping by and asking questions. Maude formed associations with other medical museums, as well as cataloguing the Canadian Army Medical Museum. She also served as editor of the *Canadian Medical Association Journal*, wrote a definitive history of medicine in Quebec and chaired the Federation of Medical Women of Canada.

It has been said that McGill University never quite appreciated the whirlwind wunderkind that it had in the woman who was often called "Maudie." Her desk was a chaos of papers. Sometimes she set such a dizzying schedule for herself that she forgot to eat. Notebooks had a habit of slipping from her fingers, and train tickets found ways of escaping her. She was consumed by her work, as evidenced by a formalin stain from one of her beloved samples that ended up on an evening gown.

Although she received offers of full professorships from other universities, Dr. Abbott strayed from McGill only once in the mid-1920s when Women's Medical College in Pennsylvannia lured her away at double her salary. When she returned to McGill, she was made an assistant professor, a designation that lasted until her reluctant retirement in 1936.

At sixty-seven, Dr. Abbott embarked on a lecture tour, which coincided with the publication of her classic work *Atlas of Congenital Heart Disease*. Always prone to accidents, she was sixty-nine when she was crushed between two streetcars in Montreal. Recovering in the hospital, she sur-rounded herself with books and papers. The following year she received a Carnegie grant to write a textbook, but she suffered a cerebral hemorrhage and died in September, 1940, before its completion.

"Work is fundamental to the onward march of sci-ence," Maude Abbott said in the valedictory address she delivered to her graduating class in 1890. "It is at the bot-tom of every great and good action that was ever done; it underlies the formation of all true character."

A scholar, a teacher and a curator, she was hailed as "a living force in the medicine of her generation." Ultim-ately, the "loveliness" of depending on herself to "get on" that Maude dreamed of as a child became her reality.

H_2O + MYSTERIOUS GREY POWDER = SUNSHINE + $$$$

Saguenay Valley, Quebec, 1892 — Turn-of-the-century industrial revolutionary Thomas Leopold Willson was one of those visionaries who could not see the forest for the opportunity. He earned several fortunes and gambled them all on the potential he saw in the uncompromising wilderness of the Saguenay River Valley.

Willson's passion was not wilderness for wilderness's sake. He saw the future in the dark recesses of that forest. To him, the raging Saguenay River represented an inexhaustible source of hydro-electric power. By 1908, Willson had acquired vast land, timber and water rights in the valley, encompassing tens of thousands of acres. As usual, he had big, big plans.

No slick grifter, Willson was a chronic and hugely successful inventor. In Canada alone, he held more than sixty patents. If even half of the proceeds had been properly managed, the return would have provided for a dozen dynasties. Willson managed to keep most of his millions and his dreams, until he met American tobacco and textile tycoon James Buchanan Duke.

Young Thomas "Leo" came from a prominent family. His grandfather was the Honourable John Willson, a member of the Legislative Assembly of Upper Canada who was known as "the Father of the Common Schools Act." One of nine children, his father (also named Thomas) became a minister, but always had a few irons in the entrepreneurial fire, which caused his downfall. He died when his eldest son was fourteen after losing everything due to a loan guarantee that went bad and a failed attempt at manufacturing.

Forced to move from the family farm in Princeton, Ontario, the family settled in Hamilton. The widow Rachel Sabina Willson, a character in her own right, supported her two sons by taking in lodgers, teaching painting and giving lessons on the Spanish guitar.

A precocious youngster, Willson built a steam-driven generator and an experimental arc light system in the upstairs loft over a blacksmith's shop. In those days, electricity was not taken for granted. It was regarded as magical rather than scientific. Willson's arc lights attracted so much attention they had to be moved from the smithy's to Dun-durn Park to accommodate the curious hordes. Forging a role for himself, the blacksmith became a business partner, taking orders for the lighting system from businesses and towns far and wide.

In the early days of electricity the big problem was the production of steady, even power, a problem that Willson had not solved. His arc lights were forever flickering and blinking on and off. Enthusiasm for them waned, transforming the buoyant business partners into bankrupts.

The faded local hero went to New York City where he worked at jobs involving electricity and smelting. He also acquired business skills and developed a new interest — aluminum.

In 1891, aluminum was a new metal that was astonishingly expensive to produce. Willson was convinced that there had to be a cheaper means of production. He needed cash and a steady source of power, sufficient to fire a blast furnace. Finding both in Major James Morehead, a wealthy mill owner from North Carolina, the Willson Aluminum Company was formed in Spray, N.C.

The way Willson talked about the process it had more in common with medieval alchemy than modern science. He even speculated about how his "New Science" could be applied to produce commercial diamonds. Many months later, Willson's talk was wearing thin and his experiments yielded nothing but frustration. He was unaware that others in the field had already just discovered a much better, less expensive way to produce aluminum in France.

The Major's patience and money had just about run out when Willson stumbled on the thing that was going to change both their lives forever.

On May 2, 1892, Willson directed his assistants to mix a specific amount of coal, lime and tar then heat the mixture in the blast furnace to 5,500 degrees centigrade.

The average person might not have seen anything revelatory in the fact that a lump of grey, turgid dirt heated to 5,500 degrees caused a violent reaction when dropped into a bucket of cold water, but Thomas Willson was not the average person.

At the heart of science is repetition. The next time he did it, Willson put an oil-soaked rag on the end of a long pole, and, just for the heck of it, lit it on fire and held it over the water in which the heated lump of dirt had been dropped.

A flame leapt between the rag and the broiling water. When he pulled the rag away, the flame disappeared.

Willson knew he had discovered something but had no idea what.

In Thomas Willson were combined two normally apostate talents. Not only was he capable of recognizing a discovery when he made one, he was amazingly adroit at realizing its commercial potential.

He knew instinctively that a gas that burns almost always has commercial value. A gas produced by dumping cheap lumps of heated dirt in plain water might have unlimited commercial potential.

Willson sent a description of his process and sample of his "unique" mixture of coal, lime and tar to the distinguished scientist William Thomson at the University of Glasgow. The response was a perfunctory "nothing new" note. Heated calcium carbide always produces bubbles of highly volatile acetylene gas in water, the professor wrote.

What was new was the actual accident of the discovery. Willson's method of producing both the carbide and the gas was tens of thousands of times cheaper than any previously discovered method.

Kerosene had virtually led the world out of the dark ages when it replaced candlelight in the 1850s. Compared to candles, the light kerosene provided was startlingly bright. The light acetylene produced was like sunlight, containing every colour in the spectrum. By the light of acetylene it was possible to grow plants. The possibilities seemed endless.

Willson's formula: Hot dirt + water = artificial sunlight + $$$$.

In 1895, "Carbide" Willson sold his American patents to the newly formed Union Carbide company and the rest is, as they say, industrial history.

Willson got married and returned to Canada with ample funds to establish an all-Canadian carbide works at

Merriton, near St. Catharines, Ontario, on the Niagara Peninsula. The new facility included the first hydro-electric plant built in Canada and the largest on the North American continent.

Those were prosperous years for Willson. He moved his family to Woodstock, Ontario, and formed a partnership with a local businessman named James Sutherland, who became a minister in Sir Wilfrid Laurier's cabinet.

Sutherland convinced Willson to move to Ottawa. In 1904, Willson established two more plants, one on Victoria Island in the Ottawa River and the other in Shawinigan, Quebec. Still, he could not keep up with demand.

By the time electricity made acetylene-fuelled light obsolete, Willson had adapted and made another fortune with oxyacetylene torches. It had just been discovered that oxygen combined with acetylene would produce a flame that would cut through steel, a technology that revolutionized industry in North America.

While his wealth continued to grow exponentially, Willson grew restless. He had already started acquiring water and timber rights in the Saguenay Valley when he was temporarily distracted by an incident in Kingston, Ontario.

Marine buoys were illuminated by acetylene but in such a way that the buoys had to be refuelled. A beacon blew while being refilled at the Kingston docks, killing four people.

A few months later Willson filed the patents on a new type of navigational marker, it effectively functioned as a mini-carbide-acetylene factory. Willson's markers generated their own light and never had to be refilled. By 1906, his Marine Signal Company was filling orders from over forty countries. Willson made another fortune.

Willson's carbide seemed to transform everything he touched into gold. It turned out that calcium carbide could "fix" or capture nitrogen, thereby making it possible to store the gas as a solid.

Suddenly it dawned on Willson that his factories that already were producing tons of calcium carbide and acetylene daily could also be used to produce a nitrogenous fertilizer.

Artificial or manmade fertilizers were already seen as elixirs of life. But they were derived from the Chilean guano fields where bird droppings were scraped from the rocks and then shipped up around the tip of South America. By the turn of the century, the guano fields were virtually exhausted.

The so-called superphosphates interested Willson. Soon he had perfected the manufacturing process, producing the most powerful fertilizer on the planet.

Willson was living at Meech Lake, where he was as restless and dissatisfied as his California-born wife, Mary, was calm and contented. All Willson saw when he looked out his window on the magnificent landscape was a source of unlimited power. A lake the size of Meech high in the Gatineau Hills had to have an outlet somewhere. Wherever that was, the water could easily be channelled.

He was thinking about the future and the Saguenay Valley and hydro-electric power. Wealthy beyond words, bored and frustrated, he began to sell off his holdings to finance further acquisitions in the Saguenay Valley. In 1909, a Buffalo, N.Y., firm bought the Marine Signal Company. He divested himself of his carbide plants. He even sold his Canadian patents.

In 1911, he damned the small river below Meech Lake and built a private hydro-electric station hidden in the woods and a factory for the production of his super-phosphate agricultural supplements. He saw in his private Meech Lake project the microcosm of his plans for the Saguenay River Valley. But it would cost more money than even Willson had stockpiled. He was in the process of mortgaging everything he owned when he met James Buchanan Duke.

Willson chartered a private train to take the fabulously wealthy Duke into the Saguenay wilderness, to show him — with style and flair — where the real future lay.

Duke agreed to lend the necessary $1.5 million, but in return he wanted as security the only thing Willson had left — the Saguenay properties. Willson foolishly agreed. A year later, the plant was up and running, but Willson found himself cash-strapped. He missed one interest payment and the wilderness belonged to Duke.

Willson was down but not out. Although he had sold his companies and his Canadian patents, there was always Newfoundland, as yet an independent colony. (Newfoundland did not join Canada until 1949.) He was able to build yet another carbide factory with impunity on the Rock, starting again from ground zero. By July, 1914, he had guarantees of over $10 million from British investors. Then the outbreak of the First World War cut off all foreign capital investments.

Thomas "Carbide" Willson was in New York four days before Christmas in 1915 hustling new sources of funding when he had a heart attack and died alone in a hotel room. He was forty-five.

James Buchanan Duke sold Willson's timber and water rights to the American industrialist Arthur Vining Davis, who established the vast aluminum industry that made the Saguenay area world-famous.

When Duke died he left his fortune, as vast as the Saguenay River Valley wilderness, to his ten-year-old daughter Doris. Until she disappeared five decades later, Ms. Duke was the richest woman in the world.

MASTICATION AS THE MOTHER OF INVENTION

Ottawa, 1907 — There once was a Canadian scientist who chewed his way to a kind of fame and fortune. Through an elaborate process of mastication and elimination, Charles Saunders discovered the wheat strain that made Canada the breadbasket of the world. Still obscure after all these years, Saunders was a reluctant agricultural researcher.

His father, William, a druggist from London, Ontario, maintained a passion for horticulture and from an early age all five of the Saunders children were taught the Latin names of plants. Charles was a frail child. Although he dreamed of studying music and enjoyed playing the flute, his father preferred him to study chemistry, so he attended the University of Toronto. "I am a docile person," he once noted. "I am always going where I am pushed."

After completing his studies at Johns Hopkins University and teaching chemistry in Kentucky, Saunders escaped the influence of his father briefly, studying singing and teaching music at a ladies' college.

But Saunders Sr. was bent on having his son carry on the work he had started in developing a strain of wheat that would ripen early enough to survive fall frosts in the West. In 1885, William Saunders became the director of the Dominion Experimental Farms where he conducted research.

At every vacation, Charles and his brother, Percy, were called upon to apply their knowledge of chemistry to developing new strains. In 1902, Charles Saunders was appointed as Dominion Cerealist — by his father.

It was a tedious task to check each sample, but Saunders was a meticulous researcher. Selection was rigorous. Strains had to be grown separately and individual seed heads demonstrating the greatest strengths were tested.

Wheat could not be milled practically in small lots, which meant it could take years of careful harvest before enough of an experimental strain could be gathered to test its flour and bread-making qualities.

Ultimately, mastication became the mother of invention, when Saunders discovered that, by simply chewing a sample of kernels, he could determine its level of gluten and the sort of bread it would make. He diligently chewed his way through more than 100 varieties before discovering "Markham," a cross between Canadian Red Fife wheat and an Indian variety called Hard Red Calcutta. Feeling that the name was not noble enough, Saunders dubbed it "Marquis" and sent a sackful to the Experimental Farm at Indian Head, Saskatchewan, for testing in 1907.

Panic set in when the boss, Angus Mackay, could not find the precious seed sample. An urgent call went out, and the wheat was returned by one of the men who had inadvertently taken it home to feed his chickens.

Marquis wheat proved to be everything Saunders had hoped for. It yielded more bushels than its predecessors and, most importantly, it ripened for harvest one week earlier than Red Fife. When it was released for commercial production in 1909, Marquis became the wheat that won the West. Northern areas were settled, and wheat returns amounted to millions of dollars benefiting manufacturers, merchants and railroads, as well as farmers. By 1920, 90 percent of the wheat grown in western Canada was Marquis.

Saunders suffered a physical breakdown in 1922. He went to Paris where he studied French literature, producing a book of verse and essays that Quebec critics extolled as "courageous." Music remained the passion of his life, although his scientific endeavours earned him a knighthood in 1934.

When Sir Charles Saunders died in 1937, the *Daily Express* of London wrote "he contributed more to the wealth of his country than any other man."

ONE WITH THE SOIL

Nobleford, Alberta, 1913 — Charles Noble was eighty-four years old when he was inducted into the Alberta Agricultural Hall of Fame. He would probably have been a Hall of Famer earlier, but the Hall was not formed until 1951. It was Noble who gave Western farmers a simple cultivation tool that protected the soil from wind erosion. He invented the Noble Blade.

Charles Sherwood Noble was born in State Center, Iowa. He left school at fifteen to help his father support the family of six boys whose mother died when they were youngsters. He was seventeen when he bought a team of horses and went into business for himself, delivering hay, straw and coal. The following year he began working with his brother, Newell, running a corn-sheller and power-saw operation. He also made time to learn about steam engines and carpentry, and he travelled to Minneapolis to take a business course.

By the time Charles was twenty-three, he had built his own homestead in Knox, South Dakota. Hail and lightning destroyed that dream twice, so one of his brothers urged the industrious Charles to consider Washington State. However, the soil there was not to Charles Noble's liking — and it was his understanding of soil and its care that was to shape his future.

He found what he was looking for in Claresholm, Alberta, in 1902. But it was not just the soil that attracted him to land across the border. Margaret Fraser, the woman who became his wife the following year, had expressed a preference to live Canada.

The region was once home to Blackfoot natives and herds of bison. In his pessimistic 1862 report, British surveyor Captain John Palliser had identified the area as part of "the Great American Desert" and suggested that what became known as the "Palliser Triangle" was "soil worthless" and unsuited for settlement. Of course, he was proved wrong.

In 1909, Noble bought four hundred acres and named the property Grand View Farm. Other acreage was soon added, along with Noble children. It was a life of hard work, and Charles Noble thought nothing of beginning his day at 4 a.m.

On February 14, 1913, the Noble Foundation Company was formed. Its purpose was to "make a contribution to the best utilization of the farmlands of southern Alberta and the prosperity of its people." The Foundation allowed the employees to share in the ownership and trusteeship of the Noble properties.

Boom years followed. Crop yields broke records. In various years, Charles Noble earned the title of World Flax King, World Oat King and World Wheat King. New businesses thrived in the bustling settlement known as "Noble," which was officially named "Nobleford" and incorporated in 1918. The Noble Foundation Company built an office, a General Store and a thirty-room hotel. By then its holdings totalled 33,000 acres, much of it purchased with borrowed money. Ten steam tractors ran day and night breaking up as many as 400 acres a day. Horse-drawn teams carried water to the steamers. Coal was hauled from the local Taber mines.

At one time, a crew of 300 men and 600 mules and horses was working sections of the land. Noble did a cost analysis on the virtues of horsepower, steampower and gasoline tractors and found that horse operations were the most economical. His findings were published in the *Grain Growers Guide*. "We believe that no matter how reasonable engines, parts and fuel may be, it would be a great mistake to neglect the breeding and working of the best type of farm horse," he concluded. Horses, after all, require "much less grief and lower bills for depreciation and repair." Tractors were used as backup for many years.

On the home front, the Noble family was ensconced in a truly noble house by 1918. Built at a cost of $30,000, it included its own 110-volt light plant, water and sewage systems and an indoor swimming pool supplied by its own well.

A drought struck Southern Alberta in 1919 and it lasted for three years. In 1920, the price of wheat tumbled from a peak of $2.20 a bushel to a low of 65 cents. In successive years, the rainfall was too light for a heavy-yielding wheat crop. In 1922, the bondholders and the Bank of Montreal foreclosed, taking the Noble Foundation's $2.5 million in assets to cover a $650,000 debt. Charles Noble had pledged everything except his furniture to support the Foundation. At the age of fifty, he started over.

By 1930, Noble had reacquired his home and more than 7,500 acres. Still, between bank interest and soil drifting, the bank statements of the period contained more red ink than black. Noble's interest in solving the problem of conserving prairie soil and moisture became a passion shared by his sons, Shirley and Gerald. Their mission was to figure out a way to work the soil without turning it. The idea was to cut below the surface, killing weeds, sealing in moisture and leaving the surface stubble of the previous year's crop to form a protective mulch.

In 1935, Noble invented a straight blade cultivator that did the job. Improvements were made, and the straight blade was changed to a V-shape with the convex blade tilting horizontally by 30 degrees, facilitating its use on rolling land conditions. In 1942, patents were obtained and a small plant started manufacturing the Noble Blade. With missionary zeal, Charles Noble demonstrated the implement all over North America, often working in conjunction with Canadian Experimental farms and U.S. Soil Conservationists. The business grew and the cultivator that Noble created was soon joined by a variety of other implements.

"The Chief," as he was known to many of his long-time employees, was also hailed as the "Grand Old Man of Agriculture." He was appointed a member of the Order of the British Empire and granted an honorary Doctorate of Laws from the University of Alberta.

Charles Noble's love of the land was as great then as it had been one summer day in 1917, when he drove over an expanse of prairie near the joining of the Oldman and Little Bow Rivers. He was with his young son, Shirley, who saw nothing much in the land except small herds of antelope and a coyote. Charles paused to examine a few badger and gopher holes that showed the subsoil. Then he drove to Lethbridge to make an offer to buy the land. Later he explained his reasons to the family, saying simply, "The land had strength and the land lay beautifully."

Charles Noble was the sort of farmer who would know such things.

RUST NEVER SLEEPS

Prairies, 1916 — The language of the plant disease known as "rust" is an ugly piece of botanical business. In ideal circumstances, when the weather is warm and moist at least one-third of the day, yellow, orange or reddish "pustules" form in raised ovals on the stems, heads or leaves of the wheat plant. Each pustule may contain as many as 1,000 "urediospores," that attach themselves as reddish-brown powder to clothing or machinery that brushes them. They can move with the wind, like a "slinking demon," until healthy plants wither and seed development is arrested. What survives is a low grade of grain, or nothing more than straw.

Production in the Canadian wheat industry soared from 63 million bushels in 1901 to 300 million bushels in 1911. The development of Marquis wheat by Dominion Cerealist Charles Saunders expanded the harvest season and earned international acclaim for Western farmers. The first harvest after Canada's entry into World War I yielded a bumper crop of 360 million bushels, despite a dry spring and a diminished farm labour force.

Disaster in the form of stem rust (*Puccinia graminis*) struck with a vengeance in 1916. Losses approached $200 million and the effect of the infection cast a pall on the fragile future of Western wheat. Previous attempts at scouring the scourge by burning straw piles and field stubble had proved useless. The spores were airborne, blown north from Mexico and the southern United States. Then they waited for the weather conditions to favour their development to epidemic proportions that spelled disaster. No amount of burning or tilling could stop the wind.

Scientists scrambled to find a solution. Conferences were organized, enjoining the talents of the National Research Council, the federal Department of Agriculture and leading plant botanists and biologists at three universities.

Margaret Newton was attending McGill University in 1917. She specialized in botany at Macdonald College, where she earned the distinction of being one of the first female students to graduate from an agricultural college, which she did with honours, including a Governor General's gold medal.

When one of her professors was called away to offer his advice about the problem of rust, Margaret was asked to maintain his ongoing experiments. In the process, she conducted her own experiments and discovered a vital clue.

Rust truly did not sleep. When ten spores were applied to ten identical wheat specimens, Newton found that the results were different. Instead of one organism, rust had many "races."

Scientists had imagined that they could control the disease by developing a single strain of wheat capable of resisting the disease. Dr. W.P. Thompson at the University of Saskatchewan had already proposed the notion of manipulating plant genetics to combine strains of wheat that showed resistance to rust with popular and profitable strains of wheat like Marquis. However, Margaret Newton had isolated and identified at least fourteen races of rust and she warned that even more could result from mutation and hybridization. The battle against rust was going to be more complex than anyone had imagined, and the young woman from McGill would devote a lifetime of study to unravelling its mysteries. In the end, it would be rust that ruined her health.

There were five children in the Newton family — three boys and two girls. Their father, John, was a chemist, and they grew up on a farm near the western Quebec town of Plaisance. Education was a family priority. Each and every one of the Newton children graduated from McGill university and each and every one of them went on to earn PhDs.

After Margaret received her doctorate at the University of Minnesota, she continued her research as a professor of plant pathology at the University of Saskatchewan.

Margaret Newton was thirty-eight when she joined the Associate Committee on Cereal Rust at the newly constructed Dominion Rust Research Laboratory that opened on the grounds of the University of Manitoba in 1925. The goal of the "Rust Lab" was to create "custom made" strains of wheat that could resist disease while retaining the bread-making qualities that Canadian wheat was famous for. As a result, new varieties such as Renown, Apex, Regent, Redman and Thatcher and Selkirk were developed by Canadian and American scientists and plant breeders.

In her career Dr. Newton isolated approximately 150 different strains of rust. She wrote forty-two scientific papers and became an international authority, lecturing around the world.

When she visited the Plant Breeding Institute at Leningrad in 1933, the Russian government wanted her to carry out research and studies on the origins of rust, which was thought to be in Turkestan. She was offered ample funding, a team of fifty scientists, even a fleet of camels for desert travel.

Margaret is said to have been tempted to accept, until her brother, Robert, who had become the Dean of Agriculture and the President of the University of Alberta, advised her that: "The overseas assignment could be a rich experience but the work in rust research in Canada would suffer." She stayed.

All of the years of working with spores took their toll. In 1945, Newton was forced to retire because of lung problems that produced a chronic asthmatic condition. When the Canadian government balked at paying her full pension, Western farmers mounted a petition in protest noting that: "This woman has saved the country millions of dollars." They were successful.

In 1948, Margaret Newton became the first woman to receive the Flavelle Medal of the Royal Society of Canada for her outstanding contribution to biological science, an award that was first presented to Sir Charles Saunders, the "father" of Canadian wheat.

AN ALLELUIA IN THE SKY

Northern Hemisphere, 1923 — To see the aurora borealis sweeping across the night sky like a shimmering curtain is to see a rare, sometimes unnerving natural phenomenon — but to *hear* the sound of light that appears to fall from the sky is even more remarkable. The few scientists who have experienced sound effects along with the visual pyrotechnics of the outer atmosphere's most vibrant visual display characterize it variously as a "crackling" and "hissing" or, more poetically, as the sound of "cellophane and steam." Clarence Chant, a professor at the University of Toronto who has been called "the father of Canadian astronomy," was watching a vivid display in 1923 when he became aware of its sound effects. He described it as "a subdued swishing sound, which grew more distinct as it approached and was loudest when the ribbon or belt of light was overhead."

Scientists are still trying to find an answer to the questions of why and how such sound might accompany the dance of the aurora. Magnetic storms, solar winds and sun spots have all been used to explain the electron phenomenon of the aurora, which was named after the Greek Goddess of the Dawn and has become more commonly hailed as the Northern Lights.

Popular science writer Terence Dickinson investigated the image of the aurora in early history and discovered that as early as 2200 BC the Chinese described the glowing, red image of a snake in the sky, which they called the "candle dragon." More than seventeen hundred years later, the Greek scholar Anaxagoras wrote that he had seen "in the heavens a fiery body of vast size, as if it had been a flaming cloud." In ancient Rome, Pliny the Elder saw the lights as "a flame in the sky, which seems to descend to the Earth on showers of blood." The Bible presents the phenomenon as "horsemen charging in mid-air clad in garments interwoven with gold." But those who live with the Northern Lights find few images of violence in their beauty. An Inuit legend suggests that the moving lights are caused by the spirits of dead friends and relatives playing a game of ball in the sky.

No two auroras are ever alike. Each one is the consequence of electrons and protons colliding with atmospheric atoms and molecules at least 56 kilometres (35 miles) above the earth's surface. Red and green colours are emitted at the highest altitudes, up to 970 kilometres (600 miles) from the ground, when atomic oxygen is released in a fixed wave of light. Ionized molecular nitrogen produces blue or reddish tinges, and sodium results in a display of yellow.

During intense displays, which usually occur in the spring and fall, pulsating curtains of light are swirled into clouds that sweep over the sky. The most brilliant and the rarest display is a coronal aurora in which even stars are obliterated by pulsing and flashing light that appears to stream in parallel lines from a magnetic zenith, although those lines never actually join.

The mighty dazzle is the result of electronically charged particles pumped out by the sun and manifest as solar winds that deflect around the earth's magnetosphere. Some of those particles become trapped in the magnetosphere and when enough of them accumulate, usually after a solar flare, they burst into an auroral ring of varying intensity and size that flows in a dome shape, centring on the geomagnetic North Pole, northwest of Hudson Bay.

More than a trillion watts of energy can be pumped into the rarefied upper atmosphere by an aurora. Geomagnetic storms have been known to cause surges in power lines. In 1982, the mining town of Buchan, Newfoundland, was left in darkness after a surge tripped a circuit breaker in the power grid. The phenomenon can also interfere with long distance radio communications. A spectacular aurora disrupted global telegraph communications in 1859. The sight alone can be disorienting. In 1939, fire brigades were dispatched to Windsor Castle in England when a red aurora was confused with a fire's glow.

Although the Northern Lights have been seen as far south as Singapore, the most spectacular view of them may be in the Northwest Territories. Today, tourists travel in droves to Yellowknife to sit in viewing stands and witness the sky show.

Two years before his death in 1977, Alberta-born artist William Kurelek created a series of paintings, drawings and observations of Inuit life that were published in his book *The Last of the Arctic*. Of the Northern Lights he wrote, "The only truly appropriate reaction seemed to be to whisper an Alleluia."

THE RAIDERS OF
DRAGON BONE HILL

Zhoukoudian, China, 1927 — Who was "Peking Man"? The answer is over 300,000 years old. From fossils and artifacts unearthed by a Canadian in Chinese caves, scientists have determined that Peking Man was a critical link in the evolution of the human species. He was *homo erectus*, the first of our kind to walk upright and the first to use fire.

The discoverer of Peking Man was a Canadian named Davidson Black. He was born in Toronto in 1884 and studied medicine and arts at the University of Toronto, taking special interest in anatomy and the study of the brain. After teaching neurology in Cleveland and serving in the Canadian Army Medical Corps, he was invited to move to China as a professor of anatomy at the Peking Medical Union College.

Once in China, Black focused his attention on the anatomical study of prehistoric man, in the belief that Asia was of strategic importance in understanding the relationship between climate, evolution and the origins of the species.

There were reports of "apelike, manlike" fossil teeth being discovered in Chinese apothecary shops, where they were prized as "dragon bones" and used in curative remedies. The Chinese excavated tonnes of such bones, but without scientific purpose tracing the origins of a few molars was virtually impossible.

In 1926, at a gala scientific meeting, the discovery of two such peculiar molars by Swedish scientists at a site 40 kilometres southwest of Peking (now Beijing) was revealed to great excitement. The Crown Prince of Sweden himself proposed that an expedition be mounted to explore the site known as Dragon Bone Hill near the village of Zhoukoudian. Davidson Black was nominated as the leader of the team, and the Rockefeller Foundation provided his funding.

In 1927, an army of workers excavated an entire hillside. After months of effort, one tooth was extracted.

Excavation continued and several caves were discovered. A skull was found in one of them and it was carefully removed to Black's laboratory, where he painstakingly copied it in casts. In honour of the country of their origin, Black named the specimen "Peking Man."

Numerous other fossil and tool discoveries followed, including evidence that Peking Man had developed quartz implements for the skinning of animals. Deep layers of ash showed early man's first use of fire.

Davidson Black, who scouted for fossils in the shale banks of Toronto's Don River as a child, earned international renown for his efforts. When he died in 1934, he was found slumped over a skull he had been working on at China's Cenozoic Research Laboratory, which he had help found.

By the outbreak of the Second World War, over 175 specimens representing 40 prehistoric individuals had been discovered at Zhoukoudian. It was the largest collection of early human fossils in the history of science.

As the war progressed, it was decided to transfer the fossils to the protection of the U.S. Marine Guard. When evacuation was ordered, the boxed fossils were prepared for embarkation on the liner *President Harrison,* but it was captured by the Japanese before leaving port.

The original fossils have never been seen again. Fortunately, the casts made by Black and his team survived and replicas of Peking Man are featured in museums throughout the world.

THE WONDER MUSH REVOLUTION

Toronto, 1930 — Although its taste has been compared to that of boiled Kleenex and wallpaper paste, the gloppy mush known as Pablum revolutionized pediatric nutrition around the world. It became the first solid food of an entire generation of Canadians. Tons of it have been dutifully ingested, scraped off high chairs and wiped away from sticky cheeks, foreheads and noses. Aside from growing bigger and healthier children, the royalties from this all-Canadian wonder food have helped fund research into everything from a cure for congenital hip disorders to the discovery of the cystic fibrosis gene. Canadian doctors, not marketers, invented Pablum.

Dr. Alan Brown, who served as physician-in-chief of Toronto's Hospital for Sick Children from 1919 to 1951, was determined to bring proper nutrition to the nurseries of the nation. Early in his tenure, he boldly claimed that he could slash the number of infant deaths by half. He accomplished that end with the assistance of research doctors Theodore Drake and Fred Tisdall.

Sixty-five years ago the cereals that babies were fed after mother's milk and sweetened formula were mostly starch. Most of the vitamins, minerals, phosphates and protein contained in the bran and wheat germ had been processed out and fed to livestock. Recognizing this, Fred Tisdall consulted with the poultry department at the Ontario Agriculture College in Guelph, which was developing a healthy feed for chicks. As it turned out, the same natural ingredients were involved for babies; the only difference was quantity.

Back at their lab, Tisdall and Drake invented a vitamin-rich baby biscuit that was "irradiated" under a mercury quartz lamp to add the so-called sunshine vitamin D. They introduced their product in a 1930 *Canadian Medical Association Journal*, and it went on to be sold as McCormick's Sunwheat Biscuits, with royalties accruing to fund their ongoing research.

The "big one" was a cereal product Drake stirred up in 1929. Wheat meal, cornmeal and oatmeal masked the flavour of the other ingredients, including bone meal, brewer's yeast and alfalfa. "We had to say we liked it whether we did or not," one hospital colleague advised years later. But adult taste buds were not the target and babies glommed the stuff down.

Drake and Tisdall were en route to Chicago to sell the idea to Quaker Oats when they met up with some friends from Mead Johnson and offered it to them. Mead's Cereal — the precursor to Pablum — was introduced in 1930. It required messy hours of cooking. Ultimately, high-pressure processing refinements were made to create a pre-cooked, vitamin-fortified cereal that was palatable within minutes by adding water or milk.

The concoction was named after the Latin noun *pabulum*, meaning food. In the midst of the Depression, it became an overnight success. There was no waste in preparation, and it cost less than two cents per serving. Convenience aside, Pablum also became a "celebrity baby food," when it was announced that the Dionne quintuplets were being raised on the new wonder cereal. Dr. Alan Brown was one of their consulting physicians.

By the time the patent on Pablum ran out twenty-five years later, Brown's brash pediatric prediction had come true. Nutrition became a recognized component of preventative medicine, and the gooey wonder mush developed by Tisdall and Drake shovelled millions in royalties into the Hospital for Sick Children's Pediatric Research Foundation.

FEETS DON'T FAIL ME NOW

Williamsburg, Ontario, 1932 — Between 1932 and 1942, millions of people from all over the world made a pilgrimage to a tiny Ontario village between Cornwall and Gananoque.

Princes from as far away as India, paupers who rode the rails, society matrons, Hollywood moguls such as Louis B. Mayer, British nobility, even the American president's wife, Eleanor Roosevelt — tens of thousands of people, day-in and day-out, found their way to Williamsburg, Ontario, to put their feet in the hands of Dr. Mahlon W. Locke.

According to the tabloids of the day Dr. Locke could virtually raise the dead. He was the Canadian "miracle man" with "x-ray hands."

On the other hand the medical profession dismissed him as "a quack."

But Dr. Mahlon W. Locke was no quack.

A fully qualified medical doctor, he held the prestigious triple licentiate from the Royal College of Surgeons, Edinburgh, the Royal College of Physicians, Edinburgh, and the Royal Faculty of Physicians and Surgeons, Glasgow.

Born on a farm at Dixon's Corners, seven miles west of Williamsburg, on Valentine's Day, 1880, Mahlon Locke showed an early aptitude for agriculture. This was a good thing because his father died suddenly in 1888 and eight-year-old Mahlon had to take on responsibility for the farm and the family including his mother and two younger brothers.

Because he was good with animals, Mahlon reasoned that he might be good with people and decided to go into medicine. He finally entered the Queen's University medical program at the age of twenty-one. An exceptional student, he graduated four years later and returned to Dixon's Corners to set up practice with his new stepfather, Dr. G.W. Collison.

With only fifteen dollars to show for six months' work, a discouraged young Dr. Locke jumped at the chance to work at Algoma Steel in Sudbury for a guaranteed $100 a month.

The following year he was accepted in a postgraduate program at the Royal Infirmary in Edinburgh, Scotland, where, among many other things, he learned the difficult techniques of foot manipulation and developed his theory of good health.

"Nobody can feel well if his feet are sick," he said. "I put my patients' feet right and Nature does the healing."

To put it simply, Dr. Locke theorized that manipulating the arches relieved pressure on the large nerve which ended in the foot. Increased healthy blood circulation in that area would, in turn, help rid the bloodstream of impurities.

In 1908, he returned to Williamsburg and began to practise the kind of medicine for which the modern age has become increasingly nostalgic. He made horse-and-buggy house calls — midday and midnight runs to deliver babies, set broken bones or stitch up split heads.

Early on, Dr. Locke observed that too many of the locals suffered from flat feet and rheumatism for the co-existence of the two conditions to be purely coincidental.

For instance, a local blacksmith named Peter Beckstead whom Dr. Locke began treating in 1908 had been as strong as the horses he shod until crippling joint pain made it virtually impossible for him to work.

To the blacksmith's amazement, Dr. Locke began fiddling with his feet, pressing his arches, spreading and pulling his toes. The blacksmith was even more surprised when the debilitating pain began to subside after half a dozen treatments.

Dr. Locke then took Mr. Beckstead to the local shoemaker and had the cobbler fit the smith's shoes with leather inserts. The doctor called the inserts "cookies." He said the cookies would keep the blacksmith's arches in place and strengthen his foot muscles.

Fully recovered, Peter Beckstead kept shoeing horses until the day he died twenty-five years later.

Dr. Locke practised his unique brand of foot-oriented medicine in relative obscurity for two decades. Because he consistently got good results, and because the locals found having their feet played with somewhat unusual, his reputation spread slowly by word-of-mouth beyond the township.

From Williamsburg to the town of Morrisburg on the shores of the St. Lawrence River is a mere six miles. From Morrisburg it is a short ferry ride to New York State.

In 1928, Frank Coughlin, an arthritic newspaperman from Lockport, New York, was referred to the Williamsburg clinic by an elderly Catholic priest who suffered from the same disorder until he put his feet in Dr. Locke's hands. Coughlin's condition had been deemed so serious that he was scheduled for potentially dangerous surgery. After Locke's foot manipulation treatment, the reporter cancelled his surgery and wrote a glowing report that was reprinted in dozens of American newspapers.

By 1930, Dr. Locke was seeing up to 300 people a day. His reputation spread like a grass fire. By the summer of 1931, the number had swelled to almost 1,000.

That summer Dr. Locke met the American writer Rex Beach. Beach had penned a dozen popular biographies, a couple of successful adventure novels and the screenplay for *The Spoilers*, a 1914 silent picture about the gold rush.

While on a golfing holiday in Ottawa, Beach kept complaining about his fallen arches. One of his companions jokingly suggested that if he was that badly hobbled, he should probably visit the famous foot doctor in nearby Williamsburg.

What Rex Beach witnessed and experienced led him to write a feature article in *Cosmopolitan* magazine, which appeared in August, 1932. After that, Dr. Locke never had another moment to himself.

The road from Ottawa to Williamsburg had been a potholed, gravel cart track, when Beach made his first visit. Three years later, he returned to find it transformed into a paved two-lane highway congested with cars, buses and trucks. Many were hung with signs such as "To Williamsburg and Dr. Locke," and "Dr. Locke or Bust."

The closer Beach got to the centre of Williamsburg (which boasted a population of a few less than 300) the slower traffic became until it virtually stood still.

People in wheelchairs rolled along the roadside. It was not uncommon to see a person on a stretcher being wheeled through the streets. Every second pedestrian seemed to be on crutches.

Two ferries were crossing from Waddington, New York to Morrisburg every quarter of an hour from 7 a.m. until midnight, seven days a week, instead of one every hour, eight hours a day, five days a week as had been the service before Dr. Locke's foot manipulation therapy seized the popular imagination. Transcontinental trains were now making regular, unprecedented stops at Morrisburg.

Two hotels, one with 125 rooms, were built and constantly full. The *Rapids Queen*, an ocean liner with sixty-five staterooms and a ballroom, was permanently anchored at Morrisburg to accommodate the overflow. Instead of three struggling restaurants, twenty-three now thrived.

While the rest of the country strangled in the grip of the worst depression in the history of North America, the townsfolk of Williamsburg and Morrisburg were literally run off their feet servicing the patrons of the foot doctor.

Rex Beach found Dr. Locke where he was most every day for the last fifteen years of his life, surrounded by a circus-throng of humanity, feeling feet on the lawn beside his house.

Dr. Locke sat at the hub of "The Circle" — a series of fourteen iron pipes that spread outward from his swivel chair, not unlike giant spokes. The pipes marked runways down which patients moved on camp stools until they reached the wooden chairs arranged in a circle around Dr. Locke.

After years of trampling, the west lawn of his house had been covered with concrete. Elderly patients pooled resources and built a wooden pavilion to shelter the hundreds upon hundreds of afflicted and infirm who waited patiently for the doctor's attention.

In his early fifties, Dr. Locke radiated strength. He was a large man with a massive head, penetrating blue eyes and thick shoulders. A little ruffled and unkempt, he worked in shirt sleeves, without a collar or tie. His diagnoses were based only on what he saw and felt in front of him. Grasping each stockinged foot, he would press up on the arch with one quick movement of his thumb while he twisted the toes down and out with the other hand. At the end of each day, he painted his aching thumbs with iodine.

Although a man of few words, Locke had a sense of humour and laughed easily. When a patient complaining of shoulder pain asked him why she had to take her shoes off for treatment, he responded with a question: "When you step on a dog's tail, which end yelps?"

He had no time for pretence. He treated everyone, rich or poor, on a first-come, first-served basis. Each consultation cost a dollar. There is an apocryphal story about a well-dressed woman who pushed her way to the front of one of the lines, proclaiming herself "a millionaire." To which Dr. Locke is alleged to have replied, "Madam, so am I. Get back in line."

With the occasional stop to unwind his chair, or go into the house and empty his pockets of dollar bills, Dr. Locke sprang from patient to patient with lightning speed, probing and manipulating as many as ten feet a minute.

During the Dirty Thirties, millions of words were written about Dr. Locke. There were thousands of newspaper columns, hundreds of magazine articles, several biographies and even a novel.

He repeatedly said that he cared nothing for money, while capriciously noting that he was probably the only man in the world who had literally made a million dollars with his own two hands. At the height of his fame, he was manipulating as many as 2,700 people's feet twice a day, seven days a week. At ten dollars a pair, 9,000 pairs of Dr. Locke's arch-support–enhanced shoes walked out of Williamsburg before he sold the patent for $30,000.

In spite of glowing testimonials from grateful patients, among them a number of his colleagues, the medical establishment stubbornly maintained that Dr. Locke's healing ways could be explained away by mass hysteria and hypnosis.

"I don't give a damn," was Dr. Locke's response. "A great many [of my patients] have been to the foremost specialists and the best hospitals both here and abroad and have been pronounced incurable."

Rex Beach wrote: "This is no mere laying on of hands: there are no instantaneous cures, no miracles. He [Dr. Locke] has a peculiar knowledge and an uncanny skill: improvement is gradual and sure."

Locke turned down an offer from the prestigious Mayo Clinic in Rochester, N.Y. He said he didn't want to work "like a mule in the back room" when he could run his own show in Williamsburg. Well-respected in the community, he declined offers to enter politics.

Although he worked year-round, with no time off except a week at Christmas, Locke found time for a hobby in farming, which grew to include seventeen properties. One of his Holstein cows set a world record for milk and butter production.

Despite the fact that he gave demonstrations and opened his clinic to examination by other physicians, Mahlon Locke was never fully able to translate the secret of his "manipulative surgery." He suffered a fatal stroke one week shy of his seventy-first birthday, after trying to push his 1942 Cadillac out of a snow-filled ditch.

UNDISCOVERED COUNTRY

Montreal, 1934 — Roughly the size and shape of a cauliflower, the human brain appears to have no moving parts, although it is composed of billions of nerve cells containing a molecular structure through which electricity moves. Dr. Wilder Penfield, a passionate neurosurgeon and scientist, was a pathfinder into the mysteries of that uncharted country.

Wilder Graves Penfield was born in Spokane, Washington. His father and his father before him had been doctors. In considering his own career path, young Penfield noted that his objective in life was "to support myself and family and somehow make the world a better place in which to live." He was inexorably drawn to medicine.

At Oxford University, Penfield met the eminent Canadian physician and teacher Sir William Osler and neurophysiologist Charles Sherrington. In Osler he secured a mentor who was both a gentle healer and fearless pioneer — "a sort of John the Baptist in a wilderness of medical superstition." Sherrington introduced him to the experimental investigation of the central nervous system in which Penfield found "the undiscovered country in which the mystery of the mind might someday be explained."

In 1918, Penfield graduated from Johns Hopkins University and determined to make neurology his specialty. His work at the Presbyterian Hospital in New York fostered an interest in the causes and treatment of epilepsy — a disorder of the brain which triggers a variety of behaviours from hallucinations to seizures.

In 1928, Penfield and his neurosurgical partner, Dr. William Cone, came to work at Montreal's Royal Victoria Hospital, where they were to establish an institute devoted to neurology. A team approach, co-ordinated by Penfield, succeeded in binding French- and English-speaking doctors and nurses in research and treatment procedures. According to Penfield: "The study of the brain is a field that a man could no more explore alone than he could paddle his way to the North Pole in a canvas canoe."

Penfield experienced one of his greatest and most tragic challenges in Montreal. His sister, Ruth, had suffered epileptic seizures throughout her life, but these were often attributed to "nerves" — the catch-all phrase for anything medical science could not fathom. Ruth's condition was growing critical and Penfield determined to operate.

He discovered a massive brain tumour, which proved too large to remove in its entirety. Nevertheless, the young woman lived for three more years. "The resentment I felt because of my inability to save my sister spurred me on to make my first bid for an endowed neurological institute," noted Penfield.

In 1934, Wilder Penfield became a Canadian citizen. In the same year, the Montreal Neurological Institute opened with the words of its founder engraved on a stone slab to mark the occasion. "Dedicated to the relief of sickness and pain and to the study of neurology," wrote Penfield, who was to be the Institute's director until 1960.

In Montreal, Penfield perfected a technique for removing scar tissue that caused forms of epilepsy in the temporal lobes. Applying only a local anesthetic, he would probe the exposed brain, relying on the response of the patient to guide him. Brain tissue itself has no sensations, but it recognizes sensations sent to it from other parts of the body and the stimulus of a mild electrical current to the specific points in the surface of the brain triggers certain responses. By stimulating the temporal lobe, Penfield discovered the source of memory, the mind's reservoir of sensation and emotion, and the storehouse of dreams.

In the space of thirty years, Penfield operated on more than 750 patients suffering from epilepsy. Despite improvements in technology and refinements in techniques, the operating procedure used today remains remarkably similar to that performed by Penfield in the 1930s.

"It is the patients who can teach one the most," Penfield wrote in his autobiography *No Man Alone.* "They open their hearts and minds. And the doctor, if he will only listen, comes to understand the inborn nature of man."

ART
&
ARTISTS

MARCHING THUNDER

THE WISE CHILD

WANDERINGS OF AN ARTIST

PORTRAIT OF THE ARTIST AS A YOUNG WOMAN

CANADA'S NATIONAL
CONTRAPUNTAL CANTATA

THE DIVA OF THE SACRED FIRE

BUCKSKIN AND BROCADE

BEAUTIFUL JOE

THE GREAT CANADIAN KISSER

THE ORIGINAL ROLLING STONE

THE PIE MAN

BORN OF FIRE AND BLOOD

THE LAUGHING ONE

SHE DID IT HER WAY

THE COWBOY FROM QUEBEC

THE MAN OF STEEL

SPONTANEOUS COMBUSTION

MORE STARS THAN HEAVEN

MARCHING THUNDER

St. Hyacinthe, Quebec, 1834 — Who has tamed the wind? Joseph Casavant was born in 1807 and he apprenticed as a blacksmith in his adolescence. Although he became known as a skilled craftsman, Casavant maintained a passion for music and dreamed of a career as a musician.

At twenty-seven, he shut down his forge to pursue a classical education. It was a bold move for a man of his age. Casavant enrolled in a seminary, where he worked as a handyman to pay for his studies.

His perseverance was rewarded when the seminary director asked him to repair an organ. A whole world suddenly opened up for the musical blacksmith. Relying on a scholarly work by a French Benedictine monk, Casavant proceeded to disassemble and rebuild the organ. Applying his blacksmith skills, he fashioned and refined its delicate and precise mechanisms.

Casavant called the newly completed organ "Marching Thunder." It was such a success that a nearby parish ordered one. The "wind tamer" from St. Hyacinthe had found a second career.

Between 1840 and 1866, Casavant completed seventeen instruments that found homes in cities and towns throughout Upper and Lower Canada. The organ that he built for the cathedral in Bytown (now Ottawa) in 1850 was the largest in North America. It consisted of 1,063 wooden and metal pipes, eighteen five-octave stops and a three-keyboard console. Sadly, none of Casavant's original masterpieces remain. However, his sons, Joseph-Claver and Samuel-Marie, inherited his love of the instrument. They studied its science and traditions in Europe.

In 1879, Casavant's sons opened an organ manufacturing workshop at the site of their father's studio. Their first commission was for Montreal's Notre Dame Church. This triumph of tonality established their reputation.

By the turn of the century just about every city and town in Canada had a Casavant organ, and the company's reputation spread throughout the world. A wind instrument manufactured in Canada since 1834 now earned an international reputation for excellence.

More than 3,700 organs have since been meticulously crafted at Casavant Frères studio in St. Hyacinthe near Montreal, and the inspiration for this thriving family business came from the musical aspirations of a village blacksmith. Today, 90 percent of the company's production is exported.

While the Casavant family's enterprising passion for excellence in large-scale organs has resulted in an on-going business, another Canadian organ innovator, Frank Morse Robb, was not so fortunate.

Robb was the inventor of the first electronic wave organ ever manufactured. In 1927, he began experimenting with recording the natural wave form of sound on the Bridge Street United Church in Belleville, Ontario. In 1928, Robb obtained a Canadian patent, seven years before any other organs were produced.

Rather than sell his idea, Robb set up his own company. By 1936 the Robb Wave Organ Company was delivering organs to stores and chapels in Toronto, but the Depression spelled doom for Robb's entrepreneurial venture.

The company folded the following year, but the multiplicity of sounds that can be orchestrated on the electronic organ continue to delight millions who can share the thrill of "marching thunder" in their own home.

THE WISE CHILD

Halifax, Nova Scotia, 1835 — If history conveys any truth, at least one axiom is that Canadians make inordinately Good Neighbours. Generous to a fault, we have, willy nilly, given our American cousins basketball, baseball, even the comic book hero Superman. Likewise, our sayings and clichés have crossed the 49th parallel as easily as a Canadian comedian with a Green Card, destined to be adopted by that larger popular culture as their own.

However, when it is "raining cats and dogs" or something happens "quick as wink," the description is purely Canadian.

Expressions and maxims, ranging from the proverbial "Jack of all trades and master of none," to the pragmatic "an ounce of prevention is worth a pound of cure," were the creations of nineteeth-century Nova Scotia judge, historian and humourist Thomas Chandler Haliburton. Americans may use the terms as freely as Canadians, but if they wish to claim them as homegrown, they are (as Haliburton would have it) "barking up the wrong tree."

A prodigious snob given to proselytizing and pontificating about the Old World and beloved England, Haliburton decided early on that the only way to reach his lazy, ignorant fellow colonists, was to employ humour "to render subjects attractive that in themselves are generally considered as too dry and deep for general reading." The son of Loyalists, he despised Americans on one hand, but also admired their industriousness and economic expansion.

American republicans called Nova Scotia "Nova Scarcity," but Haliburton was convinced that in consideration of the abundant resources of the province, a transportation initiative to improve the flow of goods and a modicum of enterprise from the citizenry could transform the region to the level of prosperity it deserved.

The vehicle for Haliburton's moral and political rails against hypocrisy and sloth was a character named Sam Slick, a wayfaring Odysseus in the guise of a Yankee clockmaker. As a travelling salesman and a con man, Sam Slick's mission was to sell clocks that cost him $6.50 to the great unwashed for $40 and in the process reveal the frailties of "human natur" and "some pretty home truths."

A cacophony of ungrammatical colloquialisms characterize Haliburton's Slick character, who oils his "marks" with "soft sawdur" before closing a deal. As Dr. Watson did for Sherlock Holmes, a Squire named Tom Poker served as the narrator in Haliburton's episodic, often plotless stories that were tantamount to an opinionated lay sermon.

"I reckon they are bad off for inns in this country," the Squire reports Sam Slick saying. "When a feller is too lazy to work here, he paints his name over his door and calls it a tavern, and as likes as not he makes the whole neighbourhood as lazy as himself."

Haliburton's Sam Slick stories were first published by his good friend Joseph Howe in his liberal newspaper *The Novascotian* in 1835 under the heading "Recollections of Nova Scotia." After the first twenty-two installments, requests for reprints spurred Howe to publish the collected stories as *The Clockmaker; or the Sayings and Doings of Sam Slick, of Slickville*. More than seventy editions of the book were published in Canada, the United States and Britain, making Haliburton the first Canadian writer to gain an international reputation.

Thomas Chandler Haliburton was aged forty when *The Clockmaker* was published. Like his father and his father before him, he was a Tory and a lawyer. Elected to the Nova Scotia House of Assembly in 1826, he proceeded to write bills and make a name for himself as a formidable orator. When the council disallowed one of his bills, Haliburton lambasted them, creating a memorable description of senators that resonates to this day.

Calling the members, all of whom in their time were men of prominence, "twelve dignified, deep read, pensioned, old ladies . . . filled with prejudices and whims like all other antiquated spinsters," he declared that he himself had no time for "petticoat government."

After three years, Haliburton found himself disenchanted with politics. The death of his father left a judgeship opening in Nova Scotia's Inferior Court of Common Pleas and T.C. filled it. He had already written two scholarly works, *A General Description of Nova Scotia* (1823), which was published anonymously, and an ambitious two-volume work, *An Historical and Statistical Account of Nova Scotia*, which received critical acclaim but left its publisher, Joseph Howe, with a heavy burden of debt.

By the time Howe published *The Clockmaker* in 1936, the variance of political opinions between the two friends had become pronounced. Judge Haliburton had urged a jury to convict Howe on a charge of libel that had been brought against him after he published a letter accusing officials of corruption. Howe defended himself in a six-hour oratory that included a description of local magistrates as "the most negligent and imbecile . . . that ever mismanaged a people's affairs." Howe won the case and his popularity soared.

Despite the strain on the friendship, Howe and Haliburton travelled to England together in 1838 for what was called "the grand tour." Howe returned to Nova Scotia to champion the cause of reform and advocate responsible government. Haliburton extended his stay in England, where he enjoyed considerable fame and success, often at the expense of Howe, whose thinly disguised exploits became the target of some of Haliburton's most pointed satire in *The Attaché; or, Sam Slick in England*.

While Howe advocated a separation of church and state, Haliburton advocated a strengthening, believing that the colony would benefit from more government by Britain rather than less. The rupture in the friendship was further scarred when Haliburton reneged on a busines deal. The two men even participated in a fruitless duel. The challenger, Haliburton, fired and missed, while Howe avoided any possibility of damage by firing into the air.

Nevertheless, Joseph Howe still found it in his conscience to endorse Judge Haliburton's controversial appointment to the Supreme Court of Nova Scotia in 1841.

That same year, Haliburton's English-born wife, Louisa Neville, died after twenty-one years of marriage and eleven children.

In less than a decade between the time Sam Slick first saw the light of day and the mid-1840s, Haliburton's realization that his political ideals were doomed turned this fun-loving hedonist somewhat dour and adversely affected his writing.

Although he continued to publish until the end of his life he never again achieved the delicately balanced chaos of ambivalence that is the hallmark of great humourists. In 1849, he published *The Old Judge*, a book of observation and reminiscence revealed through the eyes of a British tourist to Nova Scotia. It has been described as a "sad book" but critics have also suggested that "in human insight and interest, it is matched only by Susanna Moodie's *Roughing It in the Bush*.

"I am too old for romance, and what is worse I am corpulent," Haliburton wrote during that period. In 1856, he resigned from the bench and moved to England. Re-married to a wealthy British widow, he was elected to the House of Commons in 1859 and distinguished himself by receiving an honorary degree from Oxford University. He never returned to Nova Scotia.

Today, Thomas C. Haliburton is seldom remembered as a jurist, historian or for his headstrong Tory ideals, but rather as an inspired humourist, the precursor of Mark Twain and Stephen Leacock. That his writing has led him to be called "the father of American humour" would probably not have surprised the author himself. After all, it was Haliburton who wrote that "truth is stranger than fiction."

In fact, Haliburton could well have referred his Yankee admirers to yet another of his Sam Slickisms: "It's a wise child that knows its own father."

WANDERINGS
OF AN ARTIST

Hudson's Bay Company Territory, 1846 — Artists have never been known for business acumen or their ability to deal with the mundane details of daily life and Paul Kane, one of Canada's greatest painters, was no exception.

Kane began his career applying his painterly talents on household goods and signs in Cobourg, Ontario. He also almost missed the boat on the expedition to the West that resulted in the largest body of his work.

Kane was born in Ireland in 1810. The family immigrated to the village of York (now Toronto) in 1819 and Kane studied art at Upper Canada College. After practising his craft in the trades, he spent nine years roaming the United States and Europe, painting portraits and studying the works of the great masters.

In London, Kane met American painter George Catlin who was exhibiting his paintings of the prairies and foothills of the Rockies. Catlin told Kane that North American artists had a duty to record the cultures of the native peoples before they were lost to posterity.

Kane made Catlin's remarks his creed, and he returned to Canada absorbed in his dream of "devoting whatever talents and proficiency I possess to the painting of a series of pictures illustrative of the North American Indians and scenery."

He spent the summer of 1845 visiting and sketching the Great Lakes tribes. Westward travel was made possible by Sir George Simpson, the "Little Emperor" of the Hudson's Bay Company which held the whole territory west of the Lakehead under charter and licence. Simpson was so impressed by the artist and his goal that he commissioned about a dozen paintings and put in a special request for Kane to capture the annual buffalo hunt.

In the spring of 1846, Paul Kane set out to join the fur brigade with Simpson's personal letter of introduction instructing that he receive "kind attentions and hospitalities and passage from post to post free of charge."

Kane's mettle was soon challenged when he missed a steamboat at Mackinac. He hired a small skiff with a blanket for a sail and managed to catch up with the Company team.

The whole trip was an adventure of epic proportion. Kane witnessed the annual buffalo hunt at the Red River Settlement. He even participated and apparently bagged two of the mighty beasts in a flurry of killing that involved a herd of four to five thousand. Later, he survived the attack of a grizzly bear and would cross the Rocky Mountains on snowshoes.

Kane followed the Columbia River to its mouth. On Vancouver Island he sketched the northern native people, including the Haida. He encountered a gathering of 1,500 warriors of the Blackfoot nation and documented their horse races, dances and rituals.

The journey ended in 1848 and Kane spent the next decade in Toronto translating approximately 700 sketches into enormous canvases. Critics tend to prefer the immediacy and authenticity of the sketches to the larger works, which reflect Kane's European influences and perpetuate the European myth of the Noble Savage. However, in his portraits of native chiefs and ceremonies, Kane clearly captures the strength of his subjects, providing historical detail which has a photographic quality,

Along with his legacy of art, Kane also published the diary of his travels. *Wanderings of an Artist among the Indians of North America* was translated into French, German and Danish and became a bestseller.

Paul Kane died in 1871, his eyesight gone, his dream achieved.

PORTRAIT OF THE ARTIST
AS A YOUNG WOMAN

Victoria, British Columbia, 1879 — At first glance, the sepia-toned photograph looks to be nothing more than a picture of two stuffy Victorian ladies sitting for tea at a small table. One lady is primly pouring tea into a cup. The other lady looks directly into the camera, clenching her saucer. On the wall above the table there is a portrait of another woman. Or is it? There is something about the woman in the portrait. Her right arm extends outside the frame and she is pouring a full cup of tea onto the head of the lady looking obliviously into the camera. Upon even closer inspection it becomes evident that all three ladies in this photograph are one in the same person — Hannah Maynard of Mrs. R. Maynard's Photographic Gallery.

Hannah Hatherly of Cornwall, England, was eighteen when she met and married apprentice bootmaker Richard Maynard in 1852. The young couple promptly sailed to Canada, where Richard opened a boot shop in Bowmanville, east of Oshawa on Lake Ontario. Six years and four children later, Richard caught "gold fever," abandoned hearth and home and joined the rush on British Columbia's Fraser River. While he was away, Hannah began studying something new and different — photography.

The daguerreotype had been invented in France in the 1830s. In 1851, Lovell's *Canada Directory* listed only eleven daguerreotypists in the country. And for one of those, photography was a second job. He listed himself as a "surgical and mechanical dentist" first, a "daguerrian artist" second.

By 1865, Mitchell & Co.'s *Canada Classified Dictionary* listed more than 360 photographers, including 34 in Montreal, 17 in Toronto and 16 in Quebec City. One among them was Mrs. Hannah Maynard of Victoria, British Columbia.

The gold fields were good to Richard Maynard. Returning to Bowmanville, he sold his shop and moved his family to Victoria in 1862. Victoria was then nothing more than a small outpost town on Vancouver Island with maybe three dozen brick buildings. In her diaries Hannah described it as a city "of tents, gullies and swamps."

Almost immediately Richard left to go prospecting up the Stikine River. Hannah settled into a house on a dirt track at the corner of Johnson and Douglas Streets and opened Mrs. R. Maynard's Photographic Gallery.

In 1863, Mr. Maynard returned to Victoria and discovered that his wife had set up her own business.

"Everyone was astonished," said a report that was printed years later in *The Colonist*. "And like many women who start anything new she was for a very long time boycotted by the public . . . until Victoria got used to a woman photographer."

Over the next fifty years it is said that Mrs. Maynard took every single resident of Victoria's portrait — usually as a baby — at least once. Richard opened a boot store in a shop adjoining Hannah's enterprise. He must have been fascinated by Hannah's newfound career, since he was soon taking photography lessons from her. Together, Mr. and Mrs. Maynard would travel up and down the West Coast and inland through British Columbia, the Northwest Territories and Alaska, photographing the daunting and magnificent landscape. The Maynards' images were described by the *St. Louis Practical Photographer* as "the most interesting view we have ever had from those far-off regions."

Richard preferred photographing the outdoors, sometimes travelling with his eldest son, Albert. In 1868, the pair travelled by steamer and wagon to Barkerville, the terminus of the Cariboo Road. Founded six years earlier when a Cornish sailor named Billy Barker discovered gold in Williams Creek, Barkerville called itself the "largest community west of Chicago and north of San Francisco." Although it served a population of 10,000, the "town" was little more than one muddy street lined with rough wooden shacks, a few churches and sufficient saloons to satisfy a large demand.

Richard and Albert left Barkerville on September 16, 1868, shortly before an amorous miner tried to steal a kiss from a "Hurdy Gurdy" dancehall queen who was taking some time in the afternoon to do her ironing. She resisted the miner's advances and he ended up knocking over a stovepipe. Barkerville was toast. Within eighty minutes, 116 buildings were destroyed. Maynard returned to Barkerville and photographed the desolate remains.

His images of things ranging from icebergs to miners clinging precariously to sheer rockfaces have an eerie stillness. At Taku Inlet, he photographed a steamer blanketed in snow and ice. In Glacier Bay, he drifted through the mist on an ice floe to capture a poetic image of two small passenger boats surrounded by chunks of ice. Government assignments and commissions saw him photographing the construction of the Canadian Pacific Railway, native people on Vancouver Island and the seal hunt in the Bering Sea.

Hannah often joined Richard on his excursions. She also travelled by herself to the Queen Charlotte Islands. However, more of her time was spent exploring commercial portraiture. She was fascinated by faces.

After plying her craft and honing her technique for almost twenty years, Hannah Maynard's eccentricity and genius began to emerge. She started to create her "Gems of British Columbia," hundreds, then thousands, of children's little faces interlocked in greeting cards.

The "gem" was a common Victorian conceit: a small and sometimes tiny tinotype featuring three or four faces of a loved one often mounted in a piece of jewellery — a ring or brooch or pendant. Producing one required a camera with four or more lenses.

Hannah became a master of such miniatures. Then she turned the whole idea on its head, producing monumental gatherings of miniatures, fields of hundreds, even thousands of tiny baby faces in montage. These gems were painstaking, artful arrangements of miniaturized portraits of every child she photographed in a given year. They are veritable fields of faces. Her 1891 "Gems of British Columbia" was framed by years of previous gems and featured approximately 22,000 faces.

She put children's faces everywhere and in everything. She would transform something as simple as a potted plant into a frenzy of leaves covered with faces. There are even faces in the potting soil. She assembled faces in frames and diamond shapes, wreaths, palettes and crosses.

In "Sprays from the Gem Fountain," sixty babies float on clouds like well-formed droplets. They emanate from a fountain composed of children blowing streams of cascading babies out of trumpets and pouring pitchers filled with babies into a reflecting pool.

Maynard also produced something else that was popular in the period called photosculptures: unwanted parts of the subject's body, such as arms below the elbow, were draped with black cloth so they became invisible to the camera. The rest of the body, especially the subject's hair, eyebrows and clothes were caked with a white powder. The result was a picture that looked like a stone bust or a ghostly sculpture. Hannah called these photographs "Living Statuary" or "Statuary from Life."

But Hannah's most adventurous work had to do with multiple images of herself such as the three ladies at tea. More magical than cut-and-paste montage or photosculpture, they reveal a sardonic woman not at all like the conventional Victorian image of womanhood. A true eccentric, intent upon herself, she displays a mocking, even gallows sense of humour.

Aside from the technical feat of her work, Hannah also took pains to paint out lines and wrinkles from her face. She was also known to "retouch" inches from her waistline.

In 1883, the Maynards' sixteen-year-old daughter Lillie died of typhoid. Images of death and the departed began to colour Hannah's work. There was a great interest in spiritualism and seances in the late nineteenth century. Even the mayor of Victoria was a spiritualist. Hannah met with spiritualists and participated in seances. Apparitions of the grotesque started to appear in her multiples.

By the mid-1890s she had moved into a visual universe all her own, achieving an aesthetic statement unmatched by photographers until the 1920s and the advent of surrealism. At the same time, she served as the official photographer for the Victoria Police Department. For five years, from 1897 until 1902, she took mug shots in her studio, sometimes using a specially designed mirror to achieve a front and side view on a single negative. Hannah retired in 1912, five years after Richard's death. She was eighty-four when she died in 1918.

Although hundreds of images created by Hannah and Richard are held in the British Columbia Archives, the work was scarcely known until Toronto artist and visual researcher Claire Weissman Wilks discovered them while sifting through archival prints and glass plates. Wilks's book *The Magic Box: The Eccentric Genius of Hannah Maynard*, which was published in 1980, presents a rare record of Hannah's unique vision.

"She was the real thing," writes Wilks, "a parochial talent whose work is alive in the larger world because she was never provincial."

CANADA'S NATIONAL CONTRAPUNTAL CANTATA

Quebec City, June 24, 1880 — "Chant National" — the rousing cantata of contrapuntal orchestration composed by Calixa Lavallée was written in Quebec a century before it became "O Canada."

Although it was approved as our national anthem in 1967 and was designated officially by the National Anthem Act of Parliament in 1980, the song was introduced in Quebec City on June 24, 1880. It was not heard in English Canada until the turn of the century, when lyrics by Montreal-based lawyer and author Robert Stanley Weir were adopted.

In January 1880, Quebec City organizers began planning a dazzling celebration to which St. Jean Baptiste Societies in Canada and the United States were invited. The music committee boosted enthusiasm when it proposed the inclusion of a national song in the program. Reportedly, the Governor General had composed a poem called "Dominion Hymn" and asked British composer, Sir Arthur Sullivan, to set it to music as a national anthem.

This apparently riled the St. Jean Baptiste Society and they determined a counteroffer.

The words of a poem written for the occasion by
Judge Adolphe-Basile Routhier were selected and Lavallée
was commissioned to compose the music.

Calixa Lavallée was a pioneer in music, both in Canada and the U.S. He was born in Verchères, Lower Canada,
in 1842 and his first musical studies were with his father.
When he was barely a teenager he left Canada for the U.S.
and toured throughout South America, the West Indies
and Mexico. The year following his return to Verchères,
the twenty-one-year-old musician and teacher gave a concert in Montreal playing piano, violin and cornet.

Lavallée orchestrated a tour de force for the St. Jean
Baptiste celebrations, which began with a huge crowd that
assembled to attend ceremonial Mass on the Plains of Abraham.

Throughout the day, a parade moved through the
main streets of Quebec City featuring a hundred or so
French-Canadian societies and associations, preceded by
their marching bands and allegorical floats, along with
participants from neighbouring American states.

In the evening, an assembly of 3,000 vocalists and
musicians performed a program of appropriately stirring
works, leading to Lavallée's mighty climax with a composition that has been equated to a simultaneous rendition
of "God Save the Queen," "Vive La Canadienne" and
"Coming Through the Rye."

To an awed public silence, conductor Joseph Vezina
led three bands in a rousing rendition of Lavallée's "Chant"
which won the hearts of French Canadians, and approval of
the guests of honour — Governor General Lord Lorne and
his wife Princess Louise, Queen Victoria's daughter.

With a fresh triumph in hand, Lavallée then found
himself several hundred dollars out of pocket, since the

civic committee that had retained him reported with regret that it did not have the funds to pay him and the musicians.

Such luck seemed to permeate the composer's career. For example, an opera he had written in Boston was cancelled when the owner of the opera house was murdered.

Lavallée's musical accomplishments have survived him in compositions such as "Le Papillon" and his comic opera *The Widow*. However, in the hearts of Canadians the greatest legacy of the maestro can be felt in the choke of pride that swells whenever "O Canada" is played throughout our home and native land and around the world.

THE DIVA OF
THE SACRED FIRE

Montreal, 1883 — In Venice, flowers were tossed in the path of her gondola. In Africa, a Zulu warrior wearing a grass G-string asked her to sing her theme song "Home Sweet Home." The Czar of Russia presented her with a diamond-encrusted cross and Queen Victoria gave her pearls. Soprano Emma Albani was Canada's first international star, but she never abandoned her French-Canadian roots. Her triumphant return to the province of her birth in 1883 was greeted by 10,000 admirers. Poet Louis-Honoré Frechette dedicated a poem to her, and she was paraded through the wintry streets in a handsome carriage preceded by the band of the Sixty-Fifth Regiment and followed by a boisterous honour guard of snowshoers setting off firecrackers.

Albani was born in 1847 at Chambly near Montreal, where she was baptized Marie-Louise-Cécile-Emma Lajeunesse. When she was a toddler her mother began giving her piano lessons. At five, her father, a professional music teacher, took over. She practised four hours a day in a training program that included lessons in piano, harp and singing.

Following her mother's death, Emma and her younger sister, Cornelia, were enrolled at a prestigious Montreal convent school, where their father obtained a teaching position and free education for his daughters. The young woman's vocal skill was quickly recognized as advanced for her years. One reviewer described it as "a voice that seemed sent from heaven."

When she was barely a teenager, Emma performed at a musical festival honouring the eighteen-year-old Prince of Wales during his Canadian tour. By 1862, efforts were underway in Montreal to raise money for her musical education, but they met with disappointing results. "The French Canadians had the old-world traditional misgivings of a public career and especially a dislike for anyone belonging to them to go on the stage," she explained many years later. "Consequently all help, as they then honestly thought in my best interests, was withheld."

This was not the case in Albany, New York, where she found employment as a church choir leader and organist. The congregation sponsored benefit concerts that helped fund her move to Paris in 1868.

Her tutors were retired operatic tenor Gilbert-Louis Duprez and celebrated teacher Francesco Lamperti. "She has a beautiful voice and a sacred fire," Duprez once said. "She is the wood from which the finest flutes are made."

Just before her first professional singing engagement, an elocution teacher suggested a name change and she chose the old Italian family name "Albani," possibly in salute to her New York State supporters. Her debut in 1869 in Messina, Sicily, was a triumph. The *Sicilian Courier* described Emma Albani as "a privileged creature, in whom both the lady and the artist stand at the same eminence, and in whom the actress and the singer are in unison."

Accolades at Covent Garden in London followed. She enjoyed a long association with that prestigious company, which included marrying the manager, Ernest Gye.

The stunning diva performed throughout Great Britain, Europe and the United States before returning to Canada. Her repertoire included forty operas and forty-three different roles, as well as ballads such as "Annie Laurie" and "The Bluebells of Scotland" which were favourites of her friend, Queen Victoria. Kaiser Wilhelm I (Victoria's cousin) favoured her interpretations of Richard Wagner's epic operas so much that he made Albani a royal court singer. Critics praised her voice, and composers delighted in the accuracy of her interpretations.

In 1896, Albani toured Canada from Halifax to Victoria, earning the title "Queen of Song." She made two more Canadian tours before retiring, giving her last public recital in 1911. A Beethoven Medal was just one of her many honours, and in 1925 she was created Dame Commander of the British Empire. Hats and cake recipes were named after Albani, as well as a roadway in the city of Montreal.

To assist her in retirement, the British government provided a small allowance but the Canadian and Quebec governments did nothing to support the widowed singer. Her fans rose to the occasion when the Montreal newspaper, *La Presse*, sponsored a fund-raising campaign and Australian opera star, Nellie Melba, organized similar efforts in England, allowing Albani to live in comfort until her death at eighty-three.

"I have married an Englishman and have made my home in England," she noted in her memoirs, *Forty Years of Song*, "but still remain at heart a French Canadian."

BUCKSKIN AND BROCADE

Brantford, Ontario, 1884 — Poetry readings can be sonorously serious, but when self-proclaimed Mohawk princess Pauline Johnson felt her audience slipping into a trance she simply let out a whoop, called it a war cry, and got back to the business of entertaining. Her mother was British, her father was Mohawk. She drew from both backgrounds and created a persona that served her literary purpose.

Emily Pauline Johnson was a kind of sideshow in her own time, trapped in her own legend and torn between two cultures. She often wore two costumes, her beaded buckskins, moccasins and bear-claw native jewellery in the first act and a white brocade evening gown in the second. "There are those who think they pay me a compliment by saying I am just like a white woman," she told a friend. "I am Indian, and my aim, my joy and my pride is to sing the glories of my own people."

Johnson's commitment to her native heritage was grounded in a childhood that would seem the stuff of dreams. Born in 1861, on the reserve of the Six Nations near Brantford, Ontario, she grew up in an elegant, two-storey mansion known as "Chiefswood." Instead of Mother Goose stories, her mother, Emily, raised her on Byron and Keats. By the age of twelve, Johnson said she had read every line Sir Walter Scott and Henry Longfellow ever wrote, and she was well into Shakespeare and Emerson.

Her father's family claimed a Mohawk noble title that dated back to the creation of the League of the Iroquois. Her great-grandfather was baptized Jacob Johnson. He was the godson of Sir William Johnson, the first British superintendent of the northern natives of British North America and consort of Mohawk matriarch Molly Brant. Her grandfather, John "Smoke" Johnson, was a story-teller and through him Pauline kept alive her knowledge of the Mohawk language and the legends of her forebears.

Chiefswood was host to many visiting dignitaries, including Prince Arthur, the Duke of Connaught, who was initiated into the Mohawk nation at the mansion in 1869. Behind the veil of gentility, Johnson's father, Chief George, waged a battle on the Six Nations reserve against the liquor trade and theft of native timber resources. He was savagely beaten at least twice by non-native interlopers, and died after years of broken health in 1884.

Until this point, Johnson does not seem to have given much thought to a career. At twenty-three she began submitting her work to New York's *Gems of Poetry* and Toronto's *The Week*. At twenty-five, she contributed a poem at the dedication of a statue to Chief Joseph Brant but she was too shy to read it herself. Finally, at thirty, she found her "voice." Wearing her native buckskins, she launched into a rousing reading of "A Cry from an Indian Wife" at a Toronto author's evening for Young Liberals. She was a hit. A second performance was scheduled shortly afterward and Johnson composed "The Song My Paddle Sings" for the event. Performing under her family name,

Tekahionwake (meaning "double wampum") she embarked on a tour that culminated in her introduction to English society and the publication of her first book of poems, *The White Wampum,* in 1895.

Poetry, however, was the next best thing to poverty. *Saturday Night* magazine paid the grandiose sum of three dollars to publish "The Song My Paddle Sings." In her lifetime, she is said to have earned only $500 from her poetry. Johnson was forced to resume a recital career, writing nature sketches, articles and short stories for publications such as *Harper's Weekly, The Canadian Magazine* and *The Boy's World* to make ends meet. Although her work resounded with romance, she never married and suffered one ill-fated engagement to a Toronto banking inspector. As fellow-poet Charles Mair once noted: "The defeat of love runs like a grey thread through much of Miss Johnson's verse."

All told, she crossed Canada nineteen times. During this time she teamed up with Walter McRaye, an entertainer fifteen years her junior who performed the *habitant* poems of William Henry Drummond. They barnstormed from Halifax to Kamloops, speaking in churches, auditoriums and bar rooms. Along the way, Johnson kept writing and, although the results may have suffered a lack of polish, her themes remained Canadian and her personality a constant source of intrigue. In 1906, she returned to London, performing at Steinway Hall. There she met Chief Joe Capilano of the Squamish Mission of North Vancouver who was in England to appeal to King Edward VII to protest restrictions on aboriginal fishing rights.

Three years later, an exhausted Johnson retired from the stage to write prose in Vancouver. She renewed her friendship with Chief Joe and the resulting book, *Legends of Vancouver,* has been lauded by critics as "the first note-worthy rendering of Indian mythic material."

Johnson's health deteriorated and cancer of the breast was diagnosed too late to be operable. The "Mohawk Princess" died in 1913. "The inspiration of her genius was all Canadian, and all she wrote betrayed her love of the country which has passed from the rule of her fathers into the hands of aliens," declared the *Vancouver Province.*

BEAUTIFUL JOE

Halifax, Nova Scotia, 1893 — Margaret Marshall Saunders was thirty-three when she wrote *Beautiful Joe*, the "autobiography" of an ill-treated but amiable dog, which was published in 1893. The short novel took first prize in an American Humane Society competition, and became an international bestseller of over six million copies in more than fourteen languages.

Saunders was born in Milton, Nova Scotia, and enjoyed a classical education. After studying in Scotland and France, she taught school for several years in Halifax, but never warmed to the work. At the suggestion of family and friends she was encouraged to try writing fiction.

In 1889 she published her first novel, a wildly melodramatic romance called *My Spanish Sailor*. To avoid public antipathy to female novelists, she dropped her first name and published androgynously as Marshall Saunders.

Beautiful Joe was inspired by a chance meeting in Meaford, Ontario, where Saunders encountered a local miller, William Moore. He told her the story of a homely puppy he had rescued from a brutal master who had clipped the animal's ears and tail.

From this thread, Saunders wove an unapologetically sentimental story written from the point of view of the abused dog who ultimately finds a home with caring humans. *Beautiful Joe* became the first book by a Canadian to sell more than one million copies.

"I don't believe that a dog could have fallen into a happier home than I did," the mangled mongrel muses, in a conclusion reminiscent of British author Anna Sewell's 1877 bestseller, *Black Beauty*, which surely provided Saunders with inspiration. *Beautiful Joe* became the hit of the 1890s.

Over the next thirty years, Saunders wrote more than twenty-five books, most of them heart-tugging children's stories about domestic animals and birds. She travelled extensively throughout North America lecturing schoolchildren and service clubs as an advocate of legislation for wildlife protection and the humane treatment of all animals. Her humanitarian interests were also reflected in *The Girl from Vermont*, which protested the use of child labour in American factories.

In 1914, Saunders moved from Halifax to Toronto, where she lived with her sister, one dog and as many as 200 pet birds. Neighbourhood children regularly brought injured birds and animals to her for treatment. As often as not, they would find the famous author with a pigeon or two riding around on her shoulders.

Her work consistently stressed kindness and she approached human cruelty not as a lack of virtue or of understanding, but as a failure of feeling. Later critics would find much of her work maudlin and didactic, but she wrote with an entertaining grace.

While Marshall Saunders' literary ambition may have been best realized in her ability to wet the eyes and wring the hearts, other turn-of-the-century authors, such as Ernest Thompson Seton and Charles G.D. Roberts, expanded on

Canadian literature to include a whole new genre of "animal biography," featuring realistic stories of wild animals.

Subsequent naturalist and conservationist authors include Roderick Haig-Brown and Farley Mowat, whose Canadian nature tales and chronicles for adults and children are as world-renowned today as *Beautiful Joe* was more than a century ago.

THE GREAT
CANADIAN KISSER

Whitby, Ontario, 1896 — May Irwin was thirty-three years old when she puckered up for the most famous kiss she would ever deliver. The first locking of human lips in cinematic history was a close-up exchange between this Canadian actress/comedienne and American actor James C. Rice. It took inventor Thomas Edison five days to film the fulsome buss, which was promoted as "the first shocker." When *The Fifty-Foot Kiss* made its big screen debut in 1896, sermons and editorials predicted it would lead to moral decline. But few of her childhood friends recognized the famous lips of May Irwin as those of little May Campbell, who had left her hometown of Whitby, Ontario, twenty years earlier to sing, dance and amuse on the great stages of the world.

May Campbell became May Irwin around the same time as she reached puberty, simply because the shorter name fit neatly on a marquee. Her father had made a good living in the Ontario logging industry, but he was something of a spendthrift. When he died, May's mother decided to put her young daughters on the stage and presented them at an audition in Buffalo, New York. "It is hard enough being penniless in places like New York or Camden, New Jersey," the buxom entertainer recalled years later, "but nothing to jingle in Whitby, Ontario, is something terrible. Being penniless, my sister, Flo, and I were what you might call in reduced circumstances."

The "Irwin Sisters" were not reduced for long. In 1877, they began a six-year engagement at the top variety house in New York City, Tony Pastor's. By the time she was seventeen, May was married and appearing on "legit" stages in London and Paris. She was hailed as "undeniably the greatest farce actress in America" during the Gay Nineties and became known as "the personification of humour and careless mirth."

Throughout years of heady success, Irwin summered in the Thousand Islands on the St. Lawrence River where she entertained extensively. Each of her guest rooms had twin beds and twin baths. "If there were more plumbing there'd be fewer divorces," she decreed. Irving Berlin is said to have written "Alexander's Ragtime Band" at one of the six grand pianos that decorated the cottage on Irwin Island. May became the first woman to introduce ragtime songs to Broadway. She was also the first white woman to dance the cakewalk on the New York stage — a feat of footwork she learned from the black staff who worked at the tourist hotels in the Islands.

At twenty-five, May was earning $2,500 a week. Unlike her father, she sought out sound investments and purchased substantial real estate in Manhattan. She formed her own company, built her own theatre, and took time out to write a cookbook. Audiences begged for her theme song, "After the Ball is Over," and fretted when she threatened to retire in 1902. "Miss Irwin is a famous fun maker of jolly rotund figure and with a face that reflects the gaiety of nations," wrote one critic. President Woodrow Wilson was so taken with her that he named her his "Secretary of Laughter." In 1925, at the age of sixty-two, she was still a headliner and even Houdini could not upstage her.

When the stock market crashed on October 29, 1929, it took many entertainers and industrialists with it — but May Irwin was not among them. In the spring of that fateful year, she sold all of her real estate, including one lot that reportedly earned her $670,000. While the fortunes of those around her went into a tailspin, she was holding millions in cash.

When she died at seventy-four, her legacy included a body of writing on the art of comedy, as well as her best-selling recipes and several RCA Victor recordings. At her request, she was buried in a red satin dress. It was the final outrageous act of the woman who dared to kiss for the movies.

THE ORIGINAL
ROLLING STONE

Whitehorse, Yukon Territory, 1906 — Robert Service was a bank teller in Whitehorse when he was invited to prepare a reading for a church concert. It was a rowdy Klondike Saturday night when the line: "A bunch of the boys were whooping it up," popped into his head.

After returning to his apartment above the bank office, Service says in his autobiography, *Ploughman of the Moon,* he crept downstairs to the quiet of his teller's cage and commenced work. A sleeping guard awoke and assumed the midnight author was a burglar.

"Fortunately, he was a poor shot or 'The Shooting of Dan McGrew' might never have been written," wrote Service. "With the sensation of a bullet whizzing past my head, and a detonation ringing in my cars, the ballad was achieved." More than fifty years later, Service finally admitted the story was pure hokum.

Service emigrated to Canada from Scotland in 1894 with fifteen dollars in his pocket and visions of becoming a cowboy. He tramped about and took all manner of odd jobs, before he began a career in banking which led him to the Yukon.

His first book of verse, *Songs of a Sourdough,* was an accidental success. Service had intended to print a slim volume of his poems as a souvenir booklet for his friends, and his father forwarded the material to a publisher of hymnals in New York for printing. The book sold itself when pressmen were discovered laughing and reciting Service's verse, including the classic "The Cremation of Sam McGee." The book sold over two million copies and made Service one of the best-known and wealthiest writers in Canada.

In 1908, Service was transferred to Dawson City and he settled in a rustic cabin, which is now a museum. He wrote his first novel here, *The Trail of '98.* When it was finished he decided to deliver it personally to his publisher in New York.

"We expected you to arrive in mukluks and a parka, driving a dog team down Fifth Avenue," exclaimed the publisher, who was surprised to find Service rather unassuming in appearance. Far from the rough and tumble, hard-drinking womanizers and scoundrels he immortalized, Service was a teetotaller and a physical fitness buff with a particular passion for potatoes. Nevertheless, the book was deemed bawdy enough to be banned in Boston.

After one of his famous "tramps" to New Orleans and Havana, with a visit to his mother on the Alberta prairies, Service went back to the Klondike and wrote another collection of verse, *Rhymes of a Rolling Stone.* In the autumn of 1912, he took the last steamboat out of Dawson, and never returned.

His life remained action-packed. As a reporter, he covered the Balkan War, and during World War One he served as an ambulance driver and as an intelligence officer for the Canadian Army. His collection of war poetry,

Rhymes of a Red Gross Man, headed the non-fiction best-seller list in 1917 and 1918.

Dispelling rumours of his death, Service continued to publish both his memoirs and at least eight books of verse, while living comfortably in Monte Carlo and Brittany. A physical fitness book he wrote in 1928 called *Why Not Grow Young? or Living for Longevity* was reprinted when Service was a spry octogenarian. One of his health tips recommended potato eating. He claimed to eat as many as 22,000 tubers a year!

In 1958, Canadian television broadcaster Patrick Watson and journalist Pierre Berton interviewed the eighty-four-year-old, self-proclaimed "rhymer" at his villa overlooking the Mediterranean.

"Say, wouldn't it be a sensation if I croaked in the middle of this interview?" asked Service with a twinkle in his eye. The Bard of the Yukon died a few months later leaving a legacy that is the stuff of myth.

THE PIE MAN

Hollywood, 1914 — "In Canada, where I was fetched, life was cold and serious. Canadians are not congenitally comic," explained Mikall Sinott, who earned the title "King of Comedy" as Mack Sennett — actor, writer, producer and director of more than one thousand silent slapstick films. The self-described "Canadian farm boy" discovered Charlie Chaplin, invented the Keystone Kops and climaxed virtually all of his films with a wild chase sequence that could involve anything from bathing beauties to rusty bicycles, cats, dogs and babies. He is best known for the physical comedy that he brought to the silver screen, especially the delivery of a custard pie in the face of an unsuspecting subject. "There is a great deal of humour in the combination of surprise and violence," Sennett noted. "A lowering of dignity is always funny."

Mikall Sinnott was born in Danville, Quebec, in 1880, the son of Irish parents. The family moved to Connecticut when he was seventeen, and Mikall set his sights on becoming an opera singer, but ended up playing bit parts in vaudeville theatre as "Mack Sennett." One of his first roles was as the back end of a burlesque horse. That auspicious beginning led to bit parts as a five-dollar-a-week actor in the "flickers," where he worked with legendary film director D.W. Griffith at Biograph Studios. He became a screenwriter when he discovered that scripts were worth twenty-five dollars. By 1910, he was writing, directing and acting in an average of two, ten-minute comedies every week.

Sennett founded the Keystone Production Company in 1912. Legend has it that he borrowed the name from a sign he saw at a train station, and that he borrowed the money from a couple of bookies. The "studio" was a twenty-eight-acre lot in the wilds of Southern California, which is now the heart of downtown Los Angeles. The climate was perfect for filming almost every day. In its first year, Keystone turned out 140 films and Mack Sennett made his first million dollars.

Improvisation, innovation and sheer determination fuelled the comedic pace. As Sennett was fond of saying, "It's got to move." In those early days of film, the camera was cranked by hand and the film was edited by the foot. Sennett's early films were one- or two-reelers, lasting ten to twenty minutes. In 1914, he created the first full-length feature comedy motion picture, *Tillie's Punctured Romance*, which starred Marie Dressler from Cobourg, Ontario, Charlie Chaplin (as the city slicker) and Mabel Normand, the love of Sennett's life.

It was Normand who threw that first famous pie. Weary of a long day of filming, the flighty starlet caught her co-star, crosseyed comic Ben Turpin, in her crosshairs and let one fly. "His aplomb vanished in a splurch of goo and his magnificent eyes emerged batting in stunned outrage in all directions," Sennett recalled in his 1954 autobiography *King of Comedy*.

The pie toss became Sennett's trademark and a hallmark of slapstick comedy. "Non anticipation on the part of the recipient of the pastry is the chief ingredient of the recipe," he said. And there were other rules to follow. According to Sennett's instructions, "A mother never gets hit with a custard pie. Mothers-in-law, yes. But mothers, never."

The advent of cartoon short features such as Walt Disney's *Mickey Mouse* and talking pictures such as *The Jazz Singer*, produced by Montrealer Sam Warner, led to Sennett's business failure and fade into obscurity. Abandoned by Mabel Normand because he spent so much time making movies, he stuck by her through a difficult period in which she was under investigation for the unsolved murder of her playboy film director boyfriend, William Desmond Taylor. He was grief-stricken when she died in 1930 at thirty-three, amid rumours of drug problems and in the aftermath of a shooting involving her chauffeur and her gun.

In 1935, a bankrupt Sennett returned to Canada for four years, living in penury on the Quebec property his mother bought with money he sent to her during his heyday of twenty-one-room Hollywood mansions and magnificent yachts. Hollywood did not forget him, however. His protegés included director Frank Capra (*It Happened One Night*, *Mr. Smith Goes to Town*), who started his career as a Keystone "gagman," and the talents he brought to prominence included Gloria Swanson, Bing Crosby, Carole Lombard and W.C. Fields. In 1937, a special Academy Award was presented to "that master of fun, discoverer of stars, sympathetic, kindly, genius — Mack Sennett."

"Maybe people are paying too much attention to grammar today," Sennett told a reporter in 1959. "I don't think there's too many belly laughs in grammar." A year later, at seventy-six, he died following surgery for a kidney ailment. At the time, he was said to be working on a script — a comedy, no doubt.

BORN OF FIRE AND BLOOD

Ypres, Belgium, 1915 — As one officer would later recall, the wounded arrived "in batches." Sometimes they fell at the feet of the field physician who struggled to maintain some sense of sanity and some preserve of sanitation in the trenches where wounds could quickly turn to putrefaction. This was Ypres, Belgium, where Canadian troops saw battle for the first time in World War One. It was here, amid the brutal horror of bullet and bayonet injuries and the blue-green death masks of chlorine gas victims, that John McCrae wrote three stanzas which have come to symbolize the ultimate sacrifice and challenge of war.

> *In Flanders fields the poppies blow*
> *Between the crosses, row on row,*
> *That mark our place; and in the sky*
> *The larks, still bravely singing, fly*
> *Scarce heard amid the guns below.*
>
> *We are the Dead. Short days ago*
> *We lived, felt dawn, saw sunset glow,*
> *Loved and were loved, and now we lie,*
> *In Flanders fields.*

Take up our quarrel with the foe:
To you from failing hands we throw
The torch; be yours to hold it high.
If ye break faith with us who die
We shall not sleep, though poppies grow
In Flanders fields.

As a Major, McCrae was an artillery brigade surgeon during the Second Battle of Ypres. He was forty-two when he jotted the poem in pencil on a page torn from a dispatch pad on May 3, 1915. It was a moment of brief respite in the sixteen-day battle which saw more than six thousand Canadians killed and wounded. McCrae had left his dressing station at the base of a bank on the Ypres Canal and he was travelling in the back of a field ambulance. Just north of the bridge, there was a field dotted with scarlet poppies and wooden crosses. The day before, McCrae had set a cross in that field to mark the grave of a friend, Lieutenant Alex Helmer of Ottawa.

The doctor had seen the face of battle before. Following his graduation from the University of Toronto, McCrae served as a gunner in the South African War. Returning to Canada in 1900, he was appointed as a fellow in pathology at McGill University and pathologist to Montreal General Hospital. As a physician, he wrote a number of medical textbooks, and privately he wrote poetry, which he submitted to various periodicals.

Volume Two of *Literary History of Canada* describes "In Flanders Fields" as "a restrained, formal flawless expression of Canadian feeling." McCrae's commanding officer, Major General E.W. Morrison, called it a poem "born of fire and blood." The English magazine *Punch* received the poem anonymously and published it in December of 1915.

Colonel McCrae died of pneumonia on January 28, 1918, five days after his appointment as consulting physician to the First British Army. His cross is Number 3 in Row 4 of Plot 4 at Wimereux Communal Cemetery, near Boulogne, France. In memory of him, a perpetual light burns in the garden of his birthplace in Guelph, Ontario, where McCrae House is maintained as a national historic site.

One of John McCrae's comrades, Captain William Boyd — himself a former University of Montreal pathology professor — served five months at the front before joining a field ambulance unit at Ypres. He described the battlefield as a "stricken land, where death stalks you by day and takes you by the arm as you walk the road at night."

It is a wonder that a lark could sing above such grief.

THE LAUGHING ONE

Kitwancool, British Columbia, 1928 — "The woods and sky out West are big. You can't squeeze them down," she once said. Emily Carr was born in 1871, the same year that British Columbia entered Confederation. "Contrary from the start," was the way Carr described herself in her autobiography. She had no use for the tidy conventions of the society of Victoria, B.C.

She was orphaned at sixteen, and two years later her guardian granted her permission to study at the California School of Design in San Francisco. On her return, she established a studio in a cow barn and began giving drawing lessons to children, and saving her money for future studies in Paris and London.

In fact, Carr found the subjects of her greatest art before she left for Europe, when a friend took her to an isolated Vancouver Island mission called Ucluelet in 1898. The tangled, untamed and even menacing forest environment both attracted and repelled her, while the intense artistry of the ancient totem poles moved her deeply, and in the native people themselves she found a kindred spirit. They named her Klee Wyck — the Laughing One.

In Europe, Carr observed the "new art" of the Post-Impressionists. She discovered "brilliant, luscious, clean paintings." Her work hung in the Salon d'Automne of 1911 in Paris, and there was clear recognition of her talent. When she returned to Vancouver and exhibited her paintings, by her own account the result was "insult and scorn."

So she turned her back on Vancouver, packed up her paint box and easel and made a harrowing journey up the coast to the Queen Charlotte Islands and remote native villages on the Skeena and Nass Rivers, where she painted the vanishing villages and totem poles.

Unable to live from her art, she became disillusioned and built a small apartment house in Victoria, spending fifteen years as a landlady, and augmenting her income by breeding dogs, hooking rugs and making pottery.

In 1927, she was invited to include her work in an exhibition of West Coast art at the National Art Gallery in Ottawa. Carr admitted at the time that she did not even know that Canada had a National Gallery!

It was a turning point. Her work was enthusiastically received, and she was inspired by the artists of the Group of Seven, whose aspirations matched her own. "Something has spoken to the very soul of me," she wrote in her journal, finding in their canvases "a naked soul, pure and unashamed."

A burst of energy followed in 1928. Carr abandoned her tenants and headed back to the Queen Charlotte Islands to Kitwancool, a remote village noted for its impressive totem poles. She captured the totems with bold reverence, in her own brooding and solemn vision.

In later years Carr turned her brush to the large rhythms of the coastal rain forests, beaches and skies. Living in a caravan with a menagerie of pets, she painted the grand primeval brooding of the forest, translating the spiritual essence of the light in scenes of constant visual movement.

"At last I knew that I must see through the eye of the totem — the mythic eye of the forest," she wrote. Before she died in 1945, Emily Carr was in the first rank of Canadian painters.

SHE DID IT HER WAY

Montreal, 1929 — Mary-Rose-Anne Travers was a child of thirteen when she left her home in the Gaspésien town of Newport to earn her living in Montreal. Fluently bilingual, she grew up in a large family of English descent, enduring poverty as a way of life, and intuitively understanding music as its escape valve. She learned to play the violin, the harmonica and the accordian, and she was as comfortable with Irish reels as she was with the songs of Acadia.

Mary's decision to leave her home was intended to relieve some financial burden from her family. To finance her trip she fiddled on the main street and sold a popular patent medicine of the day called Red Pills. Arriving in Montreal in 1907, the teenager found work as a household maid. Later she entered a textile mill, working thirteen-hour days for pitiful wages. Shortly after the outbreak of the First World War, she married a plumber, Édouard Bolduc. Illness and poverty plagued their early years. Mary gave birth to thirteen children; however, only four survived.

Madame Bolduc began her performing career out of economic necessity. In her first public appearance, she was a replacement fiddle player in Conrad Gauthier's popular folklore show *Veillées du bon vieux temps*. When Gauthier encouraged her to sing publicly in 1927, she was such a success that he suggested she compose songs of her own.

Day-to-day life became the theme of the songstress known as "La Bolduc." Keenly observant, she found humour in subjects such as insurance agents, mothers-in-law and the police. In "La Grocerie du coin," for example, she gleefully told the public what they already knew was going on at their cornerstore. Her musical advice was to "Watch close when they weigh your meat/ Sometimes they will try to cheat." La Bolduc warned patrons not to fall prey to the distraction of a shopkeeper's yarn and her audiences — recognizing the familiar ruse — howled in delight.

Live performances on radio brought La Bolduc to popular attention. By 1929, she was ready to record. Finding no backers, she paid for studio time herself. Her first record, "La Cusinière" (The Cook), sold an unprecedented 12,000 copies in Quebec. Backers were found and soon La Bolduc was turning out a record almost every month.

The energy and the spirit of hope that La Bolduc brought to her music was a welcome respite in the bleak landscape of the Depression. Her joyous style, embellished by *turlutages* or comic ritonelles produced by clicking her tongue against her palate, made her the idol of the working class. Renowned anthropologist and ethnomusicologist Marius Barbeau found in her songs a "reckless verve and unique twist of tongue in the manner of the singers of the true soil."

She toured tirelessly in Quebec and New England and produced a total of seventy-four songs on record. In 1937, tragedy struck when a serious car accident ended her tour in Rimouski. In the course of treating her injuries, doctors discovered a cancerous tumour. Four years later, French Canada's first lady of *chanson* died at forty-six.

The musical legacy of La Bolduc has been commemorated by musicans such as Jean "Ti-Jean" Carignan and André Gagnon. In 1994, she was featured on a postage stamp, and her hometown in Newport maintains a permanent exhibit in her honour. New audiences are constantly rediscovering her music.

As CBC Radio's music archivist Adrian Shuman noted in his "discovery" of the chansonnière in 1994, "Her voice turns darkness into sunlight. It has a wonderful earthiness. You smile, and suddenly you feel like doing a jig."

THE COWBOY FROM QUEBEC

The West, 1930 — He said he was an only child, born under a wagon in Montana. He also said that his mother died when he was a year old, leaving his Texas cowboy father to raise him, until an encounter with a long-horned steer left the child an orphan.

In fact, he was born in St. Nazaire, Quebec, in 1892. He had two brothers and three sisters. His mother was still living in 1934, when he visited the family home in Montreal for the express purpose of destroying everything that could link his true identity to the fantastic fraud that he had created.

Joseph Ernest Nephtali Dufault had many aliases, but the one that finally stuck was "Will James." He was a best-selling author, a cowboy contemporary of Will Rogers and Tom Mix, and an illustrator whose detailed sketches of horses were so lifelike that one critic suggested they "seem to leap from the page and kick dirt all over you."

Even though his autobiography *Lone Cowboy: My Life Story* ranked fifth on the non-fiction best seller list in 1930, one of the few non-fiction events described by its author concerned his 1914 arrest for cattle rustling. "I often wish that I hadn't misrepresented myself as I did," Dufault/

James confessed in a letter to his brother Auguste, "but I couldn't dream of the success I've had and now it's too late to change."

The greenhorn from Montreal with a grade 8 education spent his entire adult life pretending he was "born and raised in the cow country."

He successfully deceived his wife, his publisher and his faithful readers, but the strain of deception took its toll. At the age of fifty, he died alone and broke in a Hollywood hospital of cirrhosis of the liver and kidney failure caused by alcoholism.

The groundwork for the invention of "Will James" began in 1907, when fifteen-year-old Ernest Dufault talked his parents into providing a one-way ticket to Regina. Fascinated by the lore and lifestyle of the West, he spent the remainder of his teenage years learning about ranch life and honing his cowboy skills.

He also learned English. A fellow Québécois named Beaupre is thought to have been his mentor. At one point, both men filed homestead claims at Val Marie near the Cypress Hills which spans the Alberta/Saskatchewan border. Later, in his infamous autobiography, Will James wrote that as an orphaned child, a family friend "Bopy" (Beaupre) adopted him and raised him.

In the book, the kindly French-Canadian trapper shows the boy hunting during the Canadian winters and teaches him the ways of the cowboy during summers in Montana.

According to James's story, Bopy drowns in the ice-filled Red Deer River, leaving his protegé to fend for himself with a lingering French accent that could be easily explained without revealing the truth.

By the time he reached his early twenties, the lanky, dark-haired vagabond had worked at many of Western

Canada's largest ranches and drifted around Montana, Idaho, Wyoming and New Mexico. He tried on various aliases that sounded more authentically "western" than Dufault, including Clint Jackson, Stonewall and William Roderick James.

In 1914, "Bill James" was riding bucking horses at a small rodeo in Medicine Hat where fellow cowboy Ronald "Crying" Mason noted that "Bill was as good a bronc rider" as he had ever seen.

That same year a botched cattle rustling attempt earned the self-described "Montana-born" Will James a fifteen-month sentence in the Nevada State Prison at Carson City.

After serving his time, James resumed the cowboy life. He also worked as a stuntman and extra in Hollywood westerns.

In 1917, when he was visiting friends in Calgary, he ended up driving around the Prairies in a Model T Ford that he covered in crayon drawings of bucking horses. As a part of a loose cowboy street show featuring the likes of Sleepy Epperson on harmonica and Calgary Red serving up roping tricks, James was the announcer, known as "Bullshit Bill."

From childhood, he had always enjoyed drawing images of Western life, and his hands-on experience wrangling horses, herding cattle and living the bunkhouse life gave his drawings authenticity. When he was sidelined with a concussion after a tumble from a bucking horse, a fellow patient noticed his flair for drawing and provided a letter of introduction to an editor at the popular San Francisco illustrated magazine *Sunset*.

James attempted to study art seriously at the California School of Fine Arts in San Francisco and he was offered a scholarship to Yale University. However, his inspiration came from memory, and formal studies did not suit him.

Sunset magazine published a series of his drawings in 1920, and New York's leading illustrated magazine, *Scribner's*, invited him to submit stories with his drawings.

With the encouragement of his teenaged wife, Alice, James wrote and illustrated "Bucking Horses and Bucking-Horse Riders," in one week and pronounced it "too easy done to be any good."

Scribner's paid him $300 and James became a regular contributor, with seven feature stories appearing in 1923.

"I am a cowboy, and what's put down in these pages is not material that I've hunted up, it's what I've lived, seen and went thru before I ever had any idea that my writing and sketches would ever appear before the public," James wrote in the preface to his first book, *Cowboys North and South*. Bad grammar and all, it was his unique "cowboyese" language and intimate understanding of the actual life of cowboys that separated James from the "pulp western" writers of the era. His work was celebrated for its literary achievement, which *The New York Times* described as "unvarnished but singularly salty and effective."

In 1927, his third book, *Smoky, The Cowhorse* won the coveted Newbery Medal for Children's Literature. It was translated into at least six foreign languages and became the subject of three motion picture treatments. On the strength of *Smoky's* success, his publisher advanced James money to buy a ranch near Billings, Montana.

Between 1924 and 1942, Will James published twenty-four books, but his life seems to have begun to unravel after the publication of his autobiography.

One of his biographers, Anthony Amaral, noted that in the aftermath of *Lone Cowboy* James's "career and his integrity were balanced on a precarious suppression of his true credentials."

In 1935, a year after the film version of *Lone Cowboy* premiered and a year after he returned to Canada to destroy any lingering trace of his true identity in the Dufault home, his wife, Alice, left. In 1936, James lost the Rocking R Ranch to his creditors. Years of excessive drinking and fear of discovery finally eroded his health and his talent.

Although romanticized, Will James's work is acknowledged to be among the finest examples of cowboy art ever produced. A collection of his work, including a striking self-portrait with Stetson, is permanently displayed at the Yellowstone Art Center, and singer-song writer Ian Tyson is one of James's avid Canadian collectors.

Like his contemporary, literary fraud Archibald Belaney who gained fame and notoriety as the Canadian Indian author Grey Owl, the secret truth of Will James's identity was not revealed until after his death. It passed without much notice in his homeland.

Half a century later, a society dedicated to Will James was formed. It meets once a year somewhere in North America where the cowboy from Quebec is known to have lassoed a calf, tamed a bronco or sketched a tumbleweed.

Medicine Hat educator and freelance curator Allan Jensen, who has served on the Board of Directors of the Will James Society, notes: "As Canadians, we need to repatriate Will James, his legend and his legacy as part of our cultural property and heritage."

THE MAN OF STEEL

Cleveland, Ohio, 1934 — "Truth, justice and the American way," a phenomenon administered by a muscle man wearing a cape and tights, but Superman, the king of the comic superheroes, was the creation of a Canadian.

Joe Shuster came up with the idea of a "strange visitor from another planet with powers and abilities far beyond those of mortal men" with his buddy, Jerry Siegel, when the pair were only seventeen years old. Shuster was living in Cleveland, Ohio, at the time, but had grown up in Toronto along with most of his family including cousin Frank, whose own fame would come as half of Canada's "Wayne and Shuster" comedy team. He started drawing as a child, and he drew on anything and everything that was free, including discarded butcher paper and the back-side of abandoned wallpaper rolls.

According to novelist Mordecai Richler, Superman can be seen as a perfect expression of the Canadian psyche. Shuster's mighty Man of Steel hides his extraordinary strength, speed, and superhuman powers under the bland, self-effacing guise of the weak and clumsy Clark Kent, mild-mannered reporter.

Superman is a hero who does not take any credit for his own heroism. He is a glamorous figure who could get the best table in any restaurant, but is content to live his daily life in horned-rimmed glasses and brown suits and carry his lunch to work. With his modest alter-ego Clark Kent, who, however meek, does seem to get scoop after scoop, Superman is the archetypal Canadian personality who became a "universal hero," famed throughout the world as the champion of everything virtuous.

Shuster modelled *The Daily Planet*, where Clark Kent was gainfully employed, after Toronto's *Daily Star*. The cityscape of Metropolis, the fictional city that Superman vowed to clean up, was patterned after Toronto in the 1930s. Indeed, when he was not moving faster than a speeding bullet and leaping over tall buildings in a single bound, Superman reverted to being a shy, bespectacled guy, not unlike Joe Shuster himself.

Superman leaped from comic books to radio in the 1940s, and onto the television screen by the 1950s. By the late 1970s he was a movie star. Even *Superman the Movie* had many Canadian connections. The small-town sequences were all shot in High River, Alberta. Actor Glen Ford, who hailed from Quebec, played Superman's adoptive father and Regina-born Margot Kidder played the intrepid Lois Lane.

Unfortunately, Shuster saw few of the rewards reaped by the "Metropolis Marvel's" success. He and Siegel invented their x-ray-visioned character in 1934, but it took four years for D.C. Comics to hire the persistent pair and place Superman on the cover of *Action Comics* Number One in 1938. Four issues later, it was a runaway success, but Shuster and Siegel had already sold the rights to their creation to the publisher for $130 U.S.

When the pair sued to regain control in 1947, they lost and were fired as *Superman*'s artist and writer. By 1975,

Shuster was legally blind, living in a rundown New York City apartment. Growing knowledge of his plight prompted Warner Communications, which had bought the rights to *Superman* for their 1978 blockbuster movie, to award the creators a yearly stipend of $20,000 each. As Brad Roberts, lead singer for the Winnipeg-based, internationally successful rock band Crash Test Dummies put it in his 1991 ballad "Superman Song". *Superman never made any money* ... but Joe Shuster's creation was never about anything so crass as capital gain.

Superman is about the inevitable triumph of good over evil and the ability to change clothes in telephone booths. The character stands at the top of the twentieth-century cultural pantheon, as globally recognizable as Mickey Mouse, Charlie Chaplin and Elvis. "There aren't many people who can honestly say they'll be leaving behind something as important as Superman," Joe Shuster told the *Toronto Star* on the newspaper's 100th anniversary. Two months later, on June 30, 1992, Joe Shuster died at seventy-eight.

SPONTANEOUS
COMBUSTION

Montreal, 1948 — Few Canadians have ever heard of *Refus global*, a pastiche of diatribe, essay and screed written by a group of French-Canadian artists and first published in Montreal on August 6, 1948.

"Published" can be a bit of a misnomer: 400 mimeographed copies of the 100-page document with a cover drawn by Jean-Paul Riopelle were distributed among family and friends.

Separatists and other free thinkers in Quebec have long since seized upon *Refus global* as an unofficial founding document. Certain academics and intellectuals ruefully cite it as the opening salvo in Quebec's Quiet Revolution.

In 1998, on the fiftieth anniversary of its appearance, *Refus global* — in English, "universal refusal" or "total rejection" — became the celebrated subject of exhibitions, films, radio documentaries and conferences all over the country.

The Post Office even issued a series of stamps based on paintings by a variety of contributors to the obscure manifesto, including works by Riopelle, Pierre Gavreau, Fernand Leduc, Marcel Barbeau, and the *Refus global*'s driving force, Paul-Émile Borduas, who is by now torqued by the irrepressible irony of it all, spinning furiously in his grave.

What would the brilliant painter who died an exile in Paris at the age of fifty-four, thirty-eight years before this anniversary, make of the fact that the publication that ruined the life he cherished, was now a *cause célèbre*?

A month after the release of *Refus global*, Borduas received a letter informing him that the Minister of Social Welfare and Youth for Quebec had demanded that he be dismissed "because the writings and manifestos he had published, as well as his general attitude, are not of a kind to favour the teaching we wish to provide our students."

And so Borduas, a distinguished, well-liked and eminently qualified teacher, was summarily dismissed from École du Meuble in Montreal, from a job he not only liked but desperately needed.

For his role in organizing, editing and writing the seminal essay in *Refus global* Borduas was not only fired, but denounced from the pulpit as a sinner and called a madman in the press.

Although Borduas' paintings continued to sell, the income was nowhere near enough to support him and his family. His wife, a devout Catholic, took their three young children and went home to her mother.

"We must break with the conventions of society once and for all, and reject its utilitarian spirit. We must refuse to function knowingly at less than our physical and mental potential," Borduas youthfully enthused in *Refus global*:

> Refuse to close our eyes to vice and fraud perpetrated in the name of knowledge or favours or due respect . . .
> We refuse to keep silent. Do what you want with us, but you must hear us out. We will not accept your fame

or attendant honours. They are the stigmata of shame, silliness and servility. We refuse to serve, or to be used for such purposes . . . MAKE WAY FOR MAGIC! MAKE WAY FOR OBJECTIVE MYSTERIES! MAKE WAY FOR LOVE! MAKE WAY FOR THE INTERNAL DRIVES!

In retrospect, *Refus global* seems innocent, ardent and rhapsodic. Uneven and sometimes naive, it is exactly what one might expect from a group of young, diverse artists that included experimental poet Claude Gauvreau, painters such as the now world-famous Riopelle, dancer/choreographers including Jeanne Renaud and Françoise Sullivan, and Marcelle Ferron, who created the spectacular stained-glass window for the Champs de Mars station.

The writings that sacked Borduas also earned him and his fellow contributors, many of whom were his students, police dossiers.

Believe it or not, as a consequence of *Refus global*, most of the young men and women who were signatories to the document came under surreptitious RCMP surveillance, which, in some cases, quietly lasted their lifetime. Considered subversives, they lost jobs and suffered social ostracism.

A young journalist named Tancred Marsil writing in a magazine called *Quartier Latin*, dubbed the group *"les automatistes,"* a moniker meant to describe their idealization of creative spontaneity.

Philosophically, the manifesto of *les automatistes* has a great deal in common with the sentiments and attitudes that informed Jack Kerouac's *On the Road*, which, although written in the late 1940s, was not published until 1957.

Kerouac, a contemporary of Borduas, was the son of French-Canadian immigrants who hailed from the same countryside as Borduas' family before moving to Lowell,

Massachusetts. While Borduas became a pariah, Kerouac became the philosopher-king of the "beat" generation, a generation that lionized the outsider.

Unlike *On the Road*, *Refus global* really had little or no impact on anyone except its creators. Published anywhere other than Quebec in the late 1940s, *Refus global* would have either been ignored, quietly indulged or mildly celebrated by the intelligentsia.

But it could not be tolerated by the retrograde cabinet of Premier Maurice Duplessis, controlled as it was by the staid, nineteenth-century mores of the Catholic Church. As Clarke Blaise observes in his memoir, *I Had A Father*, French Canadians were possessed of "a garrison mentality, afraid to venture forth, suspicious of outsiders, always defensive about the loss of language, culture and religion."

Garrison mentalities tend to treat usurpers, intellectual or otherwise, rather badly. And thus befell Borduas his fate, a kind of sweet oblivion.

Sweet because, although lonely, homesick and ill at the end of his short life, his art had long been recognized and rewarded for what it was — brilliant. And Borduas' last years in Paris were among his most interesting and productive.

Ironically, cultural life in Montreal during the late forties and fifties was by far the most cosmopolitan and sophisticated, outside of New York, on the North American continent. By comparison, Toronto was Hicksville. Despite the pervasive machinations of the narrow-minded Catholic junta that defined the status quo and kept Duplessis in power, it was visceral, which is why Borduas loved it so.

Paradoxically, a priest was at the centre of the orgiastic and free-thinking exposition that eventually propelled Borduas on out of wedlock and la belle province. Father

Alain Couturier was a rather worldly, expatriate, French Dominican.

In New York when the war broke, fate and the good Lord sent Father Alain north to Montreal. After God and the Virgin Mary, Father Couturier was most dedicated to the doctrine of the new, particularly in the world of art and ideas. Once entrenched, he proceeded to make a career out of disturbing fecal matter in Montreal's vibrant cultural community.

Publicly criticizing École des Beaux-Arts, the establishment art school in Montreal that Borduas had attended as a youth, Father Couturier regularly fed *les automatistes* provocative sermon/lectures on cubism, surrealism and dada.

In 1940, the Quebec-born artist Pellan, who had been living in Paris, came home in full plumage with his enthusiasms, his startling, surrealistic paintings, his books and his intimate knowledge of Braque, Picasso and their precursors.

Fernand Leger, passing through the city in 1943, gave a lecture and showed his famous, ground-breaking film *Le Ballet mecanique*.

In 1944, a travelling exhibition of Dutch paintings, including those of Mondrian, were revelations to Borduas and *les automatistes*.

One of the signatories to *Refus global*, Fernand Leduc, made contact with Andre Breton in New York. The leader of the French Surrealist Movement invited *les automatistes* to formally align itself with Surrealism, an invitation that, in the spirit of *Refus global*, was politely refused.

In 1947 the group was again invited by a persistent Breton to take part in an International Surrealist Exhibition in Paris. Although they once again declined, it is an indication that there was nothing parochial or provincial about the art scene in Montreal.

Borduas was himself classically trained. He began his career as apprentice to the last, and arguably the greatest Church painter Canada has ever known, Ozias Leduc.

Leduc (1864–1955), who lived like a recluse in Saint Hilaire, has a special place in Canadian art. Not only did he paint remarkable religious murals and altars that still define and dominate dozens of churches throughout Quebec, but he also painted radiant still lifes that were inspirational to the development of modern painting in Canada.

An excellent student and apprentice, Borduas then went to École des Beaux-Arts in Montreal and from there, on to Paris where he studied at the École d'Art Sacrés, the most important centre for ecclesiastic art in France.

After losing his job and his marriage, Borduas moved to New York where abstract expressionists such as Jackson Pollack and Mark Rothko were flourishing. By 1954, Borduas' work was included in the collection at the Museum of Modern Art.

That same year he moved to Europe, eventually settling in Paris, never to return to his beloved Quebec. Over the next twenty years he painted feverishly and produced a body of work that is among the finest in Canadian history. His paintings are characterized by the way he piled layer upon layer of paint on canvas, rich, tactile flourishes, using knives and trowels.

In Paris he was a great success. He had many dealers and museums asking for his work all over the world. Not only did Paul-Émile Borduas survive, he thrived.

His daughter, Renée, who only saw her father twice after he moved to Paris, has said that after her father left she "started talking" to his paintings.

"For me the best was there . . . So it was my job to listen to it, to understand it, to get close to it if I could."

About the austere, powerful black and white paintings produced in the last year of his life and now considered Borduas' masterpieces, his daughter said that she came to see them as the "supreme attempt to reconcile what was not reconcilable."

"He has taken extremes and made them co-exist with one another. He has made them sing . . . He's showed us the way it can be done."

MORE STARS THAN HEAVEN

Hollywood, California 1900s to Present — During the Depression the son of a Russian émigré who grew up in Saint John, New Brunswick, was the highest paid executive in the United States and one of the most powerful men in Hollywood.

Eliezer (Lazar) Mayer's father was a junk dealer and his mother sold chickens door-to-door. Their son was three when they arrived in Canada in 1888, after suffering from repeated anti-Jewish pogroms.

Three decades later, Eliezer would be famous as Louis B. (Burt) Mayer, also known as "Louis the Conqueror." He was the third "M" in the Metro-Goldwyn-Mayer Studio, whose slogan "more stars than there are in the heavens" was a virtual reality in the 1930s. Greta Garbo, Judy Garland, Jean Harlow and Clark Gable were among the stars shaped by MGM, under the patriarchal and sometimes tyrannical guidance of Louis Mayer.

L.B. Mayer was not the only Hollywood mogul with a Canadian connection whose name graced a California film studio during those early and heady days of the motion picture industry. Danville, Quebec's Mikall Sinnott transformed himself into Mack Sennett, and produced the first full-length, silent comedy motion picture *Tillie's Punctured Romance* in 1914 through his studio, Keystone Productions.

Sennett was thrown for a loop by the advent of "talking pictures." That phenomenon was pioneered by the Warner Brothers — Sam, Harry, Albert and Jack — whose Warner Bros. studio launched *The Jazz Singer* in 1927.

Like Louis B. Mayer's family, the Warners emigrated to North America to escape the persecution of czarist Russia. Their father, Benjamin, was a peddler and the family travelled extensively before settling in Youngstown, Ohio, around the turn of the century. The youngest Warner child, Jack, earned his Canadian connection by being born in London, Ontario, in 1892.

Both Louis B. Mayer and the brothers Warner entered the world of cinema from the popcorn side rather than the creative side. As the story goes, in 1904, the Warners sold the family delivery horse and bought a film projector. The following year, the brothers opened a "hole-in-the-wall" nickelodeon theatre in Newcastle, Pennsylvania. Louis B. Mayer, who had moved to Boston in his late teens, also bought a rundown theatre.

While Mayer decided to renovate his theatre and expanded his business into the largest theatre chain in New England, the Warners decided to become film distributors. By the 1920s, they were all making movies in sunny California.

There was something of a "six degrees of separation" syndrome in the early years of Hollywood. Canadian-connected Louis B. Mayer relied heavily on the brilliance of his production chief, Irving Thalberg, to guide MGM. Thalberg was married to Montreal-born Norma Shearer. Norma's brother, Douglas, the head of the MGM sound department for forty years, earned himself a dozen Academy Awards.

In 1959, Douglas Shearer received a special Oscar as co-developer of MGM's wide-screen camera system. Also honoured at the 1959 Academy Awards was Jack L. Warner, recipient of the Irving G. Thalberg Memorial Award. In 1999, the Thalberg Award was presented to Toronto-born, internationally renowned director Norman Jewison.

Of course, none of these awards would have existed if Louis B. Mayer had not suggested the idea in 1927. It was a concept that was heartily endorsed by the actor Douglas Fairbanks, husband of "America's Sweetheart" Toronto-born actress Mary Pickford, both of whom were founding members of the Academy of Motion Picture Arts and Sciences.

In fact, Mary Pickford was a mogul in her own right. In 1920 she and Fairbanks founded Universal Pictures, along with the popular "little tramp" Charlie Chaplin, who had been discovered by Mack Sennett.

Acting under the pseudonym "Dorothy Nicholson," golden-haired Mary (whose real name was Gladys Marie Smith) made her first film under director D.W. Griffith in 1908. One of her co-stars was Mack Sennett, who also took the odd acting job, having been mentored in vaudeville by Coburg-born Marie Dressler.

D.W. Griffith went on to make the legendary *The Birth of a Nation* in 1915, and it was the success of the ticket receipts from that film that skyrocketed Louis B. Mayer from the popcorn side of cinema to the production side.

Sam Warner probably deserves the title "Father of the Talking Picture" because it was his idea to use synchronized sound in movies. His brother Harry was leery at first.

"Who the hell wants to hear actors talk?" Harry asked.

Sam never lived to find out. He died the day before *The Jazz Singer*'s debut in New York City.

The star of the picture, Al Jolson, went on to fame and fortune. In 1933, while making the Warner Brothers' musical *42nd Street*, Jolson met his future wife, Halifax-born hoofer Ruby Keeler. Thirty-three years later, Ruby showed up as an extra in *They Shoot Horses, Don't They*, starring Montreal's Michael Sarrazin.

Also in 1933, Hollywood chose a Canadian to grace an ape's palm. Alberta-born Fay Wray was twenty-six when she was mauled by the movie's most famous monkey, King Kong. Twenty-one years later, New Westminster, B.C.'s Raymond (William Stacy) Burr also shared billing with an overblown primate in *Gorilla at Large*.

In 1957, Wray and Burr were united in *The Case of the Fatal Fetish*, an early television episode of Perry Mason.

Doctors were larger-than-life in Dr. Kildare, a TV series featuring young Richard Chamberlain operating under the watchful eye of Raymond Massey as Dr. Gillespie. Massey first trod the boards of a stage at Oakville, Ontario's upper-crust Appleby College. He earned a 1941 Oscar nomination playing an American politician in *Abe Lincoln in Illinois*, which co-starred London, Ontario's Gene Lockhart.

A dozen years later, Raymond Massey's brother, Vincent, was appointed as the first Canadian-born Governor General of Canada. At the time, Raymond was on the big screen playing a prophet in the steamy biblical film *David and Bathsheba*.

The Regina-born Erik and Leslie Nielsen represent another famous politician/actor combination that flew about as high as it gets. Erik served in the federal Cabinet, while his brother was buffooning somewhere between *Airplane!*

and *Naked Gun*. Early in Leslie's career he played the romantic lead in *Tammy and the Bachelor*. Fay Wray was cast as his mother.

Actresses Beatrice Lillie (born in Toronto), Deanna Durbin (Winnipeg), Alexis Smith (Penticton, B.C.) and Yvonne De Carlo (Vancouver) are only a few degrees of separation apart from many other Canadians in Hollywood.

For instance, Deanna Durbin received a juvenile Academy Award in 1939 for her contribution as a "personification of youth." She shared the award with Mickey Rooney, who was at the peak of his fame starring in Louis B. Mayer's *Andy Hardy* films. In a dozen films Cecilia Parker (born in 1905 in Fort Williams, Ontario) played Andy Hardy's big sister.

Whether as moguls or bit players, Canadians have always been "in the movies," separated by just a few degrees.

In 1992, Ottawa-born Dan Ackroyd appeared in *Chaplin*, a film about some of the early days in Hollywood when Mary Pickford was the queen of the screen. He played Mack Sennett.

And, even in death, Louis B. Mayer and the Warner brothers are not far apart.

All are resting at the Home of Peace Memorial Park in Los Angeles, California.

TRANSPORTATION

HUMPS ALONG THE FRASER

"GET A HORSE!"

BLOOD ON THE TRACKS

THE WRECK OF THE *MARCO POLO*

THE BATTLE OF THE BLOOMERS

"JUST ONCE MORE"

GETTING THROUGH THE DRIFT

THE HAPPY NEW YEAR MISSION

THE PICASSO OF BUSH PILOTS

HAVE SKI-DOO, WILL TRAVEL

IS IT A BIRD? IS IT A PLANE?
NO, IT'S AN ARROW!

HUMPS ALONG THE FRASER

Cariboo Trail, British Columbia, 1862 — The headline in the Victoria *Times Colonist* read simply "The Camels are Coming." Sure enough, they were. Twenty-three of them, to be precise, landed on the docks at Esquimalt in April of 1862. They were not particularly attractive or hospitable camels after their long journey. They had travelled from Manchurian China, across the Pacific to San Francisco, where a Seton Portage rancher named John Calbraith purchased them for $6,000 on behalf of another Victoria native, Frank Laumeister and his two partners. The hope was that the two-humped Bactrian behemoths would be worth their weight in gold on the Cariboo trail.

The Cariboo was crawling with gold-crazed miners, dreamers and adventurers who went to incredible lengths to travel the tortuous Fraser Canyon Route to Quesnel Forks in the British Columbia interior. Governor James Douglas had started a wagon road north of Yale, and road gangs of Chinese workers using pickaxes and shovels had toiled to create a passable route. This was territory explorer Simon Fraser called "so wild" that he could not find words for it. However, when Governor Douglas inspected progress on his "road," he optimistically noted that "Passes of ominous fame, so notorious in the history of the country have lost their terrors." However, according to one traveller, what passed for a trail was nothing more than "mud, stones [and] trees falling in every direction."

This was where the surefooted, two-toed camels were supposed to save the day. Freight costs to the Cariboo from Victoria and New Westminster were skyrocketing. Hundreds of mules worked the trails, carrying packs loaded with everything from candles to pianos. It could take a plodding mule train weeks to make its destination, and many a mule never made it — tumbling down the canyon walls onto the rocks below.

Camel-caravan impresario Laumeister had been advised that his camels could carry half-ton loads and travel almost twice as fast as mules. In earlier decades, one-humped dromedaries had been imported for army use in Texas and they had been used in the exploration of California deserts. Mules were expensive to feed, but a thrifty camel was supposed to be able to forage for subsistence and go for six to ten days without water. In theory, the "ship of the desert" was ideally suited to become the freight train of the gold rush.

Two of the camels that landed in Victoria stayed there. A calf and its mother (dubbed "Her Camelship") were turned loose in Beacon Hill Park where they came as quite a surprise to the unsuspecting. The pack camels were shipped by steamer to New Westminster and the start of the trail.

At the outset, the camels appeared to perform well, although their load capacity was less than anticipated. After a few weeks on the job, the *Times Colonist* reported, "They are acclimated, and will eat anything from a pair of pants to a bar of soap." The true test came when the camels hit the mountains, where rocky pathways tore into their tender toe pads. Improvised boots made from canvas and rawhide were not much help.

The real downfall of the camels was their smell, which was as intolerable to humans as it was to mules and horses. Mules would bray incessantly and stop dead in their tracks if they so much as sensed — or scented — a camel in the vicinity. Horses would panic. Camels were also prone to panic. On June 30, some fur traders startled a young camel on the trail and it slid over the edge to its demise, accompanied by a full load of Scotch whisky.

Soon there was havoc. Muleteers and horse-owners threatened to take their case to Chief Justice Matthew Baillie Begbie, and there were rumours of a petition to ask Governor Douglas to order the removal of all camels from the Cariboo. None of this was necessary. The camel syndicate withdrew the unhappy, ungainly creatures due to performance failure.

The camels were dispersed in various ways. Eight of them were let loose at Lac La Hache, about halfway between Lillooet and Quesnel, where they died during the winter. A few went to America, selling for a mere thirty-five dollars each. Some were eaten by hungry settlers, one of whom is said to have commented that "camel flesh is delicious when fried." That may have been an acquired taste or one determined by necessity, since there were few takers when camel was placed on the menu of a Cariboo Trail restaurant.

One member of the failed camel syndicate, Henry Ingram, took his losses with him and ended up with three camels grazing on his ranch at Grande Prairie (now Westwold). In 1864 he sold 181.8 kilograms (404 pounds) of camel meat to the Hudson's Bay Company in Kamloops in exchange for tools. That accounted for two of his camels.

The third camel stayed on the Ingram farm as a household pet and it outlived Henry Ingram, who died in 1879. Every spring, the camel was sheared and its hair was used to stuff pillows and mattresses. Local children enjoyed taking rides on the gentle creature. Finally, in extreme old age, the last of the Cariboo camels died in 1905. Apparently it simply leaned against a tree and died on its feet.

There are stories that claim a few wild camels survived until 1910, and an alleged bush-sighting near Kamloops in 1925 fuelled speculation that camels might be making a comeback. One thing is certain: camels were not invited to participate in the Klondike gold rush.

"GET A HORSE!"

Rustico, Prince Edward Island, 1866 — What was supposed to be a quiet Sunday celebration became an historic event, when Father George Belacourt surprised his Island parishioners by arriving in a steam-propelled vehicle, which is believed to have been the first of its kind in British North America.

The vehicle Father Belacourt imported from New Jersey was a great crowd pleaser. The mobile priest made several demonstration runs and the *Charlottetown Examiner* reported: "With wonder and delight it was observed steaming away . . . at a fast speed."

The witnessing of the dawn of a new era of transportation ended when the priest lost control of the new-fangled contraption and veered into a field.

The following year, Henry Seth Taylor of Stanstead, Quebec, built Canada's first steam carriage and the local newspaper was quick to pronounce it "the neatest thing of its kind yet invented."

The first electric automobile in Canada appeared on the streets of Toronto in December 1893. A local company built the battery-powered vehicle for lawyer Frederick Fetherstonhaugh, who proudly demonstrated its ability to travel to speeds of up to twenty-four kilometres per hour.

Motoring began to acquire an aura of glamour characterized by speed. A three-wheel car from France driven by a Quebec dentist reached the "dizzying" speed of twenty-nine kilometres per hour in an 1897 demonstration along Chemin Sainte-Foy. In the same year, George Foote Foss, a bicycle repairman from Sherbrooke, constructed Canada's first gasoline-driven car for his personal use. He drove it summer and winter for five years, and got more than eighty kilometres to the gallon.

Hamilton's Colonel John Moodie Jr. acquired the first "mass market" gasoline-engine car in April 1898. It looked for all the world like a horse-drawn buggy, with the engine in the rear. Moodie's "Winton" was such a novelty that he installed spikes around the ends to deter unwanted passengers. He once raced a steamboat from Hamilton to Toronto, winning in just less than three hours.

Despite the outrageous price tag of $1,000, Colonel Moodie contended that his car was cheaper to own than a pair of good horses. In fact, his "horseless carriage" stayed in use for fifteen years.

At the turn of the century, dozens of small machine shops had blossomed into car-makers, but many people still thought cars were a noisy and unreliable fad. Inexperienced drivers wreaked havoc on narrow roadways and the unfamiliar sound of backfires caused horses to bolt, and bicyclists to topple.

"Infernally combusting engines" became the constant butt of jokes and the roadside taunt of the day was "Get a horse." In schools, a favourite topic of debate was "Resolved: That the Motor-Car is Useless, Dangerous and Ought to be Abolished."

Prince Edward Island, in particular, did not take kindly to automobiles. In 1908, the Legislature voted to ban all autos in response to citizens' concerns about wear and tear to the roadways and the terrorization of livestock and children. "We're going to keep them cars out if we have to take a pitchfork to them," wrote one Island farmer.

Canada's love affair with the horseless carriage could not be suppressed. Ford started manufacturing cars in Canada in 1903 and Oshawa carriage maker Sam McLaughlin turned out the nation's first all-Canadian Buick in 1908. By 1911, the T. Eaton Company was selling mail-order automobiles.

The automobile became an industry, and a national passion. From 1920 to 1930, the number of cars, trucks, buses and motorcycles increased threefold to 1,235,000, making Canada the second most-motorized country on the globe after the United States. Within a decade, the number of concrete or blacktopped roads rose from 1,000 to 9,200. Still, a new word managed to find its way into the lexicon. The original "traffic jam" described autos stuck up to their hubcaps in mud on rural roads.

BLOOD ON THE TRACKS

Yale, British Columbia, 1880 — Whoever thinks of Canada's history as explosive? But it was — literally and figuratively. For instance, nitroglycerine played a very significant part in the unification of Canada.

This awesomely unstable liquid was used to blast through mountains of granite during the construction of the national railway system, and hundreds of the 30,000 workers who toiled on the railway died setting the explosive charges that carved the groundwork for tracks from sea to shining sea.

There are segments of the Canadian landscape where nature seemed to have gone to extremes to thwart the railway builders. Muskeg, bogs and sinkholes presented their own unique problems, but when it came to the Rockies the builders confronted wrinkled canyons, criss-crossed by deadfalls and sheer walls rising to lofty heights above rushing rivers.

An American named Andrew Onderdonk purchased the contracts to build the railway line west of the Fraser Valley. In 1880 he established his headquarters at Yale, British Columbia, on the Fraser River. There were four tunnels to be drilled in a 3 kilometre radius and took eighteen months to blast them out of the rock of the canyon. Twenty-three more tunnels were drilled on the Onderdonk line.

Onderdonk built an explosives factory at Yale. When the factory blew up, shattering every window in the town, Onderdonk simply shrugged his shoulders and built another factory. By 1882, the Yale factory was turning out nearly two tonnes of nitroglycerine a day.

Hell's Gate on the Fraser was aptly named according to the "navvies" who blasted holes into the rock face above a sheer drop into the foaming waters below. Men had to be lowered on ladders secured by ropes which were attached to trees on the summit until they reached the level where the tracks were to be placed. The canyon walls were slick, so they worked in bare feet to try for better footing, but the hard rock surface often frayed critically on the rope. Falling rocks or a premature blast could mean certain death.

Blasting holes were drilled into the granite, which was striped with quartz — the hardest of all rocks. Once the charge was set, the worker was hauled to the surface or he took refuge in a "secure" hiding place. Then the fuse was lit.

None of this work took place under ideal circumstances and some of the workers did not make it when the charges failed to do what they were supposed to do. Some men died when explosions were improperly timed, and rocks had a dangerous habit of catapulting off the canyon walls and into the "hiding" places. Rock slides and avalanches were triggered by the continual blasting.

Most of the railway workers had no previous experience with explosives or safety provisions.

One tried to light his pipe after handling blasting powder. Others were killed when they vigorously dumped dynamite down a chute into a waiting boat. One Chinese worker near Yale hid behind a tree 60 metres from a tunnel that was to be blasted, only to have a flying splinter shear off his nose.

Fortunes were made and boundless opportunities were opened by the building of the railway. But the human price in the lives of the labourers — French and English, Scots and Irish, Italians and Slavs, Swedes and Americans, Canadians and Chinese — was exacted in an immeasurable toll that was written in blood on the tracks.

THE WRECK OF
THE *MARCO POLO*

Cavendish Beach, Prince Edward Island, 1883 — Did the explorer Marco Polo ever visit the Cavendish coast of Prince Edward Island? The question is fanciful, although the residents of the red sand beachfront may have spread such a rumour at the turn of the century.

The only "Marco Polo" known to have landed at Prince Edward Island is a three-masted, three-deck sailing vessel that ran aground within sight of land on the morning of July 25, 1883.

The *Marco Polo* was built at Saint John, New Brunswick, in 1851 and in her day she was known as the fastest merchant ship in the world. The 156-metre, 1,475-tonne ship resembled a cross between a cargo ship and a yacht. One observer suggested she carried "the belly of an alderman on the legs of a ballet dancer."

Her spring launch may have portended her future, since the *Marco Polo* ended up jammed in the mud, and eventually capsized in the ebbing tide. Naval experts speculate that the mud may have re-shaped her hull in some way, which could account for her legendary speed. Once she had been dug out, the *Marco Polo* crossed the Atlantic in just sixteen days.

The Black Ball Line of Australia bought the clipper and refitted her as a luxury passenger vessel. On her first voyage from Liverpool to Australia she accomplished a record outward run of sixty-eight days and a round-trip record of five months and twenty-one days.

For a decade the *Marco Polo* maintained a distinguished career. Then, in 1861, she hit an iceberg on the homeward journey and had to limp to the Chilean port of Valparaiso for repairs.

By 1867, the once proud *Marco Polo* had become a tramp transport vessel under the Norwegian flag. Her final cargo was a load of pine lumber.

There are divided opinions about the cause of the wreck of the *Marco Polo*. Insurance fraud was contended, since the ship was in unprofitably poor repair. Alternately, foul wind and weather, compounded by leaking that the inboard pumps failed to stem, may have led the captain to run her ashore to save his crew and cargo.

The arrival of the wreck's twenty crew members — a colourful lot of Irish, English, Scots, Spaniards, Dutch, Germans and Tahitians — created quite a stir in Cavendish. Dignitaries from the Norwegian government, insurance adjustors and surveyors all came to examine the stranded ship.

One week later, others came from as far away as Quebec, Saint John, Sackville, Moncton, Shediac and Kouchibouguac, New Brunswick, to take part in the auction of anything and everything that remained of the *Marco Polo*. The sale raised the princely sum of $8,000 and many local residents clamoured to bid on any small item bearing the name of the ship.

One observer to the wreck of the *Marco Polo* was an eight-year-old Cavendish girl, who carefully noted the details of the tragedy and the personalities involved. Seven years later she translated her recollections in an essay titled: "The Wreck of the *Marco Polo*." It won third prize in the Queen's County division of the Canada Prize Competition of 1890. The following year, the stirring eyewitness account was published in the *Montreal Witness*. It was the first major newspaper story published by its author. Her name was Lucy Maud Montgomery and she went on to write *Anne of Green Gables*.

THE BATTLE
OF THE BLOOMERS

Anytown, Canada, 1899 — The clergy called it the work of the devil. *Scientific American* said it might change the course of world history. Advertisements suggested it enhanced overall health and temperament. Rich and poor suffered common grief when one broke down. Women's fashion underwent a radical change.

The bicycle was a revolution in its own right. Maybe it was the consequence of having spent too much time in canoes, but velocipedes seized the Canadian imagination at the end of the nineteenth century unlike anything before or since.

Early versions featured wooden wheels. These three-wheeled "boneshakers" were soon supplanted by the English "Penny Farthing," an awkward contraption that featured an oversized front wheel. Photographs of the freshly minted Montreal Bicycle Club circa 1878 feature throngs of mustachioed gentry astride a variety of high-wheelers. Some cycles had a small "safety" wheel at the rear, others looked more like delicate tricycles.

"Wheeling" started out as a pricey pastime. A suitable mount cost about half of the average worker's annual earnings. That, though, did not prevent some from creating their own homemade cycles. Some early bikes where even adapted to travel on ice, with skates replacing the small back wheel.

In the 1880s, bicycle clubs became popular. Dr. J.W. "Perry" Doolittle of Toronto headed the Canadian Wheelman's Association which held its first meeting in St. Thomas, Ontario, in 1881. The following year, a group of Canadian cycling enthusiasts pedalled their way to the world's fair in Chicago.

By the end of the decade, cycling was reaching a fevered pitch. Air-filled rubber tires invented by Scottish veterinarian John Dunlop in 1888 contributed to making the pastime marginally comfortable, along with the introduction of two wheels of the same diameter. Cyclists began lobbying for better roads.

In 1890, there were 17 bicycle factories in the United States. Five years later there were 300. Canadian-made bikes were assembled from imported parts until tariff legislation stopped the practice, giving rise to a homegrown industry.

In 1895, farm implement manufacturers Massey-Harris built a five-storey factory in Toronto and began churning out "Silver Ribbon" bicycles. Company president, Walter Massey, announced that: "The bicycle is not simply a fad, but it has become a thoroughly practical vehicle for use on the farm as well as in the city and in the village."

In 1896, a $16,000 shipment of Canadian bikes arrived in Australia and the following year the *New Zealand Cyclist* was reporting the championship racing wins on Canadian-made racers.

Three years later, Massey-Harris joined with several other manufacturers and the Canada Cycle and Motor

Company (CCM) was formed. You could get a mail-order bicycle for twenty-five dollars.

A small industry grew up around the bicycle. Cycling clubs published hotel guides for wheeling tourists. Accessories included everything from goggles to gaiters. Cycling academies urged that "ladies intending to wheel cannot do better than register at once before it becomes too crowded."

The bicycle was an instrument of liberation for women. Whalebone corsets and crinolines fell by the wayside, and chaperones simply could not keep up the pace.

Women wearing "bifurcated nether garments," commonly known as "Bloomers," were decried in *Saturday Night* magazine for the sin of revealing "the most shapeless lot of legs ever seen outside a butcher shop." A lady's bicycle suit with a shortened skirt and cycling tights sold for about fifteen dollars.

"Six or seven years ago there were no lady cyclists in Canada. Can you fancy it, my sisters?" Grace Denison wrote in an 1896 article titled "The Evolution of the Lady Cyclist."

"In one short demi-decade we have learned a new enthusiasm, gone through the battle of the bloomer, and taken into our lives a new pleasure, the like of which we never before experienced or even in our dreams imagined."

Bicycles were everywhere. Doctors pedalled to deliver babies. Telegrams were delivered by bicycle courier. Everything from policing to postal service incorporated cycling. Hotels hired bellboys to park their guest bicycles and managers of fine dining rooms complained about the "loud body sweat and road perfume" of their cycling clients.

A six-day workweek meant making careful decisions about managing one's recreational time. Piano sales decreased. Tavern owners found themselves idle when their clientele took to spending weekends riding into the country for picnics. Church attendance dropped severely, particularly during the summer. In 1894, a minister in Kingston, Ontario, railed against the "monkeyback" posture of cyclists who crouched at the handlebars and raised their rumps for a streamlining effect.

On the prairies it was said that bands of cyclists looked "like birds on a telegraph wire." But surely the oddest application of the bicycle involved those hearty fools who joined the Klondike gold rush on their bikes. In the winter of 1897, two New Yorkers got as far as the foot of White Pass near Skagway in the Yukon. They were travelling on two bicycles that were joined by iron bars, which in turn supported a canoe containing their gear.

Bicycle races attracted thousands of spectators and prizes ranged from a six-room house to handfuls of uncut diamonds. At the first annual Dunlop Trophy Race in 1894, winner Tom McCarthy was estimated to achieve a top speed of twelve miles per hour.

The bicycle frenzy peaked in 1899 when Montreal hosted the world cycling championship.

The following year, Archie McEachern became the first Canadian to win the twenty-five-mile indoor championship in Boston.

Racing teams included the Brantford Red Birds, featuring professional race champion Harley Davidson, who bore no relation to the founding fathers of the American motorcycle company.

Despite the automobile's conquest of the roadways, bicycle races remained popular throughout the 1920s. At the 1928 Olympics in Amsterdam, Canadian hopes were riding on a twenty-two-year-old racer from Victoria, B.C., who was built like a football player. Red-haired William "Torchy" Peden started the 100-mile Olympic endurance competition, but he was foiled by two punctured tires. The following year, Torchy swept the Canadian indoor championships. Then he turned professional and embarked on a racing career that made him an international celebrity.

Six-day races were the rage during the Depression, bringing in more than a quarter of a million dollars a week. Pairs of racers took turns lapping a track non-stop for 144 hours. In the tradition of marathon dances, best and brutally epitomized in the 1969 movie *They Shoot Horses, Don't They*, six-day races were gruelling affairs.

Often paired with his brother Doug "Tiny" Peden, Torchy excelled as a "sixer," and crowds marvelled at his sheer power. His trainer called him: "Muscles with a smile." To alleviate boredom, Torchy would ride on one knee or grab women's hats and tear around the track. Between 1931 and 1942, Peden won thirty-eight six-day races and his name was as well-known as baseball's Babe Ruth.

In the off-season, vacant hockey arenas were often used for six-day races. Peden started his career at the Montreal Forum. When races were held on outdoor tracks, the competitors lived in makeshift huts on the infield, never far from their bicycles.

It was a world that went round and round, slowing only during the wee hours of the morning, but never stopping. When crowds were on hand, racers would engage in sprints and jams for cash prizes. A sprint was a ten-lap dash, a jam was a team spurt.

Racers were rarely off the track for more than half an hour. They took catnaps, even while they were riding. Crashes were often spectacular. Peden is said to have fallen asleep once while doing a lap and he ended up taking a header that landed him over the boards and straight into his ringside bunk, just as though he had planned it.

Fads pass and cycling lost its glamour, only to be rediscovered by the children of post-World War II baby boomers.

After all, learning to ride is simple. It's as easy as falling off a bicycle.

"JUST ONCE MORE"

Lunenburg, Nova Scotia, 1921 — A wooden sailing boat, an iron captain and the salt-spray of the ocean — put them all together and you have a snapshot of Canada's great age of sail. It is an image that has jangled in the pockets of Canadians since 1937, when the schooner *Bluenose* took its place on the ten-cent coin. Unforgettable and unbeatable, the ship and her captain, Angus Walters, were a winning team — the crowning achievement of an Atlantic tradition.

She was a saltbank schooner and he was a fisherman skipper. As a working fishing vessel, the *Bluenose* still holds the record for the single largest catch of fish ever landed in Lunenburg. But make no mistake, she was also built for speed.

In 1920, Senator William Dennis, publisher of the *Halifax Herald*, instigated a series of races to challenge the best of the American and Canadian fishing fleets. That year the International Fishermen's Trophy was won by a Yankee schooner from Gloucester, Massachusetts. Lunenburgers did not take the loss lightly, and Angus Walters was a quintessential Lunenburger. That winter, he helped sell 350 shares at $100 a piece and work began at the Smith and Rhuland shipyards on a boat described as "deep-bellied" and "spoon-bowed." Its designer, Halifax marine architect

William Roue, had a committee of interested parties to contend with in the planning of the 43-metre (143-foot) craft. Walters had a controlling interest, so he made some modifications of his own, including raising the bow by about half an arm's length.

"My crew ain't midgets," he blustered when the hull was raised and he found the headroom so limited that even the diminutive captain would have been forced to stoop.

On March 26, 1921, the *Bluenose* was launched. Her christening title, a traditional nickname for Nova Scotians, was a natural choice. She was crafted by Nova Scotians and she was built almost entirely from wood grown in the province.

After a season on the Grand Banks where she proved herself to be the highliner of the fleet, *Bluenose* was given a new coat of paint and rigged for racing. Tall and lean, her copious sails billowed like wings over the water and her great bow rode high over whitecaps. That fall the International Fishermen's Trophy returned to Nova Scotia, never to fall into American hands again.

Only one boat ever faced its stern to the *Bluenose* at a formal finish line. The *Gertrude L. Thebaud*, a freshly minted, lithesome schooner owned by a syndicate of wealthy Bostonians challenged the toast of Lunenburg to an unofficial racing series in the autumn of 1930. Although his beloved schooner had been hampered by ill-fitting sails, Captain Walters took full responsibility for the loss saying, "They didn't beat the *Bluenose*. They beat me."

The defeat was avenged the following year, when the *Thebaud* crossed the line in the International Fishermen's Series more than a full half-hour after the *Bluenose*.

The schooner became a celebrity and an ambassador. In 1933, thousands of visitors saluted her grace at Chicago's

Century of Progress Exposition. Two years later, Walters and his crew set out from Lunenburg for Plymouth, England, the same port that Sir Francis Drake once sailed from. The occasion was the Silver Jubilee of King George V and Queen Mary. The King apparently took a fancy to the saltbanker and invited Angus to meet him aboard the royal yacht *Victoria and Albert*.

"He was a very nice, ordinary sort of fella," Walters told reporters, adding that they "chewed the rag for a while." Afterward, the King sent word that he wished to inspect the *Bluenose*, but other duties prevailed. Walters was sorry about that; he had gone to the trouble of obtaining a bottle of whisky so that he could entertain the King in style.

The *Bluenose* was seventeen when she confronted the *Gertrude L. Thebaud* in what was to be her final racing series — a challenge spread over five races off the Boston coast. The pair were locked in a tie on October 26, 1938. Millions listened to their radios and a huge crowd watched from shore as the two schooners matched each other across the water, with the *Bluenose* running a scant lead thanks to the experienced manoeuvring of her captain. Victory was just minutes away when a halyard block gave way. Repairs were out of the question.

With the *Thebaud* charging forward to take advantage of her opponent's injury, Walters did what he had always done to the *Bluenose*. He talked to her and she responded. "Just once more!" he was heard crying to the great but aged saltbanker. That exhortation, and a fortuitous gust of wind, was all it took.

The coveted International Fishermen's Cup was awarded to the *Bluenose* permanently. At the celebrations in Lunenburg, Captain Walters said simply, "The wood that can beat the *Bluenose* ain't been planted yet."

Captain Walters retired from the sea to tend his dairy business, but all the while he harboured the dream of preserving the *Bluenose* as a tribute to the age of sail that had passed with the advent of diesel engines and with war looming. In 1940, the fading schooner faced the disgrace of public auction over unpaid bills. Walters mortgaged his home to buy out the shareholders and wrest the Queen of the Atlantic fleet from the sheriff's hands. When he was finally forced to sell her to a freighting firm, Walters said he felt as though he had lost a family member.

The thoroughbred became a pack horse, plodding between the islands of the West Indies carrying bananas and rum. In January of 1946, her back was broken on a coral reef off Haiti, where the *Bluenose* was abandoned. The *Halifax Herald* called the ignominy of her death "a national shame."

In 1963, a replica of the *Bluenose* was launched amid great fanfare. Fittingly, at the Lunenburg christening, Angus Walters was made the Honorary Captain of the *Bluenose II*.

GETTING THROUGH
THE DRIFT

Montreal, 1925 — The Inuit language contains twenty-three separate words for "snow." The great frozen flakes have always been both a wonderment and a scourge of the vast Canadian landscape. As Quebec songwriter Gilles Vigneault noted in the first line of his popular 1965 song "Mon Pays": "My country is not a country: it's winter!"

Snow posed many historic dilemmas in the exploration and settlement of Canada. While the native people of North America adapted to the dictates of nature and the rhythms of climatic change, European settlers were determined to go against the drift.

The problem presented itself most dramatically in 1885, when the Canadian Pacific Railway was completed. Snowslides, avalanche debris and drifts two-storeys high closed the line through the Rocky Mountains for months at a time. Conventional wedge-ploughs were no match for such conditions.

A Toronto dentist, J.W. Elliot, took out a patent on the "Compound Revolving Snow Shovel" in 1869. Elliot's theory involved using rotary blades to slice through packed snow, but he was unable to find investors.

Fourteen years later, a fellow inventor named Orange Jull supervised the first working model of a rotary plough that was tested at the CPR yards in Toronto. Soon afterward, the Elliot-Jull snowplough became standard equipment on trains throughout North America. But it took the ingenuity of a young Quebec farmer who just wanted to get his milk to market before it soured to invent the snowblower.

Arthur Sicard was an orphan who was trying to earn his keep on a farm near St. Leonard de Port Maurice when he discovered the frustration of drifting snow. After milking the cows at dawn, he would load the milk cans into a horse-drawn sleigh to begin the 8-kilometre trek to market in Montreal. When faced with an impassable road, Sicard would be forced to return through the bitter cold. If poor weather continued, the milk would go bad, adding financial loss to frustration.

Sicard was determined to find a solution. When he was eighteen, working in the harvest fields, he observed an inspirational machine — a thresher. It separated the grain from the straw by shaking, screening and blowing the chaff away. Sicard reasoned that the same sort of blowing principle could work on snow.

Despite the derision of neighbours, he devoted himself to experimenting and tinkering with machinery that winter. In addition to the rotating blades of the threshing machine, Sicard added a fan to push the snow back into the blades, forcing it out through a discharge chute.

The following year, in 1895, Sicard was ready to demonstrate his device. While a curious crowd stood witness, Sicard blew away small snow drifts, but bogged down in large ones. The crowd laughed and went home, but Sicard persisted.

Using his own savings, he quietly worked on perfecting the machine. His fellow farmers considered him a crackpot, so he went to work in Montreal as a labourer in the construction industry, and later as a road contractor.

Finally, in 1925, Sicard displayed his snow-blowing device. The lumbering vehicle featured a conventional truck cab, with an auxiliary motor in the body. Two rotating blades replaced the bumpers and they spewed snow behind through a long ejection shoot, leaving a cleared path for traffic. No one was laughing now.

Various municipalities in Quebec purchased Sicard's snowblowers. The Department of Transport in Ottawa also saw their virtues, and eventually his snowblowers were clearing everything from roads to airport runways around the world.

Canadian ingenuity had conquered the snowdrift.

THE HAPPY
NEW YEAR MISSION

Fort Vermilion, Alberta, 1929 — There are many legendary bush pilots in the annals of Canadian aviation. At the drop of a hat, these winged *coureurs de bois* would fly, navigating over the wilderness "by the seat of their pants" and "improvising" when it came to repairs. Among them Wilfred Reid "Wop" May is a classic example. The stuff of true romance, he flew what everyone considered to be a doomed mission of mercy one frozen New Year's Eve to the northern reaches of wild Alberta with antitoxin for a village threatened by an epidemic of diphtheria.

From the beginning, flying was an adventure for May. On his first World War One combat mission, he shot down an enemy aircraft. Then May's guns jammed and he found himself being chased by the German ace, Baron Manfred von Richthofen. Captain Roy Brown, one of May's Alberta school chums, shot down Richtofen and saved his friend from becoming the eighty-first victim of the Red Baron.

After the war, May settled in Edmonton and started a commercial aviation business, along with daring "barnstorming" exhibitions. He was one of the founding members of the Edmonton and Northern Alberta Aero Club.

All of May's skill and ingenuity were called on when he was asked to fly a mercy mission on the bitterly cold New Year's Day of 1929. On December 15th, a Hudson's Bay Company employee in Little Red River, north of Fort Vermilion, died of diphtheria. Other cases were breaking out and vaccine was desperately needed to prevent an epidemic in the community of about 300 people.

The nearest radio station was at Peace River, and Louis Bourassa, the postal courier, set out on a 450-kilometre dog sled trip to send the urgent request. Fourteen days later, Dr. M.H. Bow, Deputy Minister of the Department of Health, received the telegraphed message in Edmonton. He calculated that it would take at least two weeks by train and dog sled to deliver the necessary supplies. A fly-in mission seemed the only answer, and Dr. Bow posed the question to "Wop" May, who agreed without hesitation.

Emergency workers gathered the life-saving serum while May and his co-pilot Vic Horner prepared to make the 990-kilometre trip. The only airplane available to them was Horner's small Avro biplane which boasted a seventy-five horsepower engine, an open cockpit, and no skiis for winter landing. To protect the vaccine from freezing, it was placed in an improvised thermal unit consisting of heated containers balanced on a portable charcoal stove and covered with blankets.

Blizzard conditions forced them to land on a frozen lake at McLennan Junction, almost halfway to Fort Vermilion. May realized that he would have to remove the plane's oil to prevent it from congealing, but he did not have a container. Undaunted, he siphoned the oil onto the crusty snow where it froze immediately. May carried the "oilsicle" to the village, where it thawed overnight.

When the pair arrived in Fort Vermilion the following day, their precious cargo was protected, but May and Homer were so frostbitten and chilled that they had to be physically removed from the cockpit. The serum was dispersed by dog sled to the anxious community and the epidemic was checked.

The homeward trip brought its own complications. The whole plane was coated with ice, instruments froze and the engine cut out several times due to low-grade gasoline. All the while, the media hailed their courageous "gamble with death."

A crowd of 5,000 was on hand to greet the heroes when they returned to Edmonton and May was awarded the prestigious McKee Trophy for his efforts. Six years later he was created an Officer of the Order of the British Empire, and mail-carrier Louis Bourassa was honoured as a Member of the same Order. May went on to pioneer aerial search-and-rescue techniques and he helped set up the British Commonwealth Air Training Plan during World War Two.

The bush pilots of Canada's north helped the nation enter into a new era of transportation and communication. Wilfred Reid May, who was nicknamed "Wop" by a baby cousin who could not pronounce "Wilfred," was one of the best.

THE PICASSO
OF BUSH PILOTS

Fort Resolution, Northwest Territories, 1929 — The image of the Canadian bush pilot is one that is often grounded in a romantic vision of goggled men in flowing scarves spiriting small aircraft through the wilderness skies of the North. In such an easy fairy tale, Clennell Haggerston "Punch" Dickins could have been the model. Hollywood-handsome with trim jet-black hair and the face of a curious boy, Dickins was the first pilot to survey the unmapped Barren Lands of the Northwest Territories. His legend grew to be so synonymous with northern flight that an Inuit who was giving testimony in an Aklavik court once struggled to find the proper English word for "airplane," before finally hitting on the only description that seemed just right — "Punch Dickins."

Dickins was nine years old when his family moved from Portage la Prairie, Manitoba, to Edmonton, Alberta. He enlisted at the age of seventeen and ended up serving with the Royal Flying Corps during World War I. Dickins honed his skills under perilous conditions. During his seven-month service in France, the flying teenager was credited with the destruction of seven enemy aircraft and earned the Distinguished Flying Cross for gallantry.

In 1921, Dickins joined the Canadian Air Force where he spent six years testing aircraft under winter conditions, flying forestry patrols and conducting photographic surveys. His bush flying career took off in 1927 when he joined Western Canadian Airways and started piloting prospectors over uncharted wilderness.

One such trip took him along the east shore of Great Bear Lake where his passenger, miner Gilbert LaBine, noted a curious glow emanating from the sheer rock cliffs of Echo Bay. The lustre proved to be a mixture of silver, copper and pitchblende, an ore that contains radium and uranium. The discovery became the Eldorado Mine, providing the resources that vaulted Canada into the nuclear age.

Flying north of the sixtieth parallel required extraordinary navigational skills. In August 1928, Dickins flew a prospecting party on a twelve-day trip that stretched over nearly 6,499 kilometres (3,960 miles). All told, they spent thirty-seven hours in the air, much of it over unmapped territory. Piloting over the eerie tundra landscape of the Barrens from Chesterfield Inlet on Hudson Bay to the western reaches of Saskatchewan's Lake Athabasca, Dickins relied largely on sight to navigate, since the proximity of the magnetic pole rendered his compass useless.

"This was over the real Barren Lands," he noted in his journal, "from the time we left Baker Lake we never saw a living thing until getting near the tree line again, when a few birds were seen. The tracks of caribou could be seen also." Using other means of travel, such a trip would have taken at least a year and a half.

That January, Punch Dickins was asked to explore the possibility of establishing a regular mail service to far northern communities. Since the railway line ended at Fort McMurray, remote settlements along the Mackenzie and

Athabasca Rivers received their mail by dog sled once or twice each winter. Airmail deliveries would end the loneliness and isolation, connecting the people of the north to the southern world which they called "Outside."

The first test flight ended in a farmer's field outside of Edmonton when ice particles formed in the plane's carburetor, forcing Dickins to land. Then a blizzard intervened. However, word of the experimental flight created great excitement in the North, and when Dickins finally made his first stop at Fort Chipewyan everyone in town showed up to greet him. They had cleared the snow on a stretch of Lake Athabasca and defined a "landing strip" with fresh-cut spruce trees.

On the return leg of the trip, Dickins and his engineer Lew Parmenter ran into trouble near Fort Resolution on Great Slave Lake. Landing in swirling snow, the undercarriage of the plane hit rough ice. No one was injured, but the fuselage was damaged and the propeller blades were bent out of whack.

Employing the improvisation skills that became a hallmark of bush pilots everywhere, Dickins and Parmenter scrounged a piece of waterpipe from a local priest to repair the fuselage. With moderate pressure, one of the propeller blades was coaxed back into shape, but the other one was badly twisted and snapped off, leaving it more than a hands-length shorter than its companion. Undaunted, the pilots cut the healthy blade to match the size of its diminished companion. Punch taxied the Fokker Super Universal across the ice and found that it could pick up speed. They flew out that afternoon.

Dickins's career was punctuated with adventure and innovation. During World War II he served as the operations manager of Ferry Command and managed six flight schools as part of the British Commonwealth Air Training Plan. After the war, he joined de Havilland Aircraft, where he was instrumental in marketing Canadian-made Beaver aircraft worldwide. An Alberta lake is named after him, and he was the first inductee into Canada's Aviation Hall of Fame in Wetaskiwin. According to fellow flyer Grant McConachie, who worked with Dickins during the early days of Canadian Pacific Airlines, "Of all those pioneer flyers, Dickins stands alone . . . One might call him the Picasso of bush pilots."

When Punch died in 1995 at the age of ninety-six, his family requested that his ashes be scattered along the Mackenzie River by his friend, another legendary bush pilot and aviation pioneer, Max Ward.

HAVE SKI-DOO,
WILL TRAVEL

Valcourt, Quebec, 1935 — Joseph-Armand Bombardier gave new meaning to the concept of "dashing through the snow." He unlocked the world of winter when he created the snowmobile.

Bombardier grew up in the community of Valcourt in Quebec's Eastern Townships. Throughout his childhood he enjoyed nothing better than constructing machinery.

On New Year's Eve 1922, Bombardier demonstrated his first snowmobile. His father had previously given him an old automobile, and Bombardier had promptly removed the engine, which he mounted on four runners. A large, hand-made propeller replaced the radiator fan. Joseph-Armand perched on the back, while his brother Leopold was in front, steering with his feet. To the astonishment of his neighbours, Bombardier "drove" his primitive snowmobile through the centre of Valcourt. It was a dangerous contraption, but the young mechanical genius became convinced that it was possible for a man and a machine to conquer transportation over snow. Bombardier continued to tinker with mechanical inventions. He learned English so that he could decipher technical journals. At nineteen, his father built him his own garage, which grew into a successful business. His passion remained producing snow-machine prototypes, but tragedy was to provide his ultimate impetus.

In 1934, his son, Yvon, died following an attack of appendicitis during a bitter winter storm. Roads were blocked with snow and Bombardier's various snow machines were lying in pieces in the garage. There was no way to transport the child to the hospital. With the loss of his son, Bombardier focused in earnest on the invention he had dreamed of since childhood.

The following year he designed and built a rubber-cushioned drive-wheel and track. With a model that satisfied him, he began a series of demonstrations that exhibited his impressive marketing skills as well as his remarkable invention. Travelling from town to town throughout Quebec, he invited local newspaper editors for a ride and became front-page news wherever he went. Two years later, he was granted his first patent for a snowmobile called B7 — B for Bombardier and 7 for the number of passengers it could carry. Full-scale manufacturing began in 1942.

The snowmobile was an immediate success — priests, country doctors and ambulance drivers quickly bought the new machines. Soon, "Bombardiers" were transporting everything from mail to medical rescue crews. During the Second World War, the vehicle was modified for military purposes and a twelve-passenger model gained international and commercial acceptance.

In 1959, Bombardier introduced a sport model. He considered calling the two-passenger version the "ski-dog," before settling on the now famous "Ski-Doo." By the late 1960s, ski-dooing had captured the popular imagination and revolutionized transportation in northern communities. Five years after Bombardier's death in 1964, the Royal

Canadian Mounted Police replaced their last Yukon sled dog teams with snowmobiles.

The competing brands of snowmobiles threatened to overwhelm the family firm in the early 1970s; however, Bombardier's heirs shared the innovative spirit of their founder. In 1974, Bombardier Inc. diversified and entered the public transit business, manufacturing 423 subway cars for the city of Montreal. Eight years later, Bombardier signed a multimillion-dollar contract to supply subway cars to New York City. Subsequently, the corporation has expanded into aeronautics and high-speed trains, but recreational activities remain at the forefront of operations. In 1988, the company introduced the "Sea-Doo," which demonstrates the same agility on the water as its snow-conquering counterpart.

Bombardier's inventions have been used in building dikes in Holland, herding reindeer in Lapland, laying pipelines in Scotland and hauling logs in the Peruvian jungle. But to millions of red-cheeked Canadians, Joseph-Armand Bombardier is remembered quite simply as the man who made winter fun.

IS IT A BIRD?
IS IT A PLANE?
NO, IT'S AN ARROW!

Ottawa, 1959 — Few Canadian stories transcend the details of their history and become part of the national consciousness, but that's what happened when Prime Minister John Diefenbaker cancelled the Avro Arrow C 150 project on February 20, 1959. Faster than Diefenbaker's fulmination, the Arrow disappeared into myth.

Eleven months before the cancellation, thousands of employees of A.V. Roe Canada Limited had cheered the thirty-five-minute maiden flight of the advanced supersonic twin-engine, all-weather interceptor jet aircraft.

When Diefenbaker made his announcement to a hushed House of Commons, those same employees immediately lost their jobs and their collective dream to fulfill what Minister of National Defence George Pearkes had eighteen months earlier hailed as "a new era for Canada in the air."

Four decades later, controversy and intrigue continue to surround this amazing airplane. The fact that everything to do with the Arrow including all existing planes, components, tooling, drawings and documentation were ordered destroyed certainly contributed to its mystique.

There is even a persistent rumour that one Arrow was surreptitiously saved and remains hidden away to this day.

To date, there have been six non-fiction books, two books of fiction, a play, dozens upon dozens of articles and a mini-series aired on national television about the Avro Arrow and its fate. There is an Arrow fan club and a rather elaborate and well-developed website.

Canada has a tradition of making serious contributions to advances in aviation — from W.R. Turnbull's perfection of the electrically operated variable-pitch propeller in 1927 to the Spar Aerospace Canadarm. The Avro Arrow was an exceptional example in this distinguished history.

A.V. Roe Canada, although set up by British interests, was financed in Canada. After World War II, the Canadian military, under the tutelage of their American cousins, supposed that the major postwar threat was long-range, high-altitude bombers flying over the Arctic.

What was needed was a unique, new aircraft to protect this difficult frontier. It was decided that the best approach would be to design and build it in Canada.

The CF 100, Canada's "home-designed and built front-line fighter plane" was the precursor to the Avro CF 150 Arrow. Six hundred and ninety-two CF 100s were built and successfully put into service all over the world.

In the early 1950s, the Canadian government decided to follow the same course to replace the CF 100s. Military strategists predicted that the Cold War threat to the North American continent would evolve into supersonic, Soviet bombers. A new plane would need to be ready for service in the early 1960s. But the specifications seemed to be out of a science fiction novel.

The new aircraft had to be able to cruise and fight at Mach 1.5 (one-and-a-half times the speed of sound), at an altitude of 50,000 feet (very high) and be capable of pulling 2g in manoeuvres with no loss of speed or altitude (2g in a manoeuvre means that the pilot's weight on the seat is twice that of level flight, twice the pull of gravity).

The aircraft was to have a range of at least 200 nautical miles and be capable of reaching maximum speed and altitude in less than five minutes from the time its engine was started.

No one else in the world had been able to build an aircraft that would even come close to fulfilling such stringent demands.

With its all-Canadian designed and built Iroquois engine, the Arrow exceeded the specifications. A number of innovations were tossed in for good measure. For instance, the design of a removable armament pack aerodynamically integrated with the aircraft meant that whatever was carried in the pack had no effect on the airplane's speed or manoeuvrability.

The Arrow was conceived to be the delivery component of a rather elaborate, high-tech system of defence. That system included an airplane, airborne fire control systems, weapons and a ground-based radar communications system.

The designers of the Arrow worked feverishly to build actual aircraft, testing each design and alteration with elaborate computer models and simulations. Meanwhile, their political masters fiddled and fudged.

Originally, they were to pick up the fire control system from the Americans; then they were directed to switch to a Canadian-designed system called Astra. Then it was switched back to Hughes. The choice of weapons went back and forth, at the behest of the RCAF and the government, from American to Canadian to American-made missiles. The ground-based radar system became part of the Canadian/American North American Air Defence Command (NORAD) set up in 1957.

The Arrow was nothing if not adaptable. Missiles such as the American Falcon, the Canadian Velvet Glove or modified Sparrow were debated and substituted one for the other without any noticeable effect on the aircraft's performance and manoeuvrability. During one test flight, the Arrow reached a speed of Mach 1.96, even though the plane was powered by an inferior American-built engine.

Then it was gone. There was no Parliamentary debate, no public discussion. The decision was made by Diefenbaker and a few members of his Cabinet in secret, behind closed doors. Diefenbaker simply announced the end of the Avro Arrow in Parliament on February 20, 1959, and that was that. Crawford Gordon, President and General Manager of A.V. Roe, announced the cancellation over the plant public-address system. With it came a notice of termination. That very day, A.V. Roe laid off 14,000 workers. Six prototypes went to the chopping block.

Nagging, unanswered questions still surround the Arrow. For instance, why did the government and the minister responsible lie about their immediate and inexplicable plans to destroy every Arrow prototype and everything having anything to do with the project?

The Honourable Raymond O'Hurley, then Minister of Defence Production in Diefenbaker's government, started out at first assuring the press that no order had been given to destroy the Arrow.

When caught out in that lie, he simply gave them another. He said such action was routine with classified projects; he had been mistaken in the first instance and his office had not actually been consulted. Recent revelations show exactly the opposite to have been true. A memo dated March 4, 1959, from O'Hurley's office shows he was delivering the orders for the total eradication of the Arrow.

Was the scrapping of the Arrow project in part a political payoff for favours curried from Duplessis and his Quebec liberal government?

Why was BOMARC, the American ground-to-air missile system, blithely accepted by the Canadian government as a substitute for the Arrow when BOMARC's failure was imminent and predictable?

Who initiated the Defence Production Sharing Agreement with the U.S. and why?

Why was the national media often ill-disposed to the Arrow project? Diefenbaker and his Cabinet wrongly interpreted the negative reportage as a reflection of public opinion that supported what they had wanted to do since as early as 1957.

Why was there no attempt to maintain and profit from technology transfers and spin-offs that were legion with a high-technology project which was as diverse and successful as the Avro Arrow?

Some commentators see in the Avro Arrow and its fate a turning point where Canada once and for all relinquished control over its own destiny and ceded to a diminutive garrison mentality and perpetual branch-plant economy.

Whereas these and many other questions will continue to be asked by historians and students of the Diefenbaker era and the Avro Arrow, the plane itself will always exist as a perfect machine in a special place beyond sound and light.

COMMUNICATION

THE TELEGRAPH AT HEART'S CONTENT

THAT LONG DISTANCE FEELING

PRESS PASS 110

RADIO MAN

DOT, DOT, DOT...!

THE MAVERICK MUSE OF THE WEST

HUMAN ENGINEERING IN AN UNSEEN WORLD

AS IT HAPPENED

A MAN IN A HURRY

THE CROSS-DISCIPLINE DRESSER

THE TELEGRAPH
AT HEART'S CONTENT

Heart's Content, Newfoundland, 1866 — When the telegraph came to Canada in 1846, people called it "talk by lightning," and a revolution in communication began. Current events were suddenly "current" outside of their immediate locality. Life-saving messages were sent and chess games transpired between counties. Prince Edward Island made telegraphic communication to the mainland a condition of its entry into Confederation, and telegraph lines took their place along with railway tracks, merging transportation and communication across the nation.

Like the construction of the railways, laying telegraph lines across the nation's jumble of geography was a feat of epic proportion. And the laying of a cable across the Atlantic Ocean from England to Newfoundland ranks as one of the outstanding achievements of the nineteenth century. It began as the dream of a self-educated, English civil engineer named Frederick Newton Gisborne, but the thunder and the glory of its success were usurped by an American tycoon.

Gisborne kicked around the world touring places like Australia, Tahiti, Guatemala and Mexico before settling on a farm at St. Eustache, Lower Canada, in 1845. Two years later, the twenty-five year old abandoned the plough in favour of a more exciting career in telegraphy. Shortly afterward, the understanding of electrical principles applied to communications that he had studied in books, saw him supervising the construction of telegraph lines. By 1849, he had become chief operator and superintendent of the Nova Scotia Telegraph Company, and in 1852 he laid the first submarine cable in British North America, connecting Prince Edward Island and New Brunswick.

Never one to rest on his laurels, he formed the New York, Newfoundland and London Telegraph Company and surveyed 640 kilometres of the rugged island with a stipend blessing from the Newfoundland government. Ultimately, he found himself $50,000 in debt in the midst of laying an overland line. His property was confiscated and he was arrested.

But the dreamer would not quit. Years before, he had discussed the prospect of transatlantic telegraphy with Nova Scotia Premier Joseph Howe. Flat broke, Gisborne headed for New York to find investors. Late one January evening in 1854, he met Cyrus Field.

Field had made a fortune in the U.S. paper industry and was a bored millionaire at thirty-three. Gisborne's venture was a new challenge. Four months after their first meeting, Field had drafted a company and subscribed 1.5 million dollars for the project. Gisborne's affairs were settled, and he was put on the payroll as Chief Engineer, but he lost control of the dream.

Where Gisborne had employed 350 workers on the overland Newfoundland line, Field hired 600 to confront the irregular landscape. By the end of 1856, more than a million dollars had been spent, and Field kept raising more. Despite chronic seasickness, he made more than forty trips to England seeking support and advice. Two attempts to lay a cable across the ocean failed, although communications stayed clear for four weeks in August 1858 before a spasm silenced the flawed line.

The Civil War postponed further development, but in July 1865 Field was back at it. A stronger, more flexible cable weighing almost twice as much as the original was constructed and Field chartered the largest ship in the world to lay it. When the *Great Eastern* left Ireland, she carried a crew of 500, more than 8,000 tonnes of coal, a milk cow and assorted livestock including 120 sheep. They were less than a day away from the safe harbour of Heart's Content, Newfoundland, when the cable snapped. Field raised another three million dollars and built more cable.

On July 27, 1866, the *Great Eastern* finally delivered her payload. Cheering spectators lofted Field into the village for celebrations that spread throughout the island. A few weeks later, the previous cable was salvaged and connected. Although it cost the equivalent of $100 to send a twenty-word message, more than 2,700 were sent in the first two months.

Cyrus Field began taking credit as the originator of the Atlantic cable scheme soon after a disheartened Frederick Gisborne resigned in 1857. Typically, debate ensued over who was the "father of the mighty thought," but Gisborne avoided the pettiness. He studied geology in New Zealand. He invented a shipboard flag-and-ball semaphore. In the Middle East, he was involved in laying cable across the Red Sea and, by the 1870s, he was back in Nova Scotia as a railroader. In 1879, he was appointed as superintendent of the Dominion Telegraph and Signal Service, and, before he died in 1892, he told a friend that he had a vision of a time "when messages will be sent across the Atlantic *through the air.*" Dreamers can see such things.

THAT LONG
DISTANCE FEELING

Brantford, Ontario, 1876 — When Alexander Graham Bell achieved international fame as the inventor of the telephone, Scotland claimed him for his birthright, America claimed him for the citizenship he took in 1882, and Canada also demanded a piece of the action.

"Of this you may be sure, the telephone was invented in Canada," Bell wrote and said many times. "It was made in the United States." According to Bell, Brantford, Ontario, was justifiably dubbed "the telephone city," because it was there, at nearby Tutelo Heights, that he conceived his invention in 1874. The Bell family had come to Canada four years earlier, hoping to find relief for Alexander, their sickly twenty-three-year-old son who was fighting with tuberculosis. Two of his brothers had already succumbed to the disease. "I went to Canada to die," Bell recalled later, but the change in geography proved therapeutic.

Much of Bell's research took place in the United States. It is a good bet that every schoolchild in North America learns that the first telephone conversation began with Bell's request, "Mr. Watson, come here I need you." It happened in Boston. Five months later, on August 3, 1876, the language of communication elevated substantially when Hamlet's "To be or not to be" soliloquy was recited between two buildings in Brantford. The following week, the long distance feeling became a reality when Bell's father spoke to his son over telegraph wires from Brantford to Robert White's Book and Shoe Store more than 12 kilometres (7.4 miles) away in Paris, Ontario. That first long distance phone call lasted for three hours, consisting largely of songs that ranged from the sacred to the profane.

Bell returned to Canada every chance he got. Once he came to borrow money and the result was one of the most classic business blunders in history. Senator George Brown, a Father of Confederation and the editor of the *Globe* newspaper, was a friend of the Bells and he kept a farm near Tutelo Heights. In the summer of 1875, Bell returned to the family home to rest and recuperate from his extensive American experiments — and to raise some cash. He had fallen in love with Mabel Hubbard, a former student of his at a Boston school for the deaf and the daughter of one of his principal American backers. But his inventions had sidetracked him from making a daily living. In Canada, he asked Brown for approximately three hundred dollars to tide him over until the telephone made him his fortune.

Brown and his brother, Gordon, agreed to provide Bell with fifty dollars per month, in exchange for half the British Empire and foreign patents. Brown was to file these patents when he went to England in January, 1876. But in England the specifications stayed in his trunk, suggesting that Brown was concerned about being associated with a crackpot idea.

Bell's future father-in-law finally gave up on the Canadian and filed Bell's patent application in Washington on Valentine's Day, 1876, just hours before a rival presented a similar idea. George Brown blew one of the biggest pay-days in history.

Bell married Mabel five months later. When he took his bride to Brantford, Mrs. Bell Sr. broke an oatcake over her daughter-in-law's head following a Scottish tradition to ensure that the bride would never go hungry in her husband's home. There seemed little chance of that. Three years later, Bell was awarded the $50,000 Volta Prize. Despite more than six hundred legal challenges to his patents, he won every one and became a wealthy man, a prodigious inventor and a laudable philanthropist.

In 1885, Bell began acquiring land nead Baddeck, Nova Scotia, on Cape Breton Island where he established a summer home, Beinn Bhreagh (Gaelic for "beautiful mountain"). The telephone had been just the beginning of Bell's invention spree. He was also the father of the phonograph record, but he was most proud of his work on behalf of the oral education of the deaf. He served as president of the National Geographic Society and his never-ending curiosity saw him investigate everything from radar to breeding sheep that would consistently produce twin lambs.

At Beinn Bhreagh, Bell pursued his interest in flight, experimenting with monumental kites. In 1907, Mabel Bell became the first woman to establish and endow a research organization, the Aerial Experimental Association, whose objective was "to get into the air." This culminated in the first airplane flight in the British Commonwealth by the Silver Dart in 1909.

Bell may have taken American citizenship, but when he died in 1922 he was a citizen of the world. He was buried at Baddeck, in a pine coffin built by the men who worked in his laboratory. The consummate inventor wore the medal of the French Legion of Honour to his grave, which was carved into Cape Breton rock and flanked by the British and American flags. While a Highland piper skirled him to his rest, every telephone in North America was silenced for two minutes.

PRESS PASS 110

Cuba, 1898 — "After nearly three months of despairing to get here, the great force we call will has conquered. I am looking at the hills of Cuba," read the dispatch to the Toronto *Mail and Empire* from press correspondent pass 110, who had arrived at the scene of the Spanish-American War. More than 130 members of the press had applied to "cover" the war, but Number 110 was a distinctly different voice. It belonged to the first woman in the world to become an accredited war correspondent. She was a thirty-four-year-old reporter from Canada, who became internationally renowned as "Kit" Coleman.

The bronze-haired daughter of Irish gentry, Kathleen Blake was born at Castle Blakeny near Galway, Ireland, in 1864. Educated at Dublin and in Belgium, she was unhappily married at sixteen. Widowhood at nineteen propelled her to a new beginning in Canada, where she remarried and settled in Winnipeg. Now a mother of two, she was widowed again in 1888 and moved to Toronto. The following year she submitted a story about an organ grinder to *Saturday Night* magazine, which led to a job at the *Mail* where she established a page for female readers called the "Woman's Kingdom."

Over the next twenty-two years, "Kit of the *Mail*" attracted readers of both sexes. One of her biggest fans was Prime Minister Wilfrid Laurier. Topics ranged from divorce to Western imperialism and from recipes to racism. She dished out advice to the lovelorn and wrote columns with titles such as "Waists of English Actresses," and "Is Marriage a Failure?" Her popularity was such that the *Mail and Empire* sent her to cover the Diamond Jubilee of Queen Victoria and the Chicago World's Fair. To other women of the press, she was a role model. In 1904, she founded the Canadian Women's Press Club while on a junket with a dozen colleagues to the St. Louis Exposition. Surprisingly, she was opposed to women's suffrage, calling its exponents "platform women."

When America declared war against Spain over the status of Cuba on April 25, 1898, Coleman caught war fever. Initially, she tried to persuade the Red Cross to let her tag along — undercover — as a member of the nursing staff. When that failed, she cajoled U.S. Secretary of War Russell Alger into accrediting her, with the provision that she stay with missionary or relief columns and avoid army camps.

When she arrived in Tampa, Florida, looking for a boat that would take her to Cuba, a legion of male reporters thought it a sensation. London *Daily Mail* correspondent Charles Hands described her as a "tall, healthy youngish lady with a quiet self-reliant manner and an enterprising look." Coleman told him that she knew he thought she was "ridiculous," but she did not much care. "I'm going through to Cuba," she told him, "and not all the old Generals in the old army are going to stop me." While she looked for passage, she wrote about what she saw of the 17,000 ill-prepared troops readying for battle. She called these lightweight stories the "guff." They included everything from interviews with Canadians who formed part of Theodore Roosevelt's soon-to-be-legendary Rough Riders to comments on the Canadian nickel used on American gunboats.

Unlike her male counterparts, Kit was trying to cover a war on a shoestring budget. Top American correspondents carried gold to cover expenses, but the impoverished Coleman was reduced to mailing most of her columns back to her editors. She sent only three telegraphs, and one of those landed her in hot water.

When troops assembled on the Tampa docks for the invasion, she wired the news in a coded message to her *Mail and Empire* editor. Later she wrote, "As I marched triumphantly from the telegraph office thinking how bright and clever I was to get off the news to my paper . . . a Secret Service officer touched me on the shoulder, 'I arrest you,' he said." Eventually, she was released and went back to the business of trying to arrange passage to Cuba.

On August 8, 1898, the front page of the *Mail and Empire* proudly declared "Kit Reaches Cuba's Shores." The story was datelined July 28 — the day that Coleman *left* Cuba. All told, she spent approximately one week observing a war that had all but ended by July 17.

Her biggest story of the war was about the trip home. It began aboard a cockroach-infested ship crammed with wounded soldiers in the care of a medical student who had no medicine. Coleman and three other reporters provided the sick with quinine capsules and shared their field supplies. Off the coast of Florida, the "horror ships" were quarantined for a week and conditions worsened. Despite the gruesomeness of the scene, Coleman accompanied 350 wounded on a ship bound for New York. She helped the sick and got the story.

Five months after her adventures in Cuba, Coleman addressed the International Press Union in Washington and told them, "If ever a time comes when swords are beaten into ploughshares and spears into pruning hooks, it will be for one reason, because the wielders of pens were not less earnest and may we say, not less heroic, than the wielders of deadlier weapons." Believing that the press would play a powerful role in eliminating war through the immediacy of front-line reportage was one thing, participating was another. Coleman announced that if another war came along "this pioneer woman war correspondent will stay home."

Although she offered penetrating assessments of the brutal inanity of conflicts in South Africa, Russia and China, she did not venture back to the front. Instead, she married a mining company doctor and moved to Copper Cliff in northern Ontario, where she lived and wrote for three years. When they moved to Hamilton, she resumed feature writing — focusing on crime stories. Her biggest "scoop" came in 1904, when she scored an exclusive interview with Canadian con-artist Cassie Chadwick, who styled herself as the illegitimate daughter of American industrialist Andrew Carnegie.

In 1911, the *Mail and Empire* asked Coleman to add a daily column to her workload, with no increase in pay. It was too much to ask, even of a woman who once suggested to one of her advice-seeking readers, "It is an honour to write for nothing, if you write well." For years she had been earning thirty-five dollars a week, a paltry sum by American standards. She quit her job and began syndicating "Kit's Column" for five dollars a piece to various newspapers, but never again to the *Mail and Empire*.

Mabel Burkholder, a member of the Hamilton Women's Press Club who met Kit in 1891, has suggested that in America, "She would have been considered the most brilliant newspaper woman on the continent." Burkholder concluded that, "Kit was handicapped by being too big for her position, and too progressive for her times."

Kit Coleman died of pneumonia on May 16, 1915. It was her fifty-first birthday.

RADIO MAN

Brant Rock, Massachusetts, 1900 — Before any event involving the transmission of sound begins, chances are that
someone steps up to the microphone to test the system by
intoning the words "one, two, three, four . . ." The banality of
this announcement has historic roots — those four little words
were the first ever to be broadcast by a human voice. They
were transmitted by Canadian inventor Reginald Aubrey
Fessenden on December 23, 1900, 354 days before Guglielmo
Marconi, the alleged "father of radio," managed to transmit
a mere Morse code "S" from a hill in Newfoundland to a
receiving station in Britain. Fessenden also initiated the first
two-way transatlantic voice transmission in 1906, the same
year that he delivered the first ever radio broadcast.

Reginald Fessenden may be one of the least-lauded
geniuses Canada has ever produced. Born in a small town
near Sherbrooke, Quebec, in 1865, he was teaching Greek and
French at Bishop's University at the age of sixteen. In his spare
time, he studied mathematics. By 1886, he had sufficient confidence in his comprehension of science to solicit an introduction to American electrical pioneer Thomas Edison. Without practical experience, Edison rejected the brash Canadian, but Fessenden inveigled his way into a job testing the

maestro's lighting wires in the streets of Manhattan, and ultimately into a position in Edison's research laboratory.

"An inventor must never be intimidated by what appear to be facts when he knows they are not," Fessenden once noted. It was that guiding principle that allowed him to unravel the electrical relations of the atom decades before his contemporaries. Consequently, he provided Edison with an insulating compound for electrical wire, negating the problem of "hot wires" that plagued the fledgling lighting industry. When Edison went broke, Fessenden went to work for George Westinghouse, for whom he built a longer-lasting, economical light bulb.

With more than five hundred inventions to his credit, Fessenden's output was prodigious. At the turn of the century, he cut a colourful swath in the American scientific community with his flame red beard, sweeping black cloak and irrepressible curiosity. As legend has it, his continuous-wave radio theory first dawned on him in 1896. He was en route by train from Toronto to his uncle's home in Peterborough, where he intended to take a vacation from the wireless transmission theorizing he had been doing as the Chair of electrical engineering at the University of Pittsburgh.

After a stint with the U.S. Weather Service, Fessenden found backing for a full-fledged research station at Brant Rock near Boston. Although he was supposed to be concentrating on telegraphy, he secretly devoted himself to radio.

The first transatlantic voice message was accidentally received by his assistant in Scotland, who heard voices while listening for dots and dashes. Fessenden followed this unacknowledged achievement with his historic radio broadcast.

Preparations involved adjustments at the peak of a 400-foot transmitting tower, which Fessenden undertook to do himself. He had not, however, calculated accommodating his considerable girth in the tower cylinder. Fortunately, he had invented a primitive version of the pocket pager, which was built into the headgear of his employees. When their buzzers went off, they discovered the portly Fessenden lodged in the passage. The only way to extricate the wedged wunderkind was to strip off his clothing and rub his body with grease.

On Christmas Eve, 1906, sailors on United Fruit Company cargo ships were monitoring for Morse code messages as they steamed northward from the Caribbean. Instead, they were treated to a one-man variety show. Fessenden played "O Holy Night" on the violin, sang and read a biblical passage before signing off with "Merry Christmas." Letters from incredulous shipboard radio operators confirmed the success of the experiment.

Reginald Fessenden was not the astute businessman or self-promoter that Marconi proved to be. Although the Canadian government endowed Marconi with $80,000 and granted him exclusive rights to build radio stations in Canada, Fessenden could not even get a teaching job at McGill University. Nevertheless, when war broke out he volunteered his services to the Canadian government and contributed everything from an improved internal combustion engine to tracer bullets for machine guns to the sonic depth finder.

A paucity of funds plagued the inventor, and violations of his patents resulted in countless legal battles. By Fessenden's accounting, reparations amounted to $60 million. So it was a minor victory when the U.S. Radio Trust conceded in 1928 with a payment of $2.8 million. Fessenden retired to Bermuda, where he died four years later.

"It sometimes happens that one man can be right against the world," remarked the *New York Herald Tribune*. "Professor Fessenden was that man."

DOT, DOT, DOT...!

Signal Hill, Newfoundland, 1901 — There he was, thirteen days before Christmas, a grown man flying a kite on Signal Hill in the middle of a storm. And, if one man wasn't fool enough, he had a couple of buddies helping him out. But the fool on the hill was no fool at all. He was Guglielmo Marconi and the kite he was hoisting on a 180-metre wire would serve as an aerial for the first wireless signal to be sent across the Atlantic Ocean.

At the time of Marconi's birth in Italy in 1874, Alexander Graham Bell was trying to perfect the invention of the telephone. By the age of thirteen, Guglielmo (or William) had begun to experiment with scientific principles. One of his first creations was a whisky still, which may not be surprising since his maternal grandfather was Irish whisky czar Andrew Jameson. His fascination quickly transferred to electricity. After completing a biography of Benjamin Franklin, he rigged some dinner plates on wires at the edge of a stream. Using a homemade battery, he passed a high-tension, electric current through the wires, causing the plates to "jump" and smash into smithereens.

Marconi's studies included practical experiments at the University of Bologna and summer holidays learning

Morse code. At twenty-one, he succeeded in transmitting a wireless Morse code message over 3 kilometres across the family's estate. Initially, Marconi foresaw that his new system of communication could be of great use linking ships at sea with shore bases. When the Italian government indicated that they were not interested, Marconi took his invention to England.

In 1896, he demonstrated his wireless transmission to British experts from the Army, Navy and Post Office. "The calm of my life ended then," he told a friend. Overnight, he became a famous figure. Offers poured in for his patented invention, but he would not sell. Marconi continued his experiments in Britain, extending the range to almost 20 kilometres.

In 1898, the British first employed wireless telegraphy between lightships and shore installations. Realizing that his invention needed popular support, Marconi arranged with a Dublin newspaper to provide the world's first radio sports report, covering a yachting race that summer. The publicity was tremendous. Queen Victoria herself read the accounts and requested the installation of a personal wireless device so that she could communicate with the Prince of Wales' yacht from the Royal residence on the Isle of Wight.

As the story goes, Marconi was fixing equipment one day and doffed his hat as the Queen walked by, a liberty which the monarch found offensive. A gardener instructed Marconi to leave by the back way, which he found offensive. Confronted with this state of affairs, Victoria is said to have replied haughtily: "Get another electrician." She later reconsidered, giving Marconi both an audience and her wishes for success.

After numerous experiments, Marconi was convinced that he could achieve a wireless link between Britain and

North America. With typical, boyish enthusiasm he called it "the big thing." Although many were skeptical, he was able to persuade the investors of Marconi's Wireless Telegraph Company Ltd. to finance his new venture.

A land station was established at Pohdhu in Cornwall in 1900 and Marconi was able to transmit over 380 kilometres. He tried to establish a receiving station in Cape Cod, but it was wiped out by a storm. Undaunted, Marconi ordered another station to be set up at St. John's in Newfoundland and his assistants scouted the Signal Hill location.

At first, they tried using a huge balloon filled with hydrogen gas to raise the 180-metre wire aerial, but strong winds snapped its mooring rope. Marconi suggested trying kites. The first rose to 135 metres before it shared the balloon's fate. Finally on December 12, 1901, the kite soared to its full height. The crew retired to a small building equipped with a table, one chair and Marconi's equipment. Pohdhu station was transmitting the Morse code letter "S" (dot, dot, dot) regularly for a fixed period.

With a gale in full progress, Marconi adjusted his earphone and started listening. Shortly after noon, "the big thing" became a reality as Marconi heard the three-dot transmission from Pohdhu and his assistants gathered to listen to the $200,000 signal that crossed the ocean.

Cable companies that owned communication rights in Newfoundland forced Marconi to leave the island soon after his historic triumph. However, Prime Minister Sir Wilfrid Laurier stepped in to save the day. The Canadian government provided Marconi with $80,000 to continue his experiments at Glace Bay, Nova Scotia. One year later Governor General Minto sent the first wireless transmission from Canada to Britain.

A new age of communication had begun.

THE MAVERICK MUSE
OF THE WEST

Calgary, 1915 — There are those who believe that if newspaper editor Bob Edwards had concentrated more on his
own aggrandizement and less on the local tavern, he could
have become as famous as Mark Twain. As it happened,
the boisterous newspaperman's remarkable wit and political tenacity stood him in good stead as a pathfinder for
truth. That he was one of a kind in his profession is undis-
puted. When this editor who rarely edited himself died in
1922, he was voted the most colourful pioneer in Western
Canada by his peers. "People are always ready to admit a
man's ability after he gets there," remains one of Edwards's
oft-quoted pronouncements.

Born in Scotland to a publishing family of some repute,
Edwards emigrated to Wyoming in 1894 after graduating
from Glasgow University. Three years later, the impetuous
thirty-three year old had settled in Wetaskiwin, Alberta,
where he launched his first newspaper — a "corker" that he
planned to call *The Wetaskiwin Bottle Works* until saner minds
prevailed. An itinerant publisher, he settled into a groove
when he founded his most famous newspaper, the *Eye-
Opener*, in High River, Alberta. His satirical and sarcastic

pokes were endured for several years until "the church incident" of 1904, wherein he substituted a recorded hymn with the popular ditty "Just Because She Made Them Goo-Goo Eyes." Shortly afterward, the paper was relocated in Calgary.

Direct news reporting was not of particular interest to Edwards. He preferred to expose hypocrisy and snobbery — his lampooning "Social Notes" bordered on the hysterical. "The family of Mr. and Mrs. W.S. Stott, Eleventh Ave. West, all had the mumps last week," he once reported. "A swell time was had by all. Mr. Stott will not be able to deliver his address today at the Rotary convention much to the relief of those who have heard him speak." He mocked the two-boat Canadian Navy, denounced Alberta Premier A.L. Sifton as a "liar," and once proclaimed that a statesman was "a dead politician, and what this country needs is more of them."

Always skipping the razor edge of libel, Edwards's *Eye-Opener* soon had a circulation that was greater than the population of Calgary. It boasted readers across North America who followed the adventures of delicious fictitious characters such as Albert Buzzard-Cholomondeley, remittance man. Still, Edwards remained constantly in debt and constantly facing the bottom of a bottle at the hotel bar that he frequented with illustrious pals lawyer Paddy Nolan, meat baron Pat Burns and ranch king George Lane.

The crunch of conscience pursued Edwards, however. When Alberta faced a prohibition plebiscite in 1915, the "wets" are said to have solicited his editorial support by offering him almost ten thousand dollars. The "drys" requested the same consideration, but had nothing financial to offer. Despite his personal proclivity, Edwards surprised those who thought his backing was "in the bottle" by devoting an entire issue of the *Eye-Opener* to antibooze editorials and columns. He wrote, "In a word, there is Death in the Cup and if this Act is likely to have the effect of dashing the Cup from the drunkard's hand, for God's sake, let us vote for it." When the issue was published, Edwards was confined to a hospital bed sleeping off a bout with the demon he had condemned. The temperance vote won, and Alberta remained dry until 1923.

As a maverick publisher, Edwards crusaded for soil conservation, old age pensions, votes for women, senate reform and a host of visionary social issues. Despite his derision of politicians, he was elected to the provincial legislature in 1921, but he attended only one sitting before his death.

"I live with a sort of secret hope that between drunks I'm doing something to give this new West an individuality," Edwards is reported to have confided. He had a police escort to his grave and his young wife laid him to rest with the last issue of the *Eye-Opener* and a flask filled with whisky.

HUMAN ENGINEERING IN
AN UNSEEN WORLD

Toronto, 1918 — There was no moon in the autumn sky over Hemmel Hill in Belgium as Lieutenant Edwin Albert Baker of the Sixth Field Company of Engineers reconnoitered the cratered landscape, laying a communication line between Canadian units on the front lines and their farmhouse headquarters. The year was 1915. Baker was twenty-two, a farm boy from Kingston, Ontario, who had earned his electrical engineering degree at Queen's University.

He was inspecting a caved-in trench when the sharp crack of rifle shots and machine-gun fire filled the air. One bullet from a German sniper creased the bridge of Eddie Baker's nose, destroying both of his eyes. He was the first Canadian officer to lose his sight in World War I.

"Now don't worry about me," Baker wrote to his parents, while he recovered and underwent therapy in London. At St. Dunstan's rehabilitation hostel, he adopted the philosophy of the institution's founder, Arthur Pearson: "Nothing should be done for a blind man, if he can possibly do it for himself."

Baker studied Braille, typing and business administration before returning to Canada. "Please, mother, don't ever do that again," he said gently, when he found that his "welcome home" roast beef dinner had been cut into pieces for him.

Through "Black Jack" Robinson, editor of the *Toronto Telegram*, he received an introduction to Ontario Hydro chairman Sir Adam Beck. Both men were impressed with the earnest young man. Baker ultimately married Robinson's daughter. At Ontario Hydro, he worked his way from the typing pool to a trouble-shooting, data collection position.

Baker became involved in working for the blind community when he discovered that Canada's only Braille library in Toronto was slated to close due to lack of funds. With the help of five friends and the assistance of the Toronto Women's Musical Club, the library was saved and moved to new headquarters.

Informal meetings at the library led to discussions about the need for a national organization for the blind in Canada. Such a group would extend itself into the community to help with the care, training and employment of the blind, as well as working to prevent blindness.

The Canadian National Institute for the Blind received its charter in 1918. Eddie Baker was its first vice-president, and five of the seven founding members were blind.

At first, the CNIB consisted of two small shops where men and women made brooms and sewed. Then, with government backing, Baker established the CNIB's Pearson Hall Training Centre where war-blind veterans were taught how to walk and function in an unseen world.

Baker went on to design training programs to help other blind Canadians. As head of the CNIB, he arranged for a range of services from vocational schools to Seeing Eye dogs, as well as residences for the aged and public treatment clinics. Braille services were established, "eye banks" created and research launched into the causes and treatment of blindness. In areas of education reform and pensions, Baker was a leader.

Baker received many honours in the course of his career, including the Croix de Guerre, four honorary law degrees, the Order of the British Empire and elevation to the rank of colonel. For thirteen years he served as president of the World Council for the Welfare of the Blind, coordinating the activities of forty-seven nations.

"By a trick of fate, I found myself transferred from my proposed career as an electrical engineer to one which might be termed human engineering," Baker once noted.

AS IT HAPPENED

Moose River, Nova Scotia, 1936 — In what has been lauded as the outstanding radio news story of the first half of the twentieth century, J. Frank Willis, of the fledgling Canadian Radio Broadcasting Commission (CRBC), reported every half-hour from April 20, 1936, for sixty-nine hours to fifty-eight Canadian stations and 650 American stations, while Nova Scotia draegermen struggled to save lives at a remote collapsed mine at Moose River. His broadcast held a staggering fifty million listeners across North America spellbound for almost three days.

On Easter Sunday in 1936, two Toronto men, Dr. David Roberston, chief surgeon at the Hospital for Sick Children, and lawyer Herman Magill, went to inspect a sixty-year-old gold mine they had bought in Moose River, 90 kilometres northeast of Halifax.

With their timekeeper, Alfred Scadding, the men descended, unaware that the shaft was barely supported by rotting timbers. After about an hour, the noise of shifting rock alarmed them. At the 42-metre level, the mine buckled and the men were trapped in a dark, wet cave.

A rescue mission was immediately launched, but by April 15th newspaper headlines mourned "Hope Almost

Gone." While miners attempted to tunnel toward the men, diamond driller Billy Bell succeeded in opening a shaft approximately 4 centimetres in diameter on April 18th. Just before midnight, a small steam whistle was used to attempt to signal the men, and at 12:30 a.m., Billy Bell heard a tapping response on the pipe and hope was renewed.

Food, candles and medicine were lowered to the men, and hot soup was passed through a rubber tube. Using the shell of a penlight flashlight as a casing, foreman Bill Boak, and engineer W.E. Jefferson, of the Maritime Telegraph and Telephone Company, improvised a miniature microphone. It too was sent down the drill hole providing telephone communication with the ever-weakening men, who spoke to their wives.

Newspaper reporters had already swarmed the site, when Willis, the only CRBC employee east of Montreal, arrived on April 20th. Although Michael Dwyer, Minister of Mines for Nova Scotia, had commandeered the only local telephone line for the rescue, he granted Willis permission to use it for several minutes every half-hour for a broadcast.

Between the Canadian network and the U.S. station coverage, almost anyone on the North American continent who could get to a radio could hear what was going on as it happened. Willis reported from the mouth of the hole, interviewing draegermen as they crawled out for any word about the progress.

On the first day of Willis's marathon broadcast, Herman Magill died from exposure. Prayerful listeners were glued to their radios. Teachers set up radios in their classrooms. Doctors reported increases in patients with "nervous prostration," suffering from too much excitement and too many late nights. In his rich baritone, Willis reported "the torture of doubt, the Calvary of mental anguish, the nerve-destroying sound of dripping water, the rattle and splash of falling rocks."

Not everyone was enthralled with Willis's reporting. On April 21st, Nova Scotia Premier Angus Macdonald fired off a blistering telegraph of complaint to CRBC headquarters in Ottawa. In it he complained about the "inaccurate, exaggerated and over-dramatized nature of some radio comments." But Willis persisted until he was able to announce the most-awaited of messages: "The long-looked-for victory is now in our hands, and those men are coming out alive!"

In the early hours of April 22nd, the two grateful survivors were brought to the surface, where the miners sang "Praise God from Whom All Blessings Come."

"We are cutting our wires now and heading back," advised a weary Willis. The drama was over, but through it the Canadian Radio Broadcasting Commission had come of age. Six months later, the Canadian Broadcasting Corporation came into being.

A MAN IN A HURRY

Ottawa, 1939 — "In a film you must tell a story, otherwise you are boring," John Grierson once told a gathering of students in Montreal.

The man who has been called "the father of documentary film," was himself never boring. Likewise, the stories he aided and abetted in telling as the first head of the National Film Board of Canada were never boring. The mandate was to tell Canadians about their country and inform the world about Canada.

Grierson was a child of modest privilege, growing up in Scotland as the son of two accomplished educators. He studied philosophy at Glasgow University and served a stint on a minesweeper during the First World War.

A Rockefeller Foundation Fellowship brought him to America where he studied social science and the effects of mass media. His specialty soon became propaganda, which he considered to be an educational tool.

"We can by propaganda, widen the horizons of the schoolroom and give to every individual, each in his place and work, a living conception of the community which he has the privilege to serve," Grierson once noted.

Grierson spent a decade in England, where he organized a government film unit. In 1929, he produced and directed *Drifters*, a film about the harsh and dangerous circumstances of herring fishermen in the North Sea. It became a model for British documentaries, featuring a style Grierson summed up as "working men with their sleeves rolled up."

Grierson is said to have coined the term documentary in response to the filmmaking techniques of Robert Flaherty, who turned his lens on the daily life of the Inuit in 1922 to create *Nanook of the North*.

By 1938, Grierson was acknowledged to be an expert in the field of documentary film production which he liked to call "the creative interpretation of reality."

The Canadian government, under Prime Minister William Lyon Mackenzie King, asked Grierson to come to Canada to draft a plan for a government film unit. On May 2, 1939, what became known as the National Film Board of Canada was created by an Act of Parliament, and Grierson was appointed its director shortly afterwards.

When Canada entered the Second World War, Grierson also became the manager of the Wartime Information Board. As Canada's "propaganda maestro," he embarked on an energetic program that included a monthly series of short films that were shown in theatres across the country.

Canada Carries On highlighted the influence ordinary Canadians had on the war effort, along with strategies and themes that placed the Canadian effort in a global context. *Food for Thought* offered nutritional information in times of food shortage. *Women Are Warriors* showed English, Russian and Canadian women serving on the front lines and in factory lines. The *Strategy of Metals* pitted Canada's aluminum resources and manufacturing against a backdrop of German armaments.

Along with churning out pleas for war bond support, there was some straight-up propaganda such as the anti-Japanese film *The Mark of Nippon*, which bore the French title *Les Nazis jaunes*.

Many of these documentaries became part of another series, *World in Action*, which reached an international audience of more than thirty million viewers.

In 1941, barely two years after its formation, the National Film Board of Canada won its first Academy Award for *Churchill's Island*. While illustrating the Battle of Britain, the film also focused on British civilians holding fast in the face of war with "stubborn calm." The last line: "Come — if you dare," intoned by Canada's "Voice of Doom" narrator Lorne Greene, spoke directly to John Grierson's aspiration to see the Americans join the war. Six months later, they did. "Art is not a mirror, it is a hammer," was another Grierson saying.

In the six years that Grierson served at the NFB, hundreds of films were made by a team of more than 800 filmmakers. The hive of all of this activity was an aged sawmill on John Street in Ottawa, where a barn served as both screening room and recording studio. Despite the fact that the occupants of the elegant French embassy across the road considered the NFB building a blight, composer and conductor Louis Applebaum was occasionally able to cajole them into allowing rehearsal time on their superior piano.

During the Second World War film was rationed, but with Grierson's blessing independent film producers continued to work — for the NFB.

Years later, Academy Award–winning independent film producer and director Budge Crawley (*The Man Who Skied Down Everest*) recalled the importance of Grierson to development of the film industry in Canada. "Grierson employed all of the country's film skills to do what he thought were useful things," he told a Grierson symposium in 1981. "He always encouraged us. He gave us recruiting films. I spent months moving little Dinky-Toy tanks around and making tank training films."

Grierson also imported talent to get the Film Board up and running. In 1941, Grierson asked a fellow Scot, animator Norman McLaren, to join the NFB. *V for Victory* (1941) was the first of many short McLaren war effort pieces.

Ultimately, McLaren founded an animation department at the Film Board and became world-renowned for his experimental and lyrically poetic animated films.

Grierson left the NFB under an unpleasant cloud raised by the Cold War. Rumours of a "Communist nest" at the NFB were fanned when a reference to an NFB secretary was discovered in evidence that Soviet cipher clerk Igor Gouzenko turned over to the RCMP as proof of a spy ring operating out of the Soviet embassy. A Royal Commission ensued, implying that Grierson had knowingly hired Communists and allowed them to flourish at the NFB. He resigned in 1945.

"In all the RCMP files about Grierson there was not one thing said to implicate him, except through Freda Linton. She was his secretary . . . there was nothing to tar his name," an RCMP security officer said later.

Grierson had planned to go to America and start an independent film company after the war ended. However, this plan was foiled by Federal Bureau of Investigation director J. Edgar Hoover who targeted Grierson in the midst of the "red scare." U.S. newspapers crowed "Spy Suspect Expelled" when Grierson's visa was revoked in 1947.

After a brief stint with UNESCO in Paris, Grierson returned to Britain. He became controller of the Central Office of Information and guided a government film finance corporation designed to foster new talent, including Kenneth More, Peter Finch and Peter Sellers.

Despite recurrent bouts with tuberculosis, Grierson remained active. At home in Scotland, the self-described "man in a hurry," worked on the Oscar-winning *Seawards the Great Ships*. From 1957 to 1967, he was the host of *This Wonderful World*, a documentary television series produced for a Scottish television station owned by Canadian press magnate Lord Thomson of Fleet.

In 1968, Grierson was invited to lecture at Montreal's McGill University, where he held some of his seminars on filmmaking at his apartment.

"Something *does* something *to* something," he told students. "You must reveal the secret of that interaction, whether it is a psychological story, a political story or a story about tying shoelaces."

Never stumped for an opinion, Grierson also postulated that, "People with eight mm minds shouldn't make thirty-five mm films."

As Grierson's biographer, H. Forsyth Harvy noted, "He was never happier in his life than when he was bombarding complacency."

The "father of documentary film" died in England in 1972 at the age of seventy-three. Honours were heaped on Grierson during his lifetime, but the only one he almost received from Canada — an honorary doctorate from McGill — arrived posthumously. In 1973, the Grierson Building of the NFB in Montreal was dedicated in his memory.

The energy, elegance and intelligent "eye" that was Grierson's legacy to Canadian culture has in total earned the

National Film Board more than 3,000 national and international awards.

In 1989, the NFB was celebrated with an Academy Award in recognition of its first fifty years. Despite recent restructuring and downsizing (which critics have called "gutting"), the NFB continues to produce an average of 100 uniquely Canadian films every year.

"There is a profound element of common sense and good taste about Canada and Canadian life which is a precious thing to know," Grierson wrote. "This the Film Board reflects and demonstrates."

THE CROSS-DISCIPLINE DRESSER

Toronto, 1965 — Few, if any, Canadian thinkers have ever been mentioned in the same breath as Freud and Einstein. "Suppose he is what he sounds like — the most important thinker since Newton, Darwin, Freud, Einstein, and Pavlov — suppose he is the Oracle of Modern Times?" Tom Wolfe postulated in an article about Marshall McLuhan for *New York* magazine entitled "What If He's Right?" But the big question with McLuhan has always been "right about what?"

In spite of the fact that most people did not, and do not, understand one iota of what he wrote or said, Marshall McLuhan is one of the few men in the twentieth century who became truly famous for his ideas alone. Take Sigmund Freud, for example, whom everyone considers another "oracle of the modern times."

Although both Freud and McLuhan are virtually household names, most people are willing to believe Freud's idea that there is a dark side to the human psyche for which the individual is not consciously responsible. But few, if any, understand what McLuhan meant when he wrote that "the medium is the message" in *Understanding*

Media, published in 1964. Besides, Freud was from Vienna, the zenith of European culture and learning.

Herbert Marshall McLuhan was born in Edmonton, Alberta, on July 11, 1911. By the time he died in Toronto on December 31, 1980, he was the most famous man of letters Canada has ever produced.

He had the ear of captains of industry around the world. His opinions were regularly sought out by heads of state. Revered as a teacher and often reviled by his peers, McLuhan also loved jokes and one-liners. One of his favourites was about the first telephone pole — Alexander Graham Kowalski.

Because he was a true prankster, McLuhan pretended to put more stock in his participation in the popular culture than he did in the machinations of academia. He was inordinately proud of his walk-on part in Woody Allen's 1977 film *Annie Hall*. He took great delight in the fact that he was regularly mentioned on *Laugh-In*, an enormously popular 1960s television comedy series. In the middle of every show, one of the stand-up comedians would suddenly crop up on the screen and pose the philosophical question: "Marshall McLuhan, what'er ya doin'?"

He wrote articles for magazines such as *TV Guide*, *Family Circle*, *Glamour*, *Vogue*, *The Saturday Evening Post*, and *Playboy*, publications in which no self-respecting academic would be caught, even posthumously, although they all secretly wished for such popular recognition of their work. The Beatles thought McLuhan was cool, but he, undoubtedly, thought they were "hot."

To McLuhan, his role in the popular culture as "Guru of the Global Village" was completely consistent with his other roles as academic, thinker and teacher. The thematic underpinnings of McLuhan's theories are really quite simple: to McLuhan, everything was a medium, not just the obvious such as the telephone or the newspaper. A railroad was a medium. Money was a medium. Furs were a medium. Victims of fashion were aphorisms of insight. Nothing escaped: the wheel, the spear, the stirrup. All were media.

He contended that change and the individual's relationship to the world was not driven by war, religion or politics, but by the inexorable and invisible force of new media.

When he first reportedly said "the medium is the message" at a reception following a symposium on music and the mass media at the University of British Columbia in 1959, he simply meant that the key to understanding the world in which we live is contained in the technique and technology of new media. For instance, to know the message of the miraculous invention of television, the student must first comprehend the world before television. The message of the medium of television is the effect it has on the individual and society and its effects cannot be understood unless one understands what life was like B.T.V. (Before Television). For McLuhan, the fastest way to gain an understanding of different cultures or different times was through the period's poets, writers and artists.

By training, McLuhan was an English teacher and he looked every inch the part. He was tall, with a long straight face and appropriately pallid complexion. He combed his hair straight back. If he could be said to have had a disposition, he would have been described as perpetually preoccupied. Slightly dishevelled, he worked out of a small, dilapidated office on the edge of the University of Toronto. He taught English to freshman and graduate students alike. Even at the height of his fame, he graded papers himself.

McLuhan saw poets as seers, society's antenna, and claimed he derived most, if not all, of his insights from their study. He had an uncanny ability to discover in the works of difficult writers such as Gerald Manley Hopkins, Ezra Pound and James Joyce, delightful insights into the modern world and everyday life. In doing so, he made the writers' works more accessible to his students.

McLuhan was a kind of professional student himself. After graduating from the University of Manitoba in 1933, he went to England and took a second undergraduate degree in 1936. He eventually got his doctorate from Cambridge in 1943. His first teaching job was at the University of Wisconsin in 1936. An A-1 classification from a draft board in St. Louis in 1943 propelled him back to teaching positions in Canada.

His first book, *The Mechanical Bride,* was published in 1951. The book was didactic and argued that a technologically driven society destroys family life and the free expression of thought and feeling. The book did not do at all well. From then on, he abandoned point-of-view and argued that all of his statements, insights and attitudes were merely "probes."

In 1952 he teamed up with his friend and colleague, anthropologist Edmund Carpenter, and that collaboration eventually produced *Explorations in Communications.* He went on to participate in many collaborations: with Quentin Fiore for two books, *The Medium is the Message* and *War and Peace in the Global Village; The Marshall McLuhan DEW-LINE Newsletter* with Eugene Swartz and *Through the Vanishing Point* with his friend Harley Parker. McLuhan was astonishingly widely read. An eclectic and an inordinately curious man, he could truly dress across disciplines.

In the late 1950s, he had come under the influence of a University of Toronto historian named Harold Innis who wrote books about the fur trade in Canada with titles such as *The Bias of Communication*.

In his preface to *The Gutenberg Galaxy* (1962), McLuhan gave Innis his due: "Innis explained why print causes nationalism and not tribalism; and why print causes price systems and markets such as cannot exist without print. In short, Harold Innis was the first person to hit upon the process of change as implicit in the form of media technology. The present book is a footnote of explanation to his work." McLuhan's "footnote" won the Governor General's Award for non-fiction. It was followed by *Understanding Media* (1964) and *The Medium is the Message* in 1967. These books formed a body of work that brought him international fame.

It was partly the temper of the times and partly good management — McLuhan's career as a consultant and public speaker was managed by a remarkable San Francisco public relations duo, Gerald Feigen and Howard Gossage. The more unintelligible and aphoristic McLuhan became, the more in demand and famous.

Giant corporations such as IBM, GE, Bell Telephone and others paid inordinate sums to have him lecture their senior executives about the unseen world of the electronic environment. He was fond of saying "they all know just about exactly nothing about the real business that they are in." The more he said stuff like that, the more they paid him.

In 1963 he became the director of the Centre for Culture and Technology, which was a fancy name for what was essentially a one-man band with some letterhead. It was eventually set up in a coach house on an alleyway behind the library of the St. Michael's College campus at the University of Toronto.

No matter how far he travelled or how widely he was championed, how much he was paid, or how famous he became, he always returned to his dishevelled coach house and the classroom. His true legacy takes two forms: the Centre for Culture and Technology, which has become a hub of international inquiry into the effects of mass media, and the thousands of students in whom he instilled perpetual curiosity, eclecticism and a unique understanding of poetry.

"You don't like these ideas? . . . I got others." Thus spoke Marshall McLuhan.